To Die For

*

To Die For

THE PARADOX OF AMERICAN PATRIOTISM

*

CECILIA ELIZABETH O'LEARY

PRINCETON UNIVERSITY PRESS

PRINCETON, NEW JERSEY

Second printing, and first paperback printing, 2000
Paperback ISBN 0-691-07052-0

The Library of Congress has cataloged the cloth edition of this book as follows

O'Leary, Cecilia Elizabeth, 1949–
To die for : the paradox of American patriotism / Cecilia Elizabeth O'Leary
p. cm.
Includes bibliographical references and index.
ISBN 0-691-01686-0 (alk. paper)
1. Patriotism—United States—History. 2. Nationalism—United
States—History. 3. United States—Civilization—1865–1918.
I. Title.
E661.046 1999
973—dc21 98-25235

This book has been composed in Baskerville

The paper used in this publication meets the minimum requirements of
ANSI/NISO Z39.48-1992 (R1997) (*Permanence of Paper*)

www.pup.princeton.edu

Printed in the United States of America

3 5 7 9 10 8 6 4 2

IN MEMORY OF MY MOTHER

ELIZABETH ANNE O'LEARY

AND

FOR THE NEXT GENERATION

MILAGROS, DAVID, JOAQUIN, CASSANDRA, JONAH

✻ *Contents* ✻

CONTENTS

❋ *Illustrations* ❋

* Acknowledgments *

I AM deeply indebted to many people who gave generously of their time, encouragement, and knowledge. Lawrence Levine, my dissertation adviser at Berkeley, has been a friend and mentor, teaching me invaluable lessons about the historian's craft. I am grateful to Cornelia Levine for opening her home to our dissertation group and becoming a friend in the process. I also want to thank the other members of my dissertation committee, Mary Ryan for her insights on feminism and Alex Saragoza for his interest in and support of my work since my undergraduate days.

Early in this project and at subsequent meetings, I had the opportunity to discuss my topic with Stuart Hall, who suggested theoretical approaches to national identity that I have drawn upon extensively. I also want to acknowledge the assistance of the late Raphael Samuel, who shared his work on patriotism and led me to a fruitful meeting with Hugh Cunningham. In particular, I want to thank John Bodnar, Gary Gerstle, Eric Foner, Michael Kammen, and Ed Linenthal for reading the manuscript in its entirety. Their sharp and insightful feedback has helped to guide the final revisions. Numerous other historians have read and given me comments on conference papers, chapters, and articles that pushed me to reconsider and refine my analysis and arguments. I am indebted to David Blight, Gaines Foster, David Glassberg, Michael Kazin, Leon Litwack, Waldo Martin, Stuart McConnell, Charles McGovern, Francesca Miller, Nina Silber, and John David Smith. I also want to thank my chair, Rina Benmayor, at California State University, Monterey Bay, for extending her full support as I juggled teaching and administrative responsibilities at a new university while preparing my manuscript for publication.

Several generous fellowships allowed me to do the broad research my topic required and gave me the gift of time: 1994–95, Smithsonian Fellowship at the National Museum of American History; 1993–94, Mellon Graduate Fellowship; summer 1993, Smithsonian Summer Fellowship; spring 1993, Phi Beta Kappa Scholarship; 1992–93, Phi Alpha Theta Grant and Eugene Irving McCormac Graduate Scholarship; May 1992, Western Association of Women Historians' Graduate Student Fellowship Award; summer 1991, Mellon Summer Fellowship for Dissertation Prospectus; and 1989–90, Una's Fellowship.

At the Smithsonian, Lonnie Bunch and Charles McGovern offered me friendship in a new city and helped me learn the wonders of the institution's collections. In 1995–96, my joint position as a Landmarks Scholar at the American University and the National Museum of American History allowed me to deepen my belief in the importance of public history and taught me how to use everything from advertisements and song sheets to banners and photographs to bring history to life. Numerous curators and staff have taught me how to find, interpret, and use the materials at the Smithsonian, including Amy Begg, Tom Bickley, Lynn Chase, Pete Daniel, Mary Dyer, Harold Langley, Steven Lubar, Keith Melder, Jim Rowan, Harry Rubenstein, Fath Davis Ruffins, Barbara Clark Smith, Stephanie Thomas, and Jon Zachman. I also want to thank Heather Mitchell and my other research assistants, Keith Champney, Gordon Lanpher, and Samantha Harris.

My research took me into many different archives and collections. The richness and variety of sources I have used was made possible by the guidance and help of the many reference librarians and curators at the Cubberley Library at Stanford University, the Library of Congress, the Moorland-Springarn Research Center at Howard University, the Rush Rhees Library at the University of Rochester, and the Valentine: The Museum of the Life and History of Richmond, Virginia. In particular, I want to thank John Coski, who advised me on the holdings at the Museum of the Confederacy, and Walter Hill, who helped me navigate the Byzantine corridors of the National Archives. I would also like to thank Brigitta van Rheinberg, my editor at Princeton University Press, for her intellectual enthusiasm and shepherding of the manuscript through the editorial process. I would like to thank Joanne Allen for her patient and meticulous copyediting. Finally, Janie Silveria and Nancy Relaford, librarians at California State University, Monterey Bay, provided assistance with reference checks and interlibrary loans that allowed me to meet production deadlines while teaching.

On my many research trips to Washington, D.C., June Kress and Dennis Soiberman opened their home to me; Janet Wolff also welcomed me into her home in Rochester. My brother Tim and my sister-in-law Betty saw me through the best and the most difficult of times. Thank you. Finally, I want to thank my partner, Tony Platt, who worked with me each step of the way, always giving his love, wisdom, and wit. In the words of Walt Whitman, "I ascend, I float in the regions of your love O man, / O sharer of my roving life."

To Die For

*

CHAPTER 1

"To Make a Nation"

In 1831, Alexis de Tocqueville marveled at how "a society formed of all the nations of the world" could forge such "diverse elements . . . into one people."[1] Yet only thirty years later Union generals engaged the Confederacy in a strategy of complete conquest, directed at defeating not only an enemy army but a "hostile people."[2] At the end of the bloodiest civil war of the nineteenth century the combatants left the battlefields for political, economic, and cultural arenas, where the struggle "to make a nation" continued with renewed intensity.[3]

Although the Civil War determined the survival of the United States, what it meant to be a loyal American or disloyal "un-American" remained an open question until the matter was settled, albeit temporarily, during World War I.[4] For more than half a century there was considerable disagreement and conflict over which events and icons would be inscribed into national memory, which traditions would be invented to establish continuity with a "suitable historical past,"[5] which heroes would be exemplified in national narratives, and whether ethnic, regional, and other identities could coexist with loyalty to the nation.

Most of the patriotic symbols and rituals that Americans now take for granted or think of as timeless representations of national culture are in fact quite recent. The first national observation of Memorial Day took place in 1868, but it was not uniformly observed on the last Monday of May until 1971; Francis Bellamy's Pledge of Allegiance was not written until 1891; "The Star-Spangled Banner" was finally approved as the official national anthem in 1931; and Congress did not enact a national law against "flag desecration" until 1968. Moreover, these symbols of the nation emerged, not from a harmonious, national consensus, but rather out of fiercely contested debates over, for example, the wording of the Pledge, whose memories would be enshrined in national holidays, and what exactly constituted disrespect for the flag.

3

purpose of book

This book explores the origins, development, and consolidation of patriotic cultures in the United States between the Civil War and World War I, a period in which the country emerged as a modern nation-state and global power. Before the Civil War, the process of creating a unitary sense of national belonging and allegiance had been slow and uneven. Local and regional loyalties predominated, and the drive towards becoming an integrated continental power was by no means guaranteed. National culture was highly fragmented, with little agreement about or interest in making symbols, heroes, or rituals sacred.

By the end of the nineteenth century, capitalist expansion and industrialization, coupled with military victories in the U.S.-Mexican War, the Civil War, the Indian wars, and the Spanish-American War had not only assured the existence of a territorial United States but launched the United States as an emerging world power. Nonetheless, as Eric Hobsbawm has noted, "The mere setting up of a state is not sufficient in itself to create a nation."[6] Nationalism also depends on the mobilization of masses of people and the imaginative process, to use Benedict Anderson's insight, of uniting disparate communities into a "deep, horizontal comradeship," irrespective of how much the nation is divided by "actual inequality and exploitation."[7]

Although modern nations claim to be bound together by essential unities and progressively unfolding histories—whether linked to civil or ethnic narratives—what appears as a national consensus is only accomplished through the articulation of basically unstable and often conflicting interests and their suturing into a sense of a unified national identity.[8] Never neutral, nationalism always creates, reflects, and reproduces structures of cultural power.[9] Like most nation-states, the United States did not develop coherently or homogeneously. Instead, the drive to build the nation reveals paradoxical processes of unifying and dividing, consolidating and fracturing, remembrance and amnesia.

The subtitle of this book, *The Paradox of American Patriotism*, grew out of the recognition that American identity and loyalty are historically steeped in contradictory patterns and ambivalent relationships. Deep discrepancies always have existed between the nation's political ideals and its everyday practices. Unresolved tensions between ideologies of social equality and individual liberty have driven wedges into the body politic, and sense of betrayal

4

has often accompanied the belief that dying for one's country would earn the patriot's reward of full citizenship rights. "A nation's existence," as Ernest Renan noted in 1882, is "a daily plebiscite, just as an individual's existence is a perpetual affirmation of life."[10] But as Homi Bhabha reminds us, a nation's existence is also dependent on "a strange forgetting of the history of the nation's past: the violence involved in establishing the nation's writ. It is this forgetting—a minus in the origin—that constitutes the *beginning* of the nation's narrative."[11]

Overall, American nationalism after the Civil War has been given insufficient attention by historians.[12] Some have argued that the United States was an exception to the trajectory states typically followed to become nations because of its unchanging quest for Liberty and its commitment to core civic values of democracy and individual rights.[13] According to this perspective, "America is not a nation like all others" because "its unique national character [is] based on common political ideals and shared experiences."[14] To Arthur Schlesinger Jr., "the original theory of America" is " 'one people,' a common culture, a single nation."[15]

In contrast, this study is part of a growing body of literature that revisits American nationalism—"the political doctrine that dares not speak its name," in Michael Lind's apt phrase[16]—as more typical than atypical of how disparate, local communities and social groups imagine themselves part of a national family.[17] My focus is on the development of a nationalist consciousness in the United States—with particular attention to the North, South, and Midwest—from before the Civil War to World War I, when the patriotic movements were most active in debating and forging the modern rites and rituals of the nation. Studying nationalism and patriotism over this long historical period allows us to understand the shifts and changes in national discourse and the consolidation and dismantling of alliances that took place within very short periods of time.[18]

Although this book generally follows a chronological narrative, beginning with the earliest efforts to construct national symbols and ending with the provisional institutionalization of an official patriotism during World War I, the development of U.S. nationalism defies being neatly divided into sequential stages. Undertaking the study of patriotic thought is more like entering a maze, to use John Bodnar's allusion, than embarking on an evolutionary journey.[19] Far from settling the question of American national identity, I argue that the victory of the Union in the Civil War was the *beginning* of a long and contentious struggle over who and what would represent the nation. As Joyce Appleby reminds us, "E Pluribus Unum is an ideal; it is not a description of American life in any period."[20] There was no coherent or coordinated plan to subsume all local and regional identities under the "political roof" of the nation;[21] instead, the nationalizing effort was fueled by disparate individual activists and voluntary organizations. The United States did not follow the path of countries whose activist governments played a significant role in establishing a national patriotic culture.[22] In fact, it was not until World War I that the federal government fully intervened in this process, and even then it relied on the work of tens of thousands of volunteers and private organizations.

For most of the period under study, the development of nationalism as an ideological and cultural innovation did not originate with the state. After the Civil War, mass organizations such as the Grand Army of the Republic and the Woman's Relief Corps first took up the challenge of defining the character of the new national family, while elite organizations such as the Daughters of the American Revolution searched for a national unity in a mythic, pre–Civil War past. From the white South came the United Confederate Veterans and the United Daughters of the Confederacy, who proposed an alternative nationalism grounded in regional autonomy and white supremacy. Meanwhile, black veterans, freedmen, and freedwomen, struggling to have Emancipation Day included among the nation's anniversaries, allied with white Northerners from the abolitionist tradition to expand the meaning of patriotism to include the fight for equal rights and social justice. Women's groups used their participation in the patriotic movement to move from the political margins into the center of civic life. Labor organizations also used nationalism as a route for advocating their right to participate in the nation's largesse. Far from unified, these various groups who participated in the nationalist project represented different ideological tendencies, regions, ethnicities, and class interests. Organizations battled within themselves as well as with one another over who would have the cultural authority to speak for the nation.

In the United States, where being an American is seen as a choice rather than a birthright, control over nationalist discourse has far-reaching consequences.[23] For patriots, loyalty to family, friends, church, and place are subsumed under allegiance to one's country on the assumption that each citizen's welfare can best be realized though the preservation and expansion of the nation-state. For some five decades, what it meant to be a loyal American was contested over a wide cultural terrain—in public events, newspapers and magazines, political forums, schools, advertising campaigns, and organizational meetings. In addition to the involvement of large and small patriotic groups, a wide variety of educators, journalists, politicians, and businessmen actively promoted their ideas about patriotism and worked to forge the ceremonies and symbols associated with the nation—flag exercises, pledges of allegiance, parades and other theaters of memory, statues and shrines, commemorative holidays, and inspirational songs, texts, and primers. It was not until World War I, when the government joined forces with right-wing organizations and vigilante groups, that a racially exclusive, culturally conformist, militaristic patriotism finally triumphed over more progressive, egalitarian visions of the nation. And even that moment of hegemony was short-lived, as the nation-state once again became a site of social and political struggles in the 1920s and 1930s.

An interdisciplinary approach to nationalism is required in order to capture the dynamic relationships between the political and economic structures of nation-building, the organizations that form the social bases of the patriotic movement, the specific cultural and ideological contents of U.S. nationalism, and the resulting efforts to create a national consciousness. The "processes of cultural unification," to use Geoff Eley and Ronald Suny's term, spanned several generations and unfolded unevenly and contradictorily, as the multiple participants proposed varied, at times competing interpretations of what it meant to be an American.[24]

To understand the complexities of American nationalism, it is not enough to study the role of the government and politics, which, although clearly important, do not fully reveal the conflicts that exist just beneath the surface. Nations are more than the sum of their political institutions, and citizenship means much more than the right to vote.[25] This book focuses in particular on how a sense of identity and allegiance was generated in the United

States, how popular and local movements intervened in the construction of national ideologies, and how the cultural meanings of nationalism were represented, contested, authorized, and enforced.[26] I propose that at least until World War I, the nationalist discourse was a relatively open process and the chauvinist variety of patriotism—associated with "my country right or wrong"—was an important but not hegemonic tendency.

Between the Civil War and World War I, the nationalist discourse was characterized by debates and conflicts on a number of issues. First, to what extent would militarism and claims of safeguarding the security of the nation-state take priority over democratic demands for social equality? Second, what role would African Americans[27] play within the patriotic movement, and would the legacy of Emancipation or the resurgence of white racism define national memory? Third, how did women patriots participate in national life, and to what extent did they challenge or reinforce the image of the male warrior as a central tenet of patriotic culture? Fourth, how did nationalists address the issue of dual identities, as immigrants, Southerners, workers, and leftists tried to assert their cultural identities within Americanism? Fifth, what were the tensions and agreements between government-sponsored nationalism and the patriotic projects of popular, voluntary, and private organizations? And finally, would patriotism thwart or present opportunities for expanding the circle of citizenship?

Some one hundred years after American public life was the site of widespread conflicts about the meaning of "true patriotism," the same underlying issues still animate national discourse, as witnessed by recurring controversies—Should an official language be defined by multilingual opportunities or English-only prescriptions? Is the integrity of national identity maintained by barricading the borders or by recognizing immigrant contributions and diversity? What constitutes proper use of the flag in public events and private art shows? Should the Stars and Bars be allowed to fly above state legislatures and in the streets? What role should museums, national shrines, public parks, and monuments play in celebrating or demystifying national memory? Whose stories, heroes, and heroines will be included within national narratives? And how should the history of the United States be characterized and taught in textbooks and classrooms?[28]

8

The contradictions of American nationalism—notably, whether or not patriotism can hold out the promise of more democratic forms of citizenship—remain with us today. Fears about what ties together such a polyglot, racially and ethnically heterogeneous nation have deep historical resonance. As long as there are structures of inequality, nationalism will remain conflicted over who speaks for the country, who has "a right to the flag," what memories and symbols deserve official recognition, and whether the nation-state will guarantee or limit the rights of citizenship.

"Dyed in the Blood of Our Forefathers": Patriotic Culture before the Civil War

FOLLOWING the Civil War, most of the cultural symbols and rituals that we now consider part of a timeless and consensual patriotic culture either did not yet exist or had just begun to assume their modern forms. No song had emerged as a national anthem; the flag was not yet considered a sacred national symbol; and the Pledge of Allegiance had not been institutionalized as a daily ritual among schoolchildren. As late as 1893, organizers of the Chicago World's Fair carpeted a stairway with the Stars and Stripes for a reception for West Point cadets. The "State ladies" of the California Building, despite indignant protests from local members of the Daughters of the American Revolution (DAR), insisted on keeping the forty-foot flag on the floor. While the Daughters condemned them for making the flag into a "footmat," hundreds of guests, including representatives from other countries, stepped on Old Glory.[1]

Controversies over the appropriate representation of patriotism were not new, but before the Civil War local and regional variations dominated political culture. The nation-state did not yet touch people's everyday lives, and forces of disunity figured as strongly as those of unity. National identification shifted and changed over time, winning adherents unevenly across social groups and regions. Nationalism represents just one among the many ways that people define themselves as members of a group. Consequently, the success of the national idea not only involves social engineering by elites and the state but also reflects the allegiances and sensibilities of ordinary people.[2] In the United States in the late eighteenth and early nineteenth centuries, the nationalist project had not yet won mass support. Up until the Civil War, that the United States would break up into several nations loomed as a real possibility. However, despite the numerous obstacles to achieving a unified national culture through the first half of the nineteenth century, we can still identify some emergent heroes, anniversaries, and symbols that formed the basis of an embryonic cultural nationalism.

"We, the People of the United States": Legitimating the New Republic

The problem of forging a unified national identity began with the War of Independence. As Americans, colonists shared little in common beyond their opposition to British tyranny.[3] Newspapers urged them to "Join, or Die," using the symbol of a severed snake to demonstrate their plight if they refused to support the fight against Britain.[4] Colonial elites, without "other resources to fall back on . . . appealed to the only thing they had: their masses, whom they 'invited into history.' "[5] But the requisite transference of allegiance from the British crown to an independent United States remained an open question until the very eve of the Declaration of Independence. Following the victorious outcome of the American Revolution, the new republic suddenly found itself independent but without a truly national spirit.

An American nationalism only slowly developed out of a British nationalism. The conceptualization of the rising American nation, or "empire," as it was frequently referred to, began to emerge in the course of the war as poets, publicists, and politicians contributed to the creation of a national mythos to replace the image of the "British empire-nation" that dominated the imagination of the colonial era. At first one's notion of country more often than not was affixed to an individual state. Citizens of North Carolina, for example, took a loyalty oath to their state in 1777 and pledged to defend its independence against Great Britain. Thomas Paine gradually made the journey from being an English nationalist to becoming an American nationalist in the pages of the *Crisis*.[6] "The division of the empire into states is for our own convenience," he wrote in 1783, "but abroad this distinction ceases. . . . In short, we have no other national sovereignty than as United States. . . . Our great title is Americans."[7] But while this image of an American nation developed, the pull of local allegiances remained a formidable bond that could work for or against the deepening emotional ties of a body politic.

11

legitimate vs. legitify?

The nascent United States faced the dilemma of how to legitimate the new nation-state. Compared with their new land's original inhabitants, Americans did not have a lengthy history of shared memories, symbols, or traditions. The past that many did share problematically pointed back to a monarchical, not republican, England. Furthermore, outside of a small circle of nationalist leaders who championed the Constitution, most ordinary Americans remained preoccupied with local, not national, matters. As Joyce Appleby observed, "Fighting a war for independence had not unified Americans. Rather it created the problem of nationalism."[8] Even the wording of the preamble to the Constitution—"We, the people of the United States"—arose from an ambivalent relationship between individual states and the emerging nation-state. The original draft began, "We, the people of the States of New Hampshire, Massachusetts, Rhode-Island and Providence Plantations. . . ."[9] Far from representing the idea of a "more perfect Union," the wording reflected the drafters' uncertainty about which states would ultimately ratify the Constitution.[10]

Consequently, the first national narratives dwelled on what the country was not. Late-eighteenth-century republicans, fearful that a president might reestablish himself as king, sought to purge the state of any hint of monarchical rule. Protestants, who emphasized the need for cultural separation from a ritual-laden Catholicism, adamantly rejected the use of symbols and ceremonies altogether. Only the special place accorded to religious sermons and public oratory at Fourth of July celebrations offset the meagerness of national pageantry during the early republic.[11]

In search of symbols for the new nation, early leaders looked to ancient Rome for idealized republican models.[12] Just as England's ruling class looked backwards to the classical teachings of Aristotle as a way to bring intellectual stability to changes in the polity during England's century of revolution, so early American elites returned to classical republicanism as a way to ideologically legitimate their leadership role as virtuous men over the democratic rabble.[13] A neoclassical revival dominated American art and architecture from the late eighteenth to the mid-nineteenth century, inspiring the design of the national capitol, the use of the goddess of liberty for the nation's first coins, and the incorporation of the spread eagle from Roman battle standards into the design of the

1. Horatio Greenough sculpted this neoclassical statue of George Washington, which was placed on the grounds of the Capitol in 1841. Prints and Photographs Division, Library of Congress, LC-USA7-144.

U.S. seal.[14] Benjamin Franklin even proposed the infant Hercules as a fitting allegory for the mighty young nation that was coming into being.[15]

From 1841 to 1908 a massive, twelve-foot-high statue of Washington, seated upon a classical chair and dressed in a toga, was located on the grounds of the Capitol. The sides of the chair feature two reliefs: on one side Apollo charges into the future on his horse-drawn chariot; on the other side two infants, Hercules and Iphictus, are threatened by a serpent that represents the dangers inherent in creating a new civilization. While Iphictus, representing South America, cowers in the corner, Hercules, representing the United States, takes the serpent into his hands and successfully wrestles with destiny.[16]

Paradoxically, not only did the new republic draw upon the language, architecture, and symbols of liberty but its use of forced labor paralleled that of the classical world. Slaves played a significant role in building America's "Temple of Liberty," the nation's capitol, which to abolitionists was more a symbol of oppression than one of democracy. One abolitionist book prominently featured a graphic that linked the burning of the capitol by the British in the War of 1812 to divine retribution for the young republic's sanctioning of slavery.[17]

Teachers in the early nineteenth century used lessons of bravery from ancient Rome to teach the meaning of patriotism. They exhorted their students to follow the example of Brutus, who condemned his son to death when he learned of his betrayal of Rome. Most of the early readers and spellers instructed children that "patriotism . . . must be considered as the noblest of the social virtues," but it was not until after the Civil War that examples of American patriotism substantially replaced heroic legends from ancient times.[18] The reliance on classical models satisfied an immediate need for practical symbols to represent the new nation but left the development of an indigenous patriotic culture to proceed at a slow and uneven pace.

The formation of a national ideology is never a decisive act but a process that unfolds over time. As a settler nation, the United States could not claim the blood heritage of Native Americans it was in the process of conquering, nor did most Anglo-Saxons feel inclined to recognize the multicultural heritages of enslaved Africans or most other European immigrants as part of a common American identity. The lack of ancient blood ties and a long history was both a weakness and a strength, as early nationalists such as Thomas Jefferson located American commonality in the future rather than in the past. "The earth belongs in usufruct to the living," declared Jefferson, "the dead have neither powers or rights over it."[19] John Quincy Adams, like Jefferson, also looked to a future in which immigrants "must cast off the European skin, never to resume it. They must look forward to their posterity rather than backward to their ancestors—they must be sure that whatever their own feelings may be, those of their children will cling to the prejudices of this county."[20] In effect, these early nationalists acknowledged that America was coming into being, that its national definition rested in its potentiality, not in its past reality.[21] A futurist orientation gained additional cultural legitimacy from the pervasive influence of the postmillennialist notion that God had given America an exceptional, providential destiny. The close asso-

ciation of Protestantism with what it meant to be an American provided followers with a seamless web of shared beliefs, despite the official separation of church and state.[22]

Nonetheless, the growth of a unifying national culture in the United States proved to be unusually slow. The development of an American nationalism lacked many of what Peter Parish refers to as the "building-blocks" that other nations relied upon.[23] Instead, conditions of disunity prevailed: a weak central government; persistent local and regional ties; a heterogeneous population made more diverse with each new arrival of immigrants; the absence of threatening neighbors; divisive partisan politics; and the dynamics of a population on the move. The government's view that its responsibilities did not include sponsorship of memory further ensured a decentralized transmission of political culture. The initiative to enshrine a battle site, celebrate a patriot, or remember a historic anniversary remained with the people.[24] After the War of Independence, most people chose simply to return to the mechanics of their daily existence. The process of establishing new identities and allegiances more often than not reflected people's lived reality rather than the work of self-conscious nationalists. Hector St. John de Crevecoeur, a farmer in the first decades of the republic, described immigrants' growing allegiance in practical terms of "land, bread, protection and consequence; *Ubi panis ibi patria.*"[25]

Before the Civil War, only George Washington and Benjamin Franklin ascended to the pantheon of the nation's founding fathers. Franklin's death in 1790 had allowed his image to be separated from the partisan associations that kept another founding father, Thomas Jefferson, from becoming a national symbol until the twentieth century.[26] By the 1850s, Franklin's *The Way to Wealth* had been reprinted more than eighty times, and his *Autobiography,* nearly one hundred times. People regarded both as handbooks for success. In addition to his writings, Franklin's image appeared on engravings, on one of the first stamps issued by the Post Office, and on the banknotes of more than twenty-six states. Whereas Franklin's popularity was firmly rooted in the practical image of a self-made man, Washington's image, canonized in Gilbert Stuart's disembodied portrait, was distant and heroic.[27]

Washington, like other eighteenth-century propertied republicans, belonged to a class apart from self-made men. He believed

15

that virtuous gentlemen demonstrated their loyalty by serving the common good, but the circle of virtuous men remained tightly drawn around Federalist elites, who never entertained creating a nation of equals.[28] These first cultural nationalists envisioned an America defined by the high civilization of Europe rather than a rambunctious democracy. By 1800 the defeat of the Federalists signaled a major reconfiguration of social and cultural power, as the "responsibility for creating a national identity passed down the social ladder."[29]

The popularization of the Washington legend came not from elite Federalist families but from a preacher turned bookseller, Mason Locke Weems. His book on Washington, a jumble of fact and fiction, sold more than fifty thousand copies between 1800 and 1830. The tension produced by the ethically questionable but mutually beneficial alliance between commerce and patriotism emerged as an ongoing theme in the construction of national culture. Weems understood that patriotism sold and urged prospective publishers to see his book on Washington as profitable for themselves and useful to the country.[30] John Adams deplored how little interest his own countrymen and women appeared to have for real history. Only one generation after the Revolution, commented Adams in 1809, "histories appear to me to be Romances."[31] A mythologized Washington, a Roman eagle, and a classically dressed maiden alternately called the Goddess of Liberty or Columbia, after her masculine namesake Columbus, emerged as the preeminent symbols of the early nation.[32] Nonetheless, despite Washington's rapid ascension to the status of founding father, partisan politics thwarted observance of his birthday, sectional animosities created rival claims to his legacy, and indifference stalled efforts to build a national monument in his memory.

During Washington's first year in the presidency, Congress adjourned in honor of the anniversary of his birth and Philadelphia held a spirited parade of artillery and light infantry corps. But almost immediately, celebrations of Washington's birthday became embroiled in political conflict. Washington's association with the Federalist agenda led the 1796 Congress to defeat a resolution for adjournment on the anniversary of his birth. Only his death in 1799 induced Congress to resolve that February 22 should be observed throughout the country. Boston, like other cities that had previously paid little attention to Washington's an-

niversary, finally made the day official during centennial celebrations of his birthday in 1832. However, the uniform celebration of Washington's birthday would not take place until the twentieth century.[33]

When a joint congressional committee proposed to move the tomb of George Washington from Mount Vernon to a national sepulcher in the capitol as part of the 1832 birthday celebrations, Southerners blocked the resolution. With regional tensions on the rise, Southerners protested the removal of Washington's remains, "lest a severance of the Union occur, and behold! the remains of Washington on a shore foreign to his native soil!"[34] The West protested as well, hopeful that the national capital would move in the wake of westward expansion. Efforts to build the monument in Washington, D.C., were stalled by vigorous debates over the appropriateness of a republican nation's honoring an individual with a monument, insufficient funds, and even hostility from Catholics when a stone they had donated was carved out of the monument and thrown into the Potomac.[35] Though the cornerstone was eventually laid in 1848, the monument stood uncompleted for forty years.[36] Official monuments were not yet seen as sacred tributes by ordinary people. Instead, many preferred personal souvenirs they could take home. Washington's death, for example, led to an explosion in the production and marketing of souvenirs that rivaled the souvenir industry that accompanied the Revolution. Senatorial images of Washington appeared on everything from clocks, ceramics, and glassware to yardage, homemade quilts, handkerchiefs, and banners.[37]

Besides the cult of Washington, the only other component of patriotic culture that became national in scope prior to the Civil War was the celebration of the Fourth of July. One local community after another decided to make the day into an official holiday. By the 1780s, communities regularly celebrated the Fourth with parades, barbecues, and the reading of the Declaration of Independence. July Fourth became one of the first festivals of nationalism. Lengthy orations focused on love of the land, its beauty, its abundance, and, most importantly, its potential for material progress. Speakers thanked God for giving the United States a superior destiny and praised Americans' unique love of liberty.[38] The idea of exceptionalism was very appealing as a popular motif that stressed the uniqueness of American history and life. From the early days of the young republic, millennialists like Jonathan Edwards affirmed the unparalleled spiritual mission of America.[39] The notion that the United States had a special destiny imbued the promise of American abundance with moral purpose, linked independent yeoman farmers with civic virtue, and generated representations of America that remained silent on slavery and racism.[40]

But beneath assertions of national unity, the Fourth's significance varied widely as social and regional divisions deepened. The Declaration of Independence's affirmation "that all men are created equal; that they are endowed by their Creator with certain unalienable rights; that among these are life, liberty and the pursuit of happiness" represented an open text given to multiple interpretations. The variety of celebratory styles, from Sabbath-like rituals, middle-class self-restraint, and private observances to festivals of fireworks, working-class exuberance, and public beer drinking, also demonstrated how different regions and social groups interpreted the day's significance. Although formulaic newspaper reports may have given local communities the impression that the rest of the country celebrated the day in a cohesive manner, the nationalism of July Fourth more often than not meant "little more than localism writ large."[41]

The first emancipation movement emerged in the 1780s and indicted the nation for not living up to the Declaration's principles. For artisans, July Fourth became a day to renew the principles of the Revolution against an avaricious capitalism intent on destroying their republic. In the bustling new towns of the West, civic and business leaders overwhelmingly linked boosterism with celebrations of July Fourth. Women in calicos marched in front of wagons profusely decorated with American flags and the wares of local merchants.[42] Promoters of the first railroad, the Baltimore and Ohio, recruited the last surviving signer of the Declaration to symbolically open the railroad's construction on July Fourth, 1828. "I consider this among the most important acts of my life," Charles Carroll proclaimed, "second only to that of signing the Declaration of Independence, if, indeed, second to that."[43] By the 1820s the ideological convergence of concepts of liberty and power, symbolized by a feminized goddess and a militarist eagle, had supplanted the Revolutionary generation's distrust that power would always aggressively prey upon liberty. By then, images of prosperity had even begun to replace liberty's favored place.[44] "Peace and Plenty," symbolized by the plow and cornucopias, notes Michael Kammen, became the new national watchwords.[45]

Nativists also incorporated nationalist imagery into their anti-immigrant and anti-Catholic campaigns. In 1845 they marched seventy thousand strong through the streets of Philadelphia with bands, banners, and floats on Independence Day. Marchers wore silk badges emblazoned with images of flags, Washington, and Protestant Bibles inscribed with the maxim "Train Up Your Children To Love Their Country and Guard Its Institutions."[46] Ralph Waldo Emerson opposed the "narrowness" of nativism and instead proposed that the United States be an "asylum of all nations" where the "energy of the Irish, Germans, Swedes, Poles & Cossacks, & all the European tribes,—of the Africans, & the Polynesians, will construct a new race."[47] The conflict between demands for national homogeneity and recognition of ethnic and religious autonomy persisted into the twentieth century. The meaning of patriotism was contested by optimistic Americanizers, who believed in nationalism's conversion powers, and nativists, who saw immigrants as a foreign threat and campaigned for restrictionist policies.

In the decades before the Civil War, July Fourth was celebrated in a variety of ways and reinterpreted in support of diverse causes. Abolitionists, trade unions and labor associations, temperance activists, evangelical preachers, and women's suffrage advocates all tried to use July Fourth for their reformist campaigns. By midcentury the day revealed more about what divided Americans than it did about what united them.[48] While Daniel Webster assured a July Fourth audience assembled in 1851 to witness the laying of a cornerstone for the capitol's expansion that "today, we are Americans all; and nothing but Americans," deep rifts divided the country.[49] White Southerners rejected overtures to national unity and instead used the Fourth to focus attention on their struggle against what they denounced as the "tyranny" of the federal government.[50]

Free blacks in Philadelphia and Boston initially joined in celebrations, but racial tensions increasingly accelerated into confrontations with gangs of white youth regularly harassing blacks who ventured onto the Boston Common. Reflective of geographic segregation in Philadelphia and Boston, July Fourth became a whites-only affair.[51] Black communities in the North approached July Fourth with ambivalence: some boycotted the day altogether and chose to celebrate January First in memory of the abolition of the African slave trade; others observed July Fourth not as a day of celebration but as a time to protest the racism that contradicted the ideals of independence. After the passage of the Fugitive Slave Law in 1854, William Lloyd Garrison, editor of the *Liberator* and founder of the New England Anti-Slavery Society, burned a copy of the law and the Constitution. As the documents ignited, Garrison declared to the assembled July Fourth audience, "So perish all compromises with tyranny."[52]

Only the victory of the North in the Civil War assured that the Stars and Stripes would fly as a symbol of the United States. However, the story of what became the nation's most sacred symbol began in obscurity and arrived at its place of honor by a circuitous route. The paucity of national symbols left the flag as the main physical representation of the early republic. But outside of the celebration of July Fourth or Washington's Birthday, most people had little contact with the Stars and Stripes. Rallying around the flag, the ritualistic core of the modern patriotic movement, was slow to develop. In the early republic, the flag functioned simply as a utilitarian symbol, lacking in uniformity and mainly used by commercial ships and the navy. Early Congresses discussed the national flag infrequently and with marked indifference. A drafter of a new flag act in 1818 gained a modicum of support only after drawing attention to the fact that all the flags flying over the buildings of Congress were different. This flag act, still in effect today, was the first to specify that the stripes should be horizontal, but it lacked instructions regarding the number of points on the stars or their arrangement.[53]

Like the history of the flag, the origin of "The Star-Spangled Banner" reflects little of the formality later demanded by self-conscious patriots. In place of a national anthem, bands indiscriminately struck up numerous "national airs." An eighteenth-century English drinking song, "To Anacreon in Heaven," inspired the melody for "The Star-Spangled Banner." During the Revolutionary War and the War of 1812, numerous lyrics were sung to its melody, including the poem written by Francis Scott Key.[54] Watching the British bombardment of Fort McHenry, Key wrote, "O! say does that star-spangled banner yet wave, O'er the land of the free, and the home of the brave?"[55] Opponents and advocates of temperance in turn adopted and parodied "The Star-Spangled Banner," which was popular but by no means sacred. Alternative lyrics, such as "Oh! who has not seen by the dawn's early light, Some bloated drunkard to home weakly reeling," could be heard at town meetings.[56] Reverence would not be expected until the end of the nineteenth century, when patriots campaigned to make the "The Star-Spangled Banner" into the nation's anthem. In 1893 the navy stipulated that "The Star-Spangled Banner" be played at the raising and lowering of the colors, and during the Spanish-American War the public began to follow the military's lead in standing while the anthem was played. But it was not until 1931, almost one hundred and twenty years after "The Star-Spangled Banner" was written, that it gained official recognition as the national anthem of the United States.[57]

Like the anthem-to-be, the flag also was not generally invested with an aura of sanctity before the Civil War. This began to change during the U.S.-Mexican War, when, for the first time, the army carried the national colors into combat on foreign soil.[58] Other expeditions, such as John C. Fremont's exploration of Native American territory, had not carried the Stars and Stripes. Instead, Jessie Benton Fremont had made an eagle flag of her own design for the regiment.[59] Despite the army's infrequent use of the U.S. flag, the linking of military success to the goals of the nation became a standard way to identify a true patriot. When the Whigs ran William Harrison for president in 1840, they printed thousands of ribbons, promoting their candidate as a military hero against "redskins" and "redcoats." Although Harrison was hardly from humble roots, his campaign badges proclaimed, "In Peace, the Farmer and his Ploughshare: In War, the Soldier and his Sword." Another ribbon pictured Harrison surmounted by an eagle and a stand of battle flags with the inscription

> Tis the Star-Spangled Banner
> O'Long May it Wave
> O'er the Land of the Free & the Home of the Brave
> Conquer We Must—Our Cause is Just.[60]

By the time of the U.S.-Mexican War, the association of patriotism with military expansion, masculinity, and the flag resonated broadly. The battle cry "Remember the Alamo!" reverberated within popular culture. The Texas war for independence in 1836, in which both newly arrived Anglo colonists and the Tejano Mexican elite often fought on the same side, had been transformed into a national drama about the triumph of Anglos over Mexicans.[61] The mythology of Texas, an independent republic from 1836 to 1845, was appropriated into national narratives of Anglo superiority, and the Alamo was remade into a racial and nationalistic shrine to the fighting spirit of Anglo Americans faced with "foreign" aggression. Mexican settlers who had lived in the Southwest for two hundred years became foreigners in their own land.[62] Although the chauvinism of the popular press cannot be taken to literally represent the everyday thoughts of ordinary citizens, it is worthwhile to remember Hobsbawm's caution that the construction of nationalism can only succeed "in proportion to its success in broadcasting on a wavelength to which the public was ready to tune in."[63]

Consecrated in the blood of battle, soldiers and citizens alike began to look at the Stars and Stripes as the symbolic repository of their patriotic sentiments. Even though they were still identified primarily by their membership in state volunteer regiments, soldiers jockeyed to be the first to raise the Stars and Stripes over Monterey or Chapultepec.[64] "The most beautiful of all flags," effused one officer, "dyed in the blood of our fore-fathers, and redyed in that of their sons upon the fierce battle-field . . . an emblem of American possession to the Sierra Madre!"[65] Imperialism and nationalism became inseparably linked in the symbol of the flag as the press associated it with images of blood shed in victorious battles. Wives and daughters, who were not able to go into battle themselves, made flags for departing regiments. Romantic ideas about war found their way into fanciful arrangements of stars, while the appeal of nationalist conquest often took the shape of ferocious eagles.[66] The demand for the Stars and Stripes became so great that the Annin Flag Company of New York began the mass production of flags in 1847. For the first time, standardized flags flew amidst the colorful patchwork of homemade banners.[67]

Although the United States fought the U.S.-Mexican War as a divided country, its impact on strengthening an idealistic nationalism cannot be underestimated. Despite substantial opposition to the war among antislavery forces in the Northeast and pacifists, who saw the war as an aggressive attack on a weak neighbor, the mood of the country was in support of the victorious fighting regiments.[68] Henry David Thoreau, who was among the dissenters, refused to pay his state taxes in protest of what he saw as an immoral war and spent an evening in jail before a supporter paid his bail. Two years later he delivered a lecture entitled "Resistance to Civil Government" and published his beliefs in the now famous essay "Civil Disobedience."[69] Thoreau criticized the nation-state for making men into machines marching "against their common sense and consciences." But whereas Thoreau had seen the "file of soldiers" as "agents of injustice," many more Americans saw them as embodiments of Jefferson's "Empire for Liberty."[70]

Newspapers fired their readers' imaginations with images of the "children of the Revolution" raising the Stars and Stripes over the "Hall of Montezuma and Cortez, thus establishing in the valley of Mexico, a new dominion—the Empire of Freedom." Heroic serials about George Washington circulated among U.S. army regiments in Mexico, who shared the reading by campfire light. "Shall we not follow the Banner of the Stars from the bloody height of Bunker Hill," read the men, to "the golden city of Tenochitlan?"[71] The slogan "To the Halls of the Montezumas" became popularly associated with the Marine Corps during the U.S.-Mexican War, and in 1848 the District of Columbia presented the corps with an ornate banner inscribed with the slogan.[72] The war even inspired a young Walt Whitman to envision the "common people" fighting to spread democracy. "There is hardly a more admirable impulse in the human soul," wrote Whitman, "than patriotism."[73]

"LET US DIE TO MAKE MEN FREE": THE UNITED STATES AND THE CONFEDERACY

This heady mix of jingoism and nationalism, however, proved momentary. In less than two decades the political and economic contradictions of maintaining a system of slavery overshadowed any sense of national unity. In thirteen short years two nations, the United States and the Confederacy, initiated total war against each other. "After all the threats that have rung in our ears for a long time," wrote Nancy Cunningham in her diary, the lowering of the

United States flag in 1861 at Fort Sumter "took us by surprise, as the Judgment Day will come with men unprepared." Overnight the Stars and Stripes became the inspiration of the Union effort. "Until now," confided Cunningham, "we never thought about the flag being more than a nice design of red and white stripes."[74] At first, Northerners thought the news of Sumter was a " 'sensation story' of the newspapers," but when the "telegraph declared that the old flag had been dishonored," it was clear that the dreaded conflict had begun.[75]

In New York City, businesses closed and at least one hundred thousand people gathered in Union Square on 20 April 1861 to see the battle-torn flag of "Old Sumter" fly again.[76] The New York Chamber of Commerce awarded Maj. Robert Anderson a medallion for not allowing the flag to be captured. On one side of the medal was a picture of Anderson, and on the other, the "Guardian Spirit of America rising from Fort Sumter" with an American flag in the left hand and the "flaming torch of war in the right."[77] As news of the attack spread, crowds gathered in their town squares. Northern ministers resolved to fly the flag "from the spire of every church in the land, with nothing above it but the cross of Christ."[78] In Boston, Edward Everett spoke to thousands about how "one deep, unanimous, spontaneous feeling shot through the breasts of twenty millions of freemen" when we heard that the "standard of united America" had been "outraged" at Fort Sumter.[79]

Two years into the war, its outcome uncertain, Gail Hamilton issued "A Call To My Country-Women": "When the first ball smote the rocky sides of Sumter, the rebound thrilled from shore to shore, and waked the slumbering hero in every human soul. . . . Patriotism, that had been to us but a dingy and meaningless antiquity, took on a new form, a new mien, a countenance divinely fair and forever young, and received once more the homage of our hearts."[80] Another activist, Julia Ward Howe, responded by writing a testament to the transformative power of patriotism. In the "Battle Hymn of the Republic" Howe tied people's lives to a national destiny ordained by God. "Mine eyes have seen the glory of the coming of the Lord," wrote Howe, "He is trampling out the vintage where the grapes of wrath are stored." As guardians of public morality, women like Howe easily moved between religious and patriotic themes. She set her stirring lyrics to the music of "John Brown's Body Lies Moldering in the Grave" and challenged the

Union to uphold God's sacred trust:

> He has sounded forth the trumpet that shall never call "retreat."
> He is searching out the hearts of men before His judgment seat.
> Be swift, my soul, to answer Him; be jubilant, my feet. . . .
> As He died to make men holy, let us die to make men free.[81]

Northern men and women who previously had recognized only local, regional, ethnic, and religious allegiances hammered out the meaning of patriotism as they fought to preserve the Union. During the Civil War, the inexhaustible need for soldiers necessitated a wartime draft that broke down state regiments previously made up of recruits from single localities, employments, and political persuasions.[82] Despite different backgrounds and motivations, Northerners found common cause in defending the Union. Thomas Francis Meagher, an Irish and American patriot, created an all-Irish brigade for the Union army. Peter Welsh, an Irish American who joined the brigade, wrote, "This is my country as much as that of any man that was born on the soil, and so it is with every man who comes to this country and becomes a citizen." Such clearly stated allegiance to the United States was joined by Welsh's belief that a victory for the Union would also be a victory for Ireland. He saw the Civil War as a "school of instruction for Irishmen" and hoped that the day would come when an army could be raised in the United States to strike "terror to the Saxon's heart." Irish and American in identity and purpose, Meagher's brigade carried both the Stars and Stripes and the emblem of Ireland. Welsh vowed, when selected to carry the green flag of Ireland into combat, that it would "never kiss the dust while I have strength to hold it."[83]

The North's overwhelming urge was to preserve the nation, not to abolish slavery. Responding to enormous military pressures, Abraham Lincoln made the fateful decision in 1863 to transform the war's mission by issuing the Emancipation Proclamation. Many Northerners balked. Only two years earlier Lincoln had declared that he would not interfere with the "institution of slavery in the States where it exists."[84] Military necessity forced Lincoln's decision: to win, the North needed to abolish slavery in the heart of the enemy's territory. Frederick Douglass, the leading black advocate for equality during the nineteenth century, urged black men to enlist "because the war for Union, whether men so call it or not, is a war for Emancipation."[85] Douglass believed that the question of "what shall be done to the Negro" had encompassed the nation like a "wall of fire." The "Negro and the nation," he argued, would "rise or fall, be killed or cursed, saved or lost together." Douglass rhetorically asked, "Can the white and colored people of this country be blended into a common nationality, and enjoy together, in the same country, under the same flag, the inestimable blessings of life, liberty and the pursuit of happiness, as neighborly citizens of a Common country?" Answering his own question, he advocated nothing short of the "most full and complete adoption" of black men and women "into the great national family of America."[86] The uneasy relationship between citizenship, racism, and nationalism would persist into the next century as a central contradiction in the construction of American identity and allegiance.

Regardless of individual motivations, the Civil War became more than a test of whether there would be one or two nations; also at stake was whether patriotism would be grounded in aspirations to freedom and equality for all Americans. For many antislavery reformers, the Emancipation Proclamation endowed the conflict with moral dimensions.[87] Lincoln's proclamation played a critical role in expanding the meaning of patriotism from a willingness to die for the Union to the reciprocal obligation of the nation to make the idea of liberty into a reality.[88] At the dedication of the cemetery at Gettysburg on 19 November 1863, Lincoln called for a "new birth of freedom" with the now famous words, "Four score and seven years ago our fathers brought forth, upon this continent, a new nation, conceived in Liberty, and dedicated to the proposition that all men are created equal. Now we are engaged in a great civil war, testing whether that Nation, or any Nation so conceived and so dedicated can long endure."[89]

Amidst the horrors of war, soldiers forged bonds that would have been inconceivable in times of peace. The Stars and Stripes became a symbol of their own and their comrades' endurance. For example, just before the Confederate army captured the 16th Regiment, Union soldiers tore up their flag and divided the strips of cloth among themselves to keep it out of the hands of rebels. Years later, the survivors authorized their "sacred souvenirs" to be carefully sewed back together and placed on permanent display in the Pennsylvania statehouse.[90] Even Stephen Crane, a writer known for his social realism, could not ignore the powerful mythology of the flag when he wrote *The Red Badge of Courage*. The hero's embrace of the flag reveals a potent mix of death and sexuality, eroticism and nationalism:

> The song of bullets was in the air and shells snarled among the treetops. . . . The youth ran like a madman to reach the woods before a bullet could discover him. . . . Within him, as he hurled himself forward, was born a love, a despairing fondness for this flag which was near him. . . . It was a woman, red and white, hating and loving, that called him with the voice of his hopes. Because no harm could come to it he endowed it with power. He kept near, as if it could be a saver of lives, and an imploring cry went from his mind.[91]

For the first time in military history, the army awarded medals of honor to men who captured enemy flags and kept Old Glory from touching the ground.[92]

No story captures the emerging national ethos better than Edward Everett Hale's "Man Without a Country."[93] Hale gave the nation the haunting image of a man condemned to never see his homeland again.[94] A cautionary, fictional tale of treason and patriotism, the story recounts the fate of Philip Nolan, who brashly blurts out, "Damn the United States! I wish I may never hear of the United States again!" A military court forces Nolan to live in exile from the moment he speaks those fateful words in 1807 until his death in 1863. The tragedy becomes more poignant with each passing year as Nolan's yearning to return home grows more painful. The story's narrator, a young naval officer, first meets Nolan while at sea. One night when the two are alone, an older and wiser Nolan cautions the young officer to never "look at another flag." Always remember, says Nolan, that this is "your Country, and that you belong to Her as you belong to your own mother. Stand by Her, boy, as you would stand by your mother." The narrator recalls being "frightened to death by his calm, hard passion." After the young officer swears to always serve his country, Nolan whispers, "Oh, if anybody had said so to me when I was of your age!"[95]

The story, passed from generation to generation, continues to survive in national memory as a deeply moving lesson in the importance of pledging unflinching allegiance to the United States. Hale wrote the story to galvanize support for Lincoln's war effort in 1862, when patriotic fervor had plummeted from lack of military successes. The *Atlantic Monthly* hoped to maximize the story's effectiveness by publishing it as an authentic memoir.[96] However, even after Hale became known as its author, the public insisted on retelling it as a historical saga rather than as a piece of fiction. "The Man Without a Country" resonated among a population who had sent fathers, husbands, and sons to baptize Old Glory with their blood.[97]

No one escaped the reach of the Civil War: the number of men killed remains greater than the total number of Americans lost in all later wars, including both world wars and the wars in Korea and Viet Nam.[98] Union casualties alone are estimated at 360,000 out of a population of 20 million, almost seven times greater than the comparable percentage of U.S. losses in World War II.[99] The experience of total war left the country deeply scarred. Those not directly on the battlefields formed volunteer units to nurse the sick and dying, collect clothes, sew uniforms, and make bandages. By the war's end, the social reverberations caused by the unprecedented slaughter, the walking wounded, and the mentally damaged reached even the remotest village. Patriots such as Kate Sherwood believed that the magnitude of personal sacrifice was linked to the nation's salvation. "A mighty angel, sifting, sifting as he flies!" raising "heroic men and women," wrote Sherwood.[100]

Abraham Lincoln, at the commemoration of the Gettysburg cemetery, believed that no words could be equal to the task of commemorating the bravery of the men whose graves lay around him. He asked the nation to resolve that "these dead shall not have died in vain."[101] Union veterans understood that memories would fade if they did not turn themselves into the "living testaments" of America's most awful war. In the decades that followed, Northern veterans assumed their place as the torchbearers of patriotism and took charge of Civil War memory through monuments and symbols, published memoirs and oral histories, and dramatic rituals at sacred places. In 1865 the nation first glimpsed the arrival of a new and formidable cultural force as Union veterans marched en masse into the nation's capital for a triumphant Grand Review.

"When Johnny Comes Marching Home": The Emergence of the Grand Army of the Republic

Out of the crucible of the Civil War, the cultural representation of the United States quickly became a martial affair. Spectacles of military power increasingly dominated public ceremonies by the turn of the century, while wars assumed a central importance in defining mass allegiance. Shifts in national culture towards a more militarized interpretation of freedom and liberty was evident in the years leading up to the Civil War. The nineteen-foot sculpture commissioned in 1856 for the top of the Capitol initially featured Liberty wearing the Revolutionary generation's symbol of freedom, a liberty cap. But when Jefferson Davis, then serving as secretary of war, saw the plans, he complained that the cap might be misconstrued as symbolizing emancipation. The liberty cap removed, the artist titled the statue *Armed Freedom* and sculpted a helmet topped with feathers and an eagle's head.[1]

After the Civil War, the idealization of heroic male warriors competed with both patriotism's antebellum association with virtuous men and Emancipation's promise that America would live up to its civic ideals. A broad range of nationalists sought sufficient cultural authority to reinterpret the meaning of loyal Americanism. This chapter explores the role and ideology of one of the most influential voices, the Grand Army of the Republic (GAR), which forged the first mass organization of veterans in the United States and provided an institutional framework for the concept of an *armed democracy*. Despite the ultimate, albeit provisional, triumph by World War I of a narrow version of patriotism that promoted "my country right or wrong," many ideological battles took place within the GAR over several decades. The construction of patriotic culture was by no means predetermined or consensual, as fierce debates continuously erupted across a far-ranging political terrain: over endorsement of a nonracialized or segregated vision of the nation; over the role of women as activists or subordinates within the patriotic movement; over the support of capital or labor in the class conflicts of the late nineteenth century; and over restrictionist versus open-door immigration policies. Ultimately, the Grand Army's adoption of a specifically militaristic conception of patriotism, backed by its demand that the nation economically reward its citizen-soldiers, had far-reaching consequences for future generations. This chapter explores the origins, development, and politics of the GAR, and chapter 4 explores the ideological contradictions that gave the organization its dynamic momentum.

"A Parade of Fighting Men": The Ritualization of Male Warrior Heroism

In May 1865, for the first time veterans memorialized war by marching en masse behind their tattered banners. "Fresh from the field of action" and "clad in their veteran suits of threadbare blue," they marched as the victorious and masculine embodiment of the United States. For two days, more than 150,000 Union soldiers paraded 60 abreast in a continuous line up Pennsylvania Avenue to the Capitol.[2] Strains of "Rally Round the Flag, Boys" and "When Johnny Comes Marching Home" resounded throughout Washington, D.C., as the "armies of the republic" staged a triumphant Grand Review. By virtue of their military superiority, the "Boys in Blue" had transformed what began as a Northern army into a national force. The *Boston Post* heralded them as "citizens in arms" who fought not as "hirelings nor soldiers of fortune" but for the cause of the "People."[3] The Stars and Stripes and the men who carried it into battle emerged as the most important symbols of the enduring power of the nation-state. Just as electoral politics tied male power and identity to the workings of government, images of veterans symbolically defined what it meant to be virile citizens. Throughout the second half of the nineteenth century, people from across the social spectrum participated in modifying the meaning of manhood. The GAR laid the cultural groundwork for a cross-class model of gender that later found its fullest reflection in Teddy Roosevelt's linking of "civilized manliness" with "primitive masculinity."[4]

2. The first mass veterans' parade, known as the Grand Review, took place at the end of the Civil War in Washington, D.C., 1865. Photographed by Mathew B. Brady. Prints and Photographs Division, Library of Congress, LC-B811-3316.

For the first time too, rank-and-file soldiers assembled before their commanding officers at the war's end. In previous wars, state regiments had simply returned home after the final battle.[5] We "have had wars, but no reviews," lamented the *Philadelphia Inquirer*: "We planted our flag over the steeps of Mexico, but came home separately, like folks from church. We saved our original boundaries from British graspingness, but thought it useless to do any congratulatory parading. We redeemed our age of independence, but our forefathers melted away." The Grand Review broke with all past conventions by focusing the country's attention on a dramatic military spectacle staged at the "sacred seat of popular Government," an event unequaled "in the history of our continent."[6]

Every aspect of the pageant appeared "calculated to make a loyal American's heart beat with patriotic pride and exultation."[7] Huge crowds poured into Washington, D.C., forming a virtual sea of flags. "Now and then as a flag-staff passed with less of the old colors clinging to its battered peak, the cheers pealed out more loudly, handkerchiefs shook like aspen leaves and the bands chimed in their soft-gliding notes of heavenlike airs."[8] The Grand Review provided a ritualized occasion for emphasizing the gender divide between the marching "battle-scarred warriors" and the spectators' "feminine loveliness."[9] Women, spatially and symbolically removed to the sidelines, rushed into the parade to hang wreaths of flowers around the shoulders of officers, while schoolchildren gathered before the Capitol to sing their welcome.[10] Directly in front of the White House, flags and bunting ominously inscribed with names of battlefields covered the principal reviewing stand.[11] A reporter looking out over the regiments recalled lapsing "into a dream filled with visions of Vicksburg, Chattanooga and Atlanta, and camp fires stretching on through the South to the ocean."[12]

The Grand Review initiated the ritualization of male warrior heroism on a national scale. It "was a parade of fighting men in fighting trim, not plumed, nor polished, nor set on hobby-horses, but in the worn paraphernalia of battle, with their engines of death all rusty with mud, and their flags so funereal that they seem to have been playthings in the grave rather than fashioned by the soft fingers of women."[13] Nationalists used the parade to commemorate the war's achievements and to make mythic heroes out of the Boys in Blue rather than dwell on the horrors of war. "Future years will never know the seething hell," confided Walt Whitman. "The real war will never get in the books."[14]

Parades of state and local militias were not new, but the character of the Grand Review was unmistakably modern. During the Civil War, public ceremonies had already began to lose the spontaneous character associated with community-oriented rituals. In their place, orchestrated spectacles attracted vast numbers of people, transformed from participants into spectators.[15] The powerful sights and sounds of masses of men and military equipment thrilled the crowds. The 1865 parade "was a glorious sight," effused one newspaper. Amidst the mass of blue came the relentless sound of soldiers marching to the cadence of drum and bugle corps, while the glint of polished canons and flashes of drawn swords caught everyone's eye.[16] From the Capitol, the center of the parade appeared as "a moving mass of glistening steel, reflecting the bright rays of the sun, while ever and anon was a tattered banner, or a war-worn guidon, or a bright battle flag." On either side "fair women" formed a "living framework" to cheer the soldiers' return.[17]

Beneath this dramatic display of martial unity, however, ongoing divisions, ambiguities, and inequalities persisted. The Grand Review's inclusion, omission, and subordination of different social groups, notes Stuart McConnell, created a new representation of nationhood that embodied a specifically Northern, white, and masculine identity.[18] The Confederate South was not present; nor were the tens of thousands of black soldiers who had fought for their manhood and freedom; and women, though accounted for, remained subordinate. Although the nation mobilized women throughout the Civil War, the veteran parade, the first of many theaters of memory, marginalized their role to waving handkerchiefs at the returning warriors.[19] There would be no reenactments of women's wartime effort; instead, their public performances focused on traditional themes of love paying tribute to valor. From the soldiers' ranks, the Irish Brigade appeared wearing the green, but willingness to fight for the United States was not guaranteed to halt nativist attacks.[20] Black troops were notably absent from the parade on both days. Whereas some photographs document a limited number of black soldiers at the margins of the parade, newspaper accounts only mention two tall black soldiers riding small pack mules who provided what the *New York Times* called a "comic scene" for the white spectators.[21] The black regiments, counseled the *Philadelphia Inquirer*, "can afford to wait, their time will yet come."[22] Patriotic culture emerged from war deeply fractured and ambivalent. In the ideological battle over the meanings of mass allegiance that followed, the veterans themselves became a critical force.

"THE LIVING LINK": THE GRAND ARMY OF THE REPUBLIC

The Civil War's mobilization of hundreds of thousands of armed citizens engaged in mass warfare undermined the traditional expectation that citizen-soldiers disappear back into civilian life at the war's end. Since the American Revolution the role of the military in American life had produced acrimonious debate. Supporters of a citizen army viewed the Regular Army with suspicion, often deriding its professional officers as aristocratic. They maintained that only citizen-soldiers could be expected to protect a democracy against subversion by a power-hungry professional army. The Regular Army remained isolated except during times of war prior to the twentieth century, when the ascendance of the United States to the status of a world power finally led to a closer rapport between the American people and its army.[23] Until the Civil War, veteran societies were similarly viewed as elitist, remaining largely isolated and politically ineffective.

Officers of the American Revolution formed the first veteran organization in 1783. The Order of Cincinnati, in keeping with its elitist and patriarchal sense of lineage, ceded membership to the eldest male descendants. In an age characterized by fears of a return to monarchy, the Order appeared to republicans such as Mercy Otis Warren as an effort to re-create "crowns, spectres, and the regalia of kings."[24] Samuel Adams denounced it as a "stride towards an hereditary Military Nobility."[25] George Washington, the first president-general of the Order of Cincinnati, tried to mollify popular opposition by urging the order to abolish its hereditary clause. Although his recommendation failed, Washington's gesture successfully placated the press. While popular hostility abated, the order barely survived owing to its membership's own indifference.[26]

Later, the War of 1812 produced only a scattering of local veteran groups, and officers who formed the Aztec Club after the U.S.-Mexican War limited their activities to annual dinners and toasts. Not until more than forty years after the War of 1812 did veterans attempt a belated effort to organize officers and enlisted men. On 20 June 1854, eleven hundred veterans, including a delegation of Native Americans from the Six Nations who had served in the War of 1812, assembled to march for pensions. Many veterans, too old and sick, watched from the sidelines. They came to "implore" the government to do justice by those who had fought to "retain the principles of Republican Liberty." Make your representatives remember the "bloody Saranac," where the "river ran red with soldiers' blood," resolved the veterans of 1812. Ask them to envision the "bloody obstinacy, the cool bravery, the self-sacrifice," and demand to know why such deeds remain unrewarded.[27]

The soldiers and widows of 1812, however, made little headway in their campaign for veteran pensions. They had waited too long and had grown too old to launch an effective movement.

Unlike their predecessors, Civil War soldiers founded numerous new societies almost immediately after the war.[28] Predictably, an array of officers' associations developed across the country. But just as quickly, a truly remarkable phenomenon appeared: rank-and-file men began to organize their own local veteran societies. The Grand Army of the Republic aligned itself with the egalitarian thrust of the Civil War and set its sights on becoming the first national veteran organization to include both officers and enlisted men. A romanticized version of the founding of the Grand Army, promoted in veteran lore, recounts how Dr. Benjamin Franklin Stephenson, joined by several of his Civil War comrades, formed a brotherhood of veterans in 1866 for the sole purposes of providing relief and promoting brotherly love. However, behind the legend lurks evidence of a more pragmatic interest in organizing a Republican voting machine to further the ambitions of soldier-politicians like General John A. Logan. Whatever the truth of its actual origins, the GAR did begin in the spring of 1866 in Illinois and quickly spread to other Midwestern states. In the fall of 1866, Massachusetts established the first Eastern post, enabling the GAR to hold its first national encampment in Indianapolis in its founding year.[29]

The Grand Army faced two formidable challenges. First, it had to forge a national organization out of a disparate mass of men. Within years of its founding, external forces and internal tensions almost destroyed the fledging organization. Political and economic events severely weakened its consolidation of a national infrastructure, while the pulls of localism threatened to doom the implementation of any centralized direction. Although the GAR was organized along military lines, national orders no longer carried the same kind of weight in civilian life, largely rising or falling on a local post's enthusiasm or indifference. Despite exhortations to national unity, regional loyalty remained a vibrant dynamic in GAR politics.

Second, the Grand Army confronted the challenge of gaining moral and political legitimacy as a voluntary military organization in peacetime. The membership mounted an ideological campaign to be recognized as saviors of the Union by presenting themselves as "the living monument of that momentous conflict. . . . the living link which binds the present to the glorious past."[30] In turn, the GAR demanded reciprocity for services rendered. Front-page headlines in the veterans' major newspaper, the *National Tribune*, regularly called on the government to live up to its recruitment pledge of a "nation's eternal gratitude" to men who "periled their lives in defense of the country."[31] Next to images of prosperous young men signing up for service appeared disabled veterans and needy widows lined up to receive a few coins beneath the heading "Forgotten Promises."[32]

In the years immediately after its founding in 1866, the GAR's rise to national prominence appeared assured. Its egalitarianism generated a dramatic surge in membership. Union veterans, echoing the democratic thrust of the Jacksonian era, prided themselves on how the war had equalized class differences. Throughout most of U.S. history, explained one veteran, the officers were "the best men of their communities, the civil leaders, or men trained to the profession of arms." But the Civil War transformed class relations within the army. The "college professor was often the private with his poorest under-graduate for his colonel. . . . The 'greasy mechanic' came to wear the stars of the brigadier, while the 'boss of the shop' carried a musket or sponged a gun." This kind of radical change, he insisted, "at once smashes tradition, marks our national 'make-up,' and illustrates the Republican idea."[33]

The Grand Army initially joined in demolishing social barriers by making a veteran's loyalty to the Union, rather than his rank as an officer, the only criterion for membership. When asked to justify the existence of a cross-class organization of veterans, Maj. Gen. Thomas Wood asserted that "self-dedication, even to martyrdom, for the preservation of the State" had earned every ex-soldier, regardless of rank, the rights of membership. Articulating a central tenet of martial patriotism, Wood emphasized that from the classic republic of Rome to the present day, patriotism had been the most highly valued virtue.[34]

Begun as one veterans' organization among many, the GAR quickly absorbed other local groups. But following its rapid expansion in the 1860s, the GAR suffered severe setbacks in the 1870s. The grasshopper plague dramatically thinned the ranks of the Minnesota department, while the Mountain department, in the West, lost virtually all of its membership in Custer's defeat. In the

South, the collapse of Reconstruction left black veterans politically isolated and prompted many white veterans who settled there after the war to minimize their Northern connections. Throughout the country, the Panic of 1873 scattered members in search of work or left those who remained unable to pay their dues. Most of the Midwestern posts disbanded, and the Southern posts virtually disappeared, leaving only Massachusetts, New York, and Pennsylvania as Grand Army strongholds.[35]

Moreover, the persistence of localism led many posts to resist national imperatives. Veterans, who prided themselves on the GAR's egalitarian spirit, particularly resented the national office for imposing a graded hierarchy based on the Masonic system of degrees in which new recruits entered at the lowest level. They felt that it created social distinctions and ignored men's shared experiences in the war. By 1871 the national encampment recognized its error, but the membership had already begun to steeply decline.[36] Although the Grand Army floundered, it did not perish. The organization rebounded in the 1880s and soon entered the period of its greatest expansion.

Internally, the Grand Army's resurgence rested squarely on its decision to reemphasize camaraderie over the Masonic grade system. Men who had known a similar world of death and war were drawn to an organization whose massed presence assured respect when individual veterans could become objects of scorn or pity. Also, the nationalizing thrust of postwar America swept the GAR into its orbit. Between 1865 and the turn of the century, capitalist expansion and industrialization created an integrated market system that wove the remotest regions into the fabric of national life.

"The whole people have acquired a certain metropolitan temper," marveled James Russell Lowell, "a single pulse sends anger, grief, or triumph through the whole country." The "instantaneous dispersion of news" has made the country into a "living presence, felt in the heart and operative in the conscience, like that of an absent mother." Although he painted an overly dramatic picture of national solidarity, Lowell nonetheless captured the new sense of simultaneity born of transcontinental railroads and national telegraph networks and presses. "It is not a trifling matter," Lowell insisted, "that thirty millions of men should be thinking the same thought and feeling the same pang at a single moment of time, and that these vast parallels of latitude should become a neighborhood more intimate than many a country village."[37] As Benedict Anderson noted in his analysis of the cultural construction of nations as "imagined communities," the growth of nationalist consciousness was facilitated by a mass press and the transformative power of communication technology.[38] The integration of mass production and distribution within the modern industrial enterprise in the late nineteen century provided an energized nationalism with modern media and modern avenues for ideological expansion.[39]

In 1876, only a decade after the ending of the Civil War, the United States celebrated its one hundredth birthday. The Centennial celebrated how the Revolutionary War and the Civil War had unlocked America's potential for industrial greatness and progress. An enormous statue of a rank-and-file Civil War soldier stood on the Centennial grounds in Philadelphia, while across town thousands of veterans pitched their tents for the Grand Army's national convention.[40] Yet the fortunes of the GAR continued to be uncertain as the membership reached a new low of 26,899. When the 1876 Centennial opened, the GAR took up positions as fair security along with the National Guard, but with members hard hit by the Panic of 1873, it is more than likely that many did police duty out of their need for work.[41] On July Fourth, orators from across the country paid tribute to the role of veterans in preserving the Union, but an important question remained: what would the GAR veterans stand for? Just fifteen years before, they had fought a war to save the Union that became a war of emancipation. Now, standing guard at the nation's first hundred-year anniversary, whose vision of America were they defending?

Although five thousand GAR veterans joined ten thousand workingmen in a great torchlight parade through the streets of Philadelphia on July Fourth, the Centennial was not a cultural icon of economic or racial justice.[42] Instead, members of the Eastern elite, manufacturers, politicians, and businessmen asserted their cultural hegemony, ensuring that the exhibition celebrated industrial, not racial, progress. Organized capital responded to depression headlines and the rise of class conflict—coal miners in Pennsylvania and textile workers in New England mills had just lost long strikes—with exhibits that celebrated the manufacturing future of America. Every guidebook directed visitors to Machinery Hall, where a mammoth Corliss engine powered all the other exhibits in the building. The Centennial occurred at a time of dramatic economic change: the workforce in manufacturing, construction, transportation, trade, and finance would account for 50 percent of all employment in just thirty years; in the next ten years sixty thousand miles of new railroad tracks would be added to the forty thousand miles laid after the Civil War; and monopolies like Standard Oil were just taking shape.[43] "Patriotism," notes Robert Rydell, "was explicitly linked to the need for continued economic growth as well as political and social stability."[44]

Progress had always been a theme in patriotic oration, but the 1876 Centennial made the celebration of industrial power, commerce, and prosperity the centerpiece of America's first hundred years. Commemoration of the Centennial would have remained a fragmented affair if business leaders had not intervened. The first world's fair, known as the Crystal Palace Exhibition, had been held in London in 1851 to showcase industrial civilization.[45] American industrial and commercial forces not only continued this tradition but took direct charge of historical memory by organizing the trade fair around a national anniversary. Business defined the meaning of national progress through a commercialized display of products arranged in tall glassed cabinets, abundantly decorated with U.S. flags, spread eagles, and pictures of Washington. The exhibits notably left out any visible connection to the workers who had produced them.[46]

Patriotic souvenirs commemorated the event with elegant silk ribbons inscribed with the words to "The Star-Spangled Banner" and large banners celebrating independence and prosperity by picturing Washington poised above a dock overladen with American agricultural and industrial products.[47] Trade cards, exchanged among production and retail representatives, unabashedly linked consumerism with Americanism. Cards portrayed Uncle Sam demonstrating America's new products—sausage stuffers, lard presses, and cork pullers—to eager crowds from the world's most powerful nations.[48] Beginning with the Centennial, the Grand Army made sure to link its role in the Civil War to the benefits and prospects of economic progress.

The Centennial, however, did not result in an immediate increase in GAR membership—during most of the 1870s it remained at about 27,000—but by the end of the decade the "boys who wore the blue" were on the move once again. "Yes, we'll rally round the Flag, boys, we'll rally once again," proclaimed a Nebraska songbook.[49] In 1880, GAR membership jumped to 60,678 and continued to climb as the GAR shared in the popularity of fraternal organizations.[50]

Millions of men flocked to join associations in the final three decades of the nineteenth century, christened the "Golden Age of fraternity" by the *North American Review*. Men joined such secret societies as the Masons and the Odd Fellows, such labor organizations as the Knights of Labor, and such military orders as the Grand Army of the Republic.[51] At the turn of the century, the *Cyclopaedia of Fraternities* estimated that 40 percent of the male population twenty-one years of age and older belonged to one of the hundreds of lodges, whereas less than 1 percent had belonged to a secret fraternity in the 1790s.[52] Some men sought a retreat from the pressures of modern life; others used their membership to extend business connections.[53] Whatever the individual motivations, all took part in the revitalization of a virile manhood by using gender as a dividing line of membership.[54]

For veterans, the appeal of the GAR lay in its fraternal connection to the Civil War. "I know of nothing in all the circle of human duty," explained a veteran, "that so unites men as the common dangers, sufferings, and struggles that war brings."[55] The GAR provided a place where men who longed for the "touch of a comrade's elbow as of old" could gather and space for sharing memories of the "frozen camp, the hardships of the forced march, the dangers of the battlefield, the sufferings of the field hospitals and the untold agonies of the prison pen."[56] Their brotherhood, made in the "hell of the slaughter" and in the "face of grim death," cemented "friendships that time cannot sever, mystic and blood-stained."[57] Around the GAR campfires comrades shared their favorite army ballads and sentimentally called to each other:

> Bring me the good old bugle, boy! We'll sing another song. . . .
> Sing it as we used to sing it fifty thousand strong
> While we were marching through Georgia.[58]

The Grand Army also functioned as a charitable organization, as did so many nineteenth-century associations dedicated to good works. But it was the GAR's work as a special-interest pension lobby that would have the most far-reaching consequences for American political culture. The GAR successfully coupled a concerted recruitment drive with the promise of winning veteran pensions. Thousands of men who could no longer survive on the charity of friends, family, and church now looked to the GAR as a political vehicle for economic redemption. The Civil War provided the Grand Army with a ready-made pool of potential recruits. The sheer dimensions of the Civil War's mobilization of a mass army—about 2,213,000 served in the Union army and navy—almost guaranteed that its survivors would become significant players in the postwar world.[59]

No longer confined by local constraints, the GAR grew in relation to the nationalizing forces sweeping the country: urbanization allowed local chapters to take advantage of large numbers of veterans concentrated in one place; new printing techniques fostered national veteran presses; and improvements in transportation enabled the GAR to expand its membership through the movement of veterans back into the South and out to the West. The Grand Army, organized into a national office, state departments, and local posts, gained footholds from the centers of urban power to villages isolated along the country's back roads.

"MEN FOUGHT FOR A BEDROOM SET":
THE BUSINESS OF PATRIOTISM

Business interests found a kindred ally in the Grand Army, not only because patriotism boosted consumerism but also because the GAR's emphasis on an orderly, hierarchical society, in which it would play an honored role, resonated with capital's attempts to impose social stability amidst massive economic and demographic changes. While the GAR represented a new political force to be reckoned with, it was committed to participating in, not radically redistributing, the nation's largesse. As Stuart Hall notes, capital has always had an interest in the desires of popular classes, appropriating and expropriating cultural forms in an ongoing transformation that involves both imposition and resistance.[60] Railroad barons, civic boosters, manufacturers, and advertisers all propelled the Grand Army into becoming a national presence. Railroads offered drastically reduced fares to veterans traveling across

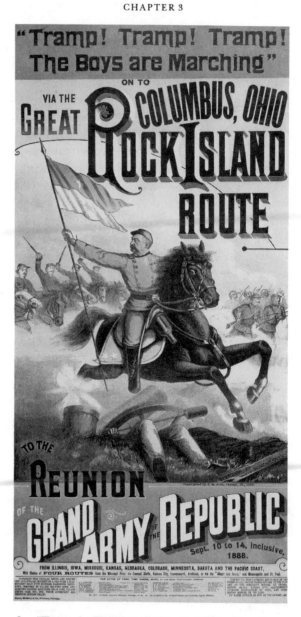

3. "Tramp! Tramp! Tramp! The Boys are Marching." The relationship between commerce and patriotism is graphically represented in an 1888 railroad poster advertising a Grand Army encampment. Prints and Photographs Division, Library of Congress, LC-USZ62-53750.

the country to attend annual Grand Army encampments. The Union Pacific called itself "the patriotic line" that bound "the Union together." Its offers of cheap tickets quickly made it a GAR favorite.[61]

Urban political leaders, eager to lure tourism and investment, competed to have their cities chosen for GAR encampments. Civic boosters mounted elaborate public displays to welcome the veterans, such as Baltimore's lavish spectacle of fireworks for the 1882 encampment, which included the explosion of the letters "GAR" into brilliant flashing lights above the acres of veterans' tents.[62] Minneapolis, chosen in 1884, built elaborate arches etched with the names of Civil War battles. On the day of the parade, "every house and store along the line of march was gaudy with bunting."[63] Not to be outdone, St. Louis constructed a massive stone arch that pictured both sides of the Grand Army badge on each column.[64] When San Francisco became an encampment site, the city engineer and the board of public works expedited plans for a massive arch that reached seventy-five feet from the ground to its summit. Hung with countless strings of electric lights, the arch illuminated the Western night.[65]

Although the commercialization of nineteenth-century culture often exploited national symbols and messages in ways that the GAR would later condemn as sacrilegious, technological changes in manufacture and the expansion of markets made patriotic symbolism a ubiquitous commodity. Beer producers literally wrapped their bottles in flags by the 1880s; companies such as Chase and Sanborn's Coffees issued free booklets entitled *History of Our American Flag*; manufacturers decorated trade cards with children dressed up as Union soldiers; and postcard companies distributed pictures of Civil War soldiers "in memoriam."[66] Retail companies also took advantage of Grand Army encampments by distributing souvenir supplements filled with activities and advertisements. Without question, patriotism sold.

The relationship between the profitability of patriotism and the veterans' sense of serving a higher mission created an ambiguous tension between promoting and exploiting sentiments of national loyalty. One soft drink company claimed that like a "group of grizzled veterans," its product at first looked like all the other "rank and file of Sarsaparillas." But like the "man with the medal," whose "measure was taken on that day of test and trial which proved him greater than the rest," so, too, Ayer's Sarsaparilla earned its medal at the World's Fair of 1893.[67] Increasingly, the memory of the Civil War and the men who had risked their lives became associated with the new values of a commercialized leisure. A furniture company's advertisement for an encampment reveals one of the many possibilities opened up by the commodification of Civil War memory:

> From Bull Run to Appomattox men fought for liberty, for patriotism and for the preservation of the Union. Liberty meant freedom in the home; patriotism meant the love of home, and the preservation of the Union meant the preservation of the home. And, strange as it may seem, aside from family ties, home simply means so much furniture in the rooms where a husband's and wife's heart are centered. From Bull Run to Appomattox men fought for a bedroom set and a fireside chair: so choose your furniture well.[68]

Cultural forms both facilitated capital's cooptation of patriotism and created conditions necessary for the Grand Army to become a national force. The mass production of flags, uniforms, and GAR jewelry dramatically heightened veterans' visibility and served as a constant reminder to every man, woman, and child of the services of the Boys in Blue. Unexcelled Fireworks Company offered GAR flags, thirty-six inches long and mounted on sticks, as well as the GAR badge emblazoned across the Stars and Stripes. Similarly, the American Flag Company promoted Grand Army flags in twelve different styles.[69] The *National Tribune* advertised veteran jewelry as an incentive to potential subscribers. The complexity of self-identity and Civil War memory became associated with objects that could be bought or sold. Pictures of GAR badges, rings, charms, watches, and chains filled the page beneath the caption: "Any man who has the right to wear this jewelry ought to have some of it. The wearing of it means vastly more than mere personal adornment. It means that the wearer bore himself manfully as a soldier in one of the greatest wars of modern times."[70]

An "Obligation," Not a "Gratuity": The Pension Crusade

While the Grand Army's alliance with entrepreneurial capital gave it national visibility, its ideologically charged campaign for expanded governmental funding of veteran pensions worked as its greatest magnet for attracting new recruits.[71] "Our present and our future," declared the GAR's chaplain-in-chief in 1878, "are indissolubly united with the past." Invoking the solemnity of a church litany, Chaplain James Farley led his comrades in prayer, "From all forgetfulness of that brave and loyal manhood by which the Union was preserved, and the constitution of the United States vindicated—good Lord deliver us."[72] One year later, in 1879, Congress answered Chaplain Farley's prayers by passing the Arrears Act, a watershed in pension legislation. The act allowed veterans with newly discovered Civil War–related disabilities to receive in one lump sum all the pension payments due to them since the 1860s. The act spurred thousands of veterans to apply for GAR membership and accelerated interest in pension legislation among GAR leaders.[73]

The Pension Bureau, overwhelmed by the number of new pension claims, urgently requested Congress's authorization of a new facility large enough to handle the flood of applications. In 1881 Congress allocated funds for the construction of what became at its completion in 1887 the largest brick building in the world. Three stories of offices line the perimeter, while a Great Hall in the center of the building floods the interior with light and air. The architect, Civil War general Montgomery Meigs, combined modern engineering innovations with motifs from the Italian Renaissance. The church of Santa Maria in Rome, which Michelangelo converted in 1563, inspired Meigs's design of eight Corinthian columns that soar seventy-five feet up to the central roof. A continuous frieze of Civil War soldiers and sailors, inspired by the Parthenon and nineteenth-century photographic studies of motion, surrounds the outside of the building between the first and second levels. The terra cotta–colored relief, three feet high and twelve hundred feet long, presents a dramatic parade of Union infantry, cavalry, artillery, navy, quartermaster, and medical units in perpetual motion.[74] The nation's history can be found throughout the built environment of Washington, D.C., where the massive Pension Building boldly attests to the powerful influence wielded by Civil War veterans.

Despite its belief in self-reliance, the Grand Army reworked notions of civic virtue to legitimate the concept of veteran entitlement and justify veterans' demands for national solutions to their individual problems. "In my mind," explained a veteran, "nothing is more clear than that it is an *obligation*," not a "*gratuity*."[75] During the 1880s, the GAR launched a powerful lobby for expanding veteran pensions, calling for a broader understanding of the government's responsibility to its citizen-soldiers.[76] Since its inception, the GAR had required local posts to provide voluntary charity to needy veterans; but systems of mutual self-help simply could not weather the cycles of economic depression.

The Grand Army's campaign to convince the nation that it had a sacred obligation to protect Union veterans proved timely. A powerful mix of ideology, economics, male suffrage, and party politics fueled the expansion of a substantial pension system for Union veterans and their widows. Tariff revenues, favored by businesses in the Northeastern core of the country, swelled federal surpluses from 1866 to 1893. These funds created a financial reserve for veteran claims, while the revival of party competition spurred generous distributive policies aimed at recruiting the soldier vote. Although high tariffs would appear to run against the interests of GAR members living in the Midwest and the West, the Republican Party was able to bring the ex-soldiers into its political coalition by funneling abundant tariff revenues into pensions.[77]

From Grant to McKinley, the Republican Party successfully ran veteran presidents. The reigns of power only fell twice, both times to Grover Cleveland, a Democrat and a nonveteran who had stayed out of the Civil War. Although President Cleveland included a sympathetic statement about destitute veterans in his annual congressional message, he enraged veterans by vetoing the 1887 pension bill. Calling the Grand Army into political combat, the chair of the GAR Pension Committee urged veterans to blanket Congress "with their vigorous and emphatic protest."[78] In June 1887 Cleveland rubbed salt into already open wounds by announcing that he intended to return flags captured by Union forces to "the Confederate states." His decision sent shock waves through GAR ranks, and the ferocity of their outcry forced Cleveland to reverse his decision. To Grand Army men, the return of captured flags gave implicit recognition to the existence of Confederate states, something Lincoln had refused to do throughout the war.[79] Not surprisingly, men who had secured authorization from the U.S. Congress to melt down twelve bronze "rebel cannons" into GAR badges steadfastly opposed the return of any war trophies.[80]

The next year, 1888, the Republican Party united with veteran dissatisfaction and mounted a successful comeback by running its "soldier president," Gen. Benjamin Harrison. Appealing to the veteran vote, Harrison made strong promises to liberalize pensions.[81] The GAR badge appeared prominently on campaign bandannas and banners. Across the "old flag," demands for "Protection" and "Pensions for Soldiers" symbolically linked economic prosperity to the veterans who had saved the Union.[82] Linking disparate forces by appeals to economic self-interest, the Republican coalition assured passage of the Dependent Pension Act in 1890. Another watershed, this act provided relief for all honorably discharged soldiers who suffered any disability, no matter how it had occurred or what the veteran's financial situation. The Dependent Pension Act paved the way for a system of disability and old-age benefits that eventually covered more than 90 percent of all surviving Union veterans.[83]

By the early twentieth century, veteran pensions proved to be more generous than European social programs in existence at the same time. In what was essentially a disguised program of national welfare, veteran pensioners and their widows received on the average between $142 and $172 a year by 1910, representing 25–30 percent of average annual earnings. But the benefits were not equally distributed. According to Theda Skocpol's study of the origins of U.S. social policy, Northern, native-born veterans benefited most from the Civil War system, along with immigrants from the North who had fought as Union soldiers. Among the 186,017 black Union soldiers who were eligible for pension benefits, the most likely recipients were free black Americans who had long resided in the North. Although the Pension Bureau, unlike other institutions of its day, was not formally racist, the applications of former slaves who lacked the documents needed to substantiate their claims were regularly denied.[84] Nonetheless, veteran pensions provided a powerful vehicle for both black and white veterans to make financial claims on having earned the rewards of citizenship.

The pension campaigns brought stunning gains to the Grand Army, its membership swelling to 409,489 by 1890. Although the GAR never gained the allegiance of all veterans, by 1890, 39 percent of all surviving Union veterans were enrolled as members.[85] The Midwest once again became the organization's stronghold, with Ohio boasting 763 local posts by 1890. Not far behind, New York, Illinois, Pennsylvania, Indiana, Kansas, and Missouri claimed more than 400 posts each.[86] During the 1890s, every state and territory was represented by a Grand Army department.

The pensions struggle, however, did not involve just economics or party politics. "Comrades, the trumpet of God is sounding. It is not the bugle call to battle," observed GAR Commander-in-Chief J. N. Walker. "The conflict of arms is over, but not the conflict of ideas, nor the trials of the people."[87] The cultural rituals crafted by the GAR dramatically countered criticisms of veteran pensions voiced by Southern Democrats and Progressive reformers, who equated pensions with governmental corruption. The veterans marched against their opponents, charging them with "stain[ing] the pages of history with the belief that . . . loyalty to country is no longer to be called a virtue."[88] Archbishop Ireland, a GAR veteran and stalwart Americanizer of the Catholic Church, castigated pension opponents by reminding them that "there would be today no United States" without the sacrifice of the veterans. Instead, the United States would have dissolved into "a dozen petty republics, writhing in the agonies of discord and revolution." The Union army, Ireland concluded, had saved the nation from the fate of Europe, assuring that "America's today" would be the "world's tomorrow."[89]

The pension campaigns drew the Grand Army out of its private world of male camaraderie into the public arena. As long-term survivors, veterans entered the fray of political combat with a sense of millennial mission, aspiring to be recognized as the authoritative torchbearers of patriotism. The GAR committee on teaching patriotism in the schools proposed that the "most effective lesson of patriotism" was the members themselves. "The record of their service in camp, on the battle field, in hospital and prison is a living illustration of patriotic devotion."[90] The GAR met the challenge of becoming a national organization by the end of the 1880s. During the next decade, it joined other nationalists in making the 1890s America's age of patriotism.

CHAPTER 4

"Living History": Crafting Patriotic Culture within a Divided Nation

THE United States secured its territorial boundaries by winning the Civil War, but the work of state formation and nation-building was far from complete. What remained was the daunting challenge of forging a shared national identity and cultural coherence among a population physically divided by region and socially fragmented by hierarchies of class, gender, race, and ethnicity. Nationalists worried that there was little in people's daily lives to inspire patriotism. As one educator lamented, "We have no frequent or great exhibitions of power; no army to stand in awe of; no royalty to worship; no emblems or ribbons to dazzle the eye; and but few national airs." He imagined that children must "wonder what kind of country this is that they have been born into."[1]

In contrast to the activist role played by the political-institutional agencies of governments as diverse as Argentina, Germany, France, and Japan, the development of patriotic culture in the United States relied on the initiative of individuals, private businesses, and organized patriots. The government would not make a significant intervention until World War I.[2] Beginning in the 1880s, organized patriots initiated campaigns to establish new national anniversaries; lobbied for additions to the nation's pantheon of heroes; urged the teaching of U.S. history and civics in the public schools; agitated for flag reverence and the daily pledge of allegiance; ushered in the greatest era in monument building, established national shrines and mapped out historical pilgrimages; and organized petition drives and congressional hearings to legislate patriotism.

By virtue of its victory, the North gained control of national history and Union veterans became its torchbearers. Where elements of a national narrative existed, patriots reshaped them; where they were nonexistent, they invented traditions and crafted new cultural productions to meet the exigencies of the hour. The Grand Army of the Republic, along with other patriotic organizations such as the Woman's Relief Corps (WRC) and hereditary societies such as the Daughters of the American Revolution, worked to inculcate loyalty to the United States by crafting what Stuart Hall describes as the "narrative of national culture"—the stories, memories, historical events, national symbols, and rituals that "stand for, or represent the shared experiences, sorrows, and triumphs and disasters which give meaning to the nation."[3] This chapter explores how the GAR developed its unities around a quasi-religious concept of nationalism, which it popularized in martial rituals and theaters of memory performed in small town halls and before tens of thousands in urban centers. But beneath this apparent harmony, as we shall see, also ran deep fissures about the rights of labor, citizenship, race, and gender. As a mass organization, the GAR by necessity reflected a wide spectrum of viewpoints, which at best could be contained but not suppressed.

"ONE COUNTRY! ONE FLAG!": LAUNCHING AN
AGE OF PATRIOTISM

The massive social dislocation created by the explosive growth in post–Civil War urbanization and industrialization fueled patriots' sense of urgency. By the late nineteenth century the United States had become the world's leading industrial nation, and for the first time, urban centers grew at a faster rate than the rural population. New York's population alone almost tripled between 1860 and 1900. In the urban centers, a new class structure emerged, with middle-class, bureaucratic-minded professionals moving into circles of political power, while immigrants swelled the ranks of labor. The 1877 railway strike heralded a long period of sharp class conflict. The belief that labor and capital could live "together in political harmony," lamented the *Nation*, had been replaced by the growing conviction among ruling elites that force would be necessary to protect society against the "dangerous class." Following the depression years of the 1870s, industry encouraged the massive immigration of cheap labor. The number of immigrants between 1880 and 1885 represented an increase of 150 percent over the previous five-year period. The proportion of unskilled labor jumped by 313 percent—with the majority of new immigrants filling the working-class districts and taking the lowest-paying jobs.[4]

Native-born, unionized workers distanced themselves from both unskilled immigrant labor and unskilled black labor by proposing their own variant of nationalism. Skilled workers demanded their right to an "American standard of living," in which they tied citizenship rights to consumer rights and the ability to live like "a respectable American citizen."[5] Racism divided working-class nationalism, as white skilled workers asserted that they alone had the character and requisite sense of consumerism necessary to comprehend and pursue an American standard of living. Sharp distinctions were drawn between the old and new immigrants, with newcomers castigated as "lesser breeds."[6] As the coercive power of the state was increasingly used against strikes, organized white labor used the political orientation and language of the American standard to press demands for a living wage as a fundamental component of what it meant to be a citizen.[7]

Nation-states have never developed neatly, coherently, or homogeneously. The United States is no exception. Although nations promote the theory of "one people," social, cultural, and linguistic heterogeneity is the norm.[8] Like other settler nations, whose histories are marked by conquest and annihilation of native peoples, the United States turned to slavery and immigration to populate its expanding economic and geographic frontiers. The construction of national culture, therefore, was by necessity selective, imaginative, and provisional. Facing an increasingly diverse nation, the GAR pursued a two-pronged strategy. On the one hand, it worked towards the longer-range goal of converting immigrants to "100 percent Americanism." But more immediately, the GAR set out to create rituals and invent traditions capable of bolstering the social order and inculcating allegiance among a population not yet unified into a single nationality. Although the veterans resolved that "there can be no Americanism which is not based upon the highest ideas of loyalty," the terms and conditions of this loyalty were by no means self-evident.[9] Faced with the reality of new divisions, unresolved conflicts, and a growing culture of materialism, many American patriots embraced quasi-religious notions of an organic nationalism.

The Grand Army moved away from an older conception of the Union as a "legal creation of contractual rights and obligations" towards one that identified the nation as a living entity with a body and soul, capable of offering its citizens moral regeneration.[10] The influence of Hegelian spiritualism and the idea of achieving national unity through the synthesis of contradictions had already begun to enter mainstream American thought before the Civil War. In the 1830s, the number of German immigrants swelled, and native-born intellectuals traveled to Berlin to study German philosophy firsthand. The diffusion of American Hegelianism was evident in nationalists' belief that the fullest expression of selfhood and freedom could best be realized through loyalty to ever larger collectivities of the family and nation-state. Not just a bureaucratic machine, the state was viewed as an organic, dynamic entity, embodying the life of society itself.[11] GAR Chaplain Lovering declared that "Love of country" was the "religion of patriotism." "Its altars are the graves of the un-forgotten and heroic. Its symbol is the flag of our Union." Its priests were GAR veterans whose "manliness today beats in hearts which have known no throb but that of courage."[12]

Educators joined the GAR in embracing organic nationalism, with its Hegelian view that nations have their "own distinctive Force" and "Moral Idea." President Raymond, of Wesleyan University, railed against an age that appeared to be consumed with selfish self-advancement, lamenting that the "multitudes, both those of native birth and those made such by a paper regeneration, are aliens to the national spirit." Defining citizenship in transcendental terms, Raymond argued that birthplace and naturalization were meaningless unless citizens felt the "breath" of patriotism and filled their souls with the "national spirit." Raymond believed that "he who feels this spirit is a citizen not only by virtue of the external insignia of birth or naturalization, but by virtue of the fact that he fills out the otherwise empty form of citizenship with ethical content. The spell is upon him, and with pride he says, 'I am an American citizen.' "[13]

Products of late Victorian society, the GAR membership infused their conception of patriotism with strains of nostalgia, sentimentality, and religion. For them the promotion of nationalism was not competitive with organized religion but rather a parallel and complementary faith. A conflict only arose when Memorial Day fell on a Sunday. All agreed that the purpose and activities associated with Memorial Day were "in tune with the highest ideals of the Sabbath." Many posts celebrated Memorial Day on Sunday and saw no conflict of interests. A small but vocal group of veterans, however, objected to anything except church services occurring on the "Lord's Day." Finally, after much discussion, the 1886 national encampment deferred to the minority opinion. Dependent on the institutional support of organized religion, the national Grand Army did not want to stimulate unwanted controversy. In the year of the Haymarket riot, the GAR sought to cement, not weaken, alliances that stood for law and order.[14]

National identification requires both the long-term process of acquiring a sense of belonging born out of everyday life experiences and the concerted and continuous political work of self-conscious nationalists.[15] The Grand Army's use of traditional religious metaphors in its modern call for mass allegiance allowed its patriotic message to resonate among a people whose commonsense view of the world already incorporated concepts of deliverance, redemption, and salvation.[16] A GAR hymn beseeched God to "make each patriot soldier's grave a sacred shrine to be . . . a high altar . . . of stalwart *loyalty*."[17] The GAR also turned to religious history for archetypes when it initiated its campaign to make Memorial Day into the "sweet, sacred Sabbath of American patriotism."[18]

Among all the religious holy days, the GAR marveled particularly at the capacity of the "great solemn feast of Passover" to sustain the national life of Jews through the centuries. Assuming the centrality of men to national narratives, it looked favorably on the ritual of fathers' passing on Jewish history to their oldest sons. "Memorial Day is our Passover," declared the veterans' *National Tribune*. Veterans had "no less reason than the Jews for solemn remembrance of our great National peril and deliverance." The Grand Army hoped to teach each son through the ritualization of Civil War memory "that the noblest act of man is to love his country."[19]

The GAR believed that by creating an expressive patriotic culture, it could translate abstract concepts of national belonging and allegiance into people's lived experiences. "Every patriotic act," explained a GAR comrade, "every gathering where patriotic sentiments are expressed help to build a wealth that can not be represented in figures, because every such act breathes the life that will perpetuate our love for the nation."[20] The GAR incorporated earlier patriotic sentiments popularized at Independence Day celebrations but gave a much greater emphasis to the role of war and singular allegiance to a God-fearing nation-state. "One country!

One flag! Eternal vigilance the price of liberty! These are the great commandments of the Grand Army of the Republic."[21] Without a war to rally behind, patriots turned to the construction of public rituals as a mechanism for mass displays of loyalty. Being a patriot became a way to claim the right to participate and influence political life.[22] In the process of creating the symbols, language, and rituals to signify the victorious Union, patriots helped to define the cultural shape of the post–Civil War nationalist project.[23]

Within the much larger movement for loyal Americanism, veterans saw themselves as "custodians of sacred memories." The Grand Army understood the politicized character of memory and sought to become its physical embodiment. Standing before a national encampment, GAR Chaplain Lovering exhorted his "comrades" to become the "living history of an immortal past. . . . You are the trustees of that living power of patriotism which looks to a great future for our great Nation. In your hands to-day history, memory, hope—the past, the present and the future."[24]

Like many American novelists and social commentators during the final three decades of the nineteenth century, the GAR practiced a selective memory. They chose to remember the Civil War in terms of redemption, ignoring the horrors of life under fire. The war had produced idealism as well as cynicism, heroic self-sacrifice along with fearful desertion; but in novels, memoirs, and the GAR's public demonstrations the subjective experiences of war were all but forgotten.[25] Magazines, such as the *Century*'s series "Battles and Leaders of the Civil War," pictured gallant generals, heroic troops, and romanticized images of soldiers advancing into battle beneath the Stars and Stripes.[26] The commanders' memoirs met Victorian expectations of a disciplined social order and focused solely on issues of military strategy and tactics.

By the 1880s, the war had already been remade into a comprehensible conflict within popular culture. There were no novels of disillusionment.[27] Stephen Crane, in his book *The Red Badge of Courage*, found masculine redemption in the war. As the smoke of battle cleared, Henry Fleming's regiment "sprang from behind their covers and made an ungainly dance of joy. . . . It had begun to seem to them that events were trying to prove that they were impotent." But just as they were about to concede, "they had revenged themselves upon their misgivings and upon the foe. The impetus of enthusiasm was theirs again. They gazed about them with looks of uplifted pride, feeling new trust in the grim, always confident weapons in their hands. And they were men."[28]

In the war's aftermath, the GAR contributed to and reflected the ideal of modern masculinity that made aggressive virility and militarism the core of national character.[29] The Grand Army measured men's loyalty by their assumed courage on the battlefield and women's loyalty by their self-sacrifice. "The Union stands for American Manhood," affirmed a GAR chaplain, "a manhood strong in physical courage. . . . It will not expose itself unnecessarily, but being once aroused has the spirit of that order given by Gen. Dix: 'If any man dare insult the American flag, shoot him on the spot.' "[30] Ironically, representations of the Grand Army's masculinity could not exist separate from feminine validation. Despite the GAR's emphasis on male camaraderie, old men could only become "boys again" before the admiring eyes of young women in veteran parades.[31] During the 1903 encampment, San Francisco newspapers published full-page graphics of an aged veteran remembering the definitive experience of his lifetime as a young soldier. Other graphics pictured old veterans marching next to appreciative young women bringing flowers down from heaven in their honor.[32] Representations of difference based on gender not only worked as a social divider between who could and could not enter the world of patriots but also served a unifying function by presenting images of heroic soldiers and solicitous women as a return to the nation's seemingly natural order. In general, notes Mary Ryan, women's presence in public ceremonies throughout the 1880s provided a culturally reassuring image, one capable of softening the harder edges of the nation-state's and modern technology's encroaching power.[33]

During the 1880s and 1890s, the GAR staged ever more spectacular encampments and parades that focused Civil War memory on the exaltation of national power and veterans' role as male warriors. Infused with a martial spirit born of their youthful baptism into national life, veterans invited citizens, newly arriving immigrants, and children to annually witness idealized re-creations of camp life. The GAR called its yearly reunions "encampments" because men literally pitched their tents and marched in regimented formation as they had done during the Civil War. The ritual drew thousands of GAR members from across the country and attracted crowds in the tens and, at times, hundreds of thousands. Encampments became living theaters, lasting several days and featuring

4. Grand Army encampments became living theaters of Civil War memory. The 1892 encampment took place behind the White House and next to the Washington Monument. Prints and Photographs Division, Library of Congress, LC-USZ62-4607.

numerous events, from parades and campfire circles to receptions with businessmen and politicians.[34] When President McKinley addressed the 1897 encampment, he spoke of coming "in the spirit of comradeship to talk with you as we have often talked in the past, around the camp fires in war as well as the camp fires in peace."[35]

Returning home, local posts organized "Camp Fire" evenings of actual gatherings around outdoor fires, as well as elaborate programs featuring music, speeches, refreshments, and taps by the bugle corps.[36] In 1890, Joseph Morton compiled a 670-page book, *Sparks from the Campfire; or Tales of the Old Veterans*, to keep the memory of the Civil War alive for future generations. The book gave its readers "thrilling stories of heroic deeds, brave encounters, desperate battles . . . and wondrous suffering as re-told today around the modern camp fire."[37] The Grand Army expected every local post to become "a school of patriotism, a school of intelligent Americanism, a school of high obedience to law and order." Activist veterans held monthly campfires with local children, visited schools in their old uniforms, and often brought a flag as an emotional reminder that patriots must be willing to fight and die to preserve the nation.[38]

The Grand Army's creation of the veteran parade, in which "battle-scarred warriors" marched behind their "tattered battle flags," became one its most of enduring legacies.[39] It epitomized the GAR's belief in law and order, its celebration of aggressive virility, and its exultation of national power. When seventy thousand "grizzled veterans" marched in Washington, D.C., in 1892, the newspapers announced: "Tramp! Tramp! Tramp! The Boys are Marching!"[40] Among the various public ceremonies that shaped notions of identity throughout the nineteenth century, none rivaled parading.[41] The GAR borrowed from the classic American parade, inscribing it with new meaning and altering it to meet the needs of the time.

Unlike earlier parades, in which class functioned as the defining signification, Union veterans marched as a great mass of Union blue, blurring social distinctions. Politicians, mindful of the soldier vote and eager to demonstrate their war credentials, joined the veterans on the streets in a show of egalitarian flourish. Former president Rutherford B. Hayes, three Cabinet officers, two state governors, as well as numerous ex-governors, joined their regiments at the 1892 encampment in Washington, D.C. More than five hundred thousand spectators crowded the sidewalks to watch the parade from "8 o'clock in the morning until after the sun had disappeared behind the Virginia hills." While bands played "Marching through Georgia" and "The Red, White and Blue," politicians marched "shoulder to shoulder with their former comrades," one hundred thousand strong.[42] All nonveterans—men who had not been part of the Union army, as well as women, children, and immigrants who had arrived after the Civil War—were relegated to the position of spectators. The distinction and social distance between veterans and the general public became even more pronounced when police cordoned off parade routes with ropes and wire fences.

Departing from antebellum spontaneity in parading, the Grand Army staged highly orchestrated military marches that followed carefully plotted routes designed to maximize the veterans' relation to sites of state power. The GAR parade reflected a trend towards orderly, legal, public gatherings begun in the years before the Civil War when parades began to be more tightly organized and the police assumed a greater role in their planning.[43] When the GAR marched in 1896, the police formed a human barrier separating the veterans from fifty thousand spectators. "For two miles there were two lines of humanity packed like sardines in a box," reported the local press. The police stationed men at all the "street intersections to keep back the irresistible current of humanity that surged in from the side streets."[44] A year later, when the GAR encampment took place in Buffalo, the police stretched wire screens along the line of the march "like an immense spider web."[45]

Flags by the tens of thousands marked the national character of GAR parades. At each encampment a "great deal of flag worship" took place, as veterans lifted their hats in reverence to the "tattered strips of silk and the few pendent scraps of what was once bright blue fringe were borne proudly past." Parents pointed to the flags and told their children "how precious those blood-defended relics were." Consecrated in comrades' blood, the flag became a spiritual icon.[46] In every region where the GAR paraded—stretching from the capital in Washington, D.C., and New York on the Eastern seaboard, through Kentucky in the South and Wisconsin in the Midwest, out to California on the West Coast—"American flags fluttered everywhere, from hundreds of street poles, from tops of buildings, from innumerable windows, and from tens of thousands of right hands raised in tribute" to the men who had saved the Union.[47]

It was not the numbers of men or the splendor of the flags that made GAR parades so memorable, mused a San Francisco reporter. In fact, "a cold critic" might even "pronounce it monotonous." The veteran parade paled in comparison with the "gaudiness" of the pageant staged by the "Knights Templar, with their gorgeous and diversified uniforms." But while the "Templars captivated the eye and dazzled the senses, the veterans captured the heart and stirred the fountains of patriotic feeling to fervor."[48] The GAR worked hard to create a martial culture that expressed Lincoln's hope that "the mystic chords of memory [would] swell the chorus of Union."[49]

"Liberty Regulated by Law": The Question of Working-Class Loyalty

Despite convincingly crafted cultural representations of national solidarity at GAR encampments and parades, the organization was far from monolithic, and the American people were far from unified. Grand Army membership cut across regional, ethnic, racial, and class boundaries, reproducing conflicts and ambivalences found in American society at large. Originally constituted at the local level, GAR posts persisted in asserting a strong degree of independence. The cross-class composition of the organization, the numbers of ethnic Americans who did not claim Anglo-Saxon roots, as well as the presence of black veterans, generated debates on a range of controversial issues. Positions varied between individuals, posts, and regions on whether the GAR should join militia units battling striking workers, support immigration restriction, or meet the demand of white veterans who had moved to the South after the Civil War and now demanded official support to impose a "color line."

Open to all men who had fought for the Union, the GAR's membership complicated taking positions on issues of class, ethnicity and race. Local posts tended to reflect the social composition of their towns. Although leadership invariably went to local elites, the majority of the GAR's membership drew from the ranks of skilled workers, clerks, and shopkeepers. At the national level, businessmen, manufacturers, and professional men dominated Grand Army policy. Overall, the GAR drew its members primarily from an antebellum, native-born, Protestant population. Yet despite the absence of representatives from southern and eastern Europe, the presence of immigrant Americans from Ireland, Canada, and Germany served as a brake upon those GAR members who advocated a nativist platform. The GAR's working-class membership also initially influenced a more sympathetic response to the plight of workingmen, but their empathy had limits. Drawn mainly from small farmers and nonindustrial wage earners, they responded with mixed sympathy to the militancy of an expanding class of largely immigrant and unskilled workers.[50]

Although the GAR met the democratic challenge of becoming the first national organization of veteran officers and enlisted men, its response to class conflict reimposed class divisions. Within a decade of its founding, the 1877 railway strike forced the Grand Army to choose sides. At first, the presence of working-class members influenced the Grand Army to take strikers' grievances into account. But the GAR's emphasis on social order, coupled with its fervent belief in individual as opposed to collective rights, ultimately led it to dismiss class loyalty as divisive and class struggle as "un-American." The 1877 railway strike was eventually denounced as "lawless." Equating loyal Americanism with the defense of capital, the Grand Army condemned labor militancy and announced that it was "willing now to take up arms in the cause of law and order as it was to crush treason and rebellion in the past."[51]

Industrialists, with the full backing of the state's repressive force, treated the labor movement as subversive outlaws.[52] The GAR joined the antilabor chorus in the growing conviction that force would be necessary to protect society against an immigrant and militant proletariat.[53] Calls for a standing army began to be sounded when local militias recruited from nearby towns took a sympathetic stance towards strikers.[54] Because of the close alliance between business and government, militant challenges to capital were interpreted as opposition to the United States itself. During the 1877 railway strike, William Vanderbilt succinctly stated, "We cannot afford to yield, and the country cannot afford to have us yield."[55] As state militias and, increasingly, the National Guard were called upon to break strikes, many workers began to see the army not as a defender of their liberties but as their enemy. Labor organizations discouraged their members from signing up for military service, when only a few decades earlier their arms had preserved the very republic that now turned its force against them.[56]

By the end of the 1880s, the growing hysteria over anarchism undermined any positions within the Grand Army that favored an identification with or even humanitarian responses to working-class grievances.[57] At the 1889 encampment, the commander-in-chief told the men that the GAR championed "civil and religious liberty" but had "no sympathy with anarchy or communism." Using the language of artisan republicanism, the Grand Army defended the "dignity of labor," but it failed to acknowledge that the rights of property no longer referred to a republic of yeoman farmers or artisans, but to the new captains of industry.[58]

During the 1894 Pullman strike, the Grand Army condemned Eugene Debs and his American Railway Union as "violently and flagrantly un-American."[59] Although the GAR grew impatient with the Pullman Company for its refusal to negotiate, the organization unequivocally denounced Eugene Debs as a "dictator" and condemned the strike as "the new insurrection." The *National Tribune* claimed to be "as devoted a friend of the workingman as any paper can be," but it saw "nothing but wicked folly in the present revolt against the well-being of the whole people."[60] The GAR declared that it stood "foremost among those ready to peril their lives for the restoration of law and order."[61] While the GAR, as the embodiment of the ideal citizen-soldier who had saved the nation, lent moral legitimacy to the use of military force against strikers, the Supreme Court codified the role of the army in its 1894 decision in favor of the Pullman Company.[62] "The strong arm of the national government may be put forth to brush away all obstructions to the freedom of interstate commerce. . . . If the emergency arises, the army of the nation, and all of its militia," the court asserted, "are at the service of the nation to compel obedience to its laws."[63]

The effects of the 1893 depression sparked labor demands for better wages across the country. When miners in Cripple Creek, Colorado, went on strike in 1894, GAR Commander Rollins condemned them for choosing rebellion rather than arbitration. "Anarchy," he proclaimed, "cannot exist in equal rank, side by side, with loyalty in the same heart, in the same society, or in the same State."[64] Rollins insisted that an "intelligent Americanism" required arbitration and compromise. The 1896 encampment resolved that the organization of industry must be filled "with the spirit of liberty regulated by law."[65]

With each major confrontation—the 1877 railway strike, the 1886 Haymarket bombing, the 1894 Pullman strike—industrialists joined publishers in branding labor activism as communist, anarchist, and un-American. Graphics regularly pictured Uncle Sam guiding American workmen away from the influence of swarthy agitators. The term *un-American* first came into significant usage as a political epithet during this period when "true Americans" used it against striking immigrant workers and later against any militant opponents of the economic order, immigrant or native-born.[66] At the turn of the century, notes John Higham, nativism assumed the "distinctively modern aspect" of equating working-class struggle with foreign ideas and agitators.[67] Traditional apprehension over foreign conspiracies and political subversion, associated with anti-Catholicism and antiradical nativism, resurfaced in the form of a "red scare."[68] Whereas Protestant nativists feared the influence of religious despotism, the new nativists viewed immigrants as too prone to political revolution.[69] A cross-class bloc of Americans increasingly held working-class immigrants responsible for the social problems associated with the era's rapid industrialization and urbanization.

"The Tide of Immigration": Nativists and Americanizers

As labor conflict intensified, the Grand Army began to discuss the question of whether to keep the "doors of the nation's welcome swinging wide to peoples of all lands."[70] Although the GAR membership remained optimistic Americanizers, a vocal minority supported restrictionist policies. George Lemon, editor and owner of the *National Tribune,* joined nativist ranks and demanded an end to the "contamination of our community with the sewage of Europe."[71] But another veterans' newspaper, the *American Tribune,* took the exact opposite position and denounced the American Protective Association as "un-American and unscrupulous."[72] The Grand Army believed in America's ability to make immigrants into citizens and worried that acceptance of immigration restriction amounted to an implicit criticism of America's powers of conversion. It resolved this dilemma by making a distinction between "desirable" and "undesirable" immigrants.

The GAR, reflecting popular attitudes as well as opinions of educators and powerful politicians, sharply distinguished between the old immigrants who made up their ranks and immigrants who had recently arrived. Typical of the prejudice and racism that new immigrants encountered, an informal line separated "white men" from Italian laborers on the docks of Brooklyn.[73] In 1892, the GAR encampment discussed welcoming "whoever comes with honest purpose to add to the brain or brawn of this free land" but enforcing restrictive measures against "that portion of the tide of immigration sweeping upon our shores which represents only the poverty and the crimes of other lands."[74]

Rocked by depression and labor strikes throughout the 1890s, members of the GAR who favored some kind of immigration restriction used each national encampment to gain support for their position. In 1894, proponents of restriction warned that "while we welcome all who intend to unite with us as American citizens . . . we have no room for those whose only desire is to destroy what has been secured by the blood and treasure of our people. The work of the Union soldiers and sailors did not end when the war closed: it only began."[75] Immigrants, who made up the poorest sections of the working class and were active participants in labor strikes, became easy targets for charges of un-Americanism.[76] Although the Grand Army did not officially endorse immigration restriction, it shared the alarm of its proponents and took up Americanization campaigns in earnest. Americanizers relied mainly on persuasion and focused their efforts on reaching the children of immigrants within the public schools. Many immigrants, however, resisted pressures to conform and continued to maintain both ethnic and American identities. But the political and cultural space for the existence of dual allegiances was not a given. Later, during World War I, state and vigilante coercion would eclipse the policy of voluntary conversion.

"ANY DESERVING COMRADE": STRUGGLES OVER
THE COLOR LINE

On issues of race relations the Grand Army of the Republic was much more ambivalent. Officially, it insisted that it would never close its doors to "any deserving comrade on account of his nationality, creed or color." But in practice the campaign to impose a color line eventually prevailed. The presence of black veterans pushed the contradictions between the national policy of promoting a color-blind membership and the reluctance and, in some cases, outright resistance of white locals to incorporating black members. Typical of other GAR locals, the membership in Post 10, of Worcester, Massachusetts, mirrored everyday practices of white unease, prejudice, and hostility towards blacks claiming their place as citizens. Amos Webber joined Post 10 in 1868, its first black member. For Webber, the formal commitment of the GAR "to equality, sealed with the blood of soldiers, was a patriotism worth embracing." Along with other veterans, he joined in the public rituals of Memorial Day processions, inserting himself into what had been an all-white enactment of national memory. Amos Webber's presence demonstrated a more inclusive representation of what it meant to be an American and underscored his own "political commitments—he was a soldier, a citizen, a black American."[77]

5. This Civil War poster urges black men to enlist in the Union Army under the banner "Freedom to the Slave." Warshaw Collection of Business Americana, Archives Center, National Museum of American History, Smithsonian Institution.

The Worcester post embodied the GAR's egalitarian principles to a point, with skilled workers, clerks, professionals, and businessmen contributing to its cross-class character. But egalitarianism had its limits; when the second black veteran applied for membership, his application was soundly rejected. Although records of the reasons for the rejection no longer exist, it is clear that Amos Webber, along with white supporters, organized against the post's racism in what became a sustained drive to enroll more black members. At a GAR fair, for example, Webber, along with the African Methodist Episcopal (A.M.E.) Zion Church, set up a "Fred Douglass table" of baked goods in order to bring the black community within the GAR's social orbit. It would not be easy, but over the next twenty years the Worcester post gradually admitted twenty additional black members.[78]

By virtue of his position as a veteran, Webber became a bridge between the white and black community. But like other black veterans, he did not limit his associational activities to the Grand Army. Although laudable for its time, the GAR's color-blind policy veiled the contradictions of white prejudice within the organization and proved inadequate to meeting the daily realities of racism within Northern society. Webber and other black veterans like him turned to all-black organizations such as the North Star Lodge, whose membership requirements were more inclusive and better prepared to provide group support against the prejudice of white Northern society.[79]

During the 1890s, the already uneasy alliance between white and black GAR members in the North and Union veterans in the border states came under increased attack as the movement for national reconciliation gained momentum. Increasingly, the valorization of battlefield deeds replaced patriotic appeals for democracy and equality made during the battles to end slavery. The struggle within the Grand Army over whether "whiteness" would become a criterion for membership emerged as a significantly divisive wedge during the 1880s, when the GAR's revival spread into the former Confederate states. Race, although an issue among the Northern departments, had not developed into a major conflict because of the relatively small number of black veterans. In the South, the issue of race also remained on a back burner as long as the only department that survived the defeat of Reconstruction remained the predominately black Department of Virginia. During Reconstruction, the Ku Klux Klan had harassed Union veterans who moved to the South, and by the early 1870s most Southern GAR posts had disbanded.

However, as an increasing number of white GAR members settled permanently in the South, the attachment of racial signifiers to membership emerged as a critical issue. The struggle within the GAR demonstrates how "race" was culturally constructed after the Civil War and politically mobilized to impose new relations of dominance and subordination.[80] In 1889, white GAR members from the Department of Louisiana and Mississippi insisted on their right to exclude black posts. When the state GAR commander contradicted their decision and admitted eight hundred black veterans, the white members launched a vehement protest.[81] The black press predicted that despite white veterans' threats to resign, the sheer numbers of black veterans would ensure their eventual victory.[82]

As black veterans in other Southern states organized posts, the issue of whether the Grand Army would tolerate the imposition of a color line could no longer be ignored. The Department of Louisiana and Mississippi stormed the national encampment in 1891, demanding that black posts be disbanded. The encampment erupted into heated debate over the memory and legacy of the Civil War. A committee appointed to evaluate a compromise proposal to create two separate GAR departments—one for black veterans and one for white—adamantly insisted that "it is too late to divide on the color line. A man who is good enough to stand between the flag and those who would destroy it when the fate of the nation was trembling in the balance is good enough to be a comrade in any Department of the Grand Army of the Republic."[83]

A veteran from Colorado took the opposite position, raging against the use of the term *color line.* The white veterans, he argued, were simply trying "to build up the organization" while having to live in the South surrounded by rebels. "Colored men belong to the Post in the city in which I live, and they are welcome there." But, he insisted, "a different condition of affairs exists down in the southern states." Immediately, a veteran from a border state, Comrade Warner, from Missouri, protested:

> Let me say to you, comrades, that during the fierce struggle from 1861 to 1865, if you lay wounded, if you were surrounded by the enemy as thick as a swarm of bees, at any moment you were liable to see a black face crawling up to you, and when he came you knew he was a friend. Yes, the color of his skin was his shibboleth and his password to loyalty. . . . He went to the field and fought for the flag of the country, a flag that never up to that time had protected him in anything but bondage. . . . Comrades, you had better tear the badge from your breasts . . . to go back upon the principles for which we fought and for which we bled.[84]

Comrade Graham, of Louisiana, passionately rejected any criticism of his department. "Should we open the doors there would be eight or ten or fifteen white men, perhaps, in a Post, perhaps twenty-five and there would be two or three hundred colored men, and it would be the tail wagging the dog." Another supporter of the "white only clause" implored, "We do not want to be sacrificed. . . . Give us a separate charter."[85]

Fearing that the mood of the encampment might shift, Comrade Johnson took to the floor and demanded to know "why it is that you want to shove us off now in a separate Department, when we always have been in one Department, and of all the institutions that we belong to no other institution has brought us so near together as the Grand Army of the Republic." Johnson indicted the hypocrisy of an organization that expected its members to be friends and brothers in the field of action but not in times of peace. For Johnson and his black brothers and white allies, the issue was not whether there would be separate posts but whether the all-black posts would be recognized within state departments. Next, Comrade Richey, of Kentucky, spoke for his "brethren in black." Richey described how in his state 182 posts, 27 of which were black, worked together in one department. "Gentleman," said Comrade Richey,

> You speak of hard times. We know something of hard times and we know just what it is to be Grand Army men. I have never heard any good reason why you should turn your backs on the colored man. I do remember that in the dark days when you were struggling for liberty, when you were struggling to maintain this country, it was the black man that came to your assistance and stood by you until the last enemy was gone. . . . Now, I say, if you want to build up the Grand Army, if you want to make her bulwarks strong, stand by the colored man.[86]

For the moment, the Grand Army upheld its founding principles, and the 1891 encampment resolved not to draw a color line. The black press applauded the decision. "All honor to the G.A.R.," affirmed the *Christian Recorder.* It appeared that the sword might yet prove "greater than the sign of the cross."[87] The white Louisiana veterans, however, remained unconvinced and unmoved. In March 1892, their commander again refused the black posts' petition to be recognized. Upon hearing of the white Louisiana veterans' intransigence, GAR Commander-in-Chief John M. Palmer suspended the state commander and ordered a reorganization of the department. Many white posts simply resigned in protest, causing the department's membership to drop from 1,058 to 332. But with the infusion of its new black members, the department's numbers rose once again, reaching 1,323 within a few months. No sooner had the reorganization of Louisiana taken place than Texas refused to recognize the organization of a black post in San Antonio.[88] The white veterans refused defeat and engaged in a battle of wills, banking on wearing down the national organization's resolve.

As preparations for the 1892 encampment began, black veterans lobbied for a place on the national planning committee. Since "we constitute a big portion of the material that makes up the GAR," reasoned the veterans, and since "all other 'races' and nationalities" who fought in the Civil War are represented, it was time to give black veterans a voice.[89] The 1892 encampment was scheduled to take place in Washington, D.C., and black veterans from the Potomac called on their brothers from Louisiana and other posts around the country to help break down the "caste prejudice" that existed in the nation's capital. Although three black veterans won appointments to the national planning committee, black GAR members criticized them for making no difference in the treatment of black delegations. "When white representatives come they are received in style, wined, dined and carried over the city in the best carriages and vehicles," but when the black delegations arrived, they were not permitted "to 'come up to the parlor.' " An editorial in the black *Washington Bee* called for the representatives to step down if they were not going to represent the "Afro-American interest."[90]

At the encampment, the struggle over the place of black veterans in the Grand Army continued unabated. Within the organizational meetings, Commander-in-Chief Palmer reiterated the stand taken at the encampment the year before, namely, that "it is too late to divide on the color line."[91] Despite the encampment's once again taking a strong position against the imposition of a color line, white Southern posts simply ignored the national policy against segregation. Black veterans could join the GAR as equals, but they then faced an informally enforced discrimination.

The GAR used a language of consensus, but beneath claims to a universal and inclusive Americanism conflicts remained and racial divisions deepened. Although black companies of soldiers marched in the 1892 national GAR parade, the grand finale of fireworks illuminated the night's skies with an ominous message.

One hundred fifty thousand people crowded around the Washington Monument for an extravaganza of fireworks. As darkness fell, lights bathed the monument in red, white, and blue. Portraits of Grant, Sherman, and Sheridan appeared surrounded by patriotic emblems and a halo of brilliant fire. Each display seemed more spectacular than the last. A flashing outline of the capitol appeared, then an eagle burst across the sky surrounded by forty-four revolving wheels, representing each of the states. More brilliant illuminations thrilled the crowds as the spectacle transformed the sky into a blaze of martial glory. Just before the finale, two fiery soldiers suddenly appeared in the sky. Looming above the cheering crowds, the Blue and the Gray faced each other and shook hands, promising the reconciliation of *white* "blood brothers."[92]

In the decades that followed, the GAR's positions on immigration and racism hardened, but the organization still reflected a spectrum of debate. Around the issue of gender, however, the veterans were adamant: women had no place in the Grand Army of the Republic. Newspaper editorials, novels, and songs all echoed the GAR's assertion that firsthand experience of the gore of battle made boys into men and women into ministering angels. The GAR reinterpreted women's role in the Civil War, even on the front lines in field hospitals, as love paying tribute to valor. But the issue of women's place in the nation was far from settled as women patriots refused to simply return to a world bounded by domesticity. At the close of the Civil War, it remained an open question whether women's participation in the nationalist movement would serve emancipatory or reactionary aims.

CHAPTER 5

"Oh, My Sisters!": Shifting Relations
of Gender and Race

Wʜᴇɴ asked to become the president of the Woman's Relief Corps, the first national organization of patriotic women, Florence Barker initially felt "like a strange pilot, removed from the harbor I knew so well, and placed in a strange port, without chart or map—only a compass to guide me." Patriotic service was not new to Barker, for she had served in the Civil War and worked in one of the thousands of voluntary associations that women organized across the country to aid returning veterans. But such local groups remained small and disconnected until 1879, when women from Massachusetts began to consolidate a regional association in the Northeast.[1] The backbone of the Massachusetts corps was formed by women like Clare Burleigh, whose parents were "antislavery workers" and whose brother was a Union cavalry officer known as "the lawyer who defended John Brown"; Lizabeth Turner, who shipped the first box of supplies from Boston to soldiers on the front lines; and Sarah Fuller, from a family of committed abolitionists, who immediately raised four hundred dollars for supplies upon hearing of the Battle of Antietam.[2]

Fragmented and narrowly focused on charitable work at the onset, local groups of patriotic women had transformed themselves into a significant nationalist force by the end of the nineteenth century. This chapter looks at how Civil War experiences changed the boundaries of women's lives and engendered a sense of citizenship that challenged earlier conceptions. No longer limited to being the reproducers of the nation, "prized and revered as objects of protection," women from various classes, regions, and ethnicities became "agents in their own right."[3] In the war's aftermath, activists in the WRC grappled with what it meant to be patriotic women. The shifting relations of gender and race became manifest in two major debates that consumed the organization.[4] First, since women had been denied the route of proving their patriotism by becoming citizen-soldiers, the WRC questioned

70

whether a woman should be defined by her familial relationship to a veteran or by her own demonstrated loyalty. Second, the Relief Corps struggled over whether whiteness and the imposition of a color line would be allowed to divide their sorority. Universal proclamations that advocated "embracing every color, every nationality, every religion," confronted the practical contradictions of racism when freedwomen petitioned to form corps in the South.[5]

"Onto Broader Freedom": Women and War

The women who joined the Woman's Relief Corps had all answered the call to arms in 1861. The popular song from the War of 1812, "The Girl I Left Behind Me," no longer seemed applicable as the war mobilized an entire generation of women into its whirlwind.[6] The song's tale of a white woman left at home while men experienced war reflected prevalent eighteenth- and nineteenth-century assumptions about gender roles. Excluded from the world of politics and bound to the home, white women became virtually invisible in the nation's narratives. Literature on the nation, with its focus on governments, public parties, and military heroes, simply ignored the roles of women.

Beginning with the American Revolution, women volunteered as spies and provided indispensable infrastructural services to the army. The ideology of the early republic, however, reinterpreted their activism differently from that of its male citizen-soldiers. Although white women's contributions to the national good were applauded, gendered conceptions of citizenship kept them subordinated: the interests of republican men and the emerging nation-state converged in masculine definitions of citizenship in which the nation's political life was restricted to white men.[7] Following the Revolution, the concept of virtue moved from its association with men in the public sphere into the home, where white women became the guardians and symbols of the nation's spiritual center. Theoretically, the creation of two spheres kept women away from the lure of self-interest, thus enabling them to concentrate on the moral training of the next generation of men.[8]

The Civil War by necessity fundamentally challenged ideological distinctions between private and public life. What quickly developed into a people's war required the mobilization of women

71

6. During the Civil War, women could be found on the homefront and on the front lines. This photograph, taken in 1862 near Washington, D.C., pictures a woman and several children alongside members of the Thirty-first Pennsylvania Infantry. Prints and Photographs Division, Library of Congress, LC-USZ62-2581.

as well as men, free and unfree. On 20 April 1861, only five days after President Lincoln called for seventy-five thousand volunteers, the women of Cleveland massed in Chapin Hall until it overflowed and organized themselves as the Ladies Aid and Sanitary Society; within three days they were fast at work collecting medical supplies for the army. Women also moved into occupations left vacant by war's endless demand for soldiers, becoming teachers and factory operatives.[9] Throughout the North, women worked as nurses in military hospitals and hospital transports, raised money for medical supplies, launched drives for blankets and other desperately needed materials, sewed uniforms, founded and ran soldiers' aid societies, assured the delivery of articles to the front lines, volunteered as spies, established homes for soldiers no longer physically fit to fight, and staffed the United States Sanitary Commission.[10] The press and politicians evoked women's patriotism in terms of bourgeois womanhood, stressing their voluntarism and depicting their efforts as generous acts of love. Women's loyalty, framed in the language of benevolence, was identified as an extension of their "natural" state.[11]

Nonetheless, women's war work proved to be far more than simply a matter of sentiment or instinct: the Civil War became a vehicle for realizing nationalist aspirations. Most women rallied to fill support roles at home, while a smaller number directly confronted the war's full brutality of mutilated bodies, disease, and sickness in military hospitals. From her home in Ohio, "Mother Bickerdyke," as she came to be known, anxiously listened as "tales of suffering began to fill the air." She heard of "sickness and neglect. . . . of cold and bleeding" and grew increasingly discontented with working so far from the scenes of battle. She wanted to have a more direct impact on the outcome of the war. "My fair sisters, stay you here at the hearth-stone, and prepare bandages and lint for them," Mother Bickerdyke told her friends, "while I go to the wars, and with my own hands bind up the wounds of our suffering boys."[12]

Hannah Ropes, an abolitionist, who believed the war represented the "special work of the nineteenth century, to take the race up into broader vantage ground and onto broader freedom," also volunteered for hospital duty on the front lines. Following the disastrous Battle of Fredericksburg, in which thirteen thousand Union soldiers lost their lives, Ropes refused to feel defeated. She confided to her diary on 14 December 1862 that the army nurse must work among the dying "as though she did not carry the whole army in her pouch, and bear crucifixion for her country!"[13] An advocate of women's rights, Ropes separated from her husband of thirteen years to pursue activities outside of her home. She became the matron of the Union Hotel Hospital, where she died of typhoid pneumonia while caring for Union Soldiers in 1863.[14] On the home front, young white women like Sarah Fuller, who later became the first president of the WRC Department of Massachusetts, sent her husband off to war, prepared hospital supplies, and organized fund-raising concerts to replenish depleted war funds.[15]

Black women, North and South, embraced the struggle for emancipation. Harriet Tubman, a runaway slave and the most renowned conductor in the underground railroad, volunteered to be a spy for Union forces.[16] When former slaves began to pour into Lawrence, Kansas, black women organized the Ladies' Refugee Aid Society.[17] Other women, living in liberated areas and inspired by the existence of all-black regiments, formed societies to care for hospitalized soldiers and newly emancipated slaves. The Colored Ladies' Soldiers Aid Society in Louisville, Kentucky, provided help to wounded black soldiers and founded a school for freed children. At the war's end, they erected a hospital for the black community.[18]

Stories of heroism abounded. Women shared stories, based in fact, mythologized in the telling, of their courage and self-sacrifice for the Union. Among the thousands of invisible acts, a mother and her daughters resolved to find a way to contribute to the Union effort despite being too poor even to purchase the material needed to sew clothing for soldiers. Left alone to farm a few acres of sterile land, they devoted all their extra time to riding a neighbor's horse twelve miles "over the mountain . . . by a road almost impassable" to procure cloth from the relief association to take home and sew into hospital garments. When asked the "secret of such fervor," they replied, "Our country's cause is the cause of God, and we would do what we can, for His sake." In the Midwest, a group of farmers' wives canvassed Wisconsin begging for contributions of wheat to sell for the "blue-coated soldier boys." They went on foot and "sometimes with a team, amid snows and mud of early spring." At market, they obtained the highest prices and forwarded all the proceeds to the Sanitary Commission.[19]

Another young women, Margaret Elizabeth Breckinridge, not satisfied to remain with the "Home-Guards," volunteered to be a nurse on one of the hospital boats that sailed up and down the Mississippi on the endless mission of picking up the "sad freight" of sick and dying Union soldiers. On one voyage she and one other nurse cared for more than 160 patients. Surrounded by dying men, she wrote home, "There is a soldier's song of which they are very fond, one verse of which often comes back to me: 'So I've had a sight of drilling, / And I've roughed it many days / . . . Yet, I think, the service pays.' " Breckinridge thanked God for the honor of letting her serve the Union. [20]

"QUESTIONS OF LOYAL LADIES": MEMBERSHIP CRITERIA
FOR THE WRC

Politicized by their Civil War experience, WRC members felt that they had "enlisted" in the nationalist project "for life, as surely as [their] husband, or father, or brother, or friend who buckled on his knapsack and donned the Union blue." Excluded from the masculine culture of political parties and fraternities, patriotic women formed Relief Corps. For almost twenty years, from 1866 to 1883, their work went unrecognized by the Grand Army of the Republic. Some women grew "disheartened" but persevered out of a sense of patriotic duty.[21] In 1879, a woman tested the GAR's gender-based criteria by applying for an honorary membership. During the Civil War she had carried Union dispatches and gathered vital information from behind Confederate lines. The Grand Army veterans did not doubt that the applicant had made sacrifices beyond the call of duty: when arrested as a spy she had barely escaped execution. But regardless of heroic service, the veterans recognized only men as citizen-soldiers, insisting that "none but the soldiers and sailors who served during the rebellion are eligible for membership."[22] Even the undisputed service of army nurses failed to win them admittance into the nation's fraternity.

Despite these rebuffs, the women of the Relief Corps refused to see their Civil War service as any less patriotic. They waited for a "true-hearted comrade" to say, "Come. Take your stand under our banner and the strong hearts of the comrades who wore the blue will stand by you as you have stood by them."[23] Finally, in 1883 the GAR approached the Massachusetts women and asked them to lead the formation of a national organization of Relief Corps. Grand Army Commander Van Der Voort confided that the "needs of the hour" necessitated a national organization of women to assist the aging veterans, since federal assistance and state infrastructure were grossly inadequate for dealing with the tens of thousands of veterans, whose situations grew more desperate with each year's passing. The GAR's opportunism was driven by the necessity of their dire situation. In turn, the Massachusetts women fully understood that the GAR's moral authority and political clout could further legitimate their patriotic activities by lending them its name. Later that year, twenty-six different women's organizations, from sixteen states, attended the founding convention of the national Woman's Relief Corps in Denver.[24]

Predictably, the Grand Army officially recognized the new organization, but not as its equal. Like other fraternal orders, the GAR rationalized women's increased participation in public life by identifying their activism as an extension, not a revision, of traditional gender roles. The creation of women's "auxiliaries" allowed men to maintain the exclusive character of their fraternal orders by designating separate and subordinate affiliations for women. Auxiliaries, in turn, provided public women with an avenue for reconciling conflicting aspirations for autonomy and masculine acceptance. The Odd Fellows and Masons had created the first fraternal rituals for women in the 1850s, each fraternity symbolically incorporating women based on their status as wives of members. In the Civil War's aftermath, these women turned their honorary memberships into actual auxiliary organizations and slowly obtained the men's grudging acceptance. Unlike auxiliaries that emerged in connection with already existing male fraternities, post–Civil War women's associations organized themselves along autonomous lines.[25]

The newly formed national Woman's Relief Corps, ambiguously poised between dependence and independence, grappled with what it meant to be patriotic women. The experience of the Civil War had already profoundly changed relations between men and women and disrupted Victorian distinctions between the home and the external world; but conceptions of citizenship still excluded women from having the right to vote, while national discourse translated women's patriotic activism into idealist associations with nurturance that were removed from their actual experience in the field. Writing about Mother Bickerdyke, a friend described the process of historical amnesia and cultural revision when she noted that "ambition and admiration delight to follow the victorious warriors with their glistening bayonets and gorgeous flags" but too often forget the work of women who left the protection of home and family to work among the mangled bodies of wounded soldiers. To remember such women, one "must strike a different chord of feeling."[26]

The Woman's Relief Corps drew its membership from a spectrum of activist women, both those who took their positions on the homefront and those who ventured out into the front lines. But without the unifying experiences of war, the women faced fundamental contradictions over the meaning of mass allegiance in times of peace. No sooner had the WRC been formed than two major questions rocked the organization to its core. The first, who constituted a "loyal woman," almost destroyed the organization. At the founding conference, when the Massachusetts WRC reported that it admitted all women who had been loyal to the nation, many in the hall balked at criteria that ignored the norms of domesticity. Instead, they urged that membership be limited to the mothers, wives, sisters, and daughters of soldiers. The Massachusetts WRC stood firm: "Let us remember that from the soldier alone came not all the sacrifice; many a brave woman's duty in the hospital—yes, in the march and in the field—compare in deeds of valor with that of the soldier."[27]

The Massachusetts WRC rhetorically asked, are we to ignore a woman's proven loyalty by only inquiring if she had a husband in the war? What of the "maiden through whose veins coursed the same proud blood, in whose heart was the same love of freedom as in that of her true, manly lover"? Never married, her lover a war casualty, would she be denied membership? Would she now come to "our doors," purified by the fire of war, and be told, "Stand aside: you are not worthy; we have only honors enough to extend over the wives, mothers, sisters, and daughters of our heroes, and, unless ranked among these, you cannot work under our banner"? No, came the refrain, "woman is loyal by birth, not marriage."[28] The WRC also gave army nurses the name "soldier-women," despite the Grand Army's insistence that only men could be given such a title.[29] The debate reflected how definitions of sexual difference are never fixed and the category "woman" is volatile and historically contingent.[30]

A year later, in 1884, Florence Barker stepped up to the speaker's podium once again, but this time backed by an overwhelming vote to open the WRC to all women who had "not given aid or comfort to the enemies of our Union."[31] She surveyed the women before her, recognizing that each one had stood by the Union in its "hour of dire distress." A "sacred duty" bound them "with ties of friendship kin to those born of camp, march and battle." Barker emphasized that although the soldiers "returned to their homes" at the war's end, "the Relief Corps was not mustered out." All understood that the journey "from camp to home, from soldier to citizen, was a long leap." Many veterans had fallen "by the wayside, the years of war telling on them." Many, too, were "without employment, home or means of support." Their condition, Barker concluded, "would have been sad indeed if women again had not taken up the work and established temporary homes."[32]

Some women, however, refused to be either as democratic or as magnanimous. The "question of loyal ladies" refused to die. Some local corps continued to challenge the national body's refusal to recognize women's familial relationships to men as the primary basis for membership. In 1887, an Indiana corps taunted the national WRC, asserting, "We are sailing under no false colors—our membership is composed only of the wives, mothers and sisters of the Veterans." The WRC president responded sharply. "I desire to urge upon every one of the 50,000 women in our ranks" who does not agree with the national policy of admitting all loyal women to immediately "take an honorable discharge from our Order." She further warned the relatives of Union veterans that they had "no right to trade on an excess of loyalty and arrogate to themselves all the patriotism of the women of the land." Remember, "wives, daughters and relatives are accidents." The WRC insisted that while loyalty differed by person, "inherent" for some, a "process of growth" for others, "no holy circle should be drawn about any class within the limits of which the loyal, patriotic or true woman may not enter."[33] In 1890, when a rival organization that made kinship to Union veterans a criterion of membership lobbied the Grand Army for official recognition, the WRC did not hesitate to beat back the competition, charging them with being "un-American."[34]

The WRC's stand against exclusive membership requirements set it off from the other most important organization of patriotic women, the Daughters of the American Revolution. Before the healing of Civil War wounds was complete, hereditary groups expanded at a rapid rate after the 1876 Centennial of the Declaration of Independence. Almost overnight, eighteen new hereditary societies emerged, bringing the total number to twenty-four by 1895.[35] Unlike patriotic organizations that required active loyalty to the Union, hereditary groups only required their members to trace their family lineage back to the American Revolution.

When the Sons of the American Revolution decided to limit its membership to men in 1890, a year after its founding, numerous women became indignant. Mary Lockwood wrote a letter to the *Washington Post* asking, "Were there no mothers in the Revolution?" Were women expected to band together with men to "commemorate a one-sided heroism"? Now is the time, argued Lockwood, "to bring forward some of the women of '76, lest the sires become puffed up by vain glory." On 21 July 1890 a call went out for "every woman in America who has the blood of the heroes of the Revolution in her veins" to attend a meeting in Washington, D.C., to found the Daughters of the American Revolution.[36] By 1900 the DAR reported a membership of 30,407, with 539 chapters.[37]

Like the Relief Corps, the DAR dedicated itself to gaining mass and official support for everything from anthems to holidays but especially for the enshrinement of the flag as the nation's most sacred symbol. Despite considerable overlap, the two women's organizations profoundly differed over issues of democracy and the inclusion of the Civil War in national memory. Over time the two groups established an informal division of labor. The DAR dedicated itself to the public history of the colonial Revolution, building monuments and reinterpreting early national history to meet the requirements of middle-class civility. The DAR's motto, "Home and Country," signified its role as the nation's social housekeeper. The members busied themselves restoring buildings, assembling genealogical records, collecting colonial and early American objects and furniture, erecting tablets to memorialize events, marking thousands of forgotten soldiers' graves from the Revolution, and holding teas with colonial china—all projects that safely by-passed the Civil War and potential conflicts between their Southern and Northern members.[38]

Intent on influencing public policy, the DAR shrewdly picked leaders from the upper and middle classes of their communities and lobbied the wives of presidents, congressmen, and generals to assume positions of national leadership. Mrs. Benjamin Harrison, the wife of the then president of the United States, became the DAR's first president general.[39] The DAR confronted the fluidity of social boundaries at the turn of the century by making family lineage an indisputable criterion of membership. When charged with elitism, the Daughters replied, "Are we would-be aristocrats because we celebrate liberty?" They resolutely maintained that there was nothing "snobbish, pretentious or un-American in collecting, preserving and cherishing the records of patriotic ancestors."[40] Deeply resentful of charges "by the unqualified and envious" that its aim was "exclusiveness," the DAR affirmed its patriotic credentials by pointing to its program of good works.[41] A picture of the DAR president general in the 1900 national report—dressed in satin and pearls, draped in furs, hair twisted elegantly about her head, her hand confidently upon her hip—captured the pose of an organization secure in its class consciousness and position. The DAR insisted that it only sought to exert an influence over those "who by reason of the lack of required ancestry can not belong to the society."[42]

Even more important than differences over membership criteria, the Relief Corps and the DAR disagreed profoundly over what to inscribe into national memory. The DAR endeavored to forge a common national heritage through a combination of historical restoration and amnesia. Its large and influential Southern membership, many of whom belonged to the United Daughters of the Confederacy (UDC), ensured that it bypassed projects associated with the Civil War and its unfulfilled promise of racial justice. Few "real daughters" of the Revolution remained by the turn of the century, but sons and daughters of Civil War soldiers abounded. The DAR erased discussion of slavery, emancipation, and the unfinished work of reconstructing race relations from its telling of Civil War history. It dismissed political debates about these issues as examples of sectional divisiveness and revised the history of the Revolutionary War so that it had neither a "North" nor a "South."[43]

The DAR hoped to mollify the bitterness that still separated post–Civil War organizations by providing a common ground for women who identified with either the Union or the Confederacy. Far from neutral, however, the DAR rarely reflected on its assumption that Anglo-Saxon womanhood defined the standard by which all others were ranked. The DAR asserted its racial dominance by both refusing to acknowledge the presence of black Americans in national history and promoting the value of the white South in building the nation. Discussions of white women's racial superiority over recent immigrants also began to appear in print in the first decade of the twentieth century. In 1904 the DAR president general reported that the founders "felt that the influx of foreign immigration . . . threatened" the nation's future and that they had "trembled for the fate of the Republic."[44]

The DAR dealt with the Civil War by heralding the patriotism of both sides. "Let us linger," wrote one of the Children of the American Revolution, "before the portraits of Grant and Lee, one in gray and one in blue, but in both the same love of Country." The men on each side fought and died for the "cause they thought best." For such sentiments, the child's essay won an honorable mention and appeared in an issue of the DAR's *American Monthly Magazine*.[45] The DAR worked actively for the rehabilitation of pride in the South. On the occasion of the Jamestown Exposition, a DAR leader reminded the nation that "if the rosary of patriotism should be counted," the South's role in building the republic could not be underestimated: "First in settlement, first, with Massachusetts beside her, in resistance to tyranny through the fiery eloquence of Patrick Henry and Richard Henry Lee; first through Thomas Jefferson in the Declaration of Independence; first through James Madison, in framing the Constitution . . ."[46] In 1912, when the United Daughters of the Confederacy decided to convene their annual convention outside of Dixie, the DAR invited its Southern sisters to hold their formal ceremonies at Independence Hall.[47] Immense bouquets of flowers decorated the DAR's hall, and Confederate flags flew next to the Stars and Stripes. The U.S. Marine Band underscored the atmosphere of national unity by playing "Dixie" and "The Star-Spangled Banner," notably leaving out the musical tribute to John Brown in their program.[48]

By comparison, the members of the WRC, like their male counterparts in the Grand Army of the Republic, found it impossible to deny that the Civil War had been the defining experience of their lifetime. Their insistence on the membership rights of all women with proven loyalty to the nation meant that they had to confront and articulate positions on the interrelationships between gender and race. Immediately after the WRC democratized its membership by opening its ranks to all loyal women, white members who moved south began agitating for the imposition of a color line. Throughout the 1890s, the WRC engaged in a prolonged struggle over the second major question facing the meaning of female patriotism: whether whiteness would be made a defining trait.

81

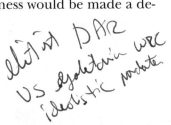

"WE ARE SISTERS, BOTH BLACK AND WHITE":
RACE AND THE WRC

Black and white women in the WRC forged reciprocal and con-flictual relations as they formed alliances, broke trusts, and shaped the changing image of what it meant to be an American. As Catherine Hall notes in her study of the national project in nineteenth-century England, cultural identity is "always complexly constituted within a field of power that never depends upon any single dimension."[49] Among the various axes of power, gender and race formed a critical and complex series of mutually reinforcing and contradictory interrelationships in the United States during the late nineteenth century. Although the WRC, unlike other fraternal organizations at that time, did not formally write a whites-only clause into its constitution, racism was an omnipresent issue as competing forces struggled for power over organizational policy.[50]

Patriots, having defined loyalty as fighting to preserve the Union, had created a slight opening in the wall of racism through which black men and women could enter. Officially, both the Grand Army and the Relief Corps committed themselves to democratic principles of equal rights. But during the 1890s, these positions were tested when white Northern women who had supported the Union cause during the Civil War moved to the South to live. Concerned that an integrated WRC would jeopardize their social standing in Southern communities, white members agitated for a whites-only clause and launched a concerted drive to segregate WRC chapters. Until then, the comparatively small number of black women in the North had worked with white women under the umbrella of the same state departments. In the South, the issue had remained dormant as long as black women dominated the few corps left in existence after Reconstruction's collapse.

As an auxiliary, the WRC organized in tandem with Grand Army posts. When the GAR experienced a revival in the late 1880s, the Relief Corps found new opportunities for creating local chapters. The WRC had a three-tiered organization that included a national office, state departments, and local corps. When a state did not have a sufficient number of members to qualify for a state organization, then the local chapters were made into detached corps that reported directly to the national office. Local chapters in the

South were so small and scattered that the national office generally placed them under its supervision. As the number of white members increased in the South, they demanded that black corps remain "detached" from the state departments they had begun to organize. The national WRC gradually condoned new categories of organization in order to accommodate segregation. By midsummer 1891, the membership of the Southern WRC—small but charged with ideological significance and symbolic importance—was 1,356 out of an overall national membership of 90,396. The WRC existed in all of the former Confederate states except Alabama. Black members, mostly freedwomen, made up twenty-four of the twenty-eight Southern detached corps.[51]

When Sarah Fuller inspected the "colored corps in the South" for the WRC in 1890, she reported on their good work. The WRC president endorsed the black corps, remembering that when the white soldiers were "flying for their lives," it was the "loyal colored people" who sheltered and gave them food. "It seems to me that the question in the Woman's Relief Corps should not be: whether a woman's face is white or black, but whether her heart is white and loyal, her life pure and generous."[52] While retaining "whiteness" as a measure of inner worth, she nonetheless articulated a position that would increasingly come under attack: that loyalty and not race should be used to define the WRC. Among the most adamant critics of the black corps were white WRC members who had moved south. As their membership grew in the 1890s, they moved to impose a color line and refused to work with the detached corps already in existence. "There can never be in our day," argued a segregationist, "a Department of white and colored Corps working harmoniously together."[53]

In 1890, the white Department of Tennessee, already set against the integration of local chapters, moved to deny the entry of any all-black corps. Hoping to diffuse the controversy, the national WRC president ruled that "where two races can not work together, there will be no Department organized, but . . . each Corps [will] be auxiliary to the National." A review committee strongly disagreed with the proposed solution, charging that it amounted to telling black members that they could wear an official badge but not participate in the self-government of a state organization. A significant number of WRC women affirmed: "We do not believe that this Organization, which knows no race nor creed, should say to the colored people, 'Because your skins are black you cannot be admitted into this sisterhood of ours.' "[54] After a heated debate, the committee's motion to grant black women a charter carried. However, by the next year Tennessee had successfully maneuvered to have the black chapters detached. This pattern repeated itself across the South as white women from Mississippi, Louisiana, Maryland, and Kentucky petitioned to make whiteness a criterion for membership in state departments.[55]

The rhetoric of equality came into direct conflict with a concerted campaign to make the face of the Southern WRC white. The attitude of Northern members reflected a range of opinions. A minority of white and black members reared on radical abolitionism during the Civil War defended the political realization of full emancipation. Others open to an alliance with Southern black members revealed the same kind of paternalism that inspired New England women to go south as educators after the Civil War. Like the Reconstruction teachers, these women hoped to remake the South in the image of New England. They offered benevolence mitigated by preconceived notions about what was in the best interest of black men and women.[56] From these disparate forces, Northern white and black members forged an informal alliance with Southern black chapters to defend the rights of black women at national conventions.

At the other end of the political spectrum, many members were largely indifferent towards issues of racial equality. The influx of white Northern members who took up residence in Southern and border states tilted the WRC' focus away from the rights of all patriotic women towards the ability of these new members to build the WRC in the white South. Demands came for the WRC to impose a racial hierarchy. Priority must be given to organizing the white corps, argued the Kentucky WRC, and "no effort [should be] made to push the formation of Colored Corps until that has been done. My experience has shown that, if a Colored Corps is organized in a town first, you will get no other."[57] Kentucky's cause gained increasing sympathy during the 1890s among Northern white members who questioned whether the organization should stand up to the dictates of white supremacy in the South.

Amidst this growing ambivalence, the Department of Kentucky marched into the 1897 Woman's Relief Corps' national convention to petition "for a division of the white and colored members."

They planned to retain control of the state organization and relegate Kentucky's black women to a detached corps. A representative from Maryland eagerly shot up her hand and asked to have Maryland added to the Kentucky petition. Lacking evidence to challenge the loyalty of black members, segregationists instead accused them of procedural improprieties, such as bookkeeping irregularities. But in fact what was operating was an assumption about the racialized inferiority of the black corps. "I lived among these people," explained a WRC member, "many of them will tell you of the help I was to them." Unfortunately, she continued, "most of the colored women in these Corps have come out of the depths of slavery. We should not expect too much of them." Ladies, she implored, "we are now discussing" a "condition and not a theory." The South is not New England. Segregation, she insisted, was the only right way to settle the question. "The colored Corps will grow just as fast, and the white Corps will increase more rapidly, and all will do infinitely better work." It should be remembered, she concluded, that "the conditions of life are entirely different than with us, and they are not yet ready."[58]

Next, Julia Layton, of the Potomac Corps, rose to take the floor. Born a slave in Virginia, Layton went on to become, in the words of the black *Washington Bee,* a "strong woman's advocate and a progressive educator." Her reputation as a national figure within the WRC was also acknowledged, and she was recognized for her work promoting kindergartens for the children of working women. Reverend S. L. Corrothers, of the A.M.E. Zion Church, described Layton as one of the "greatest women of our race."[59] When Layton rose to speak before representatives of the 1897 meeting of the WRC, she held her anger in check and delivered a dramatic rebuttal to the racism she heard on the convention floor:

Ladies . . . I have come this morning, not as a representative of a despised and ignorant race depicted to you this morning, but I come to you as a member of the Woman's Relief Corps, who joined it with the understanding that it was the one organization on the face of the globe that accorded a woman her right, be she black or white. . . . Is the colored Woman's Relief Corps dragging the white women down? No; not by any means. What we want in this organization is union, and until we have union this organization will not progress.

85

Does the Stars and Stripes, Layton asked, now only fly over "the white but not over the colored people"? Her husband, Layton reminded the members, had served in the United States Navy from 1861 until the end of the war. "He made his country free. For whom? Blacks alone? No; for the entire country." Layton argued that if the sixteen black corps in the Department of Kentucky needed more training, then the national body should simply lend a hand.[60]

Kate Brownlee Sherwood, a white WRC leader, agreed. "We are spending our money freely in every possible way; why not for this?"[61] A comrade from Tennessee, sensing that the Jim Crow forces were losing the debate, proposed instituting an educational qualification for membership. Having been denied an education, most of the Southern black members could neither read nor write. They committed organizational rituals to memory just as their treasurers frequently managed all their accounts without benefit of pen or paper. In a cruel twist of logic, this ingenuity served as grounds for detaching black corps from state departments. Deftly employing the fluid language of paternalism in support of segregation, a WRC representative from Tennessee argued that the black corps could benefit from national tutelage. Lizabeth Turner, a white member and national leader who had spent considerable time traveling throughout the South training freedwomen as members, rose in immediate opposition to instituting an educational test for membership. She recognized it as a tactic that would lead to the liquidation of the black corps. "It is the older part of the community," she argued, "who are the members, not the young ones who now have the advantage of education." Unmoved by humanitarian appeals, the Southern delegation countered that it all came down to one question: did the national WRC want "a white Department or a colored Department in Tennessee"?[62]

As the debate raged on, another black woman, Mrs. Thompkins, drew from her own experience to describe how slaves had come to the aid of Lincoln's soldiers during the Civil War. It was now time for the WRC to come to the aid of its black members. "It was my brother and sister who aided your brother, your son, to fight. . . . How can you forget what my people did for yours,—your boys, your husbands and your sons?" After such impassioned pleas the vote was called and the decision taken. Kentucky remained as it was, with white and black corps united under one state organization.[63]

Other members, however, remained resolute in their determination to racialize patriotism and simply sidestepped the decisions of the national organization. Denied formal separation, Maryland's members segregated themselves by sitting apart at their state conventions and eating at different tables during luncheons. In 1900, Maryland and Kentucky again asked for a division between white and black members. Reporting back on the inspection of the Southern WRC posts, the official report recommended that the members be divided along racial lines lest the "future of the white Corps is doomed."[64] Julia Layton again rose before the national convention, "appealing for her race." According to Layton, there were seven black women serving among the officers of the Kentucky Department and a black junior vice-commander on Maryland's staff. "If the colored women of Maryland do not want to be detached let my right hand wither before I give my voice to have them separated." Remember, Layton cautioned, "we are sisters, both black and white," and the more "you cater to prejudice the greater the prejudice becomes."[65]

Although some Northern members deplored racial prejudice, many more believed that retaining the Relief Corp's white membership should be an organizational priority. A vocal group of Northern members feared that the future of the white corps might be "doomed" if white Southern mores were not enforced. In 1900 the national convention decided to racially divide the Maryland and Kentucky Departments.[66] Even members who supported the work of black corps worried that the "social conditions of caste" prevented the black corps from getting flags and patriotic literature into the white schools.[67] Just as the suffrage movement feared antagonizing its white Southern support, so, too, the Woman's Relief Corps moved away from fighting racism by condoning segregation among its Southern membership.[68]

Even more draconian proposals continued to be raised until 1906, when a motion by the national president to deny charters to new black corps finally met a decisive defeat. Lizabeth Turner expressed the majority position: "Colored Detached Corps . . . are about all that is down there that is patriotic." During the year, she explained, they mainly took care of their sick and poor. But every Memorial Day the graves of Union soldiers were tended to by the

"Colored Corps of the South, and I think it is safe to say that there is anywhere from forty to fifty thousand graves" that they annually decorated. "The question is," concluded Turner, "shall we put them out of commission and let these graves of the South go without a flag and without a flower?"[69] The mood of the national WRC had shifted. Division along a color line was as far as the national body was prepared to go. Having decided that loyalty would be judged by personal acts, it was unwilling to formally contradict its ideological commitment to proven patriotism by banning the participation of black women.

Formally, the organization kept its membership open to all loyal women regardless of race, ethnicity, or religion. But what the national body pledged in theory, its practice negated through neglect. As early as the 1893 national convention, Julia Layton urged sending a "loyal colored woman, one who is willing to make sacrifices for her own race," down South to teach, not just for one regional training session but to stay for an extended period of time. "Oh, my sisters!" she implored, "I ask you in the name of God, and for the sake of the colored race, and for the sake of the Woman's Relief Corps all over this country, to hear this message I have brought to you." In support of the proposal, a WRC member credited the "colored women" of Washington, D.C., for making "some of the very best speeches" she had ever heard. She moved that at least two hundred dollars be allocated to pay for a full-time black organizer to go south.[70] Yet despite Layton's request and a general sense of support, the WRC provided too little in funds to make any substantial difference to the incorporation of freedwomen and their daughters into the national organization.

Groups such as the Federation of Colored Corps of New Orleans repeatedly petitioned the national body to send Georgia B. Worker, who paid her own railway fare as the national Inspector, or women like her to inspect their corps and provide them with practical assistance.[71] Finally, in 1906 the WRC made Layton an assistant national Inspector and authorized her to go south to provide local corps with instruction. But even this commitment, though important, could not meet the needs of corps like the Barnes No. 7, of Marche, Arkansas. Threats to burn their meeting hall forced these women to walk three miles into the woods to hold secret meetings.[72] The end of Radical Reconstruction had opened the doors to the reimposition of white supremacy. Mississippi ratified a new constitution in 1890 that disfranchised black men; the Supreme Court launched an assault on black civil rights and in 1896 approved racial segregation according to the fictional "separate but equal" formula; while across the South the number of lynchings of black Americans climbed into the thousands.[73] Amidst a resurgent Confederate culture, black demonstrations of national allegiance were regarded by the white South as subversive.

When Layton returned from a trip to the South in 1911, she conveyed the difficulties faced by the detached corps: "I was not permitted to sit in the ladies' waiting room at the depots but had to wait outside for the train. One place where we had to change cars I sat nearly all night outside of the station waiting for the train, sat there exposed to I did not know what danger, with my left hand in the hand of God and a six-shooter in my right." In some districts, Layton walked as much as six miles just to reach the WRC members. In Florida, she crossed a saw-tooth trestle constructed to keep cattle from crossing—"but I managed somehow to do it." At the road's end, she found twenty-two "earnest loyal black women," all born into slavery and without the benefit of education. Layton drew on their determination and spirit to instruct them in organizational regulations. Although they were in need of instruction in ritualistic work, Layton quickly clarified that "there is one thing you don't have to teach my people, and that is *loyalty*." The detached corps, left largely to their own devices, incorporated what they knew of the WRC's patriotic program into their general work of mutual self-reliance. The women raised funds to build churches, collected dues for health and death insurance, gathered flowers for Memorial Day, provided dinners for black Grand Army posts, and ensured the observance of Emancipation Day in the privacy of their own homes or, where possible, in public spaces.[74]

On a formal level, whiteness was not made into an official criterion for becoming a WRC' member, but the opportunity to forge a genuine national sisterhood was lost. The agenda of women like Layton to make loyalty stand for the full promise of emancipation remained unrealized. Although the WRC sought individual self-emancipation on many levels—from learning the nuts and bolts of professionalism, evidenced in a sophisticated level of national infrastructure, to wielding influence within local communities—it failed to give full organizational support to a social emancipation that crossed racial barriers. Insufficient national funds and infrequent national inspections left the black corps virtually on their own amidst the rising tide of Southern white supremacy. On the national level, the WRC focused its rituals of memory on fallen comrades rather than keeping the message of freedom alive through joint commemorations of Emancipation Day and Memorial Day.

The WRC's tenacious insistence that women had proven their loyalty on par with that of men did not translate into an equal insistence that black women should take their rightful place as sisters within the organization. The alliance between progressive white and black WRC members prevailed at the level of universal pronouncements but failed at the level of everyday implementation. Most white members, reflective of the Northern population as a whole, were simply unwilling to commit themselves or the funds necessary to combat the legacies of slavery. Nonetheless, the national office's refusal to ban black women altogether allowed a small number of Northern black women and Southern freedwomen to enter into the contest over the meaning of patriotism and hold back the most reactionary forces. Through this very small crack in the political wall, black women inserted themselves into the dramas of national history enacted on Memorial Day and perpetuated the memory of Emancipation within their own communities. A hierarchy based on whiteness prevailed, but not without significant contradictions and inconsistencies. A far from monolithic WRC membership took these contradictions with them as they moved into the public world and debated whether they dared to step beyond, and how far beyond, their status as an auxiliary with the sole charge of assisting Civil War veterans.

"Mothers Train the Masses—Statesmen Lead the Few": Women's Place in Shaping the Nation

U NDER the watchword "Forward!" the Woman's Relief Corp broadened its work from benevolent good works to mobilizing mass allegiance. The WRC's emergence from behind the long shadow of the Grand Army of the Republic took it into the larger "woman movement."[1] During the Civil War, men dominated the battlefields, but when the struggle for the nation moved to the terrain of culture, women took charge of its memory. Out of personal rituals of remembrance, the WRC created the most important new national holiday of the twentieth century, Memorial Day. The WRC preserved the image of womanhood as guardian of the nation's soul but transformed its ideological association with individual mothers into a social image of organized women—married and unmarried, childless and with children, wives and widows—bonded together as "mothers of the nation." In addition to relocating women's spiritual center from inside the home to within public culture, the WRC also demanded that women, in their own right, be included in the ranks of the patriotic movement.

Framed by traditions of morally inspired action, the WRC initially limited itself to acts of charitable duty. The decision to become more than a GAR auxiliary whose sole charge consisted in ministering to the needs of veterans, widows, and orphans required a prolonged debate. Some members feared that by joining with other women's groups, the WRC members would endanger their roles as patriotic mothers and wives, moving ahead of the veterans rather than walking at their sides. Others insisted that only by broadening the boundaries of its political work could the Relief Corps fulfill its patriotic mission. This chapter examines the struggles that took place within the WRC over how women should participate in the nationalist movement and what they should contribute to the cultural representations and memory of the nation.

"We Have Passed the Rubicon": Women as Patriots

Constructing the meaning of womanhood and defining gender roles assumed a central place in national discourse between the Civil War and World War I. Women's relationship to the nation-state was complex, at once affecting and being affected by their roles as biological and cultural reproducers, abstract symbols, and active participants in economic, cultural, political, and military struggles.[2] Once the WRC had opened its ranks to all women— albeit still divided along multiple lines of class, ethnicity, race, life cycle, and region—its members faced the formidable question of what positions to take within national debates about their place and responsibilities.

Historically denied the right to vote or any direct role in shaping national policy, white, middle-class women were thought to experience politics through husbands, fathers and sons. Because of their exclusion from explicitly political action, their social activities were typically characterized by men in passive and peculiarly feminine terms of quiet suffering and selfless charity. During the Civil War, however, women had proven they could be patriots, dealing an important blow to the wisdom of eighteenth-century political theory that women had "less patriotism than men."[3] Unlike the Revolutionary generation of 1776, the Woman's Relief Corps refused to remain at the fringes of a civic culture. Their wartime experiences led them to adamantly insist that "patriotism knows no sex."[4]

A wide range of women joined the Woman's Relief Corps, reflecting the divergent positions taken by women in the second half of the nineteenth century. Some argued for equal rights on the grounds that a democracy cannot deny half its people the right to shape their society; others claimed citizenship as a reward to mothers for their public service; still others believed that women's superior moral nature necessitated their assuming public roles to improve the character of society.[5] Like other women's organizations that called for temperance, created settlement houses,

7. Kate Brownlee Sherwood, a leading organizer of the Woman's Relief Corps, used this image to demonstrate the role of women patriots during the Civil War. The lines of her poem that appear next to the graphic read: "Her eye was stern, her voice a clarion blown / Across the mad tumultuous wave of doubt, / And listening souls aroused from questioning moan / Gave answering shout." *Dream of Ages: A Poem of Columbia* (New York: De Vinne, 1893), 64–65.

or demanded the right to vote, the WRC sought an alternative public voice through concerted action.

The WRC grew from forty-five women at its inception in 1883 to thirty-six thousand three years later. Women who had never been associated with any formal organization outside of their church learned how to become professional patriots. By 1890 the organization claimed a membership of more than a hundred thousand. Conscious of their historic role as female activists, the WRC members hoped to unite all "loyal-hearted women" in a union "such as no other nation on earth can boast of."[6] A substantial number of members combined religious devotion with their sense of national duty. "We ought to be consecrated to this work," preached the national chaplain, Annie Wittenmyer, "with a deeper and holier consecration than we have ever known . . . except that of the Christian church."[7] The WRC must become "an evangel to the careless daughters of the land," calling them back to meet the "high and holy obligation" of caring for "maimed and needy veterans, and the widows and orphans."[8]

The humanist orientation of the antislavery crusaders in the first women's-rights movement, in the 1830s, coupled with the post–Civil War, woman-centered ideology of suffragists, influenced the Relief Corps. Within the suffrage movement, arguments that stressed differences between men and women began to take precedence over an earlier emphasis on the common humanity of the sexes.[9] Similarly, the WRC proposed that women's unique contributions had earned them their place in the patriotic movement. Reflective of essentialist notions of womanhood, many believed that women possessed distinct natures based on their biological difference from men. "Go back through the dim aisles of the past and labyrinth of ages," argued WRC member Mary Shepherd, and "you will find that in all wars, in all the great struggles for life, woman has been first and foremost in alleviating suffering, in relieving pain, in consoling heartaches and in soothing the anxious souls." The present century, she continued, provided numerous examples of "equally noble" acts. "In times of need," she concluded, women had always been there, doing what "only a woman could do."[10]

Those members who valued the WRC as a conserving force believed that participation in the "holy work of charity" would make women into better "mothers and brighter guiding stars of happier homes." These members actively tried to maintain their separate sphere by limiting women's roles to instructing "the coming man" in Republican virtue. Women's reward, they proposed, rested in men's recognition—in men's "ever turning back with reverence and respect to the influence and teachings of women that molded their lives for the perfecting power of a nation."[11]

The majority of members endorsed the notion of women's moral superiority to men, but they were far from unanimous about limiting their work to veteran relief or staying within the boundaries of domesticity. Early in the life of the organization, a national president acknowledged, "We do not all think alike; we do not all see just alike; we have not all the same ideas in regard to the political movements and the Grand Army movement, and all other lines of legislation; and we see that we do not always agree." Yet, despite their differences, she urged the women to see themselves as sisters.[12] From the outset, some of the most articulate members raised the need for racial equality, support for suffrage, and involvement in the broader women's movement. Helping the families of the wounded, explained one member, and aiding the men whom the war had left "physical wrecks" were only the most "primitive and fundamental objects of our organization." Other "great avenues of necessary work soon claimed our attention." A WRC president credited the body's expanding patriotic agenda to the impact of historical events. "The unforgotten experiences of the sixties engendered it; the soldier environment nursed it; and the blood of our forefathers surging in our veins makes it an inborn tendency and delight."[13]

Expanding the parameters of the WRC's work and establishing organizational autonomy, however, directly challenged women's political subordination. When some WRC activists first proposed joining the National Council of Women (NCW), a coalition that included all of the major women's organizations, from the National American Woman Suffrage Association to the National Woman's Temperance Union, many members feared it might jeopardize their relationship with the Grand Army. Those in favor of the proposal countered that the women needed to move beyond being defined solely by Civil War veterans. "I tell you that this National Council," argued Kate Sherwood, will give the Relief Corps the opportunity to "bring its work before the various other bodies of women," and this in turn will allow the WRC to meet representatives from "all the branches of woman's work." Not all women in the organization, however, shared the same enthusiasm for breaking down barriers to women's expanded political activism. "I think we have glory enough," countered another member, "I can remember that we thought we had honor enough when we were accorded the permission to walk by the side of the Grand Army of the Republic. Have we grown so now that we are trying to run ahead of them, and lead their organization?" Three years earlier, the national WRC had voted against becoming an auxiliary to any other organization. But supporters of the NCW persevered, and representatives to the WRC's national convention in 1893 finally won, 136 to 92.[14]

The next year, the national president used her annual address to underscore the political usefulness of having access to the National Council of Women's extensive network. The WRC, she proposed, by its example could inspire "patriotism and love of country among the women who are likely to leave this duty to historians, rather than teach it, and live it as becomes the American woman."[15] Founded in 1888 as an umbrella organization for suffrage and temperance activists, the NCW soon included every major women's organization in the United States. The early involvement of the Relief Corps at the turn of the century revealed little of the rightward intolerance that would come to dominate the participation of patriotic organizations in the National Council of Women during the 1920s, when the American War Mothers and the DAR launched a "counter mobilization against pacifism and feminism."[16] This chauvinistic, "my country right or wrong" version of patriotism, did not gain its hegemonic place among patriotic and hereditary groups until World War I. When the Woman's Relief Corps joined the National Council of Women in 1893, its members held a more inclusive view of patriotism than the later anticommunist zealots. As a result of their direct experiences with the ravages of the Civil War, still fresh in their memory, many local corps advocated "peace and arbitration" over the use of the military to solve global conflicts. Like many progressives, the WRC supported arbitration rather than war, following the First Hague Conference on the "pacific settlement of international disputes" in 1899.[17]

On 18 May each year, local corps organized programs around the theme of international peace. In 1899 Julia Ward Howe wrote the hymn, "The Message of Peace":

> Bid the din of battle cease!
> Folded by the wings of fire!
> Let your courage conquer peace. . . .
> Let the crimson flood retreat!
> Blended in the arc of love
> Let the flags of nations meet,
> Bind the raven, loose the dove.[18]

Reflecting the views of educators who believed that too much patriotic sentiment was associated with war, a typical oration urged that "what our country needs most is men who live for her rather than die for her." Within its peace work, the WRC accommodated a range of political positions. For many, it included the peaceful reconciliation of the North and the South and resonated with Abraham Lincoln's words, "With malice toward none, with charity for all." Each year local WRC chapters were encouraged to organize a day devoted to peace and arbitration. The national headquarters provided how-to flyers of suggested program activities and outlines for talks. Paternalistic and secure in their organization's imperial position, speakers typically called for "an army of peace" in which soldiers would work for the "sake of the people," including having "friendly men in the Indian agencies, to help the Indians to become civilized." Although it did not include any critiques of domestic or international injustice, the day's themes nonetheless represented a departure from what *Leslie's Weekly* described as the prevailing glorification of the "warrior . . . the deeds of the sword, the clash of deadly combat, [and] the roar of battle."[19]

During the 1890s, just as the WRC was expanding its work within the women's movement, it also initiated numerous new patriotic campaigns. It pioneered the observance of Memorial Day; spread the campaign to fly a flag over every school; became the moving force behind the introduction of patriotic education and children's pledging their daily allegiance in the public schools; erected memorial halls and monuments; petitioned both the federal and state governments to legislate patriotism through flag-desecration laws; and agitated for the adoption of a national anthem along with a plethora of new patriotic holidays. Kate Sherwood considered the WRC's expanded program an example of what women could accomplish once they were organized. It "proves that in great national affairs the loyalty, fidelity, thrift, order, system and economy of the woman of the home finds its highest expression."[20] Flo Jamison Miller, a WRC president, maintained that the "perpetuity of this government depends on the patriotism of her women." While Grand Army veterans slowly passed away, the women marched forward as "the educators of the new generations." Miller argued that it was "far more important that we should have sensible patriotic mothers, than that we should have gifted statesmen. Mothers train the masses—statesmen lead the few."[21]

The WRC looked to the National Council of Women as the logical place to organize other women into the nationalist movement. In 1894, the WRC successfully lobbied the NCW to "take up the cause of patriotic education in the schools of the United States," and a Relief Corps' member soon assumed the chairmanship of the Committee on Patriotism within the NCW. In 1895, the Second Triennial of the National Council, scheduled to meet on Washington's Birthday, devoted the entire day to speeches on the theme of patriotism. The American Flag Company donated a twelve-foot banner, and the Stillings Publishing Company provided financial assistance for a "brilliant display of red, white and blue, including knots of ribbon worn by members of the Council and the small flags carried by the officers and the children who gave the flag salute." At long last, declared the WRC president, "we have passed the Rubicon. We have stood side by side with the other grand organizations of women and 'told our story of the flag,' and sung our hymns of loyalty, joined by the representatives of nearly one million American women."[22]

One member of the NCW candidly admitted that before the Relief Corps became involved in the council, she had only heard about Civil War veterans. When she learned that an auxiliary existed, she simply assumed that "it was a sort of a tail-end, a tag, which would do the dish-washing for them, get up their suppers and raise money for them." But after hearing those "incomparable women" of the WRC describe the "immense strides of patriotism made over this land," she had reversed her opinion.[23] Although institutionally the organization remained committed to being an auxiliary to the Grand Army, it consistently mobilized women to take independent initiative in shaping the nation. At its national meetings the WRC represented a solid phalanx of support for women's suffrage. Its principles—"Fraternity, Charity, Loyalty"— were sufficiently broad to "bind together a band of sisters" with significantly diverse points of view.[24]

The order's first two objects—"to aid and assist the Grand Army and perpetuate the memory of their heroic dead" and "to find homes for the Union veterans, their widows and orphans, and to emulate the deeds of our Army nurses"—did not necessitate the extension of suffrage to women. But the third objective—"to maintain true allegiance to the United States of America; to inculcate lessons of patriotism and love of country among our children in the communities in which we live; and to encourage the spread of universal liberty and equal rights to all"—led the WRC to conclude that women needed the "full power of the franchise in order to make better teachers" of themselves.[25] When Susan B. Anthony died, the national office took great pride in claiming that during her final hours she had worn a "badge of the Woman's Relief Corps on her breast."[26]

The WRC legitimated itself in terms of maintaining loyalty, elevating women, and upholding the purity of the home. Although the WRC denounced as un-American the notion that only women married to veterans were eligible for membership, the organization nonetheless upheld bourgeois family values and Victorian sexuality. The WRC, for example, joined forces with anti-Chinese nativists in calling for a ban against the further importation of Chinese women to the United States for "purposes of prostitution." WRC leader Kate Sherwood denounced "the reeking dives that are eating into our Republic like a loathsome cancer." Expecting men to be held to the same standards of sexual purity, she also called on the "strong arm of the law" to arrest the violators. On the question of polygamy, the WRC lobbied for legislation against a practice they saw as an attack on the "American home and subversive of the true instincts of wifehood and motherhood."[27] While statues of bare-breasted Goddesses of Liberty appeared as allegories for the nation, the down-to-earth women of the WRC stressed women's sexual propriety as a patriotic duty. Unlike later feminists, who in 1910 began to challenge gender conventions, the WRC reflected the values of "Christianity and conventional respectability" espoused by the nineteenth-century women's movement.[28] "I believe," a WRC member affirmed, that the "time has come when the Bible, the ballot-box and the flag should now and forever rest side by side upon our country's altar."[29]

"Kindergarten of Union Sentiment": Children, Commemoration, and Memory

As both conservers and modernizers, the members of the WRC ritualized memories of the Civil War by using Memorial Day to create a cultural bridge between the nation's past and its future. Having solved the challenge of secession, notes Eric Hobsbawm, the United States faced the political problem of how to assimilate a heterogeneous population. The invention of rituals, traditions, and holidays such as Memorial Day served the purpose of involving millions in a shared national history.[30] The cultural breadth of the day's language, rituals, and symbols easily accommodated a range of political views and conceptions about the meaning of womanhood and the nation. The WRC crafted a tradition that simultaneously looked backwards to fallen male comrades and facilitated the forward movement of its members as the event's central organizers and participants. The most outspoken supporter of suffrage could easily find herself working next to a member who sought neither self-emancipation nor greater political inclusion. Among a dues-paying membership that numbered more than one hundred thousand from 1892 to 1919, the majority of members limited their participation to the one day out of the year when grandfathers, fathers, husbands, brothers, and sons martyred in war could be remembered and their memory made sacred.

For many women, the larger political issues of women's role as nationalists or the cultural implications of glorifying military valor rather than principles of liberty and equality meant little in comparison with Memorial Day's capacity to speak directly and eloquently to their personal sense of loss. The day originated in private grief and spontaneous acts of placing forget-me-nots on Civil War graves. Nonetheless, the intervention of a national organization of women transformed what began as personal rituals of remembrance into the most important new national holiday of the nineteenth century, Memorial Day.[31] The U.S. government, initially dependent on volunteer soldiers, understood the symbolic importance of burial rites, and as soon as the Civil War began, the War Department assured an anxious public that the graves of loved ones would be properly marked. In 1862 Congress officially authorized the secretary of war to establish cemeteries for the Union dead. The marking of graves and the creation of cemeteries represented a major change in governmental policy and became the first significant effort to commemorate war outside the nation's capital. In turn, the government's actions reflected broader cultural shifts in attitudes towards the dead that had begun before the Civil War when the middle classes transformed cemeteries into elaborate gardens and workers formed mutual-aid societies to ensure that they did not end their lives in potter's fields. During the Civil War, military cemeteries were remade into national shrines, and the war's dead emerged as important national symbols.[32]

Whereas GAR parades celebrated the victories of male warriors, the WRC consecrated Memorial Day to "valor and love."[33] The "love" of the Relief Corps' women, however, was not just the sentimental love promoted in the numerous post–Civil War family portraits of passive women with their children grieving beneath flag-draped pictures of brave Union soldiers.[34] During the Civil War, women's love could be seen in their stoic care of the wounded in the killing fields or heard in the command of "Spartan mothers who bade their sons 'to return with their shields or upon them.' "[35] Throughout the war, women directly and indirectly contributed to the cult of courage, in which men were held to standards of heroism even when they wanted to deviate from cultural expectations.[36] Mary Livermore, one of the directors of the United States Sanitary Commission, confronted a dying soldier with the words, "Stop screaming. . . . If you must die, die like a man, and not like a coward."[37]

After the Civil War, the WRC joined Grand Army veterans in erasing any unmanly moments of doubt, cowardliness, and terror from the nation's memory of the Civil War. The women instead dwelled on sorrow and loss—conflicted memories that could undermine tragic and noble representations of the Civil War had no place in their public commemorations. The WRC made Memorial Day into a school for the nation's children in which the lessons of patriotism could be "instilled in the hearts of those who will fill our place in the future."[38] Unlike the GAR, which embodied a living history that would end with the last surviving Union veteran, the Relief Corps saw itself linked to future generations. Of all the days, a WRC president confirmed, this "one day is sacredly ours."[39]

Searching for meaning in a war that had left so many dead, the Relief Corps etched women's grief into public memory and inserted personal, emotive concerns into the political symbols of the nation-state. At a time when party politics excluded women and the GAR allowed only men to march in its parades, the Relief Corps assumed a central role in the preparation, organization, and celebration of Memorial Day. Grand Army Commander-in-Chief Jack Adams remembered a time when the sky had been "dark before Memorial Day, when it seemed impossible to place flags upon the graves of the dear boys that we loved who lie in southern battle-fields, when it seemed as if our hands were tied and that the members of the Grand Army of the Republic were forgetting their obligations to the dead." Just when all had looked lost, "up marched the Woman's Relief Corps with flags in their hands."[40]

As soon as the battles of the Civil War ended, the contest over its memory began. Women from both the North and the former Confederacy created parallel rituals of remembrance but in-scribed them with dramatically different messages. In the South, the more the war had called upon white women's labor, the more the struggle itself had been transformed from a war about the independence of Southern white men into a battle for the honor and safety of white women.[41] Out of the South's defeat, white women endeavored to reclaim their place of honor through the Confederate memorial movement. Individual acts of placing flowers on graves became formalized into Confederate Memorial Day rituals throughout the white South as state after state legalized its observance. The state of Georgia credited a young wife and mother with initiating the custom of "wreathing the graves" of the "martyred dead" with flowers. When she died, Confederate veterans recognized the "selfless devotion" of Southern womanhood by burying the young wife with full military honors.[42]

White Southern women crafted a culture of grieving that spanned years and included fashionable mourning clothes and jewelry, as well as prints for their homes and decorative ornaments crafted from the hair of prominent Confederates or lost loved ones.[43] Confederate women's expanded power increased in importance as defeated Confederate veterans increasingly turned to them for assurance that they were after all still men. The Georgia Ladies' Memorial Association, for example, turned the Confederate dead into Christ-like figures, teaching their young that just as Jesus had risen in the spring, so might the Lost Cause yet be resurrected.[44] Not until after the defeat of Reconstruction would ex-Confederates move their ceremonial life from the cemeteries back into the town squares.

For many years the national memorial ritual was known as Decoration Day, while the Southern commemoration was known as Confederate Memorial Day. Each side claimed credit for inventing the holiday. The exact origins of the day may never be known. What remains significant is how its founding story was used and remade in the cultural battle for legitimacy between the veterans of the Union and those of the Confederacy.[45] In fact, many Southerners believed that General Logan, of the Grand Army, first conceived his idea for Memorial Day during a visit to Petersburg in 1865. The often repeated story describes how he and his wife came upon women of the Confederate Memorial Association placing flowers on soldiers' graves.[46] Distressed by the white South's appropriation of the name 'Memorial Day and the growing tendency of Northerners to use the day for amusements, the GAR actively campaigned to change its name from Decoration Day to Memorial Day.[47] An important site of cultural struggle, Memorial Day validated who would be remembered as national heroes and which interpretation of the Civil War would be handed down through the generations.

In the North, the WRC used its influence to transform Memorial Day from a holiday into a holy day.[48] Unlike the regimented parades of Grand Army veterans, which followed predictable scripts, local groups exercised initiative and innovation in their orchestration of Memorial Day celebrations, reflecting their communities' distinct relationship to the nation. In remote Western areas and in the isolated chapters of the South, local corps simply assured that Union graves would not go undecorated. From the black Southern corps came bittersweet reports: "We are few in numbers and poor, but not a grave was forgotten." Another reported, "Our cemetery is too far for us to walk, so we gave a supper to pay for carriages in which to go. But seven soldiers lie there, and we just fairly buried their graves in flowers." Still another group of black WRC members described how they had "spent all day going from one cemetery to another," making sure that each Union grave would be commemorated.[49] After visiting the South in 1880, a Northern superintendent of missions stated that without the work of the "millions of souls" who are "easily known by the color given to them by their Creator," Union graves would have been forgotten. In Atlanta, he said, "they celebrate every returning Memorial day, going out to Marietta, nineteen miles, by special train."[50]

In towns with greater access to resources, middle-class women mobilized entire communities, from the mayor's office to the public schools, to participate. Only one year after the founding of the WRC, Memorial Day assumed national proportions. A local leader from Detroit, Emma Hampton, remembered that her corps had been only a few weeks old when the national office asked every chapter to make the day an organizational priority. "We were inexperienced and had little money," she recalled, but she decided to talk to the superintendent of public schools, who was a neighbor. "I went to his home, laid the case in all its bearings before him and asked would it be a proper thing to ask, with his approval, the pupils of all the schools to bring just one sweet flower to lay in holy tribute on the graves of those who died to make men free?" He did think that it would be proper, and he advised Hampton to write a letter to each teacher. "My heart was like a feather, and what mattered if two whole nights were consumed in penning the seventy-five letters!" The response was far beyond Hampton's wildest expectations. On the day of the event, wagonloads of flowers arrived. Meticulous organizers, the members of the WRC built Detroit's Memorial Day into a major celebration. In 1909 the WRC brought out 324,00 schoolchildren waving 240,000 flags.[51]

Women patriots both perpetuated notions of Victorian sentimentality and broke with Victorian conventions of separate spheres. By becoming the central organizers of Memorial Day, the WRC invented rituals that reinforced traditional relations between men and women but also literally and ideologically inserted women into public life. Many local corps made Memorial Day their year's most important project. Members devoted several months to recruiting public schoolchildren; writing, printing, and distributing flyers; meeting with mayors and city officials to gain official endorsements; publishing articles in local newspapers; lining up speakers and bands; and devising original scripts for the day's activities. On the day itself, WRC women also spoke to assembled crowds and marched along the actual parade route—still controversial and symbolically powerful poses to take in public. But such public acts did not elicit opposition because of their association with ideological images of love paying tribute to valor.

The feminine shaping of the day also gave men permission to grieve. In Grand Army parades public displays of sentimentality were scorned. Memorial Day was the one day set aside for mourning. With no intermediate state institutions available to them, women used their own initiative and creativity to reinsert feelings of loss and pain into the narratives of war. Ceremonies ached with loss but also reclaimed the dead by naming them. The women crafted rituals aimed at erasing the anonymity and randomness of war represented by the tens of thousands of soldiers who lay in unmarked graves. The WRC not only placed flags and flowers on every known veteran grave but also created the tradition of preparing floral tributes to the "Unknown dead."[52] Empty chairs, draped with flags and crepe called out for the lost souls' return.[53] In Vermont, a corps etched the words "To the men on whose far Southern graves no mother's tears shall fall, or daughter's hand plant sweet forget-me-nots," onto a large urn that they placed in front of one of the town's churches. In Palestine, Illinois, a huge mound of wreaths, bouquets, and flowers stood as a monument to the unknown dead. "Fifteen testimonials from friends, bearing cards with the name, company and regiment of the dear one remembered by some sad heart were among the flowers," reported the corps chaplain. Despite the rainy weather, ten thousand people participated.[54] For "heroes lost at sea" the San Francisco corps initiated the tradition of casting blossoms and garlands of flowers onto the waters.[55]

By shifting the locus of instructing future citizens from the home to civic spaces, the WRC made Memorial Day an important new site for public education. Imparting lessons of loyalty to the living became as essential as remembering the dead. In 1885, the national WRC president described a visit to a cemetery where the members had erected one of the first monuments to the unknown dead. At its base, baskets, bouquets, wreaths, and crosses of flowers bore the names of the unknown with dedications such as "Killed at Chickamauga, and never identified," and "To my brother—Andersonville." Children came from all directions, she recalled, "thronging around the monument and reading the inscriptions." Silently, she "prayed that these mute object lessons might each year be multiplied, that in these Kindergarten of Union sentiment our youth and children might learn the full meaning of loyalty and all it has cost."[56] The role of children in memorial services signified the perpetuity of the nation. The WRC envisioned the next generation as the "greatest standing army in the world," ready to spread their "gospel of patriotism."[57] Since the early republic, the nation had used its children to symbolically define itself as a people, but on Memorial Day patriotic women transformed children from "objects of rhetorical sentimentality" into active participants.[58]

In Michigan, the Howell corps organized the public school children to gather memorial flowers. In Owasso, New York, thirty-eight flower girls, dressed in red, white and blue, placed flowers on graves as the schoolboys sang "Our Soldier Boys." In Grinnell, Iowa, the corps organized a procession of "two wagons, one carrying forty-eight little girls dressed in white, wearing flag caps and blue sashes, bearing flowers; in the other were forty little boys, who wore red, white and blue caps, carrying flags."[59] In Plainfield, New Jersey, the corps staged a pageant, "Guarding the Flag." The schoolgirls, dressed in national colors and representing each state in the Union, recited short verses and "declared their determination to guard the flag after their fathers depart this life."[60] And in Dexter, Maine, the corps organized a procession of carriages carrying disabled soldiers followed by marching Sunday school children dressed in white with black sashes.[61]

The recognition of patriots' graves, however, stopped short of including anyone except Union men. Although the WRC played an important role in demanding autonomy and access as patriots, it carefully avoided directly challenging the social and symbolic position of the nation's masculine citizen-soldiers. Members within the WRC agitated for the decoration of the graves of women patriots, but their proposals to have a "Memorial Flag" placed on members' graves created an organizational stir. Only after much deliberation did the WRC decide that on any day except Memorial Day the graves of Civil War nurses could be honored and flags could be displayed on members' graves.[62] The WRC used Memorial Day to move to the center of patriotic culture, but,

8. At first the Northern ritual of remembering the Civil War's dead was called Decoration Day. Women used their creativity to craft a day of remembrance out of flowers. In this picture, schoolgirls and boys in Washington, D.C., have gathered daisies for the observance of Memorial Day, 30 May 1899. Prints and Photographs Division, Library of Congress, LC-USZ62-4555.

paradoxically, it obscured its own participation by focusing attention on the Grand Army veterans. The use of language and symbols on Memorial Day by which women paid tribute to men eased women's way into uncharted public spaces, but at the cost of remaining only partially visible behind the looming representation they helped to create of the heroic men.

"THE MEN WHO LOVED THEIR COUNTRY": A TRIUMPHANT PATRIOTISM

The meaning of Memorial Day remained narrowly limited by a gendered and increasingly racialized language that remembered the war as fought by white men so that the "Nation might live," rather than fought by men and women in the cause of freedom. Frederick Douglass had hoped Memorial Day would ritualize memories of Union victory and emancipation in order to help win battles ahead in the struggle for black freedom and equality. He understood the invented quality of tradition and sought to elevate Memorial Day's association with emancipation into indelible and mythic proportions.[63] Abstract declarations about liberty hung in the air, however, as the most profound reason for fighting the Civil War, emancipation, slipped from dominant memory.

The full horrors of war also remained obscured behind both the triumphant culture of Grand Army parades and the sentimental culture of commemoration. Whatever antiwar sentiment the WRC brought to the ritualized, public memory of the Civil War, the nationalist path of a rising world power led patriotic women to side with the ideals of imperial expansion, not against it. While individual corps joined the movement for "peace and arbitration," even including this work on their charts of patriotic activities, the WRC immediately endorsed the Spanish-American War as a righteous mission of the "Empire for Liberty." The ideological core of Memorial Day—the celebration of loyalty to the nation—ultimately required the WRC to join military mobilizations rather than oppose them, while the formalization of Memorial Day molded personal statements of grief into a movement to build the nation.

Memorial Day became a powerfully symbolic holiday, calling on a nation to give its "annual tribute to the memory of the men who loved their country better than they loved their lives."[64] Memorial rituals figured in the imaginative web described by Benedict Anderson, in which a fraternity of strangers, despite "inequality and exploitation," could feel that they could march off to war as comrades.[65] However, the potentially subversive quality of the memorials that the WRC crafted, with their pathos and inchoate critique of war, never materialized.[66] Organizers and participants succeeded in infusing emotive meaning into the memory of the Civil War, but their discourse centered on the triumph of the nation, not a critique of its unrealized promises.

Despite contradictions and inconsistencies, both the Woman's Relief Corps and the Grand Army of the Republic played a critical role in bringing about a massive political and cultural transformation in which identification with and devotion to the nation would take precedence over all other forms of group, ethnic, and regional loyalties. The most dramatic challenge to national unity came from the ex-Confederate, white South, which having lost the Civil War, contested the cultural terms and conditions of "one country, one people."

"One Country, One Flag, One People, One Destiny": Regions, Race, and Nationhood

THE meaning of the Civil War profoundly changed on 1 January 1863, when President Lincoln issued the Emancipation Proclamation. Thomas Wentworth Higginson, a white Union commander of a black Civil War regiment, attended one of the first freedom celebrations. Higginson recalled:

> Just as I took and waved the flag, which now for the first time meant anything to these poor people, there suddenly arose, close beside the platform, a strong male voice (but rather cracked and elderly), into which two women's voices instantly blended, singing, as if by impulse that could no more be repressed than the morning note of the song-sparrow —
>
> "My Country, 'tis of thee,
> Sweet land of liberty
> Of thee I sing!"[1]

Henry McNeal Turner, who served as chaplain to a black Civil War regiment and became a leading bishop in the African Methodist Episcopal Church, shared the initial sense of optimism and anticipation. Speaking before a large gathering of freed slaves on Emancipation Day in 1866, Turner proclaimed that "the nation's great emblem is no longer against us. . . . the glories of its fadeless escutcheon will ever bid us go free."[2]

As long as Reconstruction held, black Southerners formed the backbone of Southern patriotic celebrations. For black Americans, the answer to the most important question—"How free is free?"—hung in the balance. Neither side in the Civil War had anticipated that the national divide would develop into a struggle over the meaning of freedom in America.[3] The most dramatic opposition predictably came from the white South, where defeated Confederates refused to submit to an Americanism forged by the North. Instead, after the war they rallied behind the Confederate battle flag, celebrated the Confederate general Robert E. Lee as

110

their wartime hero, and paid yearly reverence to the bravery of Southern soldiers on their own Confederate Memorial Day.

Throughout the second half of the nineteenth century, diverse forces from the North and the South pursued national reconciliation, but cross-cutting allegiances, profound ambivalences, and political divisions disrupted and challenged the movement towards consensus. Black and white supporters of Radical Reconstruction forged interpretations of patriotism that joined the battle to preserve the Union with the realization of democracy and racial equality. Southerners who refused to be "reconstructed" relived a mythic past of social harmony, while upholding the superiority of white Southern civilization. Still others sought to negotiate a national culture capable of suturing divisions without jeopardizing social and race-based distinctions and hierarchies.

Chapters 3 through 6 focused on the organizations that participated in the nation-building movement and the struggles that took place within them over membership, activities, historical memory, and cultural politics. Now we shall return in greater depth to the fundamental issue that confronted American nationalists after the Civil War: how to build a participatory sense of allegiance to a United States of America that only recently had been two countries at war. The idealistic expectation of patriots in the GAR and the WRC that a nation is a voluntary association of free citizens would not be met by a forced loyalty imposed by the victors. The political and cultural challenge was to find some common ground on which the North and the South might envision themselves as part of a national family. Chapters 7 and 8 explore how this process of national reunification developed over several decades, with particular attention in this chapter to the conflicts that took place between African American and Confederate views about race and to the role of war and the military in promoting national unity at the expense of social equality.

"Sweet Land of Liberty": Battling for America's Conscience

At the end of the Civil War, black Southerners emerged as the region's patriots, while most Confederates retreated from the public sphere in despair. For a brief historical moment, newly freed slaves became participants in the expression of national culture. In the nineteenth century, black leaders and spokespersons represented a range of positions, but the majority were not ambiguous about their identity and allegiance: they were both black and American. During the Civil War, black abolitionists seized the ideological initiative and claimed the language and symbols of the American Revolution in the cause of their freedom. They proposed that the struggle for liberation and equality would not only affect the future of slaves but also purify American ideals and redeem America's destiny.[4]

Patriotism carried a distinctive meaning for black and white defenders of Radical Reconstruction. They expanded the language of patriotism from traditional conceptions of willingness to die for one's country to include the reciprocal responsibility of the nation-state to guarantee social, political, and racial equality. Black leaders held America's republican values up to the nation as a mirror and warned that as long as slavery and inequality endured, America would never be able to "raise her flag of liberty and spread it out unstained and uncontaminated for the world to look upon and admire."[5] Following emancipation, most black Americans refused to abandon their claim to an American nationality. "We are Americans," declared the citizens of Norfolk, Virginia, "our fathers as well as yours were toiling in the plantations of the James River." Recovering their history in the Revolutionary War, the black Virginians claimed that it was a "colored man, Crispus Attucks," who shed the "first blood," and on every engraving of "Washington's famous passage of Delaware the dusky face of a colored soldier" can be seen.[6] Another group of Virginia freedmen and women resolved that America was "now our country—made emphatically so by the blood of our brethren."[7]

At no other time during the nineteenth century would blacks consider themselves so fully American as they did during Reconstruction. Newly freed slaves created freedom celebrations after the issuance of the Emancipation Proclamation in 1863. For the first time, the nation-state represented not just abstract American ideals but an institution obligated to correct historical injustices. After Abraham Lincoln established the doctrinal basis for an activist liberal state,[8] Frederick Douglass predicted that Emancipation Day would become the "most memorable day in American Annals." July Fourth marked the political birth of the nation, but

Douglass believed that the Emancipation Proclamation promised to "put peace forever between the conscience and the patriotism of the people."[9] Only eleven years earlier, at a July Fourth celebration in 1852, Douglass had told his white audience that "your high independence only reveals the immeasurable distance between us. . . . The sunlight that brought life and healing to you, has brought stripes and death to me. This Fourth of July is *yours*, not *mine*. You may rejoice, I must mourn." Emancipation, however, opened the possibility that the "rich inheritance of justice, liberty, prosperity, and independence" might yet be realized by black as well as white Americans.[10]

Freedom celebrations reflected regional variations, and dates differed by state depending on the timing of liberation. In Texas, freedmen and freedwomen initiated "Juneteenth" following General Gordon Granger's 19 June 1865 reading of a governmental decree granting freedom to slaves in east Texas. Local churches and communities developed their own distinctive traditions by combining cultural elements from slave holidays, religious observances, and patriotic rituals. Some communities borrowed the singing of a freedom anthem and the reading of a freedom document from ceremonies created by West Indians after their emancipation in 1834. Abolitionist songs such as "John Brown" and anthems such as "America" were sung in public. Rituals like the pit barbecue of pork served as earthy reminders of slavery, while "eating higher on the hog" symbolized the social distance traveled since bondage. Clothing also became an important representation of freedom. Just as revolutionaries in France changed their style of dress to demonstrate their desire to abolish class distinctions in the 1790s, so too ex-slaves paid careful attention to the neatness of their clothing to communicate their emancipated status.[11]

Black men and women fully participated in all of the patriotic holidays, leading a white man from Charleston to bitterly complain that on July Fourth the "Niggers now celebrate, and the whites stay home and work."[12] Although only black men ran for elective office and voted, black women visibly participated in political mobilizations too. Breaking racial and gender barriers, they joined the men in the streets for rallies and parades. In 1868, during a political campaign in Mississippi, black maids and cooks defiantly wore buttons portraying General Grant when they went into the homes of their white employers.[13]

The assertion of citizenship rights and equal participation in national culture, however, would not go unchallenged. The Hamburg Massacre, in South Carolina, erupted in 1876 during the centennial celebration of July Fourth by the town's black militia. By the end of the rampage, Hamburg, once a stronghold of black Reconstruction power, lay ransacked, with seven black Americans dead. "We may not be able to carry the State at the ballot box," the *Sumter True Southron* triumphantly announced, "but when it comes to a trial of the cartridge box we do not entertain any doubt of the result."[14] Mississippi's *Weekly Clarion* blamed the violence on "Negroes drunk with power," who had driven the whites to desperation. "One demand should be made," asserted the newspaper: "Let Grant take his heavy hand off of the South. Of our soldiers we may say to him as Richard III said to Stanley: 'What do they do in the South when they should serve their country in the West?' Why should Mississippi be strongly garrisoned while troops are wanting to fight Sitting Bull in Dakota and all that region which is now threatened with a long, cruel and possibly disastrous war?"[15] Despite the governor of South Carolina's report of the "brutal murders" and his request for additional federal troops to restore public order, President Grant refused to comply and insisted that the state take sole responsibility for enforcing its laws.[16]

The language of patriotism continued to speak in universal terms of equality and democracy, but conflicts and divisions deepened along racial lines. The next year, 1877, Reconstruction irrevocably ended with the inauguration of Rutherford B. Hayes and the subsequent withdrawal of federal troops and Republican support for biracial government. Black Americans, forced out of the South's political life, turned to their own communities to perpetuate their traditions and memories.[17] Many stopped celebrating July Fourth, with its unfulfilled promise of "unalienable rights."[18] From one generation to the next, parents taught their children that Emancipation Day was "our day," recalled a woman, and "the 4th of July was for the white folks."[19] In 1883 the Supreme Court, by ruling the Civil Rights Act of 1875 unconstitutional, allowed white Southerners to claim that the "people of the United States have, by their suffrages, remitted to the Southern people, temporarily at least, control of the race question."[20]

Upon hearing the decision, Bishop Turner issued his condemnation in A.M.E.'s weekly newspaper, the *Christian Recorder*: "It absolves the Negro's allegiance to the general government, makes the American flag to him a rag of contempt instead of liberty. It reduces the majesty of the nation to an aggregation of ruffianism . . . revives the ku klux klan and white leaguers, resurrects the bludgeons, sets men to cursing and blaspheming God and man, and literally unties the devil."[21] Benjamin Tanner, the newspaper's editor, insisted that black Americans had paid "as great a price as any, and greater than most" for liberty: "To say nothing of our enforced immigration and our passive suffering, we absolutely won the boon by helping fight the battles of '76, which made the Republic possible, the battles of '12, which made it respected, and the battles of '60, which made, as the glorious Sumner said, 'the Nation national.' We say, therefore, we have won the right of American citizenship, which no power on earth can make us willingly surrender."[22]

Deaf to constitutional appeals, the Supreme Court retreated from extending federal protection to anyone who suffered racial discrimination. In 1896 the Court upheld the South's introduction of a "separate but equal" policy in *Plessy v. Ferguson*, opening the floodgates of discrimination and inequality as segregation regulations spread throughout the South.[23] The obstacle of Reconstruction removed, political and cultural space opened for building a New South that did not challenge the reassertion of white supremacy.

Symbolic of alliances to come, news of the Hamburg Massacre appeared in Northern presses in 1876 next to stories of General Custer's defeat. Within a month of Custer's death in the Battle of Little Bighorn, some Confederate veterans had volunteered to fight the new common enemy. "As this is the Centennial year of American independence," wrote a former Confederate commander from Kentucky, "I desire to let the world see that we who were once soldiers of the 'lost cause' are not deficient in patriotism." He went on to request that his congressional representative from Kentucky intervene on his behalf and offer President Grant the "services of a full regiment, composed exclusively of ex-Confederates to avenge Custer's death."[24] Ex-Confederates increasingly linked their demand for the removal of federal troops from the South with the need to fight Indian wars more effectively in the West.

115

"Leaders and Battles": The Role of Militarism
in National Reconciliation

The first signs of national reconciliation emerged during the Indian wars as the army pursued a strategy of annihilation toward Plains Indians who refused to be forced onto reservations. Immediately on the heels of the Civil War, the U.S. government implemented a new policy of abolishing the "Indian Country" in order to clear the way for Western expansion.[25] Without the enthusiasm of a popular imperialism first generated by the Indian wars and later dramatically consolidated during the Spanish-American War, the impetus for cultural reunification would have been significantly delayed.[26] Combat against a new enemy laid the basis for Southern support of national expressions of heroism, while expansion in war allowed the North to revel in the might of Union. As important to the geopolitical consolidation of the nation as the outcome of the Civil War, the final destruction of the Indian nations' military power had assured the existence of the United States as a continental power by 1890.

Regimental stories of life on the frontier abounded in a decidedly male culture of nickel-and-dime novels that flourished at the turn of the century. Young men in the East became avid readers of authors such as Captain Charles King, a retired officer and "Indian-fighting cavalryman."[27] This genre dug such deep roots in national memory that as late as the 1950s, John Ford adapted images of Northern and Southern reconciliation from turn-of-the-century army stories for his cavalry films. Ford's scripts were based on stories by James Warner Bellah in the *Saturday Evening Post* in the 1940s. Bellah, who had links to the South and was born in 1890, most likely drew upon his characterization of ex-Confederates and Union soldiers from King's bestselling novels.[28] In Ford's *Rio Grande*, Union officers sit in review as the regimental band plays "Dixie" in honor of the metaphorical reunion of a Northern Captain and his Southern wife.[29] In a scene from *She Wore a Yellow Ribbon*, an ex-Confederate officer expresses his hope to John Wayne, who plays Captain Nathan Brittles, that General Lee will soon be added to the nation's pantheon of heroes.[30] Although Ford made his Westerns with a Cold War audience in mind, his depiction of ex-Confederates' belief that it was time to resurrect

Robert E. Lee came directly out of turn-of-the-century popular culture.

Although the glorification of soldiers became the standard fare of patriotic memoirs and histories, the army itself was largely demobilized after the Civil War, with further dramatic reductions following the end of Reconstruction. Professional military schools barely escaped extinction. However, despite the army's reduced size and physical isolation fighting the last of the Indian wars, it proceeded to professionalize and prepare for the time when it could assume a place of power within civic society.[31] Citizen-soldiers like John Logan, major general and senator, warned against the emergence of a military clique and argued that professionalization would give too much power to West Point.[32] On the other side of the debate, Emory Upton, also schooled in the Civil War, wrote bitterly about the loss of life and materials resulting from volunteers' lack of training. Upton, a leading spokesmen for a professional army, condemned the "Anglo-Saxon prejudice against 'standing armies as a dangerous menace to liberty' " and asked, "Is death on the field of battle no evidence of love for one's country? Have the officers of our Army to-day no sense of duty? In time of universal peace are those who continually expose their lives in Indian wars to open up to civilization the rich lands of the far West, actuated by no motive other than love of promotion?" Upton demanded that the public at least "concede to the Army a patriotism as bright and enduring as that which prevails in civil life."[33] Though it would be many years before public support for a professional army replaced commitment to an army of volunteer soldiers, the opinions of Civil War officers carried significant influence throughout the country.

Just as war was pivotal in promoting male warrior heroism, Civil War officers assumed a critical role in promoting Northern and Southern reconciliation in the 1880s. Union officers, mostly trained at West Point, respected their former classmates and recent adversaries. Possibly only the memories of lost Union comrades kept them from acquiescing to President Johnson's pro-Southern program for reunification. Officers trained at West Point formed a class apart from rank-and-file citizen-soldiers; many were prepared to resume past friendships developed while classmates at the academy and forged as comrades in arms during the U.S.-Mexican War. Enlisted men, less conflicted by personal and professional relationships, maintained that loyalty to the Union, not valor, should receive the nation's respect.

The rituals accompanying the surrender of General Lee at Appomattox illustrate the shared culture of the officer corps. Horace Porter, a Civil War veteran who wrote his memories of that day twenty years later, emphasized the pathos of Appomattox and the overtures of reconciliation made by Grant and his officers. Porter recalled that Generals Grant and Lee were already seated when the officers softly walked in and took their positions along the sides of the room. Grant finally broke the silence by reminding Lee that he had first met him while serving in Mexico. Later, when Grant began to commit the terms of surrender to writing, he looked at Lee. "His eyes seemed to be resting on the handsome sword which hung at that officer's side. He said afterwards that this set him to thinking that it would be an unnecessary humiliation to require officers to surrender their swords ... and after a short pause he wrote the sentence, 'This will not embrace the sidearms of the officers, nor their private horses or baggage.' " For the first time, Lee showed a slight change in his demeanor, "evidently touched by this act of generosity."[34]

While the terms of surrender were being copied, Lee shook hands with Grant's officers and staff, including one Union general who had been Lee's adjutant while he was superintendent at West Point before the war. Lee departed after signing the letter of surrender, surrounded by an aura of great solemnity. Grant stepped outside and saluted him by raising his hat, a gesture followed by all the other officers present. The next day, several officers, including Sheridan, visited the enemy's line to seek out old friends. When they returned, they brought back Confederate officers to pay their respects to Grant, who received them cordially and talked with them until it was time for them to leave.[35] Porter mentions more contradictory responses, but only in passing, for he chose not to explore the sentiments of enlisted men. Unlike Grant's officers, Union troops began to fire salutes when news of the surrender reached them. Upon hearing this, Grant immediately sent orders for them to stop and cautioned the men that "the war is over, the rebels are our countrymen again."[36] The officer class closed ranks against a more popular rowdyism, but emotions proved hard to contain.

By 1884, officers from both sides were ready to contribute to a series of war recollections that would appear during a three-year period in a popular illustrated magazine, the *Century Magazine*. The magazine attracted leading generals from both sides, including Grant and Sherman from the North and Beauregard and Johnston from the South. The series emerged out of its editors' entrepreneurial recognition that the public was ready for a dialogue among former enemies. The editors carefully chose the series' title, "Leaders and Battles," to signal that the magazine did not intend to address either the Emancipation Proclamation or the condition of freedmen. The decision met with great success, increasing the magazine's circulation by one hundred thousand in the first year.[37]

Enthusiastic letters flooded the magazine's offices, leading the editors to add a section called "Memoranda of the Civil War" featuring letters from readers. One veteran wrote of an incident after Lee's surrender, in April 1865, when a group of Union and Confederate officers shared an evening of song. Knowing that paroled Confederate officers were nearby, the Union officers decided not to sing any patriotic songs. To their surprise, the Confederate officers sent a request to join them. After singing some glee songs, the Confederate officers requested them to sing some of the old army songs. They enthusiastically took up the request and concluded their concert with "Rally Round the Flag, Boys." Throughout the evening, "many a foot beat time as if it had never stepped to any but the music of the Union." After the applause subsided, the reader recounted, a "tall, fine looking fellow in a [Confederate] major's uniform" confided his parting hope that the "time may come when we can all sing the 'Star Spangled Banner' again."[38]

The magazine featured dignified graphics of handsome and heroic generals, as well as romanticized battle scenes. Images of soldiers marching under the Confederate battle flag were a far cry from cultural representations of only twenty years earlier.[39] At the war's end, gendered imagery and language lauded Union veterans for their masculine exploits as citizen-soldiers, while Northern presses caricatured the leader of the Confederacy, Jefferson Davis, as a "President in Petticoats."[40] Numerous songs, cartoons, and newspaper graphics depicted Davis dressed as a woman in flight before the triumphant advance of manly Yankees.[41] Though the nation praised white women for their maternal affection and self-sacrifice, they were still denied the just rewards of full citizenship owed to patriots. No more demeaning insult could be made of Davis than to humiliate his manhood. Cartoons contrasted the ambiguous sexuality of Davis with the unquestionable virility of Union soldiers. Davis, notes Nina Silber, became the symbol of a feminized Confederacy. Pursued by the Michigan Cavalry, Davis had tried to disguise himself by dressing in some of his wife's clothes. Although he probably had worn only a woman's cloak or shawl, his cross-dressing at the moment of his humiliating defeat allowed the Northern press to popularize an image that fit its view of an emasculated South.[42] Catchy tunes lampooned Davis's capture by describing how "just on the out-SKIRTS of a wood, his dainty shape was seen. His boots stuck out, and now they'll hang old Jeff in Crinoline!"[43]

By the 1880s, however, the *Century*'s editors believed that the time was ripe for reconciliation and condemned as public enemies anyone who attempted to "revive or trade upon the dead issues of the war." The magazine's commitment to a "new era of common interests and mutual sympathy" framed its editorial policies. The magazine's staff worked against what they considered a "narrow, sectional, and embittered tone" coming from certain quarters of the North.[44] Articles on the South also remained silent on resistance to the Northern triumph and only hinted at its ambivalence towards being once again a region within the Union.

In 1885, a letter signed by "A Southern Democrat" described his support for New South doctrines of economic modernization and reunification but also called for reciprocal compromises. The reader objected to Southern novelist George Cable's assertion that the "cause of the North was just." History, the southern Democrat retorted, was still "holding her grand inquest," and with the jury still out, "who shall say how many compromises of opinion or prejudice are necessary to give us a clear view of the truth? Assuredly compromises are necessary, and thus it happens that all the concessions need not come from the South."[45]

Most white Southerners mixed acceptance of national reunification with demands for Southern control of race relations. By emphasizing valor, rather than treason, white Southerners provided the country with an interpretation of the Civil War that obfuscated their attack on the nation and their defense of slavery.

Northern patriotic groups, who refused to concede the righteousness of fighting a war to preserve the Union, proved much more malleable when it came to recognizing the integrity of Southern heroism and endorsing a nostalgic view of the antebellum South. Officers again led the way. Once the federal government made the decision to recall Union troops from the South in 1877, officers from both sides began to appear in a growing number of "Blue and Gray" reunions. The occasion of Grant's funeral in 1885 testified to the increasing willingness of Confederate officers to publicly endorse national unity. The *Century*, wanting to promote images of harmony over outstanding feelings of hostility and ambivalence, predictably chose to emphasize how leading generals from both sides "mingled their tears in a common grief."[46] Representative of shifting relations of power, at the dedication of Grant's tomb in 1897, the elite Richmond Light Infantry Blues marched at the head of the contingents from Virginia, with a battalion of black troops bringing up the rear.[47]

The full exoneration of Confederate officers came with the onset of the Spanish-American War, when, for the first time since secession, the U.S. Army appointed ex-Confederates to the officer corps. Officers, who were among the most ready to promote a national dialogue, clearly gained from the expanding role of the military within society. But the most significant influence over negotiating the cultural terms of reunification came from the rapidly growing patriotic organizations, who assumed enormous cultural power over national discourses during the 1890s.

THE LOST CAUSE: CONFEDERATE TRADITIONS
FOR THE NEW SOUTH

Between the 1880s and the early twentieth century, developments within patriotic organizations profoundly influenced how the nation came to see itself. Grand Army veterans grappled with the contradictory impulses of sectional animosity and their ardent passion for national unity. Initially, they had been more willing to respect individual Confederates than to accept rituals, symbols, or monuments that implied respect for the Lost Cause.[48] Closely related to this issue was whether Confederate soldiers would forever be denounced as traitors or would be recognized as brothers who had fought for what they believed to be right. The debate reemerged each year as veterans prepared to celebrate Memorial Day. Determined to recognize only the graves of Union soldiers, the GAR and the Woman's Relief Corps often clashed with Confederate veterans attempting to honor their dead. The GAR initially dedicated the "nation's Sabbath," Memorial Day, to only "those who sought to preserve the Union, and not those who sought to destroy it." Long after the Civil War, Union veterans continued to insist that they did "not seek to commemorate valor, but patriotism."[49]

However, by the era of the Spanish-American War, the memory of the Civil War and the tenets of patriotism had been sufficiently revised to allow Confederates to be remembered as loyal sons rather than as traitors. The GAR and the United Confederate Veterans (UCV) laid the groundwork for this cultural reunification at the turn of the century. In the process, each also attempted to define which rituals, symbols, and interpretations would be incorporated into the nation's great patriotic "traditions."

Beginning in the late 1880s, when the GAR's membership approached its zenith, a coalition of middle-class forces breathed new life into the Confederate movement. Empowered by the removal of federal troops from the South and the ending of national support for Radical Reconstruction, the UCV attracted a mass following. Earlier veteran organizations, dominated by the traditional Southern elite, had failed to generate much popular support. After the death of Robert E. Lee in 1870, a small coalition of Virginia veterans had attempted to keep the Confederate tradition alive. Largely isolated from enlisted men, aristocratic Virginians led the first Confederate veteran organizations. They felt that defeat had called their manhood into question and, unable to reverse the war's outcome, sought to rehabilitate their honor through assertions of their superior valor. Virulently racist and unwilling to accept the terms of Reconstruction, these veterans invoked images of the prewar Confederacy in opposition to postwar change.[50]

Exerting little influence beyond its own two hundred members, the Virginia coalition nonetheless constructed an interpretation of the Civil War that endured. Jubal Early, a central figure in the organization, warned his fellow veterans that it was up to them to determine whether Confederates would be remembered as rebels

122

and traitors or as patriots who had followed the true principles of the nation's founding fathers. Adamant about the justness of the Lost Cause, Confederate veterans argued that the South had waged a legal war over constitutional principles. Loss, they insisted, resulted from overwhelming numbers on the Union side and a lack of resources on the side of the Confederacy, not from a lack of principle or honor.[51] Unable to accept patriotism as defined by loyalty to the Union, the Virginia coalition revised the meaning of a war fought to defend slavery into a war about "honor." The coalition made belief in the righteousness of their cause, self-sacrifice coupled with courage on the field of battle, and devotion to duty the defining characteristics of a patriot.

The importance of the Virginia coalition's legacy would not become fully evident until the 1890s, when a revitalized Confederate movement attracted a mass following. Instead of railing against the North and dwelling on defeat, the United Confederate Veterans demanded Northern acknowledgment of Southern heroism in exchange for sectional reconciliation. The new movement, led by a town-based middle class, recognized the benefits of economic reintegration and mobilized veterans of all classes in affirming loyalty to the Southern past as they offered new visions of the future.[52] Confederate veterans worked toward reunification at the same time that they maneuvered to create autonomous traditions. Commercial concerns and Confederate patriotism easily coexisted as Southern cities in search of urban renewal saw that an active Confederate culture also meant added revenue. Ready to capitalize on the awakened spirit, real-estate interests promoted building Confederate statues on what was to become Monument Avenue in Richmond, Virginia, when all that existed was empty farmland and real-estate maps of vacant lots promising a boon to the local economy. The intersection of commerce and the new Confederate culture took the shape of a vast new assortment of products, including Robert E. Lee wood-burning stoves, featured in the pages of official souvenir pamphlets from the dedications of Confederate monuments.[53]

Unlike in the period of the Civil War, the growth of Confederate monuments and rituals neither resurrected the demand for independence nor served as a basis for rebellion. Instead, as Gaines Foster has shown, the Confederate movement created a model of political order that ritualistically affirmed social unity and deference to authority. Alarmed by threats to white supremacy during Reconstruction, challenged by the revolt of farmers in the Populist movement, and determined to silence the demands of a militant labor force, the UCV hoped that a redefined Confederate culture could mobilize loyalty and defuse competing class allegiances.[54] "Anarchy will never get a hold in the South," affirmed the *Confederate Veteran*, "while the Confederate soldier element predominates."[55]

The UCV members believed that only by becoming legitimate members of the nation could they be left alone to manage race relations and preserve the memory of the Confederacy. Broad enough to accommodate a spectrum of viewpoints and interests, the membership swore allegiance to the Stars and Stripes without undermining a more visceral loyalty to the Lost Cause. Such flexible and opportunistic sentiments characterized much of the invention of the Confederate tradition. Across the South communities erected monuments to Southern generals and privates, thousands participated in Confederate Memorial Days, and cities enthusiastically embraced annual UCV reunions. At the 1896 reunion, ten thousand veterans paraded through Richmond. A Northern visitor described how "men, women, and children welcomed the old battle-scarred heroes with yells of triumph and enthusiasm that knew no bounds." In fact, the excitement seemed even greater than that at a Grand Army reunion parade the visitor had attended just a year earlier.[56]

In cities such as Richmond, Raleigh, Columbia, Atlanta, Tallahassee, Montgomery, Jackson, Little Rock, and Baton Rouge, statues dedicated to Confederate soldiers graced the grounds of statehouses. In the legislative halls hung portraits of Confederate officers painted by leading artists, displayed in the most prominent places. Confederate swords and battle flags were also tenderly preserved in glass cases where everybody could see them.[57] At the dedication of a monument to the Confederate dead in South Carolina, a military demonstration of twenty companies, more than a thousand men, and an audience of eight thousand attested to the vitality of Confederate culture.[58]

In May 1890 a statue of Robert E. Lee was erected on Monument Avenue in Richmond. John Mitchell Jr., a leader in Richmond's black community and editor of the *Richmond Planet*, argued against appropriating city funds for the statue when money was desperately needed for social services. But his position was over-whelmed by white popular support, and the city council pledged ten thousand dollars from the city's strapped budget.[59]

Not just observers, celebrants participated in the creation of a living Confederate history. When the unassembled statue arrived in Richmond, thousands of volunteers helped to pull the long ropes attached to boxes containing sections of the statue. Before the war, the people of Richmond had similarly dragged sections of a statue of Washington to its site. Robert Munford Jr. reminisced about his boyhood excitement when he and hundreds of other white schoolboys, "impelled by their patriotism and the zeal of their youth," had taken turns "tugging away at the precious ropes."[60] Those standing on the sidelines soon "caught the infec-tion, and, with an enthusiastic yell, took hold of the hemp" when the statue of Lee passed by.[61]

Three weeks after the arrival of the statue of Lee, more than one hundred thousand people from across the South gathered in Richmond for its unveiling. The city was decorated with pictures of Washington and Lee, as well as miles of bunting. Countless Con-federate and American flags waved above the festivities, but the sentiment went overwhelmingly to asserting a Confederate iden-tity and patriotism. During the early morning hours, a group placed the Stars and Bars in the hands of a bronze statue of Wash-ington.[62] The line of the march stretched four miles as some twenty thousand paraders made their way to the statue. At the beginning of the official ceremony the band played "Dixie," and soldiers fired canons and muskets at the statue's unveiling. Pas-sionate cheers and rebel yells came from the crowd as men repre-senting the cavalry and the infantry reenacted a mock battle be-fore the statue.[63] The unveiling was the largest Confederate celebration since the war.

Parallel to the creation and consolidation of a national patri-otism, Confederate symbols and rituals persisted as part of an au-tonomous regional culture.[64] The Lost Cause, never just a concept, gained added substance from the stories, songs, paintings, monu-ments, and statues generated by the United Confederate Veterans. Although the Confederacy lasted only four years, the relics of Con-federate culture continued to be used and redefined by each suc-ceeding generation. Typical of grass-roots organizing in the 1890s, Sumner A. Cunningham, founder of the *Confederate Veteran* maga-

9. A separate Confederate culture developed simultaneously with a national culture after the Civil War. In this postcard picture, schoolchildren have formed a "Human Confederate Flag" in front of the Robert E. Lee Monument for a United Confederate Veterans reunion in 1907. Copy photography by Katherine Wetzel, Eleanor S. Brookenbrough Library, The Museum of the Confederacy, Richmond, Virginia.

zine, organized fund-raising drives to raise money for memorials to Sam Davis, the "Boy Hero of the Confederacy." Virtually unknown, the legend of Sam Davis grew as veterans presented him to the South's youth as an example of the "courage and firmness of the Confederate soldier element." Captured by Union troops, Davis was hung for not revealing Confederate secrets.[65] Many Southern towns erected strikingly similar statues of rank-and-file Confederate soldiers standing with one leg bent and apparently at ease. A model of propriety and the new social order? Yes, but the casual stance belies a soldier with arms crossed in the determined defiance of Sam Davis.

Today, memorials to the Lost Cause remain; hundreds of Confederate statues are still centrally located in town squares. In 1889, the Alexandria UCV erected a statue featuring a soldier with his back to the national capitol. Rather than looking North, the soldier purposely faces South in the direction of Richmond, Virginia, the former Confederate capitol. Representative of the complexity of regional and national relationships, a substantial contribution for the erection of the statue came from a Confederate commander who donated his government pension from the U.S.-Mexican War.[66] Although an increasing number of white Southerners realized that they had to work within the Union, reconciliation remained precarious, since many were opposed to being a section within, not outside, the nation.

The United Confederate Veterans played a critical role in negotiating cultural terms favorable to the white South. By the 1890s, many Northerners, influenced by anti-immigrant xenophobia, were more than prepared to turn society's "race problem" back to the South. Heartened by its pro-Southern sentiments, the largest Confederate journal, the *Confederate Veteran*, reprinted an article in 1895 from the *Ladies' Home Journal* that praised the South as "the heart of America." Between tyranny and anarchy, stated the article, the South remained a place where "men and women are guided in their action by wholesome sentiment, where people live righteously, where the best of our customs are perpetuated, [and] our own language is spoken by all."[67]

Northern veterans' acceptance of Southern valor emerged slowly, however. Having survived a war in which a generation of men were sacrificed, Grand Army veterans often expressed strong hostility towards the South and wanted to affirm the victory of the Union. But as a selective memory of the Civil War moved from pondering its causes to stressing moments on the battlefield, aging veterans on both sides became more receptive to looking at the commonality of their experiences. With the passage of time, the GAR's attachment to the cause of the Union and its desire to forge a national brotherhood made it more willing to accept that it was not treason but the South's belief in the righteousness of its cause that had led the South into rebellion.

During campaigns for veteran pensions, the tendency to idealize citizen-soldiers also led to judging former Confederates in a more favorable light than noncombatants. To the editor of the leading Northern veteran newspaper, the *National Tribune*, angered by public and governmental indifference to veteran campaigns for increased pensions, the main enemy of the Union veteran was not the ex-Confederate but the "selfish, cold-blooded, low minded fellow, who cared too little for anything outside of his own mean little interests to be even an active rebel."[68] The leading

Confederate paper expressed similar sentiments of disgust towards slackers and noncombatants. "Hold a moment, my friend,"
went a poem published by the *Confederate Veteran.* "Pray, where
were you then, in the sixties, when the Gray was / fighting the
Blue? / . . . For tis proof to me of a loyal soul, that will never desert
a fight. / But will bravely defend to the bitter end the cause he
deems is right."[69]

Despite such common sentiments against those who had not
fought, rank-and-file veterans from both the North and the South
remained profoundly divided. A magazine graphic expressing the
tension just below the surface portrayed a Union general with a
"bloody shirt" wrapped around his eyes, preventing him from
seeing the fraternal reunion of the "Boys in Blue" and the "Boys
in Gray." The caption sardonically asked when he would stop
blinding himself to the spirit of reconciliation. Could he not see
"that the Gettysburg of 1887 is not the Gettysburg of 1863!"[70]
When a Grand Army comrade proposed making the surrender of
the Confederate army at Appomattox and the freeing of slaves
into a national holiday, a lengthy debate erupted. Opponents denounced the proposed holiday on the grounds that it would foster
sectional antagonism. "We fought for the Nation," declared a GAR
veteran, "not for the North, and we want the Nation undivided in
sentiment and loyal to a common flag." Others agreed, raising the
specter of the United States' perpetuating the same kind of hatred
that had divided Europe for centuries.[71] Under the slogan "One
country, one flag, one people, one destiny," the 1897 encampment
encouraged a rapprochement between Northern and Southern
veterans.[72] The change from viewing Confederates as traitors to
embracing them as brothers, however, necessitated compromises
over the writing of Civil War history. This would be facilitated by
the development of a popular imperialism that provided new common enemies both regions could agree upon.

CHAPTER 8

"Blood Brotherhood":
The Racialization of Patriotism

At an early observance of Memorial Day, in 1871, Frederick Douglass spoke before a memorial to the unknown dead: "We are sometimes asked in the name of patriotism to forget the merits of this fearful struggle, and to remember with equal admiration those who struck at the nation's life, and those who struck to save it—those who fought for slavery and those who fought for liberty and justice." But, he warned, we must never "forget the difference between the parties to that terrible, protracted and bloody conflict."[1] Douglass maintained until the day he died that the Civil War had been an ideological conflict with profound moral consequences. Against the spirit of sectional reunion and the celebration of martial heroism, Douglass continuously insisted that it had been a "war of ideas, a battle of principles . . . a war between the old and the new, slavery and freedom, barbarism and civilization."[2] Christian Fleetwood, an Afro-American recipient of the Congressional Medal of Honor, speaking to Grand Army men in 1894, also urged them to remember that until Emancipation the flag had meant "nothing to five millions of her children, but the lash of the master, and the blood-stained back of a beaten slave." The flag's "grand march" must proceed, he urged, "until every man, white or black" is assured its full protection.[3]

Motivated by different perspectives, interests, and aims, the former enemies—the Grand Army of the Republic and the Woman's Relief Corps in the North and the United Confederate Veterans and the United Daughters of the Confederacy in the South—engaged in a process of cultural negotiation over three interrelated issues that profoundly affected whether the broadening of democracy and racial equality articulated during the struggle to end slavery would prevail against a resurgent white supremacy. This chapter examines, first, the contest over whose interpretation of the Civil War and Reconstruction would be inscribed in national memory and recognized in official history; second, the debates

129

over the place of Confederate ideology, symbols, and rituals within the nation's cultural life; and third, the negotiation of terms for the reentry of Confederate veterans into the national fraternity they had left. The reunification of the North and the white South provides us with a lens for looking into the complex processes through which national identity and loyalty were forged, and the price of that new unity.

"LIES AGREED UPON": REWRITING CIVIL WAR HISTORY

The first area of contention centered on each side's insistence that its interpretation of the Civil War be taught to succeeding generations. Through the 1890s, Grand Army veterans vigorously demanded that the language and interpretation of the Civil War make it clear that Southern "withdrawal" from the Union had represented an insurrection.[4] Southern authors, in turn, insisted on depicting the war as a "heroic struggle for constitutional freedom." The United Confederate Veterans took particular offense at Civil War histories that referred to Confederates as rebels and traitors and lobbied textbook companies to replace the phrase *war of rebellion* with *Civil War between the states*.[5] The writing of history became a consciously political act as textbook writers and censors waged ideological battles over what should be taught.

In several cases the Grand Army lobby forced publishers to make revisions. At stake in the textbook campaign was not just the description of the battles but the GAR's overall interpretation of the nation-state. The GAR insisted that the South had never existed as a separate nation. When a "Populist Commission" in Kansas adopted a text that the GAR felt was "devoid of patriotism," the local post wrote up its objections to *Taylor's Model School History* and distributed more than ten thousand copies throughout the state. The post organized for five years until the governor finally appointed a new textbook commission sympathetic to the Grand Army point of view.[6] The perceived restraint on Southern historians prompted Woodrow Wilson to send his condolences to a Southern colleague: "In a word, you have gotten into a chair whose incumbent is expected to present, not the scientific truth with reference to our Constitutional history, whether that truth be on the side of Webster or of Calhoun in the great historical argument, but 'Yankee sentiments'—sentiments agreeable to that eminent body of scholars, the Grand Army of the Republic."[7]

The growth of public education lent added urgency to textbook debates. Before 1860 only six states had required the study of history, but with general approval for tax-supported public education following the Civil War, numerous states passed legislation aimed at regulating textbooks. By 1900 twenty-three states required the study of history.[8] Equally vehement as the Northern patriots, the United Confederate Veterans' History Committee demanded that Southern teachers not be expected to "instruct children that their fathers were traitors and rebels."[9] Agitation for a Southern viewpoint in history textbooks dates back to before the Civil War, when white Southerners, alarmed by abolitionist teachers from the North, launched a movement for "home education." The UCV infused the textbook campaign with new organizational energy in 1892 by establishing its own History Committee.[10]

The education campaign not only allowed Confederate patriotic societies to counter Northern condemnations of the South but also served as a vehicle to bolster the embattled status of Southern patricians against the challenge of discontented black and white agrarians. Linking the need for white supremacy with lessons from the antebellum social order, Southern historians hoped to perpetuate Old South values among a new generation.[11] Organized along lines similar to those of the GAR, Confederate organizations worked at the national, state, and local levels to ensure that white Southern teachers taught from Southern texts. The passage of uniform textbook laws in states throughout the South greatly aided their work.[12] The Daughters of the Confederacy were at the forefront of this campaign, using the moral status of suffering Southern motherhood to wage a relentless ideological campaign for the adoption of histories "just and true" to the Lost Cause.[13]

Negotiation of a mutually acceptable interpretation of the Civil War did not begin to emerge until professional historians at the turn of the century sought a consensus around a "usable past." Most Southern historians grudgingly accepted the GAR's demand that the unconstitutionality of secession be recognized. Northern historians, while maintaining a pro-Union view, were increasingly influenced by Social Darwinism and found common ground with their Southern colleagues in a shared racism. They willingly made concessions, softening, even romanticizing, their depictions of slavery, condemned Reconstruction for its "excesses," and expressed admiration for General Lee.[14]

Within the emerging historical profession, Woodrow Wilson and John Burgess led the revision of Civil War and Reconstruction history at the turn of the century. Wilson, in *A History of the American People*, eliminated the role of black Union soldiers altogether from his narrative of the Civil War. Instead, he wrote about the "extraordinary devotion and heroism" of men from both armies who shared the "same race and breeding." Taking the view that Reconstruction was a tragic aberration, Wilson described the early Ku Klux Klan as "frolicking comrades" and titled his chapter on the end of Reconstruction "Return to Normal Conditions." At last, Wilson wrote, "the hands of political leaders were free to take up the history of the country where it had been broken off in 1861."[15]

John Burgess revised U.S. history along similar lines. "Slavery was a great wrong, and secession was an error," he conceded, "but Reconstruction was a punishment so far in excess of the crime that it extinguished every sense of culpability upon the part of those whom it sought to convict." Burgess identified the "change of mind and heart on the part of the North" as the critical causal element in the "now much-talked-of-reconciliation."[16] These patently racist reinterpretations of Civil War and Reconstruction history would not be significantly challenged until the 1930s, when W. E. B. Du Bois condemned the degeneration of history into "lies agreed upon." Far from depicting Reconstruction leaders as scoundrels whose corruption led to their failure, Du Bois argued that white fear of black success had fueled reaction and led to Reconstruction's defeat.[17]

By the early 1900s, organizations of both Confederate and GAR veterans decided that the compromises within official history sufficiently met their perspectives to shift priorities from textbooks to other campaigns. In 1904 the GAR concluded its special commission on textbooks had satisfactorily met its objectives.[18] The Confederate veterans also slackened their vigilance. "We do not fear the bookmaker now," they declared in 1910. "Southern schools and Southern teachers have prepared the books which Southern children may read without insult or traduction of their fathers."[19]

The organization of Confederate women, however, was not prepared to end its textbook campaign so quickly. The UDC protested Northern interpretations of the Civil War well into the twentieth century. In 1921, Mildred Lewis Rutherford, the state
historian for the UDC, published *Truths of History*, which argued
that Abraham Lincoln had deliberately forced the Civil War upon
the South and was not a fit example for schoolchildren. The publication of the pamphlet created an uproar in Northern presses and
rekindled the sectional issues so passionately debated during the
1890s.[20] Despite continued agitation for the Confederate point of
view, Northern historians had in fact made significant concessions
to the white South in their interpretations of both slavery and
Reconstruction.

"A War of Ideas": Memory and Amnesia
in National Culture

National amnesia, historical revisionism, and the racialization
of patriotism took place not only within the new historical profession but also within national culture. Throughout the 1890s
and the early twentieth century, reunions of the "Blue and the
Gray" embodied the price of reconciliation. "The army of Grant
and the army of Lee are together," President McKinley declared
in 1897, ". . . the country is no longer in danger."[21] As Confederate
veterans reentered the national fraternity, racist caricatures of
blacks permeated popular culture: from cartoons, advertisements,
and songs, to children's stories, novels, and plays. Thomas Dixon's
racist play *The Leopard's Spots* became one of the most popular
Broadway productions of the 1903 theater season. Three years
later, Dixon's glorification of the Ku Klux Klan and his condemnation of Reconstruction appeared in his bestselling novel *The
Clansman*.[22]

In 1903, W. E. B. Du Bois compiled essays he had written since
1897 to counter the racism in American social, political, and cultural life into the *Souls of Black Folk*. It was in his essay "Of the Dawn
of Freedom" that Du Bois declared, "The problem of the twentieth
century is the problem of the color-line." In juxtaposition to the
national metaphor of veterans clasping each other's hands in mutual respect at Blue and Gray reunions, Du Bois presented his

133

readers with the disturbing image of "two figures": an old Confederate, "who stood at last, in the evening of life, a blighted, ruined form, with hate in his eyes," and a slave woman, "a form hovering dark and mother-like," who had come "to see her dark boy's limbs scattered to the winds by midnight marauders." These "two figures," wrote Du Bois, represented the "saddest sights of that woful day," a deepening of the American tragedy. "No man clasped the hands of these two passing figures of the present-past; but, hating, they went to their long home, and hating, their children's children live to-day."[23] As David Blight eloquently notes, the legacy of slavery lives in Du Bois's image of the meeting of the "present-past," showing that "racial reconciliation, unlike sectional reconciliation, demands a serious confrontation with the hostility rooted in rape, lynching and racism." This was a confrontation that white America was unwilling to undertake at the dawn of the new century.[24]

Against expressions of national amnesia, Grand Army and Woman's Relief posts in black communities continued to organize both Memorial Day and freedom commemorations. Marchers carried the Stars and Stripes and banners inscribed with freedom slogans such as "Emancipation, 1863, Liberty, 1887."[25] On Emancipation Day, black veterans marched through the main streets of their towns, often ending their processions at a local A.M.E. church, where the minister gave the day's oration. For the twenty-third anniversary of the Emancipation Proclamation in New York City, young girls dressed in white each carried a small flag with the name of one of the states printed on it in gilt letters. Black veterans also continued to march in Grand Army parades. In 1897, the black community of Buffalo, New York, took particular pride when black veterans marched beneath the arch they had erected for the GAR parade. When black veterans marched at the anniversary of the Battle of Antietam, their appearance elicited thunderous applause.[26]

The visible participation of black veterans, however, rapidly lost cultural ground as the prominence of Confederate ideology and symbols gained a foothold in national culture. At the turn of the century, a selective memory shaped American identity. In official and public history, in textbooks and in monuments, the participation of black Americans in winning the Civil War was largely forgotten.[27] Memorial Day ritualized an interpretation of the Civil

War that narrowed its redemptive meaning from that of a war to end slavery to that of a war to preserve the Union. The early post–Civil War protests against any visible signs of Confederate symbols within national culture also began to recede as Confederate veterans were accepted as brothers in the numerous Blue and Gray reunions that took place throughout the 1890s. Regardless of whether the highly publicized activities of the Blue and Gray actually reflected the feelings of veterans who did not participate, they nonetheless created a visual image of reconciliation for public consumption.

"THE CAPTURED BANNER": CONFEDERATE SYMBOLS AND NATIONAL CULTURE

The second disputed issue—the place of Confederate symbols and rituals within public culture—generated passionate debate. Initially, Grand Army veterans adamantly refused to march next to Southern veterans still in uniform or carrying the Stars and Bars, the battle flag of the Army of Northern Virginia. Both Union and Confederate veterans felt passionately about the symbols under which they had fought. Emotions ran high on both sides as Confederates lobbied for the return of their battle flags stored in a federal facility, along with other enemy flags captured by the United States and dating back to the War of 1812. In the eyes of Union veterans, Old Glory had been bathed in soldiers' blood.[28] At first, the GAR refused to accommodate the public display of any Confederate symbolism. Each attempt by the United Confederate Veterans to have the U.S. government return captured battle flags created a massive outcry. The GAR viewed the hard-won flags as their "trophies of patriotism."[29]

Confederate Captain Carlton McCarthy countered that the Stars and Bars was not a symbol of the Confederacy but simply the flag of the Confederate soldier—the "unstained banner of a brave and generous people whose deeds have outlived their country." As such, he continued, "it should not share in the condemnation which our cause received, or suffer from its downfall." McCarthy proposed instead that the "whole world unite in a chorus of praise to the gallantry of the men who followed where this banner led."[30] In a nation traditionally lacking in formal symbols, veterans from each side turned to their tattered banners and infused them with sacred meanings. Not unlike the cultural adjustments following the Viet Nam War, the nation attempted to heal its divisions by separating individual soldiers from the larger political context in which they had fought.

But the process of negotiating the return of Confederate flags was not straightforward. Objections from each side stalled the shaping of a cultural consensus for some time. White Southerners refused to accept cultural defeat and sustained a Confederate tradition in spite of the South's reincorporation into the United States. Confederate veterans, though willing to show loyalty to the national flag, were not prepared to "surrender their affection" for the Stars and Bars. The *Confederate Veteran* affirmed that the "God of ensigns never witnessed among His creatures a devotion more after divinity than those who suffered willingly under its pure folds. It went down without other stain than the blood of martyrs."[31] "The Captured Banner," a poem by Father Abraham Ryan, lamented the furling of the flag but predicted that it would yet live on in "song and story."[32]

Even in the months immediately following the Spanish-American War, the return of Confederate flags was still contested. The GAR commander-in-chief disagreed with "well-meaning comrades" who proposed the return of captured Confederate flags. Instead, he supported the building of a national depository in Washington, D.C., where captured flags and "all such emblems and trophies of each side" could be properly collected. To return the flags was out of the question: "We have never recognized the proposition that the War of Rebellion was a war between States; it was a war for union and the union today is all the States. Those lately in rebellion are as thoroughly a portion of it as are those which battled for its life and supremacy. All captured property belongs to the Government of this Union."[33]

A large number of Confederate veterans took particular offense when the UCV's own Historical Committee recommended that the U.S. government keep captured or surrendered Confederate flags. "Confederate veterans are unquestionably loyal to this government . . . but they are not satisfied to have it keep our flags." The time has come, the veterans continued, for the North to stop cherishing "trophies" of war. "We love our relics, and we want to keep them ourselves." Others criticized the report for excessive "fraternalism." One only needed to have seen, still another wrote, the twenty-nine battle flags carried in the grand procession of the last reunion in Charleston to understand "how dear they are to the hearts of the Confederate veterans."[34]

Only in the jingoistic aftermath of the Spanish-American War did Congress finally approve the handing over of battle flags to the white South.[35] Their return not only represented the new alliance between the white North and South but also signaled the popular acceptance of a rewritten Civil War history and the relinquishment of federal control over the cultural meaning of Confederate symbols. Now that the banner was no longer held as an emblem of treason or the slave autocracy, it was left to the white South to determine its ideological significance. Some Confederate veterans argued that the Stars and Bars represented individual heroism, whereas others defiantly held it as the flag of an older, superior Southern civilization against the influence of a crasser Northern capitalism. Still others voiced what to many was implicitly understood: the Stars and Bars once again could fly as the banner of white supremacy. The popular imperialism generated by the Spanish-American War played a critical role in creating the conditions for the reincorporation of Confederate veterans and their sons into the nation's fraternity.

"Americans All": Popular Imperialism and the Spanish-American War

The experience of new wars in which all regions could assert their American-ness against a Spanish and later Philippine Other revitalized national celebrations of unity and power. The wars not only provided the two veteran movements with increased opportunities for reconciliation but also gave a new generation a way to prove their manhood through the "restorative" act of war.[36] "Over all of us in 1898," wrote Carl Sandburg, "was the shadow of the Civil War and the men who fought it to the end."[37] Militarists like Theodore Roosevelt and other Progressives believed that a war with Spain would give the young men of the 1890s the kind of experience needed to resist the corrupt influences of urban life and the pursuit of individual interests.

137

Frederick Jackson Turner, in his 1893 address at the World's Columbian Exposition, had sounded the national alarm over the end of the "frontier." The westward movement of settlers into "free land," he argued, had provided the essential conditions for "American social development." The West, not the East, had forged the "American character," for the "perennial rebirth" of the nation depended on the "frontier as the outer edge of the wave—the meeting point between savagery and civilization."[38] Turner posed what he saw as the central question of the new century: how would America remake itself with each new generation without the frontier experience? Whereas Turner chose to nostalgically remember a lost epoch of yeoman farmers who had shaped an agrarian republic, Roosevelt celebrated the frontiersmen as heroes who had regenerated the nation by winning the war against a backward Indian race. Looking forward to an imperial future in which world expansion would provide the new "instruments of American progress," Roosevelt agitated for war and grew increasingly frustrated by the apparent loss of the nation's masculine vitality.[39] "I wish to Heaven we were more jingo about Cuba and Hawaii!" he wrote in 1897. "The trouble with our nation is that we incline to fall into mere animal sloth and ease, and tend to venture too little instead of too much."[40]

The nation's opinion of whether to go to war with Spain over the "liberation" of Cuba remained divided, however, until the sinking of the *Maine* in the waters outside Havana on 15 February 1898. In April, President McKinley finally capitulated to mounting political and editorial pressure, including his own party's fear of defeat in upcoming elections, and signed Congress's war resolution.[41] Hearst's *New York Journal* printed full-page images of the Stars and Stripes with headlines announcing: "WE'RE FIGHTING FOR HUMANITY, FREEDOM. SHOW YOU'VE NO OTHER FLAG. CUT THIS OUT. DECORATE YOUR HOME."[42] Across the country tens of thousands of businessmen, labor associations, and college students organized their own regiments and offered their services. States mobilized National Guard units even before receiving an official call to duty. A fierce rivalry broke out between the Regular Army and National Guard enthusiasts over who would be used in the assault and who would be left behind.[43]

Though most were now too old to reenlist, both Union and Confederate veterans volunteered to fight the "Spanish oppressors." For the first time since the Civil War, former Confederates once again served as high-ranking officers. President McKinley made a calculated decision to court the South by awarding major generals' commissions to Joseph Wheeler of Alabama and Fitz-hugh Lee of Virginia. The appointment of "Fightin' Joe" Wheeler symbolized the final end of Reconstruction for the white South. Intent on increasing Southern support for his administration and eager to demonstrate that sectional animosity was a dispute of the past, McKinley also awarded numerous brigadier general's stars to less prominent Confederate veterans.[44]

McKinley's appointments enthused the South, and applications poured into recruitment offices for the newly organized volunteer army. Regiments from all the Southern states filled their quotas quickly, and their numbers compared in strength to those of units raised in the North, East, and West.[45] Theodore Roosevelt welcomed Southern recruits to the Rough Riders, including former Harvard classmates from Virginia and hardened frontier fighters from the Texas Rangers.[46] He omitted immigrants, proletarians, and black Americans from his troop of heroes, instead choosing men he felt represented the nation as a white race advancing to a new stage of world power.[47] The military set up camps in the South, where suddenly places like Chickamauga, Huntsville, and Tampa became the meeting grounds for white soldiers from the North and the South, as well as all-black regiments.[48] A martial spirit infused national culture. Advertisements in support of a war tax, for example, appeared on everything from sleeping-car tickets to chewing-gum labels stamped "Remember the Maine." When the Virginia troops set out from Richmond, the Lee and Pickett camps of Confederate veterans cheered the Southern soldiers, and thousands lined the streets to bid them farewell. The Richmond Blues, now made up of the sons of Confederate veterans, were marching once again.[49]

Col. Leonard Wood, the commander of the First Volunteer Cavalry, wrote to his wife about seeing American flags in the hands of white Southerners as enthusiastic crowds came out to greet the Rough Riders, who were passing through New Orleans on their way to Tampa. "Everywhere we saw the Stars and Stripes," added Col. Theodore Roosevelt, who had never dreamed in the "bygone days of bitterness" that ex-Confederates would be out in force to greet the old flag or send their sons "to fight and die under it."[50]

10. Flag-draped coffins of U.S. soldiers who died during the Spanish-American War are exhibited in newly dug trenches at the nation's shrine, Arlington Cemetery, 1898. Copy photography by Arthur Timothy Wells, Prints and Photographs Division, Library of Congress.

Northern and Southern brigades mixed for the first time since before the Civil War in divisions of the volunteer army. Maj. Gen. Joseph Wheeler commanded brigades from states as diverse as Arkansas, Alabama, Florida, Kentucky, New York, Tennessee, and Wisconsin.[51] In the Northern classrooms and playgrounds, schoolchildren recited, "They've named a cruiser *Dixie*— / that's what the papers say— / An' I hears they're goin' to man her with / the boys that wore the gray."[52]

In just over three months, Spain agreed to sign a peace treaty. "VICTORY!!" declared the *New York Journal* above the wings of an enormous eagle. "Complete! Glorious! THE MAINE IS AVENGED!"[53] But the war did not stop with the defeat of Spain: the United States placed the whole of the Philippines under martial rule. Within weeks revolutionaries declared independence from the United States and established republics on several islands. Between 1898 and 1902, when the United States finally consolidated its domination of the Philippines, 126,000 U.S. soldiers would serve in the nation's first war in Asia.[54] Conscription was not necessary, as young men from the West and the South eagerly volunteered for military service and the promise of martial adventure. The war in the Philippines, though publicly justified as a civilizational campaign to uplift "little brown bothers," had more in common with the wars of annihilation fought against American Indians. Most of the high command had honed their military expertise while fighting Apaches, Comanches, Kiowas, and Sioux. Some commanders who had participated in the massacre at Wounded Knee brought tactics learned in the West to the theaters of war on the new imperial frontier. Eager to end what had developed into a protracted guerrilla war, a soldier from Kansas expressed the feelings of many soldiers when he argued that the "country won't be pacified until the niggers are killed off like the Indians."[55] News of atrocities in the Philippines generated anti-imperialist critiques of expansionism, but a mass antiwar movement never materialized. Anti-imperialists objected on constitutional, economic, strategic, and moral grounds to the transformation of what had begun as a war of liberation in Cuba into a imperialist campaign in the Philippines. But racism played as strong a role among opponents of the war as democratic commitments to principles of self-determination.[56]

The popular imperialism of the Spanish-American War combined aggressive American nationalism with racialist theories of progress. A national narrative in which the United States was represented as the embodiment of Manifest Destiny was popularized in touring performances, such as William F. Cody's Wild West. Roosevelt and other expansionists drew parallels between the "savage" Filipinos and Apaches, recasting the Spanish-American War in terms of a struggle between Anglo-Saxon progress and the forces of reaction.[57] Teddy Roosevelt's Rough Riders, the charge up San Juan Hill, and the rapid victory over the Spanish were all celebrated and promoted in newspapers, fiction, and song. Roosevelt believed that the Darwinist struggle between nations required not only "virile fighting virtues" but also the civilized impulses of America's leading race.[58] Roosevelt's nationalism was firmly based in a racialized male authority in which white women were responsible for reproducing the nation's children and white men were responsible for revitalizing the nation through expansion.

The Grand Army rejoiced that the war not only had resulted "in arousing the patriotism of our people to the highest conceivable point, but has [also] had the effect of bringing the people of all sections of the country into the most harmonious of relations."[59] The Woman's Relief Corps similarly extended its "loving tribute" to the next generation of fallen comrades. In Memorial Day services across the country, the conflation of militarism with patriotism was expressed in the "firing of guns and cannon," in brigades of schoolboys executing flag drills, and in speeches that claimed a direct link between the battle for liberty during the Civil War and the liberation of the Cubans in the Spanish-American War.[60]

Drawing upon the language of Manifest Destiny, the Spanish-American War was reshaped into a religious mission. "Old Glory is God's chosen banner," proclaimed a GAR veteran. "When our flag was raised on these islands and proclaimed freedom and independence to the inhabitants, it was like a voice from heaven." National hubris, missionary zeal, and a racist paternalism towards the "poor, ignorant people" of Cuba, Puerto Rico, and the Philippines proved a powerful combination. The politics of nationalism and imperialism, however, belied the proclamations of Memorial Day speakers who upheld the United States as a nation that stood for "truth and justice" and heralded the flag as the protector of the citizens of the world.[61]

The Spanish-America War provided a structural basis for the ideological alliance of white supremacists in the South and advocates of imperialism in the North. "What does all this mean for every one of us?" asked Senator Albert Jeremiah Beveridge in a speech advocating the annexation of the Philippines in 1900. "It means opportunity for all the glorious young manhood of the republic—the most virile, ambitious, impatient, militant manhood the world has ever seen."[62] Though politicians and the press would popularize the war as a mission of liberation against an old world power, Beveridge more accurately claimed it as a mission for the realization of American power within the modern world system of nation-states.[63]

While the heroes who emerged from the New South during the Spanish-American War embodied a modern representation of American manhood and nationhood, they also perpetuated the traditions and prejudices of the antebellum South, albeit in a changed political context. Southern newspapers praised Southern officers such as William Montgomery and Keller Anderson for bringing "honor to the whole country, and eminently so in representing the South." The *Confederate Veteran* acknowledged Montgomery for having impeded the advance of Grant's army during the Civil War and then for leading the "revolution" that allowed "white people to redeem Mississippi in 1875." The magazine recognized Colonel Anderson for surviving three wounds during the Civil War before going on to quell the "mobs" during the "mining troubles" of Coal Creek, Tennessee, between 1891 and 1893.[64]

Though the nation briefly extolled black soldiers as American heroes during the summer of 1898, the war did not result in any new enthusiasm for expanding civil rights. Instead, it served to reinforce racism at home as the United States assumed what Rudyard Kipling described, in a poem written to inspire Americans onward in their conquest of the Philippines, as the "the White Man's burden."[65] Postcards, newspaper cartoons, and stereographs depicted the people of Cuba, Puerto Rico, and the Philippines as little children in need of Uncle Sam's guiding hand. Similarly, black Americans, when not pictured as beasts and rapists, were parodied as childlike simpletons, incapable of self-government.

Black church leaders warned that the ascendance of "race supremacy" was undermining the "finest impulses of American citizenship." The meaning of Emancipation, asserted one minister, was to "celebrate the aspiration, the purpose, the destiny of the Republic of the United States. Take out the meaning of the Negro's presence in this country and you remove from our history the touchstone by which we may test every element of the original ideal."[66] Despite such appeals, the triumph of a militarist nationalism defined by overseas expansion and the pursuit of world empire exacerbated domestic racial divisions. George W. Prioleau, a chaplain in the black Ninth Cavalry, wrote to the *Cleveland Gazette* about the different receptions given white soldiers and the black members of his own unit. Upon arriving in Kansas City, Missouri, the members of the white First Cavalry were invited into the townspeople's homes and furnished with free meals in the local restaurants. The black Ninth Cavalry, whose members had fought valiantly and "returned home with victory perched upon their country's banner," were not even allowed to stand up and get a bite to eat at the restaurant counters. "You call this American prej-

964—The Philippines, Porto Rico and Cuba—Uncle Sam's Burden.
(With apologies to Mr. Kipling.)

11. An 1899 stereograph entitled "Uncle Sam's Burden"
portrays a U.S. soldier carrying three children, symbolizing the Philippines, Puerto Rico, and Cuba, in the Stars
and Stripes. The Spanish-American War was visually represented within turn-of-the-century popular culture as a
civilizing duty the United States had assumed rather than
as a war of imperialist conquest. Prints and Photographs
Division, Library of Congress, LC-USZ62-93327.

udice," wrote the chaplain, "I call it American hatred." No longer
confined to the South, "there are but few places in this country, if
any, where this hatred of the Negro" is not present.[67]

A typical *Atlanta Constitution* editorial celebrated the reunion of
white brothers and a "national spirit" that could "conquer the
world in peace, and if need be, hold the world at bay in war."[68]
"Just think!" wrote a veteran from Columbus in 1898, "five years
ago the Grand Army opposed the Confederates coming here and
decorating their comrades' graves; now they were with us." The

GAR drill corps fired a salute as thousands arrived at Camp Chase to place flowers on all the soldiers' graves. A Union veteran, skeptical at first, reportedly declared, "Comrades, I went there, and I am converted."[69]

Some Grand Army veterans remained steadfast in their commitment to equal rights and to the black comrades with whom they had fought side by side during the Civil War, but large numbers of GAR members sanctioned or remained indifferent to the racialization of patriotism. Some had shifted their concern from federal commitment to Reconstruction to federal commitment to veteran pensions; others shared racial resentments toward new immigrants and sympathized with the predicament of white GAR veterans in the South; still others refocused their memories to allow for feelings of camaraderie rather than continued animosity towards former enemies. The GAR, after all, based its brand of patriotism on the belief that it had preserved the Union, not radically restructured the nation.[70]

By 1899 it was common to see monuments on battlefields such as Chickamauga commemorating the valor of both the Confederate and the Union army. A Kentucky monument dramatized the reunion of brothers by sculpting a Union and Confederate flag, crossed with the staff of each flag grasped in the claws of an American eagle.[71] By 1901 the impetus to erect a national memorial to Lincoln in Washington, D.C., had been appropriated by an elite group of Republicans as part of their City Beautiful program. Earlier proposals to have the sculpture memorialize Emancipation and represent principles of racial equality lay abandoned. Instead, the only monument to Emancipation stood some distance away from the Capitol and the national mall. The statue, known as the Freedman's Memorial to Lincoln because its funding came from the donations of freedmen and women, features a black slave kneeling before his liberator, Lincoln. At the statue's unveiling in 1876, Frederick Douglass was so angered by the sculptor's transformation of black people from active participants in the struggle for equality into passive objects of benevolence that he criticized the statue for showing the "Negro on his knees when a more manly attitude would have been more indicative of freedom."[72]

The inclusion of Confederate soldiers within patriotic culture received official sanction when, in 1903, Confederate veterans were allowed to hold services for their dead at the nation's shrine to her martyrs, Arlington National Cemetery. During the celebration of the Spanish-American War peace treaty, President McKinley had toured the South and made the first official overture towards the assumption of federal responsibility for the care of Confederate graves. At his stop in Atlanta, McKinley declared the now familiar interpretation that "every soldier's grave made during our unfortunate Civil War is a tribute to American valor." In 1900, the United Confederate Veterans convinced Congress to authorize the reinterment in Arlington National Cemetery of the remains of 128 Confederate soldiers who lay in graves across Washington, D.C.[73] The Daughters of the Confederacy lobbied further for the erection of a magnificent monument to the Confederate dead. In 1906, the secretary of war authorized the building of a major memorial to the Confederacy on the grounds of the cemetery.[74]

The movement toward reconciliation generated by the Spanish-American War also led the GAR commander-in-chief to call on the membership to revise the meaning of Memorial Day. No longer used as an occasion to demarcate Union veterans from the Confederacy, the day was transformed into an opportunity to weave and blend the "peoples of this country, obliterating differences." The commander-in-chief encouraged his comrades to place flowers on the graves of former opponents, not in honor of their cause, but because of the valor they had demonstrated in battle.[75] The Spanish-American War, he concluded, had finally verified Lincoln's prediction that "the mystic chords of memory, stretching from every battlefield and patriot grave to every living heart and hearthstone all over this broad land, will yet swell the chorus of the Union."[76] "We only needed a common danger to arouse our people," another GAR commander explained. "No section of our country responded to the call to arms more readily or more enthusiastically than the young men from Dixie." Participation in the war served as the litmus test for Southern "devotion" to the nation. "From that date [1898]," the commander concluded, "we had a new Union, no Northerners, no Southerners, but Americans all."[77]

The emergence of the United States as a world power during the Spanish-American War ratified and accelerated cultural reconciliation between former enemies. An anecdotal Memorial Day story, retold at the 1906 Grand Army encampment, demonstrated the extent to which differences had dissipated. The story described an old man who appeared at a national cemetery and placed flowers on the grave of a soldier who had died under the Stars and Bars. When he stood, he reached into his pocket and "drew forth a flag. It was old, tattered and torn, and its center showed where the banner had been pierced by bullets." When some GAR veterans spotted the Confederate banner, they demanded that it be taken down. "The old southerner straightened up. One sleeve of his coat was empty but there was a look of defiance in his eyes." The old man explained that he had come to see if his son's grave had been decorated. "You fellows have forgotten him. He was killed in the seven days of fighting round Richmond. He was my boy, the only boy I ever had." He refused to remove the Confederate flag until the Stars and Stripes were placed above his son. Immediately, the GAR men found a flag and placed it on the grave. When they tried to take the Confederate flag away, the old man vehemently objected. "That was my regimental flag in Stonewall Jackson's brigade, it wasn't taken away from me then, and it won't be given up now." The Grand Army veterans let him keep it and began to entertain the idea that perhaps Southern manhood could be honored after all.[78]

Imperialism profoundly affected and shaped internal conceptions of what it meant to be an American.[79] Entrepreneurial capitalists, eager to take advantage of the new nationalism, appropriated patriotic sentiments so that their products could appeal to both the North and the South. Businesses as diverse as publishers of textbooks or dime novels, producers of sheet music, and flag manufacturers agreed that what was good for business was in the national interest. Widely read magazines and graphics on music sheets began to include General Robert E. Lee on their lists of "American heroes."[80] *Beadle's Half Dime Library*, famous for adventure stories like *The Comanche Captive*, excluded any mention of the Civil War.[81] As Indian warfare became part of America's historical past, new adventure stories increasingly featured former Indian fighters battling the new enemies of civilization, identified by their Spanish names and brown complexions.[82] The silence surrounding the Civil War and its aftermath in Beadle novels, published weekly and read by thousands throughout the country, reflected the publisher's understanding that selling to a national market required enemies that people from different regions could agree upon.

Flag companies, also eager to capitalize on national sales, advertised "flags of our country" alongside "Confederate flags." In the Annin Company's catalogue, the badges and colors of GAR posts are followed by pages advertising "hand embroidered silk stars" for Confederate flags. On pages featuring "patriotic novelties," Irish-American flag bows appear next to "Confederate Bows—Red & White." And on opposite pages, Revolutionary flags with the icon of the rattlesnake and the motto "Don't Tread on Me" appear without intended irony next to Confederate battle flags.[83] As producers of patriotic symbols, flag companies both reflected and promoted the growing movement towards reconciliation in the interest of commercial progress.

Nonetheless, contradictions, divisions, and cross-cutting allegiances remained. Rather than reflecting an indissoluble unity, the Grand Army and the United Confederate Veterans sought reunification for very different reasons. The North demanded the priority of one nation-state, whereas Confederate veterans pursued reunification for economic reasons but insisted on maintaining autonomous Confederate traditions. The national abandonment of Reconstruction was the most critical term of reconciliation, for the withdrawal of national support for racial equality effectively silenced its black and white supporters within the dominant political culture. Emancipation continued to be celebrated by black Americans but failed to be included among the nation's great traditions.

From being a "people in arms," the military, its officers, and veteran organizations committed themselves to keeping the flame of patriotism alive between wartime mobilizations. Members of the officers' corps had been among the first to promote reconciliation. Patriotism, traditionally associated with willingness to die for one's country, was renegotiated to once again include ex-Confederates in the national fraternity. The final conquest of the continent and the subjugation of the Plains Indians permitted ex-Confederates to identify with the Regular Army. But even more important, the popular imperialism inspired by the Spanish-American War endorsed *American*, not Northern or Southern, male warrior heroism. As immigration soared, these former enemies reinforced their unity by identifying a new threat to the nation. Convinced that "no one is born a patriot," Americanizers refocused their energies on remaking immigrants and their children into 100 percent Americans.[84]

"I Pledge Allegiance . . .": Mobilizing
the Nation's Youth

Some thirty years after the Civil War, nationalists believed the United States faced its most serious challenge in having to "deal with an alien element" that needed to be "Americanized in the common schools of the nation, or not at all."[1] Confronted by the dilemma that Americans are made, not born, educators and patriotic organizations questioned what more they could do to create an expressive culture of loyal Americanism. Chapters 9 and 10 focus on some significant changes that took place in the organization and ideology of nationalism between the 1880s and World War I. This period witnessed the aging and decline in power of the generation that had built the Grand Army of the Republic and the Woman's Relief Corps, as well as an unprecedented shift in the demographics of the U.S. population as a result of immigration from Europe.

Activists in the patriotic movement could no longer rely on the lived experience of the Civil War to activate a sense of national allegiance in a generation that in large part were Americans by immigration rather than by birth. Beginning in 1888, organized patriots, progressive reformers, and civic-minded businessmen launched what became popularly known as the schoolhouse flag movement. Despite differences in politics, goals, and constituencies, nationalists cooperated in their efforts to raise the flag over every schoolhouse; institutionalize a daily pledge of allegiance; introduce patriotic rituals aimed at galvanizing children's hearts; and create civics and history curriculums aimed at securing children's minds.

What distinguished this movement from earlier efforts to forge a sense of mass patriotism was its emphasis on youth as the standard-bearers of the nation and on the public school as the primary locus of instilling patriotic values. This chapter focuses on a new breed of professional nationalists who drew upon modern technology and newly powerful means of communication to organize the first, national propaganda campaign on behalf of the nation. Chapter 10 explores how educators played a critical role in elaborating the ideology and rituals of patriotism within the growing system of public education. Despite the effectiveness of these new nationalists, both in public discourse and in the classroom, the movement continued to include a variety of ideological perspectives and encouraged a degree of debate about who and what stood for the nation. But as we shall see in chapter 11, this pluralism was not extended to African Americans, who, despite segregation and repression, continued to keep alive the most progressive traditions of American patriotism.

"Badge of Citizenship": The First
Pledge of Allegiance

In the late 1880s, the GAR, under the motto "The school-house stands by the flag, let the people stand by the school," took its patriotic campaign into the public schools.[2] "Let the children," resolved the veterans, "learn to look upon the American flag 'By angels' hands to valor given,' with as much reverence as did the Israelites look upon the ark of the covenant."[3] The Woman's Relief Corps, whose Memorial Day work had given it experience in crafting memory, understood the importance of shaping the next generation. Soon, public-school teachers began experimenting with flag ceremonies aimed at teaching an emotional patriotism; this in turn developed into the ritual of children's daily pledging their allegiance.[4] Even though the Constitution does not prescribe a daily oath, the notion of pledging loyalty had become more commonplace during the Civil War and Reconstruction, when teachers from Southern border states were required to swear their allegiance to the Constitution of the United States and denounce the tenets of the Confederacy.[5]

George T. Balch, an educator, veteran, and GAR spokesman, wrote the first pledge to gain widespread recognition: "We give our heads and heart to God and our country: one nation, one language, one flag."[6] He began his research on flag rituals while working as an auditor for the New York City Board of Education in the late 1880s. Balch recalled being particularly impressed with morning exercises before a newly purchased American flag at a large, immigrant school.[7] Working closely with Margaret Pascal, credited by the WRC as being among the first teachers to introduce flag exercises into her classroom, Balch wrote *Methods for Teaching Patriotism in the Public Schools* for national distribution.[8] First published in 1890, the book used the flag as the basis for teaching devotional rites of patriotism. Balch's work inspired numerous children's books, including *A Patriotic Primer for the Little Citizen.* Children were expected to memorize questions and answers modeled along the lines of a catechism. A typical question, "What is the aim of the Public School?" was followed by the answer, "To train us in such habits of behavior as will best fit us to become GOOD MEMBERS OF CIVIL SOCIETY and PATRIOTIC AMERICANS."[9]

Both Pascal and Balch promoted values of citizenship grounded in self-reliance and individual duty to the nation-state. Although Pascal believed that every immigrant was a potential citizen, she distinguished between male and female models of patriotic behavior. Like many women who entered the public workforce after the Civil War, Pascal could justify her own entry into the teaching profession as an expansion of women's traditional work in the home.[10] The ranks of these new social housekeepers grew rapidly in the public schools as men moved on to better-paying jobs and communities increasingly viewed schools as the "natural" place for their neighbors' daughters. Local school boards underpaid women in relation to the salaries they paid to men and saw women's work as teachers linked to their education as future mothers.[11] Rather than seeing political activism in contradiction to their domestic roles, activists like Margaret Pascal extolled public values associated with feminine virtue.

Following in the footsteps of Betsy Ross, whom she regarded as a domestic and patriotic model, Pascal organized schoolgirls to sew flags, while she encouraged male pupils to make flag staffs out of "genuine Lincoln rails" or join the Balch Cadets, in which they could execute military drills fashioned after parades of Grand Army veterans.[12] Pascal worked closely with Balch, filling her classroom with patriotic songs and recitations, adding and adapting Balch's flag rituals to her work with immigrant children.

Balch's book became an immediate success. Its opening pages invoked the nation's best-known minister, Henry Ward Beecher, to explain why the flag stood at the core of Balch's educational system. "Our flag carries American ideas, American history and

American feelings," declared Beecher in 1861. "Every color means liberty, every thread means liberty, every form of star and beam of light means liberty. Not lawlessness, not license, but organized institutional liberty through law, and laws for liberty. Accept it then, in all its fullness of meaning. It is not a painted rag. It is a whole national history. It is the Constitution. It is the Government. It is the emblem of the sovereignty of the people. It is the NATION."[13]

Trained at West Point and an ardent Christian, Balch devised a series of flag rituals and rewards intended to create an environment for children between the ages of four and nine that mixed religious fervor and military discipline. He understood that children this age were too young to appreciate the full significance conveyed by the word *nation*. Nonetheless, he believed that patriotic teachers could foster sentiments that would predispose children to feelings of love and duty for their country, just as religious teachers taught love of God before students grasped its full significance. "Punctuality, regularity of attendance, personal neatness and cleanliness, cheerfulness, and evenness of temper, truthfulness, ready obedience to rules and instruction, respectful bearing towards superiors in knowledge and years, and studiousness," according to Balch, constituted the elements of moral discipline and good citizenship. Children who met these criteria could wear a colorful "Badge of Citizenship," a miniature silk flag hung from a metal coat of arms. Those who failed were separated from their class at the weekly award ceremony and made to march at the rear.[14]

Balch's system, aimed primarily at immigrant children, reflected Progressive Era strategies of implementing social control through public agencies. Balch based his method on the belief that "there is nothing which impresses the youthful mind and excites its emotions" more than the "observance of form." Through a mixture of flag pageantry and public rewards or humiliations, Balch intended to "reach and permanently touch the heart" of each child.[15] The implementation of educational programs, like Balch's use of flag rituals, made the schools one of the most important institutions for political socialization in the late nineteenth century. As Eric Hobsbawm has noted about comparable developments in Europe, the state made use of the "increasingly powerful machinery" of public education "to spread the image

12. Working-class children are taught to salute the flag in the Mott Street Industrial School, New York City, in the early 1890s. Photographed by Jacob Riis. Prints and Photographs Division, Library of Congress, LC-USZ62-13077.

and heritage of the 'nation' and to inculcate attachment to it." Although nationalists such as Balch and Pascal were clearly engaged in "conscious and deliberate ideological engineering," it would be a mistake to understand their efforts as only manipulative propaganda.[16] Without authentic popular resonance among immigrant families seeking ways of identifying with their new land and among hard-pressed schoolteachers in need of effective lesson plans, the flag would not have been waved so vigorously or so uniformly.[17]

By 1893, New York teachers from the twenty-one schools of the Children's Aid Society organized more than six thousand children, representing sixteen nationalities, to salute the flag each morning.[18] Using Balch's patriotic manual, the teachers taught students their "first lessons in the duties of American citizenship." The Presbyterian Board of Home Missions also adopted Balch's patriotic curriculum for its mission schools in the West and the South, and the federal government adopted Balch's plan for use in its "Indian Schools." On Washington's birthday in 1893, government teachers led twenty thousand Native American children in saluting the U.S. flag. Balch's plan, with its stress on regulated and uniform behavior, appealed to teachers charged with Americanizing immigrants in the new urban schools and to government schools, which aimed to assimilate more than 250 Native American tribes by removing Indian children from their homes and placing them in government-controlled boarding schools.[19]

"A MESSAGE TO THE PUBLIC SCHOOLS OF AMERICA": ADVERTISING PATRIOTISM

Although organized patriots and educators laid the groundwork for patriotic education by lobbying for flags to be flown over every schoolhouse and through experimentation with flag rituals in the classroom, it was not until a national paper, the *Youth's Companion*, added its expertise in modern advertising techniques that the schoolhouse flag movement became a truly national phenomenon. Oratory had formed the most important medium for communicating nationalist ideology throughout the eighteenth century and the first half of the nineteenth century, but with the explosive growth of national magazines and newspapers after the Civil War, the locus of communication shifted from individual speakers addressing local communities to mass newspapers and magazines. As a result of the increased availability of capital, advances in printing technology, and favorable mail rates, the number of periodicals increased from seven hundred in 1864 to more than three thousand in 1885. By 1900, some national magazines claimed a circulation of more than one hundred thousand subscribers.[20]

The spread of national markets also meant that advertisers increasingly looked to newspapers and magazines to reach prospective buyers. Advertising, once seen as simply the sale of space and the listing of products, began to undergo important changes. In the years immediately following the Civil War, selling advertising, according to the president of the American Sugar Refining Company, had been on the "same plane as selling second hand clothes." Weekly papers publicized long lists of commodities, making no attempt to fit the products to the needs of the buyer. Advertising was not yet seen as a dynamic social force capable of molding public opinion. But by the late 1880s, advertising companies had begun to spend their customers' money as if it were their own, measuring success in terms of how effectively they reached tens of millions of prospective buyers.[21] The *Youth's Companion* welcomed these changes in advertising and made its own pioneering contributions. Under its motto—"The more we can do for our subscribers, the faster the *Companion* will grow"—the paper expanded from 140,000 subscriptions in 1876 to 410,000 by 1888, becoming one of the most widely read weeklies in the country.[22]

Founded in 1827 in Boston, the *Youth's Companion* was a family paper to be read by parents with children, and teachers with students. A weekly, it published short adventure stories, reports on national and international events, editorials on issues of the day, and illustrated serials.[23] From the paper's inception, its owners understood that the interests of the *Companion* were inextricably linked with the emerging public school system.[24] "Our school's greatest task," announced the *Companion*, is to make each child into a "thorough going American." Citing statistics from the Census Bureau, the paper reported in 1892 that one-third of all children in the country between the ages of five and seventeen had foreign-born parents or had themselves been born in another country. "It is the problem of our schools," asserted the *Youth's Companion*, "to assimilate these children to an American standard of life and ideas."[25]

The paper threw its advertising know-how and its access to teachers into the mobilization for raising the flag over the schoolhouse. As in every other *Companion* campaign, the paper launched the flag drive from the paper's promotion department.[26] To encourage the idea of "flag decoration in the home and schoolroom," the paper advertised and sold U.S. flags at a substantially reduced cost. To build enthusiasm among students, the paper offered free flag certificates, which students could sell for ten cents each and then apply the proceeds towards the purchase of a sixteen-foot flag for their school. Mixing appeals to patriotism with values defined by the Protestant work ethic and the emerging spirit of corporate capital, the flag cards entitled the holder to "one share in the patriotic influence of the school-house flag."[27]

Next, the *Companion* sponsored a national essay contest on the topic "The Patriotic Influence of the American Flag when raised over the Public School." Teachers from forty-one states and six territories sent in the best essay from their schools. The winning schools received a flag, which they raised over their schoolhouses during July Fourth ceremonies in 1890. To promote community involvement, the paper advertised free canvas storage bags inscribed with the name of anyone who bought a flag for his or her local school.[28] Teachers, students, and their families responded enthusiastically to the schoolhouse flag movement.[29] With a national distribution that reached 560,000 subscribers by 1892, the paper articulated a vision that combined its own self-interest with the cause of the public schools and the promotion of patriotism.[30]

"WHO WILL . . . START THE MOVEMENT?": MOBILIZING FOR THE COLUMBIAN CELEBRATION

Upon hearing news of the upcoming Columbian Exposition in Chicago, the *Companion* seized the initiative and launched a campaign for the Columbian Public School Celebration. Its editors envisioned the exposition as an opportunity for the nation's schoolchildren to simultaneously pledge their allegiance to the flag on Columbus Day as a prelude to the main event. With 1892 marking the four hundredth anniversary of Columbus's "discovery" of America, the *Companion* proposed to place the public schools at the center of the celebrations and to make children feel "their coming power as the citizens of the new century."[31]

The paper charged Francis Bellamy with organizing and leading a national campaign. A nationalist and Christian socialist, Bellamy believed in the social gospel, agitated for the broadening of governmental powers to correct social injustice, and preached that the "Savior was emphatically the poor man's friend." After graduating from the University of Rochester Theological Seminary, Bellamy had spent eleven years as a Baptist minister. Just before he started to work for the *Youth's Companion*, the Bethany Church had forced Bellamy to resign because his supervisors found his views on labor too radical and his theology too unorthodox.[32]

A proselytizer by trade, Bellamy joined the promotion staff at the *Youth's Companion* after resigning from the ministry. His job at the paper required hands-on organizing, and Bellamy often spoke on the Lyceum League lecture circuit, trying to win converts to the schoolhouse flag movement by preaching on the topic "The Spirit of Americanism."[33] After the Civil War, he explained, "patriotism had been worked too hard; and men plunged into money making." Now, "amid the incoming waves of immigration," many were beginning to question whether they would even "be able to retain that which is American."[34]

Unlike George Balch, Bellamy denounced the privileging of individual liberty over social equality and fraternity. Society "is much like a sand heap," he explained, "where there is liberty for every atom," but it has been transformed into freedom for "great corporations to oppress the people . . . for the atoms on top of the sand heap to press down harder and harder on the atoms below." He called for a new nationalist spirit that would turn to notions of equality and fraternity for inspiration. Equality must mean equal rights to employment and education; *fraternity*, Bellamy proposed, "is a word which, when applied to the nation, means that we are not a sand heap, but a family."[35]

Bellamy, like most social reformers at the time, identified his cause with loyalty to the nation and used patriotic language and symbols to articulate his program. For those who chose this route, patriotism was not yet the property of any one political persuasion. As a committed patriot but also a Christian socialist, Bellamy drew upon a different source of inspiration than did Balch, who joined his penchant for militarylike discipline with a property-centered, individualistic model of civil society. Whereas Balch indicted the poor for producing criminals, Bellamy looked to the broadening of governmental powers to correct social inequalities.[36] Balch's program aimed to police the poor, whereas Bellamy dedicated himself to their moral uplift. He allied himself with other reformers who envisioned a "social citizenry," in which every member of civil society would share a common set of institutions and services that would guarantee everyone a decent standard of living.[37]

In a time of major class formation and social dislocation, Americans debated what kind of society they wanted their country to become. Most national presses stood behind the rights of property, condemned calls for economic justice, and denounced mili-

158

tant labor demonstrations for the eight-hour workday as the work of aliens and anarchists preaching "doctrines wholly un-American."[38] Francis Bellamy moved in socialist circles that advocated a United States in which all could share in the nation's peace and prosperity. His cousin, Edward Bellamy, wrote one of the most influential books on the "new nationalism"—*Looking Backward*, published in 1888. In sharp contrast to the perpetuation of inequality based on class, the book envisioned the realization of a utopian society by the year 2000. Rather than leaving economic planning to the vicissitudes of the market economy, the government would assign all jobs according to the needs of the nation, and, as shareholders in the nation, citizens would receive equal incomes.[39]

The novel is set in the year 2000. On a rainy night, Doctor Leete explains that the "difference between the age of individualism [1880s] and that of concert [2000] was well characterized by the fact that, in the nineteenth century, when it rained, the people of Boston put up three hundred thousand umbrellas over as many heads, and in the twentieth century they put up one umbrella over all the heads." Doctor Leete's daughter, Edith, looks up at the waterproof awning stretched over the street and walks out into the stormy night confident that all the city's citizens will be protected from the rain. "The private umbrella," she explains, "is Father's favorite figure to illustrate the old way when everybody lived for himself and his family. There is a nineteenth century painting at the art galley representing a crowd of people in the rain, each one holding his umbrella over himself and his wife, and giving his neighbors the drippings, which he claims must have been meant by the artist as a satire on his times."[40]

By 1890, *Looking Backward* had already sold two hundred thousand copies, making it one of the most popular novels of the decade.[41] Francis Bellamy's cousin Edward also identified his brand of socialism under the rubric "nationalism." Unlike many European socialists who advocated internationalism, the Bellamys believed that the goals of socialism could best be met within the boundaries of the United States.[42] The concept of nationalism, explained Edward Bellamy, was fitting because "its purpose was to realize the idea of the nation with a grandeur and completeness never before realized, not as an association of men for certain merely political functions affecting their happiness only remotely and superficially, but as a family, a vital union, a common life."[43]

On another occasion, Edward Bellamy confessed that he used the term *nationalist* because it made it more difficult for opponents to stigmatize what in essence was a socialist movement. Another social reformer clarified that "Nationalism and Christian Socialism" in the United States differed from European socialism in two ways. First it made the "dividing line between the two contending forces vertical instead of horizontal, thereby dividing all classes, so that we have still on one side the poor, the suffering, but also the noble, the progressive and patriotic, opposed to the ignorant and the selfish." Second, nationalism in the United States "stands for Patriotism, while European Socialism considers that sentiment a vice rather than a virtue. . . . We are proud of Uncle Sam, and what we intend to do is to enable him to grow on the very lines that were laid down by the Pilgrims when they landed on Plymouth Rock."[44] This was not the first time that reformers and social activists tried to locate their political programs within the parameters of Americanism, nor would it be the last.

Looking Backward inspired people across the country to form Nationalist Clubs, attracting a diverse membership of reform-minded newspaper editors, Civil War veterans, writers, progressive educators, and Christian socialists. Eugene Debs was among the admirers of *Looking Backward*, but he was critical of the middle-class sensibility of the nationalist movement, describing it as the "Yankee Doodleisms of the Boston savants." Debs detected in Bellamy's novel a paternalism towards workers, and he worried that its call for an expanded federal government might lead to absolutism.[45] The Nationalist Clubs attracted a large middle-class membership, including a number of people who played key roles in the contested terrain of American culture, such as William Dean Howells, a major literary spokesmen, Edward Everett Hale, author of "The Man Without a Country," and Thomas Wentworth Higginson, an author and longtime abolitionist who had served as a Union commander of a black Civil War regiment. With 167 clubs, the movement reached its apogee during the People's Party's congressional and presidential campaign of November 1892.[46]

Francis Bellamy's intervention into the nationalist discourse demonstrates the complexity of the struggle over whether the American political tradition would be defined in terms of governmental responsibility to its citizenry or by a liberal ideology that championed the individual in the social sphere and the rule of free-market transactions in the economy. The campaign to teach patriotism in the public schools became an important arena in which diverse kinds of patriots tried to influence the next generation and win them to their conceptions of what it meant to be an American.

Bellamy shared the conviction of most self-conscious nationalists that American patriotism was very different from the patriotism of European nations. "Over there, patriotism is in the blood," but in the United States a sense of national loyalty had to be constructed and reproduced. Bellamy used the *Companion* to play a direct role in popularizing a civic-minded patriotism.[47] When called upon to write a pledge for the Columbian Public School Celebration, Bellamy decided to move beyond what he considered a simplistic formula in Balch's pledge—"I give my hand and heart to my country, one nation, one language, one flag."[48] Bellamy dismissed the earlier pledge as a "pretty childish form of words, invented by an ex-military officer."[49] He wanted to infuse the pledge with a sense of U.S. history.

In August 1891, Bellamy undertook the writing of the pledge for the official program of the Columbian Public School Celebration. Bellamy recalled that the first line came quickly and that he wrote down the idea of "pledging allegiance to the flag." The word *allegiance* resonated with the great call to union during the Civil War, and the flag stood for the republic that had survived the bloody conflict. Bellamy then began to think about the scope of the nation's history and how to strengthen the idea of one nation. Recalling that Webster and Lincoln had used the word *indivisible* in their most memorable speeches, Bellamy added the words "and to the Republic for which it stands, one Nation indivisible."[50]

But still he wondered, "What of our purpose as a Nation?" Bellamy was tempted to use the "historic slogan of the French Revolution which meant so much to Jefferson and his friends, 'Liberty, Equality, Fraternity.' " He weighed whether the nation was prepared to move beyond a philosophy of individualism, but in the end he decided that the language of equality and fraternity would be too much for most people to accept. Instead, he settled for the final line, "with liberty and justice for all." This way, he reasoned, the pledge would be ideologically "applicable to either an individualist or a socialistic state." He left the option open for future generations to decide. Only two hours after beginning his task, the Christian socialist and muckraker emerged from his office with the text for what would become the nation's official Pledge of Allegiance.[51]

"Apathy Must Get Repeated Shakings":
A National Mobilization

With only eight months to organize the Columbian Public School Celebration, Bellamy realized that an event of this magnitude would require nationally coordinated activities. He carefully developed a strategy "to mobilize the masses to support primary American doctrines," while his staff plotted out an elaborate organizing drive. Nationalists had found that expressions of patriotism emerged spontaneously in times of crisis or war but that in periods of peace patriotism required careful cultivation. Bellamy also understood that the day's success depended on the idea's resonating with the lived experience of millions of people. He knew from his experience with advertising that how a message was communicated meant everything. First, slogans needed to be created in which "simple words" conveyed the essential "doctrines of our Nationality." The idea "must be so close to the crowd that the crowd, as soon as it hears, thinks it is its own. The idea must be so close to the crowd's present feeling that, when stated, the crowd's reaction must be 'Why, of course.' "[52]

The *Companion* crafted its appeal to meet different constituencies. Students were asked, "Is Your School to Celebrate? Ask your teacher about the Celebration." Just as the magazine urged teachers to organize their students, it also used students to mobilize their teachers. Each issue encouraged students to make sure that their school had a flag. "Who will be the FIRST boy in your district to start the movement?" queried the *Companion*.[53] Once the paper's promotion staff was organized, Bellamy secured the approval of the World's Congress Auxiliary to the Columbian Exposition for the public-school celebration.[54] With the aid of William Harris, U.S. commissioner of education and president of the National Education Association (NEA), Bellamy next met with superintendents of education at their national convention. Harris's backing of the public-school celebration assured the NEA's unanimous endorsement. The association immediately lent its name as sponsor of the celebration, appointed the state superintendents of public instruction as a general committee to lead the movement in their states, and named an executive committee to be in direct charge of the celebration. Bellamy headed up the executive committee in recognition of the *Companion*'s initiation of the proposal and promise to take responsibility for overseeing the campaign.[55]

Mass mobilizations require delegation of responsibility and a division of labor based on clearly defined goals and tasks. The executive committee divided the work among the state superintendents of education, who in turn were to reach out to the teachers, students, parents, and press in their states. Bellamy in particular recognized that the campaign required constant appeals if communities would be convinced to abandon their local orientation in favor of a national event. His organizing techniques were built on the unique recognition that getting each locality to think nationally required a combination of centralized ideology and decentralized activism. Each state superintendent appointed a working committee that sent letters to local superintendents, teachers, and the press asking them to activate their communities to make the public school the center of their Columbus Day celebration.[56] Teachers were personally asked to assist in bringing about a "patriotic demonstration which will have a place in history." Remember, predicted the *National Columbian Public School Celebration Bulletin*, the "public school of today sways the hundred years to come."[57]

Following a sophisticated, intergenerational strategy, the campaign organizers tried to activate as many people as possible across the country. "Pushing the movement" meant asking the GAR not only to give its endorsement but also to have veterans personally escort the children when they raised the flag and pledged their allegiance. Organizers contacted ministers across the country and asked them to preach on the "relation of Free Education to our American life" and persuade their congregations to participate in the public-school celebration. The twelve hundred Lyceum League of America clubs also agreed to promote the campaign. Meetings were scheduled with elected officials, from the president of the United States down to local politicians, to secure their endorsements and see what political weight they might bring to the campaign.[58]

Knowing that the success of the campaign depended on "newspaper talk," organizers launched a full-scale letter-writing campaign aimed at every type of press.[59] The executive committee issued "A Message to the Public Schools of America," to be published in all the national and local presses. The message targeted every segment of the population, encouraging students to involve their teachers, lobby their superintendents of education, and, if one did not exist yet, help form a Columbian school committee. Reflecting progressive ideas in education, the paper urged students "to be the first to move." They should not wait for the adults, it cautioned; "it is for you to begin." The response surpassed all expectations as students from across the country inundated the *Companion* office with thousands of enthusiastic letters.[60]

Maintaining enthusiasm for the Columbian Public School Celebration was not easy. The "general apathy must get repeated shakings," observed Bellamy, until "every locality will at last wake up and produce at least one man who will say 'This thing must be done.'" To arouse interest, the executive committee used the press to communicate in groundbreaking ways. Press releases, providing free advertising, became the backbone of disseminating Columbian Public School propaganda. Inexpensive plates imprinted with news of the public-school celebration proved to be the next major breakthrough. City and village papers, with small local reporting staffs, relied on the American Press Association for the bulk of their news coverage. By sending circulars, editorials, and news items to the Press Association, the organizers of the public-school celebration reached far beyond the major newspapers. At its own expense, the American Press Association made up a stereotype plate of news and information, sending out advance proofs sheets to all the small presses. Those who were interested could then use the plate for a small fee. Provincial newspapers, chronically understaffed and in need of material, eagerly used the plates as a way to fill out their paper and save on the costs of typesetting.[61] Thus the dissemination of a new patriotic "tradition" directly benefited from technological breakthroughs in printing and communication.

The next most pressing problem was how to create news. "It is easy to foresee," wrote Bellamy, "that shortly the great din of the Presidential Campaign will drown out our noise unless we make preparations for keeping our rumble going." The press was not interested in "general effusions." Bellamy knew that he had to

164

keep providing "newsworthy materials." In the spring of 1892 he worried that "already the fire is slackening" and began to explore how to make the public-school celebration news. As a way to gain the official endorsement of the government, Bellamy developed a plan based on publishing and commenting on the views of the president and the leading statesmen whom he lobbied. At meetings with political leaders he asked for their endorsement as well as their opinions. "Such a general course," proposed Bellamy, would cost little and would "give the *Companion* really magnificent advertising."[62]

Bellamy sent letters to members of Congress in which he requested a meeting with President Harrison in order to gain his official support.[63] Harrison's Democratic opponent in the presidential race, Grover Cleveland, had already given his backing. Henry Cabot Lodge arranged the meeting with President Harrison and accompanied Bellamy. The president gave his endorsement without hesitating, and at the end of the discussion Bellamy asked him if Columbus Day could be made into a national holiday. Bellamy recalled President Harrison replying, "Why sir, that can't be done without the authority of Congress." Afterwards, Lodge chided Bellamy for going too far. Determined to gain the full backing of the government, Bellamy replied that he would now ask Congress to authorize it as a holiday.[64]

Bipartisan support for any issue was exceedingly difficult, particularly on the eve of a presidential election. Bellamy recalled that the atmosphere was so politically charged that Western Union Telegraph officials held up Cleveland's endorsement for a day while the Democratic Committee verified that it had come from its candidate.[65] In the end, the breadth of public support for the schoolhouse flag movement overwhelmed partisan considerations. Although official approval of the proposed public-school celebration represented a significant political intervention, governmental support came only as a result of massive grass-roots organizing. The government's laissez-faire approach to public commemoration necessitated decentralized initiatives by individuals and organizations who pushed each state to endorse their patriotic projects at the turn of the century.

Columbian Public School Celebration themes proved to be diffuse enough to incorporate a wide variety of viewpoints and political positions. Appeals to celebrating progress and expanding mass education found genuine popular support. Bellamy's interviews with congressmen revealed differences but also demonstrated how the themes of progress and enlightenment could be fashioned to conform to each congressman's political agenda.[66] The propaganda work of the *Companion* bore fruit as Bellamy listened to politicians echoing back the themes that he and the press staff had so systematically communicated to the nation. Many spoke of Columbus's voyage as a far-sighted mission against the ignorance and conservativism of his day and credited the public schools for being a "direct product of what Columbus stood for."[67]

The Columbian Public School Celebration and the 1892 Chicago Exposition both articulated an expanded vision of Manifest Destiny. Just as Columbus had brought "civilization" to the "New World," the youth of the United States were pictured as the new explorers bringing enlightenment and "redemption" to the world's "backward" nations. A typical *Companion* graphic featured three boys navigating the seas in a small boat, just as Columbus had done four hundred years earlier. The graphic showed one boy holding the Stars and Strips against the sky, while another waved his sword and the third peered through a telescope at the world.[68]

Bellamy and his ideological colleagues at the *Companion* opportunistically linked the sense of the United States as a rising world power with Enlightenment imagery. "No other thing had been so important to the human race," Theodore Roosevelt reportedly told Bellamy, as the "Discovery of America." Just as the opening of America to Europe was the first step in the revolution of the whole world, he claimed, the United States would have a dramatic impact on the world in the twentieth century. Roosevelt urged the use of all means necessary to inculcate the "most fervent loyalty to the flag." The Columbian Public School pledging of allegiance, asserted Roosevelt, would demonstrate that "we are one people" and communicate what no local celebration can, namely, that "we are a solid nation."[69]

After weeks of lobbying, leaders from both houses passed a joint resolution on 29 June 1892 authorizing the president to proclaim Columbus Day a national public-school holiday. In less than a month, President Harrison made 21 October a day that would link the "discovery" of America with the schoolhouse flag movement. "Columbus stood in his age as the pioneer of progress and enlightenment," announced Harrison; "the system of universal education is in our age the most prominent and salutary feature of the spirit of enlightenment. . . . Let the national flag float over every school-house in the country and the exercises be such as shall impress upon our youth the patriotic duties of American citizenship."[70]

The momentum built over months of painstaking organizing finally peaked with the president's endorsement. "A movement instantly secures a numerous following," observed Bellamy, "when success is assured." Hundreds of papers that had "been conspicuous by their silence" now "applauded the undertaking." Thirty-five more governors no longer hesitated to issue state proclamations and 120,000 public schools, more than half of all the schools in the country, pledged themselves to the celebration.[71] As the day approached, school bands practiced playing "America" and the "Star Spangled Banner," while pupils learned drills and memorized the new Pledge of Allegiance.

"WE LOOK BACKWARD AND WE LOOK FORWARD": THE COLUMBUS DAY PLEDGE OF ALLEGIANCE

The Columbian Exposition, not scheduled to officially open until May 1893, moved its dedication ceremonies up to October 1892 to coincide with the four hundredth anniversary of Columbus's "discovery of the New World." Half a million foreigner visitors came to Chicago for the three days of receptions, concerts, parades, and tours of the exhibition grounds.[72] Chartered trains brought in the highest-ranking government officials, members of the U.S. Supreme Court, and diplomats representing countries around the world.[73] Decorated by a sea of flags and bunting, Chicago played host to the most elaborate exhibition ever produced in the United States.[74]

The Columbian Exposition was an unprecedented opportunity to boost the image of the United States as representing the highest degree of industrial civilization.[75] For the tens of thousands who visited Chicago for the dedication ceremonies and the millions more who would read about them in the national and international press, the exhibition promotion department intended the preliminary festivities to stimulate people's imaginations, beckoning them to see the wonders of the United States for themselves.[76] The exposition, aptly called the "White City" because of the color of its buildings, embodied themes of white supremacy, imperial greatness, and masculine power in it program, exhibits, and architecture.[77] Black men and women, excluded from any important positions on the Exposition Commission and barely represented in any of the exhibits, called the exposition "the white American's World Fair."[78] The spatial arrangement of the Columbian Exposition divided the white, "civilized" nations, represented by achievements in iron and steel, from the Midway, where villages of imported "natives" and other "exotic" peoples provided, according to the *Chicago Tribune*, an opportunity to travel the path of evolution from its heights of progress to its savage beginnings.[79]

During the first day, attention momentarily shifted from the Columbian Exposition to Chicago's youth. Across the city, contingents of children gathered en masse at their schools to pledge allegiance to the flag of the United States.[80] "Wouldn't it be a most tremendous lesson in patriotism if the school pupils should take over the celebration?" asked the originator of the idea, James Upton. "Let them feel that this is their day," he continued, "to show to the older folks that they are going to be the patriots."[81] Chicago took the lead in carrying out the flag exercises that would be repeated across the country. By the end of Columbus Day, 21 October 1892, millions of schoolchildren had participated in the first nationally orchestrated day devoted to raising and saluting the flag.[82]

Large crowds gathered at Chicago's schools to see the children execute their "military salute."[83] Three hundred of them, each holding a small American flag, lined the front of Chicago's Froebel School in preparation for the arrival of GAR veterans who had agreed to make "common cause" with the schools and function as the day's official patrons.[84] At the Garfield School, flags flew from every window, and red, white, and blue draperies covered the archway at the school's entrance. The children assembled in their classrooms, and at the signal they marched with GAR veterans into the yard, forming two divisions around the flagpole. Immediately following the grammar-school contingent, the students from the primary school marched in step to the sound of fife and drum.[85] All of the teachers and children wore official Columbian Public School badges, which featured a silk flag with a fanciful arrangement of stars and a cameo of Columbus's arrival showing him staking claim to the "New World" by his own flag-raising.[86] The *Chicago Tribune* noted that the badge gave a "distinguished air to even the tiniest child."[87]

Throughout the country, public schools followed the standardized scenario outlined in the day's official program: When the color guard and veterans had taken their positions at the flagpole, the principal gave the command "Attention!" All faces turned towards the featured speaker, who read the president's proclamation.[88] Whereas only four years earlier the flag had seldom been flown over schoolhouses, on Columbus Day, 1892, more than one hundred thousand schools raised the flag. When it reached the top of the staff, the old GAR veterans could be heard leading assembled students in shouting, "Three Cheers for Old Glory." The principal then gave another signal, and the students repeated in unison: "I pledge allegiance to my Flag and the Republic for which it stands: one Nation indivisible, with Liberty and Justice for all."[89] At the words "to my flag," the children raised their right hands and extended them palm upward towards the colors, then returned them to their sides. The band struck a chord and the whole school joined in singing "America." Pausing for a moment of prayer, the children concluded with a song specially written for the day:

> . . . Humanity's home! The sheltering breast
> Gives welcome and room to strangers of the oppressed.
> Pale children of Hunger and Hatred and Wrong
> Find Life in thy freedom and joy in thy song.[90]

In school after school, the United States was held up as the most perfect expression of enlightened progress since Columbus's discovery of a "virgin world." Throughout the country, speakers followed a common text of the national narrative:

We look backward and we look forward.

Backward, we see the first mustering of modern ideas; their long conflict with old World theories, which were also transported here. We see stalwart men and brave women, one moment on the shore, then disappearing in dim forests. We hear the ax. We see the flame of burning cabins and hear the cry of the savage. We see the never-ceasing wagon trains always toiling westward. We behold log cabins becoming villages, then cities. We watch the growth of institutions out of little beginnings. . . .

We see hardy men with intense convictions, grappling, struggling, often amid battle smoke, and some idea characteristic of the New World always triumphing. We see settlements knitting together into a nation with singleness of purpose. We see the birth of the modern system of industry and commerce, and its striking forth into undreamed of wealth, making the millions members one of another as sentiment could never bind. An under it all, and through it all, we fasten on certain principles, ever operating and regnant—the leadership of manhood; equal rights for every soul; universal enlightenment as the source of progress. These last are the principles that have shaped America; these are the true Americanism.[91]

Finally, speakers implored the assembled children to unite as "one army under the sacred flag" and build the twentieth century on principles of Americanism.[92] Local newspapers carried front-page headlines about the activities of their cities' schools. Cincinnati boasted that the afternoon parade of boys had been one of the "most inspiring spectacles" in its history. People lined the streets to greet them and broke out in enthusiastic cheers at the sight of children dressed in uniform caps and carrying small American flags.[93]

"Young America Leads Off," announced the *New York Times*. A parade of twenty-five thousand schoolchildren and college boys was the first of the great parades planned for New York's Columbus Week. Crowds of children, each wearing a cap of either red, white, or blue, filled the reviewing stands and when in position formed a sea of immense national flags. Primarily made up of boys, the contingents reflected a military model defined by masculinity and disciplined drills as the foundation for robust citizenship. Hundreds of thousands of spectators "banked themselves up so densely that the paraders literally marched through a multitude from the order 'Forward!' until the order 'Break ranks!' " The press reported that many had been particularly moved at the sight of a contingent of "Indian boys and girls" from the government's school at Carlisle and by the five-year-old boys from the Hebrew orphan school marching behind their "tiny Drum Major." For nationalists, the sight of these children provided a visual testament to their efforts to mold future citizens through patriotic education in the schools.[94]

Not since the Civil War, reported the national press, had such a "patriotic and thoughtful uprising of the people taken place." Whereas only thirty years earlier the nation had appeared doomed, the "conspicuous presence and patronage of the war-worn veterans, under the nation's flag, seemed like the bequeathing of a sacred trust to those who are to command the future." Every village and town, announced the *Youth's Companion*, has now "placed the nation's flag, not over her forts and battle-grounds, but over her public schools." The children, marching with "drilled precision" into the new century, formed the latest addition to America's army.[95] The Pledge of Allegiance represented a critical step in transforming schools into machines for political socialization, but the nationalist campaign to make patriotism a fundamental component of educational programs had only just begun with the Columbian Public School Celebration.

"The Great Fusing Furnace":
Americanization in the Public Schools

Although nationally coordinated events like Columbus Day and nationally distributed propaganda like the *Youth's Companion* played a critical role in promoting a sense of the nation, the day-to-day work of mass patriotism shifted beginning in the late 1880s from grand public events to practical routines in the local schools. This chapter examines the role of educators as the new nationalists who took up the challenge of converting "deserving immigrants" into "100 percent Americans." As one of the earliest examples of the Americanization campaigns that during and after World War I would turn fiercely intolerant, the schoolhouse flag movement was by no means monolithic in either its ideology or its methods of inculcating patriotism. Like the previous generation of veterans and women activists, the postwar cadre of activists debated the meaning of the nation.

As a captive public, schoolchildren were potentially the easiest constituency to mold into a loyal and disciplined citizenry. Nationalists saw it as their duty to actively inspire millions of future citizens and newly arriving immigrants through the rational study of civics and history, augmented by expressive lessons that appealed to people's imagination and stimulated their patriotic enthusiasm. Just as veterans knew from their battlefield experiences that successful mobilizations required more than appeals to civic responsibility, so, too, educators and organized patriots understood that the flag could become the most important emotive ingredient in the repertoire of nationalist symbolism. Through dramatic rituals, they hoped to make immigrant and native-born children begin to see themselves united within a larger national community. Viewing schools as an agency of social cohesion was not new, but before the Civil War advocates of universal education had received little federal support for their attempts to broaden schooling.

As the government assumed greater responsibility for the public school system, moral majorities, who previously had used persuasion to influence local school boards, increasingly turned to state legislators to make their values an integral part of compulsory standards of education. From the 1890s on, nationalists, along with advocates of temperance and Bible reading, worked with educational leaders to compel immigrant children to participate in Americanization programs.[1] In 1891 the Committee on State School Systems of the National Education Association warned that foreigners were "destroying distinctive Americanism" by spreading a "system of colonization with a purpose of preserving foreign languages and traditions." Compulsory education in the public schools, the committee resolved, would be the most effective remedy. "The majority sentiment of this country," declared an educator, holds that immigrants "must be intelligent and moral before they can be free, and before they can become an essential and vital part of this republic." It was educators' responsibility, he contended, to maintain the American "standard of civilization" by legislating moral and political standards for newcomers.[2]

"BULWARK OF OUR SAFETY": DEVELOPMENT
OF THE PUBLIC SCHOOL SYSTEM

The Revolutionary generation had also worried about how future generations would be taught a national spirit. Republicans such as Noah Webster promoted the common schools as a vehicle for instilling the next generation with "an inviolable attachment to their own country."[3] Benjamin Rush called for a standardized system of education "to convert men into republican machines."[4] Each stressed the key role of moral education in reconciling freedom and order through the training of a class of virtuous citizens who would be prepared to subordinate themselves to the common good.[5] Although their arguments were compelling, these early advocates made little progress in actually establishing a national system of education. Locally controlled, most schools were organized on a voluntary basis with short sessions and little or no financial assistance from the state. Only the North could claim to provide elementary education to most white Americans by 1830.[6]

The spread of mass public education, like the construction of patriotic culture, depended on the existence of social movements throughout the first part of the nineteenth century. One of the strongest factors in the creation and spread of public schools was the efforts of rurally based activists who shared a common, "Protestant-Republican millennial" ideology. For believers, the "redeemer nation" could best be realized by an agrarian-based capitalism made up of "purified citizen-members," freed from the chains of sin, ignorance, and aristocracy. Promoters of public schools originally emerged out of church groups and civic boosters in the North and the West who linked education and salvation to the future possibilities of the United States.[7]

During the 1830s and 1840s, commitment to universal education gained additional support among elite and middle-class Americans. The "common school revival" held out the promise of becoming a bulwark against "social dangers" associated with declines in landholding, the fragmentation of Protestantism, and the extension of white male suffrage, as well as the destructive consequences of manufacturing and unlimited immigration.[8] Many feared that without education, liberty would degenerate into license and universal suffrage would devolve into a tyranny of the majority.[9] Some took the long view that state-supported education might promote self-discipline among workers and cultural conversion among immigrants.[10] Reformers such as Horace Mann, disturbed by the leveling prospects of Jacksonian democracy and the specter of class antagonisms exacerbated by industrialization, argued that universal education could become the "balance wheel of the social machinery."[11] Equally if not more important than intellectual instruction and job training, schools would mold students' characters and foster an internalized sense of duty and self-discipline.[12]

Nonetheless, the organization and scope of education would not be radically transformed until almost forty years after the Civil War. The processes of cultural unification took place over generations as the centralizing machinery of the nation-state slowly expanded into the area of schooling.[13] The bureaucratization of the public school system and the increased role of the state in standardizing courses and compelling attendance grew out of the broader Progressive movement, which lobbied the state to assume greater responsibility for the nation's social welfare. Public schooling—free and often compulsory, age graded and hierarchically organized, taught by a trained staff and administered by full-time experts—began to replace locally run schools across the country.[14]

Finally, educators had access to an institution capable of "fus[ing] all discordant elements into a homogeneous whole."[15]

It would be a mistake, however, to see the broader reach of the nation-state into the school system only in terms of "ideological engineering." State-imposed patriotism works best when it reflects and interacts with vernacular sentiments already in existence.[16] The teachers at the end of the nineteenth century were not just cogs in the expansion of state machinery, for they responded enthusiastically to the challenge of inculcating nationalist ideals and patriotic sentiments among their students. As upwardly mobile members of the lower middle class, teachers were among those most likely to see themselves as members of a national family with a stake in the future. "The public schools are the great fusing furnace," noted one teacher. "From the plastic stream of American childhood we must mold American patriots."[17]

George T. Balch, author of an early version of the Pledge of Allegiance, saw the public schools as the key to solving the "pernicious influence" of immigration and crime.[18] Nationalists were concerned that immigrant parents would pass on to their children an "instinctive" ethnic identity that would foster "divided allegiances." Mary North, a patriotic instructor in the Woman's Relief Corps, later reflected:

> I have stood at our ports . . . and have watched the incoming thousands, and a horror fixed upon my heart as I looked down the years which stretched before my imagination, and I thought, "Who is able for these things?"
>
> Will our order awake to the opportunities which confront us? "Wide open and unguarded stand our gates, and through them presses a wild, motley throng," and in that throng are children . . . and we should feel that the burden is laid upon us to teach these children what patriotism is.[19]

The new nationalists agitated for state-supported schools and looked to the new cadre of women teachers to make them into the "nursery of American patriotism."[20] This demand radically departed from the role assigned to women following the American Revolution, when republicans counted on mothers to train future citizens in the privacy of their homes.[21] For patriots like Balch, the conditions of the 1890s called for "heroic remedies" if the schools were to be transformed into a "mighty engine for the inculcation

175

of patriotism." Balch warned of "fifteen millions of aliens, speaking more than forty distinct languages and dialects," radically modifying the "social and political conditions which in the past have characterized our national life."[22] He shared Thomas Jefferson's earlier concern that too many immigrants from absolute monarchies would "warp and bias" the direction of the nation, rendering it "a heterogeneous, incoherent, distracted mass."[23]

For professionals like Thomas Morgan, a member of the National Council of Education in the 1890s, the huge cost of public schooling could be justified by the potential contribution of education to promoting the "common weal." Love of country was not simply a natural impulse; it required cultivation. Since patriotism was the source of "public good," reasoned Morgan, it should be the "prime object of public education." His logic made sense to a generation who feared that the "tide of patriotic fervor" that had carried them through the "costly struggle for the preservation of the Union" had "spent its force."[24]

The veterans' *National Tribune* warned that the arrival of adult immigrants, "entirely unfamiliar with our system of Government, and who are unable in their ignorance to comprehend the principles which underlie a Government of the people," threatened the nation's future. Although "it is next to impossible to educate the adults who are thus flocking to our shores," warned the newspaper, we can "look to the enlightenment and development of their children. The public schools of the United States are the bulwark of our safety, and through this channel we must build for the future."[25] Whereas rural-based social movements dominated the spread of common schools throughout the early and mid-nineteenth century, organized patriots and urban professionals took charge of public education at the end of the nineteenth century.

"Americanize the Alien Child": Flags over the Public Schools

The schoolhouse flag movement harnessed the combined energies of patriotic organizations to the self-interests of civic-minded businessmen, teachers, professional organizations, Progressive politicians, and religious reformers. The breadth of its support secured endorsements from a variety of dignitaries, including presidents of the United States and commissioners of education in the fledging public school system. Between the late 1880s and 1900, the movement successfully campaigned for the flying of flags over schoolhouses and the daily pledge of allegiance; the introduction of invented heroines such as Betsy Ross, the mythic maker of the first American flag, as well as narratives of the nation, such as Edward Everett Hale's "Man Without a Country"; the incorporation of flag pageants, drills, and rituals into daily school life; the participation of teachers and students in regular essay contests devoted to patriotic topics; the observance of national anniversaries accompanied by the distribution of free guides to ensure their uniform celebration; the hanging of plaques and portraits of national heroes and events in every classroom; and the scheduling of visits from original "daughters of the revolution" and GAR veterans to animate the study of history.

William Harris, the U.S. commissioner of education, actively enlisted the participation of top-level educators and local schoolteachers from the National Education Association in the initial campaigns of the schoolhouse flag movement.[26] From its founding in 1856 through the first half of the twentieth century, the NEA devoted considerable attention to teaching citizenship.[27] Educators, disturbed by the decline of patriotic fervor in the two decades following the Civil War, promoted the notion that the flag might serve as an emotional rallying point for reawakening nationalist sentiment.[28] Innovative teachers began to use the flag as a practical means for teaching immigrant children about loyalty to the United States. In the early 1890s, Francis Bellamy, author of the officially adopted Pledge of Allegiance, witnessed the "astonishing results" produced by flag exercises. He reported seeing in New York schools "the children of Italy and Germany and Portugal and Ireland" singing " 'Watch the Rhine' and other European national Aires followed by 'The Red, White and Blue,' 'America,' and the Stars and Stripes." The enthusiasm of the children when they gave their salutes confirmed for Bellamy that the flag had "as great a potency to Americanize the alien child as it has to lead regiments to death."[29]

Heralding the success of the schoolhouse flag movement, the *Youth's Companion* reported in 1891 that "thousands of schools have raised the flag whose pupils seldom saw it before." Even more important, the paper received numerous letters from teachers attesting to the positive effects displaying the flag had on their pupils.[30] Beginning in the late 1870s, teachers tried to meet demands for compulsory teaching of citizenship by introducing U.S. history, national poetry, and biographies of the nation's great men. Throughout the 1880s, they gradually began to add singing and drama to enliven traditional approaches based on memorization.[31] The young women schoolteachers, the majority of whom lacked any professional training, welcomed patriotic how-tos that helped them organize their classroom activities and manage their students.[32]

A teacher from Minnesota wrote that the "flag has come to mean something" to her students, "whereas before it was a meaningless piece of cloth." Many reported a "distinct growth of real patriotism," and a teacher from Maine described how "almost every day after the flag-raising one could hear the children cheering the old flag." From the West, a teacher wrote about her efforts to instill sentiments of loyalty among immigrant children. "Eighty-six percent of my scholars were either born in other countries, or are the children of foreign born parents. The effect of the flag upon my school had been to make every one of my pupils enthusiastic Americans."[33]

Francis Bellamy later acknowledged that the schoolchildren probably understood little about the deeper meaning of the flag or the Pledge of Allegiance, but he also understood the importance of rites and rituals in building future loyalty: "To most of them it is a chance to yell all together, and an all-together yell is more fun than a mere song. They know at least that it is what children everywhere are shouting. . . . While the full thought and meaning of all the words are too big to be taken in by the young children, the whole thing sinks in as a general impression, which by repetition becomes a memory that sticks by as they grow older. . . . It is the same way with the catechism, or the Lord's Prayer."[34]

The optimism of patriots like Bellamy, who thought the United States would be enriched by the new immigrants, was paralleled by an intolerant brand of flag-waving patriotism that would later develop into a full-blown nativism and anticommunism. In the 1890s it became commonplace for patriots to invoke the flag against "un-Americans" and all the "grave political and social evils" confronting the nation. At a national meeting of the NEA, for example, the Mississippi state superintendent of public instruction revealed both the progressive and the reactionary side of patriotic ideology when he catalogued the conditions and forces tearing at the fabric of national unity:

> Corrupt municipal administrations . . . an overflow of immigrants in the great North-west; three millions of paupers, living parasites on the body politic; eight million Negroes producing political congestion in the South; party politics in the hands of spoilsmen, who buy and sell the votes of freemen; monopolies and vast combinations of capital sweeping the wealth into the coffers of the few; a brutal conflict between labor and capital; the tiller of the soil striking defiantly for relief from unjust discrimination against their interests; [and] the poor glaring fiendishly at the rich because, through existing conditions, twenty-five thousand persons have been able to get possession of half the wealth of sixty-four millions.

The Southern superintendent argued that in a nation lacking the "cohesive forces of a nationality"—tied together by "common sympathies, identity of race and descent, the same language," and "identity of political antecedents"—only the public schools could develop a "dominant national patriotism" capable of prevailing as a counterforce to anarchy.[35]

Public education placed great emphasis on service to the community and the debt each citizen owed the larger polity.[36] The Grand Army of the Republic joined educators in emphasizing the civic nature and social utility of public-school education. "We fought for our children," declared a veteran, and "have given them a heritage of peace and prosperity." Now it was time for the children to "learn how much devotion and sacrifice it cost to preserve the unity of the nation."[37] Nationalists hoped that in the long run the spirit of civic fraternity would override class and ethnic cleavages. To emphasize the price that had been paid to maintain an undivided nation, the Grand Army resolved that the "8,000,000 boys and girls in our elementary schools" should receive the Stars and Stripes "from the men who placed their bodies as a living wall between it and those who would tear it down."[38]

The GAR garnered significant cultural authority through its relationship to the Civil War and was an important symbolic force in the schoolhouse flag movement. Poignant memories of comrades fighting and dying under the Stars and Stripes led veterans to believe that its mere presence as a sacred icon could inspire national loyalty. "Raising the flag on a schoolhouse," explained a veteran newspaper, "is an act of the same nature as putting a spelling book in a child's hand." The one taught citizenship, the other the basics of knowledge. "When the child sees the Flag floating from the place where he receives his daily lessons, his mind absorbs the idea of the supremacy of the Nation."[39] A GAR committee charged with recommending a "systematic plan" for teaching loyalty called for flying a flag over every schoolhouse so that the flag would come to mean "something more than so many yards of textile fabric."[40]

The Woman's Relief Corps also committed itself to teaching "the rising generation LOYALTY." More than symbolic participants, the members of the WRC provided the infrastructural backbone for the patriotic education movement. Often the WRC combined Memorial Day organizing with outreach into the public schools. For example, in 1890, WRC members in Colorado and Wyoming worked closely with public-school teachers to mobilize more than five thousand students to distribute flowers to the "old soldiers" as they marched in procession to the graveyards. The California department similarly activated 3,235 children to participate in memorials to the Civil War dead. That same year, Connecticut and other WRC departments also began presenting flags to public schools as part of their Memorial Day activities. The WRC felt that schoolchildren should learn to love and honor the flag under which so many had fought and died.[41]

"ONE COUNTRY, ONE LANGUAGE, ONE FLAG":
TEACHING THE SPIRIT OF PATRIOTISM

The success of the Columbian Public School Celebration brought enormous legitimacy to the schoolhouse flag movement. But patriots understood that winning the "very souls of the pupils" required the repetition of patriotic rituals as well as the continual reiteration of patriotic ideas.[42] Also, the public school system was still growing. Although U.S. school enrollments in 1892, about 20 percent of the entire population, exceeded enrollments in almost all the nations of Europe, attendance varied dramatically by region. Educators faced the challenge of creating public schools in newly admitted states, bringing attendance in the South up to the national average, and meeting the constant demand for more schools to accommodate newly arrived immigrant families.[43] The effort to institutionalize patriotic education had just begun. To create the new American man and woman of the next generation, nationalists looked to extending the schoolhouse flag movement to include studying U.S. history, learning patriotic selections and songs, observing national anniversaries, and studying civics in the upper grades.[44]

Although activists disagreed over whether to give greater stress to a martial or a civic-oriented patriotism and whether to stress the rational or emotive components of that patriotism, all stood behind an expanded program for patriotic education. Some groups, such as the National Education Association, worked from above, issuing centralized policy directives; others worked at the grass-roots level, endeavoring to influence local schools and school boards. Other organized patriots pressured state bodies to enact legislation directing public schools to include nationalist subjects in their curriculums. In the 1880s, only eleven states required the study of U.S. history or civics and only nine states required instruction in English. The legalization of patriotism, however, began to gain momentum in the 1890s, when grass-roots organizing began in earnest.[45]

In 1893, Capt. Wallace Foster, a decorated Grand Army veteran, approached the WRC membership and asked them to commit themselves to advocating patriotic instruction in the public schools.[46] Foster believed that women were better suited for "emotional instruction" and could "win over the love of the child by natural forces."[47] In 1893 the WRC's eleventh annual convention gave its unanimous support, priding itself on becoming the "first great body of workers" to embrace the patriotic movement in the schools.[48] Led by the WRC, women soon assumed major responsibility for grass-roots organizing within the public schools.

The GAR endorsed patriotic instruction in the schools in 1891, but unlike the Relief Corps, it did not set up a committee on patriotic education until 1898.[49] During the intervening years, the GAR lobbied for flags over schoolhouses and visited schools during Memorial Day ceremonies, but the national organization concentrated its main energy on trying to introduce military drills into the public schools and censoring history textbooks that did not present a Unionist interpretation of the Civil War.[50] In the late

1890s, the GAR School History Committee announced that its textbook campaign had accomplished its mission and that the organization had decided to join the WRC in securing "patriotic instruction and observances in the schools."[51] The Grand Army felt that the introduction of military drilling into the schools would assure a new generation of citizen-soldiers. Its efforts to add military drilling to school curriculums, however, proved much less successful than its textbook campaign.

The GAR's emphasis on militarism grew out of its conviction that patriotism in itself could not save the Union; it must be coupled with the symbolism and rites of power. Weakness in defense or offense, argued a colonel in the cavalry, is "the greatest menace to the permanence of the Republic."[52] Born of war, veterans tried to recapture and pass on their wartime experience to the next generation of young boys. With no mandatory draft in effect, the GAR counted on military drilling to build character and prepare young students for the possibility of war.

The GAR promoted a martial patriotism rooted in the belief that there could be no "land of the free" if the United States was not also the "home of the brave."[53] Martial patriotism demanded that every young man be taught how to defend his government.[54] Furthermore, drilling would produce the "kinds of citizen qualities" needed by an "industrial America." The "American boy," editorialized the *National Tribune,* "needs to acquire self-respect, obedience, respect for others, regard for the law, and to know his responsibility as the coming citizen."[55] These methods, boasted a military instructor, produced disciplined behavior even among "incorrigibles" by fostering a spirit of "prompt obedience, 'to do right because it is right.' "[56]

What is most important, the GAR believed that drills would provide an essential foundation for maintaining a system of citizen-soldiers in a nation that depended upon volunteers in times of war.[57] Many veterans who had risen through the ranks opposed the professionalism of West Point and counted on the nation's animosity towards a standing, or regular, army to generate support for their plan to train students as future volunteer soldiers. Historically, Americans have equated the existence of a Regular Army with the mercenary armies of a corrupt Europe and prided themselves on the superior qualities of citizen-soldiers. In fact, throughout the nineteenth and early twentieth centuries the Regular

182

Army was "sufficiently isolated to sometimes resemble a monastic order."[58]

John A. Logan, soldier-politician and prime mover behind the early GAR, became one of the most outspoken opponents of military academies, vehemently denouncing their exclusiveness as "aristocratic" and "un-American."[59] During his last years, Logan wrote *The Volunteer Soldier of America*, in which he warned that as "long as the strong arm of the American citizen-soldier is extended in protection to the American republic, it will endure as a blessing to all races of men, but when that protecting arm falls, the American Union must fall with it."[60] Looking back to the independence of the yeoman farmer, veterans like Logan believed that virtue rested in the common man. They feared that the closing of the frontier meant that the nation had to find other arenas for molding the American character. The Grand Army offered military drilling in the schools as a democratic alternative to a professionally trained army. GAR veterans were not the first to introduce the idea of using schools for military training. The Morrill Land Grant Act of 1862 set the precedent by including military tactics among the subjects to be taught in the land-grant colleges.[61]

Hoping to create a "manly, self-respecting spirit" in its "loyal little American soldiers," the GAR made special efforts to reach immigrant students, convinced that military instruction would bind the children to their new country and its institutions. The GAR's efforts bore some fruit when "16 regiments of 10,000 drilled boys, some 3,000 of whom were uniformed and armed," paraded in New York City on Memorial Day in 1895.[62] A similar display of student regiments took place when four thousand boys from New York's public and parochial schools executed military drills at the dedication of General U. S. Grant's tomb.[63]

Nonetheless, many parents and teachers were reluctant to embrace such an overt expression of the culture of militarism in their schools. The GAR's Massachusetts department confirmed the existence of widespread opposition to military drills in the schools and blamed the fear of "militarism" for the lack of support. "You know," stated the patriotic instructor, "most new fads have their rise in Massachusetts, and it is not singular that our supersensitive, over-educated people should be opposed to the drill."[64] Many of the same teachers who supported teaching patriotism drew the line at training their students for war. Quakers, known for advocating nonviolence, strenuously objected to the Grand Army's patriotic scheme, while the Woman's Christian Temperance Union opposed the plan on the grounds that it would make young boys "blood thirsty." The GAR also found that "ethical writers," such as Henry George and William Dean Howells, opposed promoting "a spirit of militarism" in the schools.[65]

Within the Woman's Relief Corps there was also opposition to preparations for war in times of peace. In 1903 the WRC joined the National Council of Women in pledging to hold annual demonstrations on behalf of peace and arbitration as alternatives to military conflicts. The WRC national president declared that the WRC rejoiced that "women throughout the world are beginning to feel their responsibility for human conditions outside of the home as well as within its sacred walls." She asked all women "to adopt as their own the task assumed by the International Council of Women, which is the application of the Golden Rule to society, customs and laws."[66]

Even some members of the GAR who enthusiastically supported flying flags over schoolhouses and teaching patriotism balked at backing military drills in the schools. According to a GAR commander from New York, the "youth of the country should be educated in something higher and better than the science of murdering their fellow men." Teachers opposed the proposal because it would take time away from academic studies. Some community groups objected because they did not want to incur additional educational expenses, others feared that arming the "children of the masses" would "endanger the property of the country," and organized labor opposed the plan because of its potential to create an army capable of threatening the "liberties of the masses."[67] The use of the National Guard against striking workers had led Samuel Gompers to urge the American Federation of Labor to lobby against an 1894 amendment to New York's constitution that would have made National Guard service mandatory for young men.[68] Gompers warned that its passage would mean that workers could be arrested for treason if they "refuse to perform military duty and shoot down their fellow workers." Gompers stressed, "Mark my words . . . if this amendment is adopted it will be put into operation only in the case of some dispute between some unscrupulous corporation and its outraged employees."[69]

Among sympathetic schools, a shortage of instructors thwarted the institutionalization of military instruction. The GAR lobbied the government for passage of an act that would allow the War Department and the president to detail retired officers of the army and navy as instructors. After much effort and compromise, in 1901 President McKinley signed an act of Congress authorizing the assignment of navy and army officers to schools requesting their assistance.[70] Still, the adoption of military instruction did not advance significantly except in New York City. A principal from the Bronx, for example, organized young boys into drill teams that paraded on school grounds in military uniforms with rifles at their shoulders. Other public schools organized bugle corps and advised young girls to stand at attention and salute the flag when the color guard of male students passed by.[71] But beyond New York, only a few other cities implemented the program with any appreciable vigor. In a rare example of enthusiasm, the city of Portland, Maine, authorized the drill in its schools and spent six hundred fifty dollars on equipping one hundred boys with Springfield cadet rifles for use at a training camp.[72] To gain broader support, the Grand Army altered its proposal to specify that military drills would take place off campus and on the students' own time.[73] Yet this particular component of patriotic training still made little headway.[74]

Unlike military drilling, flag exercises were quickly incorporated into school curriculums. In 1895, the NEA formally and "heartily endorsed" the patriotic work of its membership, "which finds expression in placing the national flag upon our schoolhouses, in the increased attention to school exercises which tend to a greater love and veneration for the flag, and in the observance of national holidays."[75] As publishers caught up with the expanding market for patriotic textbooks, the Relief Corps joined forces with private companies like the American Flag Company to distribute millions of copies of flag-salute leaflets, drills, Memorial Day and Flag Day instructions, the charts of the Declaration of Independence, the *Patriotic Primer for the Little Citizen*, along with numerous other classroom teaching aids.[76] Interested teachers could easily obtain free copies of the "Flag Ritual" in bulk by simply writing to the American Flag Company and sending a two-cent stamp to cover the cost of return postage. By 1896, the national WRC reported that a number of state institutions, such as the Indiana Reform School for Boys and the Kansas State Soldiers' Orphans Home, had adopted its patriotic primer as a textbook.[77]

Although men continued to be the spokespersons, women provided the organizational backbone of the schoolhouse flag movement—canvassing neighborhoods and schools across the country, bringing the message of patriotism to the women's movement, and implementing daily lesson plans in the public schools. Every year, each WRC department reported on the number of classrooms visited, flags presented, literature distributed, patriotic essay contests conducted, and national anniversaries observed. The national patriotic instructor then tabulated the figures and prepared a detailed report for the national convention. Additionally, the national office urged department committees on patriotic teaching to investigate and report on conditions in the schools. "How many children in each school?" queried the national. In how many schools is there "instruction in citizenship?" pressed the national patriotic instructor. Many women, unaccustomed to professionalized methods, required ongoing instruction in how to conduct surveys, use forms, and tabulate statistics. Training the membership in the new skills of professional organizing as they proceeded, the national body attempted to account for local conditions when devising their strategies.[78]

"The Color-Touch in History":
Training Hearts and Minds

Although the nationalist movement was reinvigorated when the United States declared war against Spain on 29 April 1898, militarists again faced opposition and debate after Spain's surrender four months later. State-sanctioned rituals of patriotism became much more common, however. The day immediately after the declaration of war, New York enacted a law that made it the duty of the state superintendent of public instruction to prepare "a program providing for a salute to the flag at the opening of each day of school."[79] The law also required the special observance of Lincoln's Birthday, Washington's Birthday, Memorial Day, and Flag Day. The Spanish-American War gave added impetus to the Grand Army's campaign to bring military instruction into the schools, but as the war escalated into a prolonged guerrilla combat against

Filipino rebels who had fought for independence against Spain and now fought against U.S. occupation, a small but vocal group emerged in opposition to imperialism. Williams Jennings Bryan, who had organized the Third Regiment of the Nebraska Volunteers to defend "Cuba against foreign arms," urged the country in December 1898 to refuse to enter "upon a career of conquest." Some opponents denounced the "spirit of militarism" as "savagery, not less so because it glitters with its helmets and moves to the rhythm of banners."[80]

For the time being, a less militaristic approach to teaching patriotism proved more popular. In 1900, New York's State superintendent, Charles Skinner, published a 350-page *Manual of Patriotism*, as directed by the state legislature for use in the public schools.[81] In close cooperation with the GAR, Skinner compiled songs, quotes, and flag rituals aimed at inculcating a spirit of "unselfish patriotism and virtue" in students' hearts.[82] Skinner did not intend his manual to replace textbooks in American history, but he disagreed with educators in the NEA who argued that "patriotism is a rational sentiment, and its health and growth require a diet upon which the reason can feed."[83]

Whereas a Massachusetts superintendent of schools promoted teaching the "essential facts" of U.S. history to the youngest pupils, Skinner proposed that teachers let the "light of sentiment and imagination play over facts and theories—tingeing all with the beautiful Red, White and Blue of the Flag."[84] Unlike the instrumental campaign of the *Youth's Companion*, with its carefully laid out political goals, Skinner's approach fostered an expressive politics aimed at creating a national ethos. "Put yourselves in the place of the child," he advised New York's public-school teachers. "When your mind is thus made responsive to the color-touch in history, try to make your pupils see and feel the illuminating power of great and worthy deeds."[85]

Between 1900 and World War I, many teachers took up the call to bring the spirit and drama of patriotism into their students' lives. For the most part, organized patriots joined Progressive educators in their campaign to facilitate students' active participation over passive memorization and repetitive drills. Following John Dewey, they promoted active learning as one of the most important "terms by which knowledge is acquired and used."[86] Rather than just studying civil government, superintendents of schools such as William A. Mowry, of Salem, Massachusetts, urged teachers to involve their students directly with the "doings of citizens in town meetings, in county conventions, the State legislature, and the courts." During elections, argued Mowry, teachers should organize their pupils to conduct their own elections, form party caucuses, run campaigns, and follow state laws regarding balloting.[87] "History is made and done," explained another educator, whereas "civics is history in the making."[88]

Some educators even began to advocate a civic rather than a martial patriotism by stressing U.S. accomplishments in promoting the general welfare of all peoples rather than wars.[89] The president of Brown University argued against the "turgid rhetoric [and] the pulmonary athleticism" displayed on Memorial Day and at flag-raisings and instead called for teaching children a "high patriotism." There are three kinds of patriotism, he explained. First, a practical loyalty springs from "more or less selfish considerations," illustrated by what can be called a "bondholder patriotism." Second, there is a "sentimental patriotism," in which the "country has come to stand before the patriot's soul as the veritable chief good, to be fought for to the death if need be, he knows not why." Third, there is a "rational patriotism," which develops out of the "reasoned conviction" that one's "country has been called by the Power above to an eminent role in the upward evolution of humanity." Public schools, he argued, do not exist for "the sake of any man as man, but to complete each pupil's civic character" by stimulating a rational patriotism.[90]

Of course, the kind of patriotism and the level of knowledge developed out of civic-oriented activities varied widely and depended on the ability and philosophical orientation of the teacher. As Richard Hofstadter has argued, the primary intent of public education was not to contribute to the expansion of knowledge but "to take a vast, heterogeneous, and mobile population, recruited from manifold sources and busy with manifold tasks, and forge it into a nation, make it literate, and give it at least the minimal civic competence necessary to the operation of republican institutions."[91] Progressive teachers and patriots optimistically responded to the challenge of nation-building and endeavored to bring the full infrastructural potential of the public school system to the project, insisting that students actively partake in the process.

13. Working-class immigrant and black children are taught a lesson in civics by their teachers, who have organized the class to vote on whether to salute the flag. Beach Street Industrial School, early 1890s. Photographed by Jacob Riis. Prints and Photographs Division, Library of Congress, LC-USZ62-34557.

The Relief Corps agreed that patriotic education required, even demanded, the teaching of good citizenship, but it also believed that citizenship's "homely virtues"—obedience to law and order, discipline, honesty, sobriety, and industry—failed to arouse sufficient "enthusiasm in the average child." The organization concluded that "true education" required the training of the "heart as well as the mind." To touch children's emotions, the women called on their comrades in the Grand Army, "not simply because they were soldiers—for war is not always righteous. Not because of their bravery—for bravery is not a synonym for patriotism," but because they embodied "all the glamour and romance of their service as soldiers." The WRC believed that "living lessons in patriotism" could "catch the attention of children" far better than dull texts. "They will gladly learn from such a book, whose pages will soon be closed forever!"[92]

14. An old Grand Army of the Republic veteran in uniform, his GAR badge pinned to his chest, carries a child to a patriotic celebration in 1914. Prints and Photographs Division, Library of Congress, LC-USZ62-064124.

The veterans tried to reproduce their war experiences through a hands-on approach to education. One patriotic instructor visited more than six thousand children in the course of a single year. He always carried a "relic of the war," often bringing the flag presented to his regiment or an eight-pound shell from combat, to bring the war to life for the children. A cadre in the patriotic movement, Comrade Barney felt that "when the old soldiers have all passed away, these same children will tell their children and grandchildren that they saw the soldiers of the Rebellion and heard them tell their stories."[93] For the next generation of children, the GAR appeared as authentic actors in the living theater of Civil War history.

In the 1890s and 1900s there was a flurry of textbooks, produced to teach patriotism through inspirational quotes, poems, and short stories, as well as practical how-tos on flag rituals, plays, and pageants for the classroom. "A Message to Garcia" became the most popular morality tale from the Spanish-American War, reprinted in numerous textbooks and added to *The Patriotic Reader*, published for seventh and eighth graders. The hero of the story, Rowan, is asked by President McKinley to deliver an urgent message to Garcia, the leader of the Cuban insurgents, asking for his cooperation. With the mail and telegraph shut down, the situation grows more dire. Immediately, "Rowan took the letter and did not ask, 'Where is he at?' By the eternal! There is a man whose form should be cast in deathless bronze and the statue placed in every college of the land. It is not book learning young men need, nor instruction in this or that, but a stiffening of the vertebrae which will cause them to be loyal to a trust, to act promptly, concentrate their energies: do the thing—'Carry a message to Garcia!' "

The story's narrator tells students that even though the war in Cuba is now over, they too can follow the example of Rowan by becoming disciplined and self-promoting workers in the economic struggle of life. Let us stop the "maudlin sympathy" for the "down-trodden denizen of the sweat shop," he advises. When they grow up, he tells them, they should not be like the clerks who ask for detailed instructions; instead they should be like Rowan and reply, "Yes, sir," and accomplish their task! "It is the survival of the fittest. Self-interest prompts every employer to keep the best— those who carry the message to Garcia." The world is calling for such a man, he says. "He is needed, and needed badly."[94]

Clara Walker, a New York principal, organized her entire elementary school into a theater of patriotism each Flag Day. After a day of poetry, songs, and stories, the younger children would march up onto the stage and, with a flurry of colored streamers, transform themselves into a "living flag."[95] The new flag rituals allowed both children and adults to become actors in the drama of nation-building. No longer relegated to the sidelines of patriotic celebrations, students marched in formation at parades, participated in Memorial Day activities, and frequently appeared at veteran events. In 1896, twenty-two hundred schoolchildren formed a massive living flag in honor of the GAR's thirtieth national encampment, in St. Paul, Minnesota. As the long line of veterans marched by, all looked up and applauded the youngsters outfitted in red, white, and blue.[96]

Until World War I, political complexity rather than hegemony characterized patriotic culture. The authors of the first pledges of allegiance, Balch and Bellamy, demonstrated the spectrum of

191

political positions initially taken by patriots. The two authors articulated radically different visions of American society, Balch standing for competitive individualism, while Bellamy promoted the vision of a social citizenry. Disagreements over how to teach loyalty
also surfaced between those educators who advocated teaching
an emotionally charged patriotism based in dramatic classroom
rituals and those who gave greater emphasis to what they called
an "intelligent patriotism," organized around students' participation in the practice of democracy.

Many Progressive teachers advocated civic patriotism, in which
the "work of a patriot is not so much to fight and die for his country, as it is to work and live to make it a grand nation." A small
minority, including John Dewey, proposed that national patriotism was only a step towards reaching the greater goal of internationalism. Some progressive educators in the NEA even envisioned a future "when the whole world will be organized, and the
armies of the world will be turned into the paths of productive
industry, and international law will control and settle all the affairs
of the world."[97]

On the other hand, the GAR and the new nationalists led by
Teddy Roosevelt championed a martial patriotism filled with heroic images of virile soldiers, war, and the honor of dying for one's
country. Highly influential textbooks promoted this genre of patriotism among children of all ages. A typical child's primer published in 1903 taught the alphabet through the military adventures of the army during the Spanish-American War. B stood for
battles, F for the flag, P for the Philippines, R for Roosevelt, and
Z for the zeal "that has carried us through / When fighting for
justice / With the 'Red, White and Blue.' " Next to each letter,
romanticized battle scenes illustrated the lure of the Rough Riders
and "their many brave deeds," while primitive Filipinos dressed as
exotic African natives waited for young white boys to "help them
to govern / Their rich fertile land." Opposite a picture of an ad-
venturous Teddy Roosevelt, a white male child snapped a whip
above the head of his rocking horse, urging him forward into the
fray of battle.[98]

Although many groups drew the line at allowing the GAR to
introduce drilling in the schools, the call for military training resurfaced in the summer of 1914, when Progressives like Theodore
Roosevelt and military evangelists like Maj. Gen. Leonard Wood

successfully rallied the nation around the need for preparedness.[99] The GAR's brand of martial patriotism, though a minority perspective in the public-school debates during the 1890s, was a harbinger of the more jingoistic brand of patriotism that would triumph during World War I. The narrowing of nationalist debate was fueled also by the racialization of patriotism, which, at least since the collapse of Reconstruction, had virtually silenced African Americans in the discourse about the nation. Policies of segregation and repression meant that the emancipatory tradition was essentially ignored by the new nationalists as they developed their civic-minded education. Moreover, the rise of the New South to national political power in the elections of 1912 was an ominous sign that racism and preparedness for war would once again be compatible allies.

"Clasping Hands over the Bloody Divide":
National Memory, Racism, and Amnesia

O<small>N</small> 3 July 1913, "Johnny Rebs" and "Yanks" met once again at the "Bloody Angle." Old men now, the survivors formed two lines one hundred feet apart and waited under an intense Pennsylvania sun for the order to advance. Fifty years earlier, Pickett's brigades had broken through the Union lines at the stone wall only to fall before Union bayonets and bullets. The "high-water mark of the Confederacy had been reached" and the waters had receded until Appomattox.[1] The United States dealt a blow to the Confederacy from which it would not recover. Overall, 160,000 soldiers fought at Gettysburg. At the end of the three day's carnage, almost 44,000 men from both sides had been killed, wounded, captured, or reported missing in action. One out of every four soldiers lay dead or brutally wounded. When the armies moved out, they left behind a grisly scene of silenced guns, emptied cartridge boxes, bloodied clothing, rain-soaked daguerreotypes, and miles of rotting bodies.[2]

Fifty years later, cameras flashed and reporters prepared nostalgic accounts of the fiftieth anniversary of the Battle of Gettysburg. The Blue and Gray, now reunited as white "blood brothers," stood where they once had slaughtered each other. Uniformed Confederate veterans filled the afternoon air with rebel yells and marched up Cemetery Ridge brandishing the Stars and Bars to sounds of "Dixie."[3] At the wall, the men stopped and the standard-bearers crossed their battle flags. A Union veteran unfurled a silken Stars and Stripes and presented it to the Confederate contingent. "It was your flag and our flag," proclaimed a Pennsylvania congressman, "in the closing days of the Revolution," during the "march upon the Mexican capital" and in the recent war with Spain. Today "it is still your flag." Before thousands of cheering spectators, the former enemies reached out and shook hands.[4]

Reconciliation came with a price, however. The anniversary marked the decisive turn towards victory for Union troops at the

Battle of Gettysburg and the critical decision by President Lincoln to link the meaning of the Civil War to the freeing of slaves. But by 1913, national amnesia had erased Emancipation from Civil War commemorations and history books. The fiftieth anniversary of Gettysburg and the issuance of the Emancipation Proclamation never occupied the same ceremonial or imaginative space. "It is through this syntax of forgetting," proposes Homi Bhabha, "that the problematic identification of a national people becomes visible."[5] In the name of national unity, the struggle for black rights was all but eradicated from Civil War commemorations, and the nation's commitment to equal rights was in full retreat.

The year before, in 1912, the United Daughters of the Confederacy had laid the cornerstone for a massive monument to the Lost Cause in Arlington National Cemetery. Beneath a larger-than-life figure of a woman representing the white South, the monument features a Confederate interpretation of the Civil War sculpted into a circular frieze. A "faithful slave" is shown marching behind his master, while a black "mammy" is represented as the devoted guardian of her master's children.[6] The same year, the presidency went to Woodrow Wilson, a Southern son. Southerners made up more than half of the Democratic majority in the Senate and more than two-fifths in the House. The white South now held the largest proportion of influential administrative and diplomatic posts since before the Civil War.[7] At Wilson's inauguration, white Southerners filled the nation's capital with rebel yells and strains of "Dixie."[8] This chapter explores the momentous struggle between memory and amnesia in national culture and the battle of black men and women to reclaim their place as Americans during World War I.

"SOJOURNER TRUTH CRIES: 'FREDERICK, IS GOD DEAD?' ": THE FIFTIETH ANNIVERSARIES OF GETTYSBURG AND EMANCIPATION

During the first four days of July 1913, the United Confederate Veterans and the Grand Army of the Republic gave memory a tangible shape and place through their theaters of memory at Gettysburg. The media arranged staged scenes between reenactments.

15. The struggle for freedom is eliminated from Civil War memory by sculpted images of "faithful slaves" on the Confederate Monument in Arlington National Cemetery. The United Daughters of the Confederacy unveiled the monument in 1914. Photographed by Arthur Timothy Wells.

When a "motion-picture" man found a Confederate and a Union veteran talking near a cannon, he asked them to clasp hands over the gun for a perfect shot of reconciliation.[9] Under the spotlight of electric lights, which transformed blood-soaked fields into what the GAR's *National Tribune* described as a glittering "fairyland," a Disney-like scene unfolded, reshaping historical memory in the service of national solidarity.[10] Such representations allowed the former enemies to symbolically retrace their steps and emerge

16. Photographs such as this one, taken at the 1913 celebration of the fiftieth anniversary of the Battle of Gettysburg, popularized the image of reconciliation between Grand Army and Confederate veterans. Prints and Photographs Division, Library of Congress, LC-USZ62-88416.

transformed into comrades.[11] From one generation to the next, the veterans transmitted a particular interpretation of the past through their crafted acts of memory. Their commemorative performance provided a dramatic vehicle for making remembering in common possible.

More than 50,000 veterans attended the four-day commemoration—44,714 from the Union and 8,694 from the Confederacy.[12] Although the number of Confederate veterans was significantly less than the number of Union veterans, their presence satisfied the needs of politicians and the press for scenes of national solidarity. In the official speeches and choreography of Gettysburg, veterans were urged to forget their past animosities and emotional wounds. What mattered was that images of forgetting were presented as the norm.[13] The setting was carefully orchestrated, with massive dirt boulevards criss-crossing the miles of tents in the "Great Camp," named for the United States, the Confederacy, and individual states. Tens of thousands of guests, Regular Army soldiers, Boy Scouts, state and federal officials, reporters, and local citizens joined the veterans, bringing the daily attendance to an estimated 100,000.[14] Railroad companies, eager to capitalize on free publicity, chartered special trains to bring passengers from all over the country. The veterans' home states paid most of their transportation costs, while Pennsylvania and the national government assumed all the expenses for food and housing.[15]

Veterans who could not attend participated vicariously through the "wonderful modern mechanism" of motion pictures. From early in the morning until late at night, Californians thronged a local San Francisco theater to watch the hour-length film *Battle of Gettysburg*.[16] Posters and special releases in magazines publicized the film as the "most faithful reproduction of the most bitter conflict in the war annals of the world . . . where men, maddened with the fury of the combat, asked no quarter and none was given. . . . Father and son, brother and brother, opposed each other in a maelstrom of death, the tide of battle alternating through brilliant charges and acts of daring."[17] When the movie first opened in New York, theatergoers "went wild as the stirring scenes . . . were once more enacted before their very eyes." Reviewers claimed that such a "spectacle" had never before been "witnessed by any audience in the world. Thousands of men battling to death, hand-to-hand conflicts, scenes of the most awe-inspiring sensationalism and heroism."[18] In living and cinematic theaters, people who had not participated in the war borrowed memories for their own recollections.[19]

The imaginative power of national memory no longer depended on lived experiences, for now it could be learned through movies, photographs, and articles in the mass media. To meet the popular demand for films, the expanding motion picture industry increasingly turned to "patriotic melodramas and crinoline romances of the North and South." Theaters changed their bills daily and needed a constant supply of new silent movies to satisfy their customers. A handful of interchangeable plots could be found among the numerous one-and two-reel Civil War films.[20] By 1913, ninety-eight different Civil War films were appearing in theaters across the country, vividly portraying split families, life and death, and moments of nobility and cowardliness. Originally the films' sympathies were overwhelmingly with the North, but as directors heeded protests from the South they introduced heroic figures from the Confederacy.[21] In 1913, films such as *Between Home and Country, The Soul of the South,* and *A Dixie Mother* painted empathetic portraits of Confederate self-sacrifice, courage, and family honor; *Devotion, Old Mammy's Secret Code,* and *A Slave's Devotion* romanticized an idealized relationship between black slaves and their masters; and films such as *The Colonel's Oath, A Daughter of the Confederacy,* and *The Great Sacrifice* portrayed the tragedy and triumph of love between Northern and Southern sweethearts.[22]

The Civil War according to Hollywood favored personal stories and happy endings rather than narratives that revealed ongoing conflicts, unresolved questions, and unfulfilled promises of liberation. Hollywood movies often conflated nation and family, frequently portraying the divisions of the Civil War as differences among brothers and friends. In *Two Kentucky Boys,* two fathers, both veterans of the U.S.-Mexican War, bitterly part ways at the beginning of the Civil War when one pledges loyalty to the United States, and the other, to the Confederacy. Their sons, despite having vowed never to be separated, also have to choose sides. One night, Gum Jenkins's father points to the flag over the fireplace and asks, "Are you for the flag or against it, son?" Realizing that he must take a stand against his boyhood friend, the young man answers, "I—I reckon I'm for the flag." After the war, though their friendship has been "tried by fire and sword," the two young men reunite, "true to their convictions—and, better yet, true to their love for each other."[23] Like the men in the officer corps who put aside political differences out of respect for the military professionalism of their enemy, the boys' personal bonds triumph over political convictions.

At one level, the fiftieth anniversary of the Battle of Gettysburg represented a moving national reconciliation, a solemn moment of acknowledging the common humanity of former enemy soldiers. But the fiftieth anniversary was not only a commemoration that recognized the horrors of the most devastating civil war of the nineteenth century. It was also a national ceremony and a symbolic performance that refashioned the historical memory of the Civil War to make it suitable for a twentieth-century nation aspiring to world power. At the heart of this renegotiation of memory stood the issue of race. Behind the veneer of transformation and reunification was a long and bitter struggle over race relations. The commemoration physically embodied the renegotiation of political language and symbolism that occurred within national culture between 1863 and 1913.

Following the end of Reconstruction, Afro-Americans almost single-handedly waged a battle against racist revisions of historical memory. At a time when written texts, public monuments, and national holidays excluded black experiences from the historical record, freedmen and women passed on their living memories through commemorative performances. Every year the repetition of freedom rituals at Emancipation Day celebrations allowed generations to identify with those who had come before them. The vibrancy and meaning of Emancipation Day could be heard in the communal singing of "Nobody Knows the Trouble I See," from slavery; "John Brown," from the abolitionist struggle; and "My Country, 'Tis of Thee."[24] But these ceremonies remained segregated, and as the fiftieth anniversary of Gettysburg and Emancipation neared, the national government refused to acknowledge their dual significance.

Several years before the joint anniversary, Booker T. Washington had requested President Taft and the Congress to endorse a national celebration of Emancipation.[25] Washington proposed having an industrial exposition to "show the progress Negroes have made, not only during their period of freedom, but from the time of their coming to this country." The proposal generated mixed support among black communities because of its inclusion of slavery. But before the debate could unfold, the joint resolution failed to garner the necessary two-thirds vote, despite President Taft's endorsement.[26] Other black leaders lobbied Congress again in 1912 for an appropriation of $250,000 for a national exposition.[27] The bill's preamble and first section eloquently described Emancipation as "one of the great events in American history and in the history of the human race." A national commemoration would make Emancipation "tangible . . . to the present and future generations of American citizens and all the sons of men encouraged to struggle to improve their condition" and gain the "ultimate possession of equal rights and . . . the blessings of liberty protected by law for themselves and their children."[28] The Senate immediately struck out the bill's historical framework and political vision, leaving only matter-of-fact details about the appropriation.[29]

All the major black institutions, from religious organizations such as the African Methodist Episcopal Church with its 640,000 members to political organizations such as the National Association for the Advancement of Colored People, advocated its passage. The majority of black America—through newspaper editorials, church sermons, petitions, and congressional delegations— overwhelmingly urged the federal government to recognize Emancipation Day as a national anniversary. Having risked death and proven their patriotism, argued a college president, the "Negro deserves the recognition."[30] But the Democratic House mired the bill in its bureaucracy, and committees passed it back and forth until it died.[31]

Although national and state governments provided significant appropriations for Gettysburg, the federal government's lack of support for a nationally sponsored commemoration of Emancipation ensured that it would not become one of the nation's great traditions. Only three states—Pennsylvania, New Jersey, and New York—appropriated funds for expositions in 1913. Throughout the rest of the country, committees of black Americans independently assumed responsibility for organizing state and local activities, from church conferences and parades to pageants and exhibits. The largest commemoration of Emancipation took place in New York City just one half block from Broadway.[32] W. E. B. Du Bois had appeared before the Senate in 1912 to present his ideas on how to develop an exposition, but his plans would not take shape until New York finally appropriated twenty-five thousand dollars for the project.[33]

The governor appointed a commission made up of the "most influential and representative colored men of the state," who frowned on the "country fair type of exposition" and instead advocated conferences and congresses on religion, sociology, and the role of women in furthering the goal of education.[34] A global perspective informed the New York exposition's themes; its organizers used cutting-edge techniques of artifacts, moving pictures, and photographs in the design of a "fine and dignified presentation of great facts in simple form, with a frame of beauty and music." The first presentation displayed "industries of Africa"; the second looked at the black diaspora; others concentrated on women, religion, civics, science and inventions, music, and art. A small central temple designed by a black architect featured Afro-American sculptures, paintings, books, and newspapers.[35] Designers fashioned the exposition's decorations after Egypt. "The Obelisk and Sphinx are everywhere," reported the *New York Sun*, "for as one of the colored Boy Scouts said, 'We all came out of Africa.' "[36]

A pageant entitled "The People of Peoples and Their Gifts to Men," written by W. E. B. Du Bois, generated the most excitement. "It promises," predicted the *Afro-American Ledger*, to be a "great educational" experience for the cast and those who "will view this brilliant historical living picture."[37] The pageant involved close to 1,000 people, with 350 in costume.[38] DuBois believed that the "full spiritual message" of Afro-Americans had yet to be heard. "We are Americans, not only by birth and by citizenship, but by our political ideals, our language, our religion," argued DuBois. But we are also

> Negroes, members of a vast historical race. . . . We are that people whose subtle sense of song has given America its only American music, its only American fairy tales, its only touch of pathos and humor amid its mad money-getting plutocracy. As such it is our duty to conserve our physical powers, our intellectual endowments, our spiritual ideals; as a race we must strive by race organization, by race solidarity, by race unity to the realization of that broader humanity which freely recognizes differences in men, but sternly deprecates inequality in their opportunities and development.[39]

The pageant comprises six episodes in African and American history and reflects Du Bois's attempt to present the unique history and civilization of Afro-Americans.

Unlike the commemoration at Gettysburg, Du Bois's pageant does not attempt to conceal conflict. The fourth episode opens onto the sale of slaves by Mohammedans and black Africans to European traders. The desperate moanings of captives, bound in chains, become slavery's sorrow songs. The final episode presents the struggle for emancipation. The transformative experience is not of enemies into comrades but of slaves into freedmen and freedwomen. Images of John Brown, Abraham Lincoln, Frederick Douglass, and Sojourner Truth fill the stage. "Sojourner Truth cries: 'Frederick, is God dead?' . . . . Douglass answers: 'No, and therefore slavery must end in blood.' " As a single voice sings "O Freedom," a company of black Union soldiers marches onto the stage. Troops of Boy Scouts followed by little children join the chorus. With a "blast of trumpets" the pageant ends and the heralds sing: "Hear ye, hear ye, and forget not the gift of black men to the world. . . . Men of America, break silence, for the play is done."[40]

But although crowds packed the Sixty-second Regiment Armory, almost no white New Yorkers came to see the exposition or listen to the pageant's message. White press coverage was virtually nonexistent except for a few short columns.[41] Meanwhile, the black contribution to the Civil War was similarly erased from the ceremonies at Gettysburg. The *Washington Bee* rhetorically asked whether "the heroic valor displayed by the Negro, in his fight for freedom and the defense of the Union [was] less virtuous, less meritorious . . . than that shown by those who fought for disunion and the perpetuation of the infamous blot of human slavery." Then why, demanded the *Bee*, was the reunion at Gettysburg between Union veterans and Confederates? How fortuitous for Northern reconciliationists and their "over-sensitive white brothers," concluded the *Bee*, that the Battle of Gettysburg, while decisive, had been a battle in which few black soldiers participated.[42] Only a handful, if any, black veterans attended the commemoration at Gettysburg.[43] In their place, Confederates marched in uniform alongside the Boys in Blue, tattered Confederate battle flags flew next to the Stars and Stripes, and dozens of bands played both Union and Confederate war songs.[44]

It would not be an overstatement to conclude that the white South won in the cultural arena what it had lost on the battlefield. There was no mistaking the central place of racism in constructing a usable past within the emerging historical profession, public-school textbooks, and the rituals of nationalism performed at the fiftieth anniversary of Gettysburg. No longer a war of secession and treason, the Civil War was recast by orator after orator as a heroic struggle between brothers whose blood had strengthened the nation.[45] The chairman of the Gettysburg reunion articulated the official position on opening day. "It matters little to you or to me now," he asserted, "what the causes were that provoked the War of the States in the Sixties." What mattered, he continued, was that veterans from the Union and the Confederacy had survived to see their sons stand shoulder to shoulder to "sweep San Juan Hill, sink Spanish fleets in Santiago and Manila Bays, and thundering at the gates of Peking, establish our country as a power second to none on earth."[46]

The Gettysburg commemoration served domestic and international purposes. To the nation, a symbolic face of white solidarity asserted itself against double-edged fears of the New Negro and the new immigration. Internationally, the United States appeared united again after the bloodiest civil war of the nineteenth century. "It is a spectacle to inspire the world," wrote the *Philadelphia Evening Bulletin*. "It means that out of the fiery furnace of civil strife, which burned with an intensity fierce enough to consume the ties of blood brotherhood, the nation emerged stronger and better than ever, purged and purified, with a new spirit and a new resolve."[47]

To achieve this symbolic unity, the nation had been called upon to remember and obliged to forget. To the extent that commemorative performances transformed the white South's treason into valor on the battlefield, they eradicated from historical memory the roles of slaves behind enemy lines and the contributions of armed black soldiers at the front. National amnesia played as strong a role as remembrance when rebel yells, not Emancipation's freedom songs, filled the Grand Tent. During the opening ceremonies, the commander-in-chief of the United Confederate Veterans demonstrated the South's appreciation of its cordial reception at Gettysburg by leading former Confederate generals and a thousand Confederate veterans in the rebel yell.[48] When President Wilson arrived on the Fourth of July, he was flanked by a white Union veteran carrying the Stars and Stripes and a white Confederate veteran holding the Stars and Bars, thus communicating that the healing of regional divisions rested on deepening racial divides. In his speech, Wilson explicitly invoked depoliticized images of men shedding their blood "to make a nation." He did not once mention the issuance of the Emancipation Proclamation, despite its sharing the same anniversary year as the Battle of Gettysburg.[49] The president's highly selective interpretation of the Civil War carried the imprimatur of national memory, a history W. E. B. Du Bois later denounced as "lies agreed upon."[50]

Speaking at an Emancipation celebration in Nashville in 1913, Booker T. Washington warned that "when the white men who wore the blue and the white men who wore the gray met upon the

17. On July Fourth, 1913, President Wilson arrives at the celebration of the fiftieth anniversary of the Battle of Gettysburg flanked by a Grand Army and a Confederate veteran, who fly the Stars and Stripes and the Stars and Bars. Photograph in Pennsylvania Commission, *Fiftieth Anniversary of the Battle of Gettysburg* (Harrisburg: WM. Stanley Ray, 1913), 176.

field of Gettysburg a few days ago and clasped hands, it means to say to the Negro that no more would the white man of the North and the white man of the South become enemies and do battle with each other because of the Negro."[51] For this cultural moment, the nation had been reunited, but at the price of severing patriotism from the aspiration to social equality and full democracy. By 1913, a shared racism legitimated interpretations of the Civil War that lent historical credence to the continuation of white supremacy in the South and the extension of segregation in the North.

"THE BIRTH OF A NATION": RACE, GENDER, AND MILITARISM IN POPULAR CULTURE

Two years after the anniversaries of Gettysburg and Emancipation, nostalgia for the antebellum South and explicit support for Jim Crow reached new heights as the next generation shaped the old contradictions of racism into modern forms for the twentieth century. In the South, lynching became a modern spectacle, a grisly festival for white amusement. Newspapers, telegraph offices, and radio stations announced the time and place of lynchings. Fathers and mothers drove their children to the bloody carnivals; other lynchers arrived on excursion trains. Cameras in hand, onlookers took pictures and gathered body parts for souvenirs. For those unable to attend, the local press carried stories in lurid detail.[52] For many white Southerners, lynchings solved the dilemma of not having a state government strong enough to enforce their demands for "an impossibly high level of racial mastery." Generations of black men lived with the threat that they could be tortured by a white mob for simply looking at a white women or not stepping aside to give a white person the right of way on a sidewalk.[53] Richard Wright remembered that the "dread of white people . . . came to live permanently in my feelings and imagination." He grew up in the South with the omnipresent fear "that there existed men against whom I was powerless, men who could violate my life at will."[54]

As regeneration through violence took place in actual lynchings in the South, D. W. Griffith nationalized the Southern ritual through his carefully crafted film, *The Birth of a Nation*, designed to "revolutionize Northern sentiments" and win support for the "White Man's party."[55] Released in 1915, *The Birth of a Nation* became the most popular film of the era.[56] With the U.S. entry into World War I just two years off and the occupation of Haiti and the Dominican Republic underway, the film celebrated the reunification of white male warriors and the reassertion of white supremacy. Based on Thomas Dixon's *The Clansman* and drawing upon Woodrow Wilson's *History of the American People*, Griffith's film depicted Reconstruction as the "agony that the South endured that a nation might be born."[57] On the film's opening night at Liberty Theater in New York, Thomas Dixon told the audience "that he would have allowed none but the son of a Confederate soldier to direct the film version of *The Clansman*." Dixon's favorite scenes were "those stretches of the film that follow the night riding of the men of the Ku Klux Klan, who look like a company of avenging spectral crusaders sweeping along the moonlit roads."[58]

In the film, chivalrous white men free the South from the death grip of black anarchy. The assertion of black manhood rights is depicted as a reversion to primitive lust and political savagery. A white cloth with the blood of the hero's little sister is held up as

206

the banner of the Klan and proof of the threat of black rapists to the body politic. Just as white heroines in sentimental novels chose death when faced with the threat of sexual abuse, the sister had remained virtuous when pursued by a black Union veteran by leaping to her death. Unspoken, but inferred, was the belief that black women had failed the test of true womanhood by surviving their institutionalized rape during slavery. Within literature and popular culture, white men were excused for their sexual assaults, the blame for their attacks being shiften onto the dark forces that inhabited the bodies of black women.[59]

The convergence of race, gender, and militarism is dramatically expressed throughout the film, but the scene of reconciliation within the Union cabin dramatizes the critical negotiation necessary to actualize the alliance of white men. In a final scene of fiery redemption, the paternalistic slave owner Dr. Cameron and his wife are placed under arrest for harboring the Klan by a rampaging mob of white actors in black face. Helped in their escape by the son of a radical Northern congressman, the couple seek refuge in a cabin belonging to white Union veterans who settled in the South after the war. Their safety is soon threatened, however, by a mob of black men who swarm around the cabin in a scene evocative of images of wild Indians popularized in frontier movies of the day. As the cabin is attacked by emancipated black men, the Yankee veterans declare that though they had been divided from their Southern brothers during the Civil War, they stood reunited in the common "defense of their Aryan birthright." Moments away from being overwhelmed by black militants, they are rescued by the Klan. Griffith's Union veterans play the same role as the GAR men who campaigned so relentlessly for the imposition of a color line within the GAR. After disarming the black population, the film ends with a metaphorical double marriage between the sons and daughters of the Northern radical and the Southern patrician.[60]

When the National Association for the Advancement of Colored People began to organize against the film's showing on the grounds that its representation of Reconstruction history was "immoral and unjust," Dixon maneuvered to get favorable reviews from the president, members of the Supreme Court, and the Congress. Chief Justice Edward D. White agreed to view the movie after learning that it narrated the "true" story of Reconstruction.

According to Dixon, the judge leaned forward and confided, "I was a member of the Klan, sir."[61] Woodrow Wilson was impressed when he watched a special viewing at the White House. "It is like writing history with lightening," effused the president. "My only regret is that it is all so terribly true."[62] Mildred Lewis Rutherford, of Athens, Georgia, the historian-general for the United Daughters of the Confederacy from 1911 to 1916, believed that the film would do more to bring the white North and South together than anything that had happened since the Civil War. "All these years we have been trying to make the North see that we had a grievance, and now that they acknowledge it, we can without bitterness or prejudice discuss our troubles with them."[63]

As the country prepared to enter World War I, a popular song proclaimed that "there are no boys in blue or gray. It's just one country" beneath the "Stars and Stripes of Dixie Doodle and the good ole U.S.A." From the Indian wars to the Spanish-American War and onto World War I, martial culture facilitated sectional reconciliation by reuniting white male warriors. Another song, "For Dixie and Uncle Sam," urged white men to enlist and defend their Southern legacy:

> Your Grand-dad fought in the war of Sixty-One,
> He wore a suit of gray.
> Your Daddy, too, in a suit of navy blue,
> To Cuba sailed away.
> Though the one wore gray and the other blue,
> The blood of both's in you.[64]

"The Fight for Democracy Must Begin at Home":
World War I and Black America

But to the white South's consternation, the outbreak of war also brought about the first possibility of significant structural change for black Americans since Reconstruction. Within a year of Europe's going to war, the number of new immigrants entering the United States plummeted from 1,218,500 to 300,000, while many other immigrants returned to their native lands to join the fighting forces there. Just as immigration into the United States plunged, Northern industry had to quickly double and triple its

208

workforce. A typical packing plant in the Chicago stockyards expanded its workforce from 8,000 to 17,000. Facing a staggering need for labor, the industrial North looked South.[65]

Word spread quickly. Barbershops and grocery stores hummed with talk of opportunities in the North. Black Southerners shared letters from friends and passed on news from the *Chicago Defender*, a black weekly that condemned the conditions of injustice in the South and carried news of jobs and success waiting in the North. Numerous Southern towns outlawed its sale because the paper emblazoned the words "Bound for the Promised Land" upon the minds of black folk.[66] The newspaper's editor, Robert S. Abbott, took a coldly realistic attitude towards the war. Like other black leaders, he found the war deplorable but also believed that it represented opportunities for his people.[67] Letters asking for help flooded into the offices of the *Chicago Defender*. A man from Mississippi wrote, "I sometime think that life for me is not worth while and most eminently believe with Patrick Henry 'Give me liberty or give me death.' "[68]

According to Carter Woodson, the Northern migration represented the "best chance" for securing the "rights of citizenship."[69] Approximately a half-million black Southerners moved north between 1916 and 1918. Between 1910 and 1920 the number of blacks living in Chicago increased by 148.5 percent; the number living in Gary, Indiana, increased by 1,283.6 percent; and the number in Detroit, Michigan, grew from 5,741 to 41,532, an increase of 623.4 percent. The whole social structure of the North changed at an incredible speed as black laborers crowded urban centers seeking to realize their dreams.[70] The economic self-interest of industry had broken the color line between the North and the South.

Just weeks before the United States declared war on 6 April 1917, Rev. A. Clayton Powell, of New York's Abyssinian Baptist Church, urged his Sunday congregation to support the demands of four hundred thousand railroad workers who threatened a walkout. Newspaper headlines in the black *New York Age* announced: "Tells Negroes to Wage a Bloodless War for Their Constitutional Rights." Powell compared the situation of black Americans to that of the Irish, who continued to fight for home rule even as war raged in Europe. "If this kind of talk is not loyalty, then I am disloyal; if this is not patriotism, then I am unpatriotic;

if this is treason, then I am a traitor." It was time to "say to the white American people," asserted Powell, "give us the same rights as you enjoy, and then we will fight by your side."[71]

James Weldon Johnson believed that "at no time since the days following the Civil War had the Negro been in a position where he stood to make greater gain or sustain greater loss in status."[72] On the one hand, economic opportunity had opened the possibility of real structural change. With expectations on the rise, black Americans assumed that demonstrating their patriotism would be rewarded by a postwar reconstruction of race relations. "When we have proved ourselves men, worthy to work and fight and die for our country," reasoned a Southern teacher, "a grateful nation may gladly give us the recognition of real men, and the rights and privileges of true and loyal citizens."[73] On the other hand, President Wilson had already undertaken the resegregation of the federal government, and a mean-spirited racism had led to more than a thousand lynchings between 1900 and 1915.[74] The stakes were high. Afro-Americans faced the resurgence of white supremacy at the same time that opportunity beckoned.

Echoing nationalist themes, black spokesmen heralded the battlefield as an arena where they could prove their loyalty, believing that fighting "to make the world safe for democracy" would earn them full rights and opportunities of citizenship at home. Robert Russa Moton, Booker T. Washington's successor at Tuskegee, was among the first to commit support. Moton wrote President Wilson that he could "count absolutely on the loyalty of the mass of Negroes of our country." Moton pledged that as in previous wars, black Americans, "almost to a man," would rally to the flag. During the war, Tuskegee taught 1,229 draftees technical skills and led a campaign among black farmers to put in a full week's work rather than taking Saturdays off. Moton also personally maneuvered to have Emmett J. Scott, Washington's former secretary, appointed as a special assistant to the secretary of war. In the Tuskegee tradition, Moton worked to strengthen the confidence of his constituency in the government and in turn increase the government's faith in black Americans.[75]

Within a week of the U.S. declaration of war, a record number of black men volunteered, bringing the existing black units up to full strength. The War Department, facing the difficulty of absorbing large numbers of black soldiers on a segregated basis, suspended further enlistment until Congress decided on the organization of black troops. It appeared, quipped one black leader, that a black volunteer would have to break into the war "like a burglar."[76] After the suspension, Afro-American spokesmen engaged in a grim debate in the pages of the *Baltimore Afro-American*, the *Chicago Defender*, the *Cleveland Gazette*, the *Crisis*, and the *New York News* over whether to continue volunteering for military service. Du Bois argued that by not volunteering, blacks only added "treason and rebellion to the other grounds on which the South" already promoted discrimination.[77]

James Weldon Johnson entered the debate through an editorial in the *New York Age* advocating "The Right to Fight." Johnson spoke against two positions: that the "Negro, on account of his grievances, would be justified in not fighting the country's battles" and that it was time for the black American to "strike a bargain for his rights before offering himself to take up arms."[78] Johnson's support for volunteering, however, was calculated. He did not agitate for a blind allegiance; like other black leaders, he attempted to negotiate a fuller meaning of American patriotism that included a fight for civil rights. As far into the war as 1918, a reader wrote to the *New York Age* again raising the question of why "a Negro man should go to protect a country" that did not even allow him to take a drink in a public place. Johnston replied, "America is the American Negro's country. . . . the plain course before him is to continue to perform all of the duties of citizenship while he continually presses his demands for all of the rights and privileges. Both efforts must go together: to perform the duties and not demand the rights would be pusillanimous; and to demand the rights and not perform the duties would be futile."[79]

Before the debate over patriotic duty could be resolved, the government put the Selective Service Act into effect on 18 May 1917. Some Northern congressmen had wanted to include provisions outlawing discrimination against blacks in the draft. Senator James K. Vardaman, of Mississippi, not only denounced their proposal but attacked universal conscription altogether. There is "no greater menace to the South," Vardaman warned Congress, than arming "millions of Negroes."[80] Despite Vardaman's protests, black men were not eliminated from military service, but any mention of banning discrimination was removed from the draft act. The navy and the army remained segregated.[81]

Over threats from the white South and the government's legiti-
mization of segregation, most black Americans decided that patriotism still held out the possibility of realizing greater freedom.
When the "call for American manhood came," the public debate
over allegiance almost disappeared and the black movement aggressively pressed for inclusion in the army. In a nation that traditionally linked patriotism with the willingness to die for one's
country, the highest honors and rewards were theoretically reserved for the most loyal sons. Many black Americans vowed to
carry on the patriotic tradition begun by grandfathers and grand-
mothers when they answered the call "To Arms! To Arms! Now or
Never" in the Civil War.[82]

The Civil War, fought some fifty years earlier, had brought
Emancipation. It was not unreasonable to believe that fighting for
the nation once again could bring new gains. Mass meetings and
rallies encouraged young men throughout the country to enlist.
At Howard University, idealistic young students organized a "flying
squadron" to tour the South. Walter White, who later became executive secretary of the National Association for the Advancement
of Colored People, remembered being in Atlanta when "intensely
patriotic young Negroes" arrived to "whip up patriotism." For the
first time in the history of Atlanta, blacks met in the city's audito-
rium. Following an "eloquent appeal," White leapt to his feet to
be "one of the first to volunteer."[83] A national conference called
by the NAACP in May 1917 urged "fellow citizens to join heartily
in this fight for eventual world liberty" but to "never forget that
this country belongs to us even more than to those who lynch,
disfranchise, and segregate."[84]

Once the United States declared war, there were few public
voices of dissent. Among the most vehement were Chandler Owen
and A. Philip Randolph, editors of the *Messenger.* Practically speaking for themselves, they refused to be "drown[ed] by prayers of
patriotism" and the "gospel of obey and trust." Instead they called
upon their readers to "rebel and demand." As with other opposi-
tional presses, the Justice Department soon shut down the *Messenger.*[85] Most Afro-Americans who opposed the war kept their
thoughts to themselves. A young E. Franklin Frazier, at the beginning of his distinguished academic career, published a fifteen-
page antiwar pamphlet, *God and War.* But with no support for con-
scientious objectors within the black community, when Frazier's

draft papers arrived, he served without enthusiasm.[86] Benjamin E. Mays, the youngest child of former slaves who later became the president of Morehouse College, also disagreed with the war. Mays's earliest memory from childhood was when a group of armed vigilantes galloped up to his house and forced his father to remove his hat, salute, and bow. When the United States entered the war, many of his friends applied for the Negro officers' training camp in Des Moines. "What was I to do?" Mays asked. "I had known everything *but* democracy in South Carolina." Mays did eventually register for military service, but he refused to volunteer for officer training. On his draft form he purposely stipulated that he was a ministry student in the hope that it would earn him a deferment.[87]

Though motivations for enlistment were multifaceted, a record number of black Americans registered for the army, two million in all. Although the language of mobilization often referred to manhood rights, the goal of black participation included a broader agenda for the realization of citizenship rights for both black men and women. A black captain about to depart for France expressed a shared hope: "I am leaving today a wife and three children. As great as the sacrifice is, I shall be satisfied never to see America again, if my wife and children will share greater opportunities and enjoy more liberties than I now enjoy."[88]

Harry Haywood, a Northern nineteen-year-old, joined the Negro Eighth Illinois prepared to fight. Like many others in his unit, he had never crossed the Mason-Dixon line before. As his train took him South, he felt like he was entering "enemy territory." Whole towns lined up at the train platforms, blacks on one side and whites on the other, each waiting to see the amazing sight of armed black soldiers. "We pulled into the station," Haywood recounted, "with the windows open and our 1903 Springfield rifles on the tables in plain view of the crowd. We were at our provocative best." Many a man "undoubtedly retained bitter memories of insults and persecutions from the past and quickly took advantage of what was perhaps his first opportunity to bait a cracker in his own habitat." After the war, during the Chicago riot of 1919, Haywood and the men of the Eighth Illinois would also prove to white Chicago that they could not be intimidated.[89]

While black men enlisted to fight in Europe, black women volunteered for the fight at home. Patriotic service was not just about restoring black manhood or celebrating the inclusion of black men in the fraternity of male warriors. Women like Ida B. Wells, who had begun the antilynching crusade in 1892, understood that black people were fighting the war on two fronts. Nannie Burroughs, an activist in the movements for suffrage and civil rights, agreed. Black Americans must fight, but the "fight for democracy must begin at home."[90]

As always, black people lived with the paradox that though they were denied the full rights of citizenship by white America, they were expected to be equally patriotic.[91] Walter J. Stevens recalled how proud it made him when his son "offered his services to his country." Walter Jr. was "only sixteen years old, the same age my father was when he enlisted in the Civil War, and I was when I enlisted in company L." Stevens described how three generations of his family had all offered their services in the hope of making America a "more humane country in which colored citizens might live." His hope, however, was dashed by the end of the war. Stevens saw his son return home to the "same inhumanity, the same hatred and the never-ending crucifixion of our race upon a cross of lies."[92]

Throughout the war, the tension between America's patriotic rhetoric and the reality of prejudice festered just below the surface. Even as Afro-American citizens were urged to do their share, news of the East St. Louis Massacre on 2 July 1917 swept the country. White mobs had deliberately murdered and maimed hundreds of black Americans, driving more than six thousand from their homes.[93] "In the name of world democracy," noted the *Crisis*, "we land black soldiers in France to fight for our white allies, while white soldiers kill black Americans for daring to compete in the world of labor with their white fellowmen."[94] As soon as Ida B. Wells heard of the riot, she attended a hastily convened meeting of the Negro Fellowship League. She suggested singing "America" or the "Star-Spangled Banner," but "nobody wished to do so."[95]

On the afternoon of 18 July 1917, fifteen thousand black Americans dramatically challenged America's conscience. They marched silently through the streets of New York City to the sound of muffled drums, protesting the race riots in Waco, Memphis, and East St. Louis. The marchers, led by women and children, made their sentiments heard through a sea of placards and banners: "Mr. President, Why Not Make America Safe for Democ-

18. In 1917, black women and children led a silent parade to the sound of muffled drums through the streets of New York. They demonstrated against the lynching of black men and women and the East St. Louis race riot. Banners with messages such as "Patriotism and Loyalty Presuppose Protection and Liberty" linked patriotism with its emancipatory tradition. Prints and Photographs Division, Library of Congress, LC-USZ62-33789.

racy?"; "Two Hundred Thousand Black Men Fought for Your Liberty in the Civil War"; "Patriotism and Loyalty Presuppose Protection and Liberty." In front of a man carrying the American flag, a banner emblazoned with the inscription "Your Hands Are Full of Blood" stretched halfway across the street. The march eloquently linked the demand to "make the world safe for democracy" with the demand to "make America safe for the Negro."[96]

Black women stood at the heart of the homefront campaign. Drawing upon the experience and organization generated by the turn-of-the-century Negro women's club movement, they led petition and letter-writing drives, organized pray-ins, published pamphlets, held conferences, and organized marches to protest lynchings and race riots. During World War I, Afro-American

215

women utilized their influence both in the home and in the political arena to challenge the dominant systems of race and gender. They identified demands for the overall progress of the race with their own advancement as women.[97] At the beginning of the war, the National Association of Colored Women launched a prayer and petition campaign against lynching. Addressing more than five thousand women gathered at the Metropolitan Baptist Church, speakers unequivocally declared that there would be no world democracy "until the burning of innocent women and babies, aged men and innocent citizens of color is taken from the list of 'sports' of civilized America."[98] Antilynching petitions poured into Congress, while people flocked to church at six o'clock in the morning for prayer protests in cities across the country. According to the *Baltimore Afro-American*, the women displayed a determination reminiscent of the days before the Civil War.[99]

The antilynching campaign directly addressed how sexuality had been historically used against black women. Culturally barred from "true womanhood" and stereotyped as licentious, black women had long been held responsible for the sexual assaults forced upon them since slavery. At the turn of the century, white southerners also turned the weapon of sex against black men, whom they systematically lynched for allegedly raping white women. Through the antilynching campaign, Afro-Americans sought to dismantle the stereotypes of black men as rapists and black women as morally wanton.[100] Turning the tables on "true womanhood," the National Association of Colored Women delivered their antilynching petitions to the House of Representatives with a message denouncing white mothers for their role in lynching and raising their children to race hatred and savagery.[101]

But despite the concerted effort to fight the war on two fronts, lynching continued at home, while the long arm of racism reached over to the battlefields of France. Of the 380,000 blacks serving in the wartime army, only 11 percent saw combat. The army assigned all the other black soldiers to service units.[102] When troops arrived in a French port, they were greeted by the sight of black stevedores. "Our drilling," recalled a black soldier, "consisted in marching to and from work with hoes, shovels, and picks on our shoulder."[103] According to a song popular with stevedores, "black man fights wid de shovel and de pick; / Lordy turn your face on me."[104] A Louisiana work-gang song leader never received a gun; his only weapons were a guitar, a shovel, and a mop. His "Trench Blues" included the lyrics, "Uncle Sam sho' don't know that I'm here, / Uncle Sam sho' don't feel my care."[105] Two Young Men's Christian Association workers observed black soldiers working "day and night, week after week, through drenching rain and parching heat." But these physical hardships paled in comparison to the "trials of discriminations and injustices that seared their souls like hot iron, inflicted as they were rendering the American army and nation a sacred service."[106]

When the war ended the message from the States grew loud and clear: "Niggers, as you were."[107] Following the armistice in November 1918, the black press was particularly aggrieved by army efforts to write black troops out of the war. "The fact that no American Negro troops were entered in the great peace parade in Paris on July 14th," noted the *Savannah Journal*, "comes to us as a distinct shock."[108] Historical amnesia had already denied the significance of the battle for emancipation during the Civil War. At the end of World War I, national rituals and discourse again imposed a color line. Beneath all the flag-waving lay the blood and sweat shed in Europe. "Fifty thousand privates died for Democracy," went one Negro song, "Dirty little job for Jesus."[109] Returning home, black soldiers felt that they had more than earned their rights to democracy. W. E. B. Du Bois denounced the United States for lynching and disfranchising its own citizens. "We sing: This country of ours, despite all its better souls have done and dreamed, is yet a shameful land." Reversing his earlier position on the need to close ranks with fellow white Americans, Du Bois declared:

> We *return.*
> We *return from fighting,*
> We *return fighting.*
> Make way for Democracy![110]

Shortly after black troops began to arrive home, the country erupted in violence. Radicals found themselves repressed by government agencies and vigilantes, labor strikes provoked industrial warfare, and Afro-Americans faced as many as twenty-five race riots during the "Red Summer" of 1919.[111] Carter Woodson, editor of the *Journal of Negro History*, maintained that "the very uniform on a Negro was to the southerner like a red rag thrown in the face of a bull."[112] The black press demanded that "America be made and maintained safe for black Americans."[113] In the year the war ended, white mobs killed fifty-eight black Americans; in 1919 the number was seventy-seven, including ten former soldiers. One black veteran still wearing his uniform was murdered in Georgia when he refused to surrender to Jim Crow by obeying a "whites only" sign.[114] Carrie Williams Clifford took her pen in hand and wrote:

> And when to his loved Dixie he came back
> Maimed, in the duty done on foreign shore
> where the hell of war he never flinched
> Because he cried, "Democracy" was lynched.[115]

Chicago erupted on 27 July 1919, and the spirit of the postwar New Negro met white terror in full force. The Chicago Commission on Race Relations found that "for the first time in American history the Negro group fought in the 1919 riot as a body against mob violence." A black veteran told the commission, "I done my part . . . and I'm going to fight right here until Uncle Sam does his." Another veteran described what it felt like to be hunted and chased by a mob. " 'Nigger; let's get him!' those words rang in my ears—I shall never forget them." He had asked himself, "Had the ten months I spent in France been all in vain? Were those little white crosses over the dead bodies of those dark-skinned boys lying in Flanders fields for naught? Was democracy a hollow sentiment?"[116]

The *New York World* made it clear that black people did not want pity; they wanted "what we have earned by every rule of the game."[117] Wartime promises, however, remained unfilled. "White people," a black seamstress from Kentucky explained, "had promised the Negro people a 'right to the flag,' and they had never given it to them."[118] Ned Cobb, an Alabama sharecropper shared her views: "After the battle is fought and the victory is won—I'm forced to say it—it all goes over to the whites. . . . I had white people tell me, 'this is white man's country, white man's country.' They don't sing that to the colored man when it comes to war. Then its *our* country, go fight for the country. Go over there and risk his life for the country and come back, he ain't a bit more thought of than he was before he left."[119]

By the end of the war, a central paradox in American patriotism—the conflict between the realities of racism and the ideal of democracy—loomed over all the death and sacrifice. The bitter betrayal of heightened expectations later prompted Langston Hughes to write a dramatic recitation about a young soldier whose dead brother appeared to him in a vision. In a half-dark theater the soldier describes how his brother asked him what had happened to the dreams of equality for which he died? Alone on the stage, with martial music playing in the distance, the surviving brother explodes in anger telling the audience,

> It's a lie! It's a lie! Every word they said.
> And it's better a thousand times you're in France dead.
> For here in the South there's no votes and no right.
> And I'm still just a "nigger" in America tonight.[120]

The wartime experiences of black soldiers in a Jim Crow army and the persistence of racism back home, culminating in the riots of the Red Summer of 1919, left most black Americans feeling thoroughly betrayed. The promise of democratic patriotism, predicated on equal rights for men going off to war and for women fighting on the home front, never materialized. Moreover, the systematic exclusion of black Americans from the national family served as a model for a new type of official, prescriptive patriotism, in which for the first time the U.S. government led the way in promoting national conformity and silencing political opposition as "un-American."

"My Country Right or Wrong": World War I and the Paradox of American Patriotism

Between the Civil War and World War I, the cultural politics of patriotism were by no means fixed, definitive, or saturated with jingoism. There was considerable motion and flux regarding who possessed sufficient authority to speak for the nation and which memories, icons, and rituals could represent the nation's symbolic meanings. On one side stood the emancipatory and democratic tradition, which saw the state as the potential guarantor of rights and freedoms. On the other stood the militaristic tradition, which emphasized a faithlike loyalty to the nation as the highest form of allegiance. The patriotic movement was dynamic not only because of its complex mass character but also because these two broad traditions were themselves crosscut by internal differences and contradictions of class, race, and gender.

Until the era of World War I, there was a relative degree of openness about who and what should represent the nation. Organized labor interpreted the national ideal in terms of wages commensurate with its citizen workers' ability to consume. Women's and black organizations envisioned the patriotic route as a means to participate in the public life of the nation and broaden the meaning of democratic citizenship. Despite nativist exhortations for "100 percent Americanism," liberal principles of association and expression also allowed immigrant Americans to maintain dual allegiance to their homelands and the United States. As the numbers, influence, and variety of radical groups and political associations reached a historic high point, the nation reflected a broad range of ethnocultural and ideological diversity. Moreover, it was still possible for many communities to live in protected insularity, "remarkably autonomous," according to Gary Gerstle, "of the Protestant, republican, commercial culture around them."[1]

This chapter examines how this moment of political-cultural pluralism was narrowed during World War I, when for the first time the state itself became a major participant in articulating the nationalist discourse and in enforcing a specifically antiliberal, chauvinistic conception of the nation. It was during this period that the institutional and ideological basis for what later became the national-security state assumed its modern shape. The government became an active participant and catalyst in mobilizing the patriotic movement and in promoting a particularly intolerant and authoritarian brand of patriotism. During World War I, Congress passed legislation aimed at silencing free speech through censorship and imprisonment; the media supported and amplified anarchist, red, and other scares; political groups who opposed U.S. involvement in the war faced extensive repression, from tarring and feathering, beatings, and jailing to lynchings and deportations; and state-supported right-wing vigilantism grew at an unprecedented rate—taking on a very different character from the earlier mass patriotic organizations, which, by comparison, had been much more inclusive and tolerant of different viewpoints.[2] Previously, internal and external wars—the U.S.-Mexican War, the Civil War, the Indian wars, and the Spanish-American War—had played a significant role in defining the standard-bearers and symbols of the nation. But with the growing participation by the United States in the spoils of imperialism, militarism gained a much more central place in the "national idea." Progressive views persisted, but like its counterparts in Europe, the U.S. government began to promote the notion that war and military preparedness had a "revitalizing impact on national culture."[3]

With the increasing involvement of the national government in managing rituals of mass allegiance, the narrative of Americanization—which before and after World War I accommodated a "multiplicity of political visions"—shifted sharply to the political right and was used to justify nativism, Anglo-conformity, and political repression of dissident groups.[4] During the war, an activist state prescribed the terms of loyalty though public mobilizations and in the courts. The campaign to consolidate national cohesiveness criminalized political dissent, segregated black soldiers, and demonized immigrant Americans unwilling to renounce dual allegiances. Whereas President Lincoln had used state machinery to turn the Civil War into a battle for emancipation, the nation-state under President Wilson expanded its antiliberal powers while fighting a war that was supposed to make the world safe for democracy. The association of the military and the national ideal, first articulated in the pageantry of the Grand Army of the Republic's representation of an armed democracy, became officially linked in national culture during the course of the first world war.

"What Is My Country?": National Culture
and Wartime Debates

Until the United States declared war on 6 April 1917, national culture remained an open arena for political debate. Americans of European origin publicly divided along ethnic lines over whether to back the Allies or the Central Powers: Anglo-Americans backed the Allies, German Americans identified with the Central Powers, while most Irish Americans supported England's enemies out of solidarity with Ireland's struggle for independence. Preparedness advocates and activists in the peace movement debated the meaning of national loyalty and the role of war. Militarists crisscrossed the country urging intervention, while newsreels gave local preparedness parades national coverage. Initially, opposition to the war crossed class, racial, ethnic, and gender lines as peace groups such as the Women's Peace Party called for mediation and American Socialists pressed for a national referendum before any declaration of war.[5]

In January 1915 the Woman's Peace Party, later known as the Women's International League for Peace and Freedom, held its founding conference. "As women," the party's preamble resolved, "we feel a peculiar moral passion of revolt against both the cruelty and the waste of war. As women, we are especially the custodians of the life of ages. . . . We will no longer endure without a protest that must be heard and heeded by men." Speakers such as Jane Addams evoked women's superior "sensitiveness to human life" and called on them to halt the slaughter. Women, she contended, had taken part, along with men, in creating a "higher type of patriotism" that contained "liberty as well as loyalty." But "at the present moment," patriotism had degenerated into the imposition of brute force. "Women" insisted Addams, "have a right to protest against . . . a world in which they can play no part." Their experience with protecting, nurturing, and passing life on from one generation to the next carried a historical obligation to end war.[6]

Socialists condemned the war as capitalist greed and cautioned against interests that were working to stampede the United States into war. After the sinking of the *Lusitania*, the National Committee of the Socialist Party issued a manifesto warning the people of the United States that "short-sighted 'patriots' and professional militarists are inflaming the minds and blinding the reason of their fellow citizens by appeals to national vanity."[7] Later, the socialist leader Eugene Debs would condemn the imprisonment of socialists who opposed the war, caustically noting that "it is extremely dangerous to exercise the constitutional right of free speech in a country fighting to make democracy safe in the world."[8] In 1918, Debs received a sentence of ten years in prison for violating the espionage law following his Canton, Ohio, speech to a crowd of more than one thousand people, in which he indicted the "Wall Street Junkers" and the "gentry who are today wrapped in the American flag." Debs described how, with "their magnifying glasses in hand," the government scanned the "country for evidence of disloyalty, eager to apply the brand of treason to the men who dare to even whisper their opposition to junker rule in the United States. No wonder Sam Johnson declared that 'patriotism is the last refuge of the scoundrel.' "[9] But in 1916 there was still political free speech for newspapers like *The Masses*, which graphically linked war and profit by representing Patriotism as a flag-draped businessman, minister, and politician stepping over the war's dead.[10] Opposition to the war was not yet considered treasonous behavior. "I love the flag, I do, I do, / Which floats upon the breeze," wrote Charles Wood in his satirical poem about patriotism.

> I also love my arms and legs
> And neck and nose and knees.
> One little shell might spoil 'em all
> Or give 'em such a twist
> They wouldn't be no use to me—
> I guess I won't enlist.[11]

Anarchists such as Emma Goldman and radicals in the Industrial Workers of the World (IWW) denounced patriotism altogether as the ideological creation of capitalists intent on masking

MOTHER EARTH

Vol. VII.   JUNE, 1912   No. 4

SAN DIEGO EDITION

PATRIOTISM IN ACTION

19. "Patriotism in Action," cover graphic of *Mother Earth* 7 (June 1912). Copy photography by Arthur Timothy Wells.

class exploitation in the name of national brotherhood. "What is my country?" asked Emma Goldman's *Mother Earth* in 1912. "Is it the bit of soil that my fathers had cultivated and that afterwards fell into the hands of the speculators, when the price of land rose? Is it the vast areas that have been stolen by the railroads and other monopolies? Is it the city park, where the homeless and jobless man hopes to pass the night and whence he is brutally driven out by the policeman?" The answer was no. "My country is where men, united in solidarity, reach out hands across all artificial barriers in the common work for liberty and equality for all." In 1914, a front-page graphic in Goldman's magazine featured Patriotism dressed as a warrior marching over the outstretched body of Liberty. Another writer for *Mother Earth* decried how patriotism had become normalized into one of the "fundamental tests of character." The author hoped for a time "when national prejudices, national egotism, national selfishness, even national love shall be swallowed up in a new spirit—the spirit of humanitarianism."[12]

According to the IWW, the flag of the United States meant little to workers. "Love of country?" asked the *Industrial Worker.* "They have no country. Love of flag? None floats over them. Love of birth place? No one loves the slums."[13] As a migrant worked explained in 1913, "If you were a bum without a blanket . . . if you slept in a lousy, sour bunk-house, and ate food just as rotten as they could give you . . . if every person who represented the law and order and the nation beat you up . . . and good Christian people cheered and told them to go to it, how the hell do you expect a man to be patriotic?"[14] The IWW deplored the war in Europe as an example of imperialist competition and warned American workers that capitalist greed would soon plunge them into the battle. At its 1916 convention, the IWW membership officially declared themselves "determined opponents of all nationalistic sectionalism, patriotism, and the militarism preached by our enemy the capitalist class."[15] Although the IWW denounced imperialism in its literature, it did not organize against the draft, focusing instead on building "One Big Union" in preparation for postwar class struggle.[16]

Initially, many black leaders also condemned the war as imperialist competition among European powers. "To-day," wrote W. E. B. Du Bois in 1914, "civilized nations are fighting like mad dogs over the right to own and exploit . . . darker peoples."[17] A significant number of Americans favored neutrality, while peace groups actively organized in support of arbitration and nonintervention. In New York City, the country's foremost theatrical organization staged a morality play titled *Why?* to protest the "wanton wastefulness of war." One of the characters, Valor, describes a dream in which "all that were human became as beasts," gnawing at one another's throats. "Hell vomited forth her legions of destruction and the stars around us stopped in their flight to watch a world gone mad with savagery and hate."[18]

Despite the growing reach of the preparedness campaign, pacifist songs still made it to the top of the music charts. In 1914 Americans sang "Don't Take My Darling Boy Away," and in 1915 "I Didn't Raise My Boy to Be a Soldier" became a national hit.[19] In the cover illustration for the sheet music for the latter, a mother holds her grown son close to home as she imagines armies marching to their slaughter:

> I didn't raise my boy to be a soldier,
> I brought him up to be my pride and joy,
> Who dares to place a musket on his shoulder,
> To shoot some other mother's boy?
> Let nations arbitrate their future troubles,
> It's time to lay the sword and gun away,
> There'd be no war today, if mothers all would say,
> I didn't raise my boy to be a soldier.[20]

Military enthusiasts countered with their own songs, urging "In Times of Peace Prepare for War" and "Prepare the Eagle to Protect the Dove, That's the Battle Cry of Peace." Their graphics pictured Uncle Sam, his sleeves rolled up, sternly urging boys to leave their childhood toys behind and pick up their guns.[21] Both sides of the wartime debate used gendered images to reach their constituencies. Pictures of beautiful white girls in patriotic colors symbolized the ideal for which boys marching off to war were expected to give their lives, and graphics of mothers trying to save their sons from war appeared on songbooks and magazine covers.

As the war raged in Europe, military enthusiasts steadily gained the nation's attention. Each week, moviegoers watched newsreels of flag-waving Americans line their city streets to applaud martial demonstrations by army regiments and troops of Boy Scouts.[22] In 1916, Hollywood pioneered "preparedness serials," which exposed eager fans to episodes of patriotism, love, and intrigue.[23] One of the most popular serials, *Pearl of the Army*, warned audiences that spies had "infested" the United States and were seeking "our destruction." Each week record numbers of moviegoers watched "America's Joan of Arc" battle the dark and mysterious "Silent Menace." In a dramatic finale, Pearl victoriously wrestled with the shadowy traitor on a rooftop, stopping him from lowering the Stars and Stripes.[24]

"JOHNNIE GET YOUR GUN": THE MILITARIZATION
OF NATIONAL CULTURE

The many-sided debate that characterized the years leading up to the United States' entry into the Great War came to an abrupt end when the government declared war on 6 April 1917. Recognizing the broad appeal of the antiwar movement, President Wilson emphasized, when he asked Congress for a declaration of war, that the government would respond to any expression of disloyalty "with a firm hand of stern repression." Two months later, he warned that the "masters of Germany" were using "liberals . . . socialists [and] the leaders of labor" to "carry out their designs."[25] In June, the Espionage Act, designed to criminalize opposition to the war, became law. One year later, the Wilson administration gave its full support to the Sedition Act, which implicitly made any criticism of the war, the flag, or the government illegal.[26] States such as Minnesota passed laws that made it a crime to speak out against enlistment, while nine states passed laws making it illegal to verbally oppose the war effort and fifteen states passed criminal syndicalism statutes.[27] These antiradical statutes had their precedent in legislation passed by New York and three other states in 1902 and 1903 to curb labor militancy. But the proliferation of antisyndicalist laws between 1917 and 1920 represented both a qualitative and a quantitative shift in governmental policy: the targets of repression were now political as well as labor organizations. Moreover, it was now acceptable to criminalize dissidents for their ideas and associations, in addition to their actions.[28]

Police and detective forces also expanded during World War I, and private organizations such as the National Security League and the American Protective League (APL) were set up to crush political opposition.[29] The new militarism resonated within popular culture. George M. Cohan's song "Over There" called the nation to arms: "Johnnie get your gun, get your gun, get your gun. . . . Hoist the flag and let her fly, Yankee Doodle do or die."[30] As men marched off to war, popular songs replaced pacifist mothers with women who promised Uncle Sam, "If I Had a Son for Each Star in Old Glory, I'd Give Them All to You."[31] Another song pledged, "My Country Right or Wrong."[32]

Hollywood films and military spokesmen glamorized the idea that boys too young to enlist could serve their country as scouts. The Boy Scouts, originally organized in England to make patriotic men out of "unruly" working-class youths, was established in the United States in 1910.[33] As soon as the United States entered the war, the Scouts pledged 100 percent patriotism and dedicated three hundred thousand boys to fighting the war on the home front by selling liberty bonds, growing vegetable gardens, and patrolling the nation's coastline. A poster titled "Weapons for Liberty" captured the bond between men and boys with a larger-than-life scout handing the sword of "preparedness" to an American warrior.[34] In a single day, 14 April 1917, the Boy Scouts blanketed New York City with twenty thousand army recruitment posters.[35] In the film *The Boy Who Cried Wolf* the hero is a young scout who dreams of catching his very own spy. After a series of harrowing mishaps and adventures, the scout finally accomplishes his mission. In the end, he is rewarded for his vigilance against the threat from within as the final scene fades on the child soldier saluting the flag.[36]

Militant nationalists, who had failed to institutionalize military drilling in the public schools at the turn of the century, now succeeded in creating a masculine culture of order and discipline among the Boy Scouts. Trained to express an unquestioning and jingoistic allegiance, Boy Scout troops across the country staged massive operettas in celebration of "America First."[37] The "great scout citizen," Theodore Roosevelt, enthusiastically embraced the quasi-military organization of young boys, while encouraging young girls to emulate Betsy Ross by tenderly sewing stars onto flags for boys to carry into life's battles. Women's patriotic duty, Roosevelt contended, was to bear children for the nation. He maintained that a wife, just like a soldier in battle, must be judged by how she did her duty.[38] In 1911, Roosevelt charged women who gave birth to only one or two children with committing a "crime against the race" and denounced women who "in their thirst for their rights, forget their duties."[39] Men, on the other hand, were encouraged by Roosevelt to achieve "manliness in its most vigorous form," bravely carrying out their duties like soldiers on a battlefield. He offered himself as an example of a skinny child who had "built bodily vigor . . . for national service." After gaining physical strength in the "Wild West," Roosevelt had gone on to com-

228

mand the Rough Riders in the Spanish-American War and later led safaris into "primitive" Africa, inspiring images of Rudyard Kipling's imperial and manly prose in popular newsreels that documented his adventures.[40]

In addition to the Boy Scouts, hundreds of thousands of Americans joined homefront campaigns. President Wilson's administration worked in tandem with patriotic organizations, as well as representatives from advertising, the press, and the entertainment industry. The government not only lent the full authority of the state to volunteer efforts but also directly intervened in supervising a nationally orchestrated campaign to spread an officially approved patriotism. Just days after the United States' entry into World War I, President Wilson took the unprecedented step of setting up a federal agency to shape public opinion and mobilize unconditional support for America's role in the war effort.[41]

The Committee on Public Information (CPI), headed by Progressive reformer and journalist George Creel, worked with the secretaries of state, war, and the navy. Since the committee was staffed by a relatively small number of paid administrators, the vast majority of its work and finances came from volunteers. Advertising agencies donated acres of billboard space, as seventy-five thousand Four Minute Men fanned out across the country to advertise patriotism by giving short talks in movie theaters, churches, and fraternal lodges. "The idea," wrote Creel, "had the sweep of a prairie fire." Theater owners gave the organization exclusive access to their audiences, and thousands of men from every state volunteered to be speakers. The head of an advertising agency drafted the first bulletin for the men's talks. Encouraged by the CPI's scope and effectiveness, government departments turned to the Four Minute Men when they needed to "arouse the nation swiftly." The CPI flooded the country with vast amounts of information, its Washington office producing a relentless barrage of news stories, editorials, war bulletins, educational material, advertisements, billboards, photographs, cartoons, movies, war expositions, and conferences.[42] Under the slogan "Every Scout Boost America," troops across the country canvassed their neighborhoods with CPI literature.[43]

The Committee took up the challenge of molding public opinion into a single "white-hot mass instinct" for war.[44] It mobilized millions of Americans who just months before had supported isolationism or pacifism by drawing on the political prestige of government officials, the intellectual legitimacy of university professors, and the marketing know-how of advertising executives. One of its first pamphlets, *The War Message and Facts behind It,* featured speeches from prominent politicians and historians. Franklin K. Lane, the secretary of the interior, described the war as a struggle "against feudalism—the right of the castle on the hill to rule the village below. It is a war for democracy—the right of all to be their own masters."[45] The moral themes in government pronouncements resonated within Progressive circles and among suffrage groups and black Americans who believed that by entering into the social contract of war they could gain full citizenship rights. But the intrusion into civic life of state institutions went far beyond mobilizing public opinion favorable to the war effort. Volunteer organizations—including the American Defense Society, the National Security League, and the APL, all of which coordinated their surveillance activities with the Department of Justice—fanned out across the nation to hunt down radicals and immigrants suspected of harboring disloyal sentiments. In a three-day raid, the APL and the Bureau of Investigation arrested tens of thousands of men for draft evasion, only to have all but a small fraction released. Before World War I, the Justice Department's Bureau of Investigation had limited responsibilities and no clear mission for law enforcement, but demands for surveillance and prosecution of suspected spies and slackers quickly led to what Frank Donner calls the "federalization of intelligence."[46] By 1918, the attorney general could confidently claim, "it is safe to say that never in its history has this country been so thoroughly policed."[47]

The movement to legislate patriotism, initiated during the flag movement of the 1890s, created a vast web of new laws during World War I. Precedents for government-promoted patriotism had first occurred in the public schools. By 1913, twenty-three states required public schools to display the flag. During the Progressive Era, states legislated nationalism by requiring the compulsory teaching of subjects ranging from flag exercises and civics to instruction in English and courses on U.S. history. But the most dramatic increase in state directives took place during the years surrounding World War I. Unlike legislation at the turn of the century, which delegated broad discretionary authority to school boards and mandated educational practices already in existence, World War I enactments reflected lawmakers' determination to enforce a national will.[48]

Even the specific text of the Pledge of Allegiance came under close scrutiny. In the 1900s, organized patriots and educators had been too busy spreading the word to worry about standardization. Versions of the pledge multiplied as teachers, textbooks, and patriotic organizations boosted their favorite wording and form of presentation. During the war years, however, Americanizers worried about immigrants who maintained dual allegiances and debated whether the wording of the Bellamy pledge allowed immigrants to swear a secret loyalty to another country. The Woman's Relief Corps proposed a solution: replace the words "my flag" with "the flag of the United States."

As war continued in Europe, nationalists upped their demands for national conformity, making the daily pledge of allegiance by every student and in every public school the normative expectation. On a Chicago morning in 1916, an eleven-year-old black student, Hubert Eaves, stepped apart from his classmates and refused to salute a flag that to him represented Jim Crow, disfranchisement, and lynching. Such dissent caused considerable controversy. "I am willing to salute the flag," Eaves explained, "as the flag salutes me." The *Chicago Defender* broadcast his story in bold headlines: "Youngster, Eleven Years Old, Starts New Philosophy of American Patriotism—Tells Judge Dudley that Flag is a Dirty Flag that Will Not Protect Its Unhyphenated Citizens." For his crime, Hubert Eaves was arrested, brought before a juvenile court, and tried. Judge Dudley, unable to locate a criminal statute that governed Eaves's behavior, ordered him to return to school.[49]

In the South, rumors spread that Germans had launched a propaganda campaign aimed at convincing black Southerners that they were being asked to fight abroad for rights denied to them at home. The newly formed Bureau of Investigation took the rumors seriously and initiated a full-scale surveillance program aimed at black Americans, assuming a dubious loyalty from citizens it considered un-American. Rather than protecting the rights of black citizens against a resurgent racism, the bureau forwarded reports to the State Department on anyone who complained of discrimination or lynching.[50] White Southerners sent frantic letters to the bureau about the changed "demeanor of the colored people," blaming the "propaganda that has been very vigorously carried on by German influences in order to upset the racial situation, and drive away the agricultural labor in the South." White employers reported seeing black servants reading the *Chicago Defender*, gathering in small groups to discuss the war, and practicing the un-American behavior of refusing to step aside when white people passed them on the sidewalks. The investigation of black citizens reflected the bureau's belief that spies and traitors, rather than the forces of white reaction, had incited the race riots of 1917.[51] As racists dismissed black demands for social justice, nativists condemned anyone who did not act or appear sufficiently assimilated as "un-American." Increasingly, those under suspicion were expected to prove their true Americanism through public acts of loyalty.

"Emblem of National Authority": The Flag Protection Movement

During World War I, attitudes toward the flag became the litmus test of patriotism. Although the first flag protection bill was proposed in the House of Representatives in 1878 and flag laws had been in effect since the 1890s, only small groups of patriots worried about their enforcement and mainly targeted advertisers and candidates from both parties for what they considered flag desecration. Business interests and patriotism were so interwoven in the national culture that William McKinley popularized his 1896 election campaign with flag banners inscribed with his name next to the slogan "Patriotism, Protection & Prosperity."[52] While most Americans felt ambivalent about whether to support laws aimed at outlawing the use of flags by political parties or in variety shows, they agreed that businesses had gone too far when manufacturers imprinted the flag upon urinals and pictured it on toilet-paper wrappers.[53] Nonetheless, prosecutions between 1895 and 1917 remained few and far between.[54] A number of prominent leaders, such as the president of Brown University, opposed making the flag into a fetish and warned that "true patriotic sentiment" came from "what the stars and stripes stand for: liberty, union, rights, law, power for good among nations."[55]

The Daughters and Sons of the American Revolution, on the other hand, were among the most morally indignant opponents of popular and entrepreneurial use of the flag, which they regarded as a form of lowbrow treason. But congressmen remained ambivalent about abandoning their own use of the flag in political campaigns, and many did not believe that commercial use of the flag, particularly among financial supporters, necessarily undermined patriotism. Flag protection committees broke through this impasse by refocusing their efforts on community organizing. Hereditary societies, unable to pass legislation at the federal level, took their campaign against flag desecration to the states. Between 1897 and 1905, they secured spectacular victories at the local level, passing flag legislation in thirty-one states, including the New Mexico and Arizona territories.[56]

But state appeal courts almost doomed the whole flag protection movement by overturning convictions on the grounds that they violated the right to pursue an occupation and advertise a business.[57] In 1900, the Supreme Court of Illinois declared its state's flag law unconstitutional and overturned a lower court's conviction of two businessmen for picturing a national flag on cigar box labels. Judge Magruder saw no reason to penalize commerce for imaginative use of national symbols in advertising. When flags are combined with "objects to catch the eye," he reasoned, they "appeal to feelings of patriotism, and win purchasers of the merchandise to which they are affixed."[58] Businessmen and political parties alike felt emboldened by the courts' decisions. Despite an order by New York's police chief to refrain from using flags for campaign banners, both William McKinley and Theodore Roosevelt displayed their own images along with slogans on national flag banners in their 1900 bid for the presidency and vice-presidency.[59]

In 1907, however, the flag movement gained new life when the U.S. Supreme Court upheld the constitutionality of flag desecration laws in *Halter v. Nebraska*. A lower court convicted two businessmen for selling bottles of "Stars and Stripes" beer. When the businessmen appealed their case to the Supreme Court of Nebraska, the judges legitimated the state's duty to prescribe the norms of patriotic culture. The flag, according to the court, must be protected just as religious symbols are kept sacred: "The flag is the emblem of national authority. To the citizen it is an object of patriotic adoration, emblematic of all for which his country stands—her institutions, her achievements, her long roster of heroic dead, the story of her past, the promise of her future."[60] The U.S. Supreme Court agreed. "A duty rests upon each State in every legal way to encourage its people to love the Union with which the State is indissolubly connected."[61]

Although the patriotic lobby was finally successful in getting the government to enforce reverence for the flag, the new laws were used, not against the businessmen and politicians who routinely draped their products and campaigns in the country's colors, but against political opponents of the war and immigrant Americans suspected of divided loyalties. The politicization of flag laws during World War I, unlike the earlier flag prosecutions that waxed and waned in the first decade of the twentieth century, spurred nationalists to prosecute "un-Americans" with a vengeance. In the highly charged atmosphere of World War I, avid nationalists wielded the Stars and Stripes as a weapon in their cultural arsenal.

Patriots also increasingly turned to vigilante justice. "The victims of mob violence were varied," recalled the IWW organizer Elizabeth Gurley Flynn, including "Christian ministers, Negro and white, advocates of peace on religious, moral or political grounds; Socialists, IWWs, members of the Non-Partisan League . . . [and] friends of Irish freedom." Gurley also described how "inoffensive Germans, residents of this country for years, parents of American-born children, were suspected as potential 'spies' and attacked merely for being German."[62] Typical of individuals who took the law into their own hands, a Milwaukee marine placed a man in his own custody after hearing him make disparaging remarks about the flag.[63] Similarly, a group in Santa Cruz, California, made a man accused of "insult[ing] the colors" kneel on the sidewalk and "kiss the flag."[64] At a New York supper club, an angry crowd surrounded and attacked a former reporter for a socialist newspaper and two suffragists after they refused to stand when a band played the "Star-Spangled Banner." Later, the diners turned the three over to the police on charges of disorderly conduct.[65] Numerous states responded to the rise of such public incidents by dramatically stiffening their penalties for flag desecration. Texas passed a "disloyalty act" in 1918, raising its prewar penalty of thirty days in jail for desecrating a flag to twenty-five years. No longer limited to actual acts of desecration, the new law applied to anyone who used "any language," privately or publicly, that "cast contempt" on the Stars and Stripes.[66]

Undivided loyalty became the watchword of "true Americans." The Department of Justice issued a warning to all new immigrants that they would be arrested immediately if they abused the American flag.[67] But the wrath of the courts was not directed solely at immigrants; it also extended to native-born, ethnic Americans. In a typical case, a New York judge sentenced a native-born man of German descent to twenty days in the county jail for "using profane language in reference to the American colors." The man's denial of disloyalty fell on deaf ears despite his four years of service in the U.S. army and his appearance in court wearing a U.S. flag on his jacket lapel.[68] In Illinois, vigilantes took people from their homes and forced them to publicly profess their loyalty, and a volunteer of the county council of defense in Tulsa, Oklahoma, shot a waiter for allegedly making pro-German statements. When the jury returned a not-guilty verdict at his trial, the courtroom broke into cheers. In Missouri, Robert Paul Prager, a German by birth, became another victim of patriotic murder after he talked to fellow miners about the merits of socialism. A mob went after Prager, stripped him of his clothes, and wrapped an American flag around his body. When the police rescued him, the mob simply broke into jail and hung Prager on the outskirts of town for allegedly being a German spy.[69]

In 1918, Kansas convicted Frederick Shumaker Jr. for insulting the Stars and Stripes while visiting a blacksmith's shop. Among the evidence marshaled against him was a witness's report that months earlier, when Shumaker had seen flags flying at half-mast, he had said, "What in hell is going on? I see you got the rags on the poles." The Kansas Supreme Court upheld his conviction on the grounds that any "man who uses such language" lacked the kind of respect "that should be found in the breast of every citizen."[70] The court maintained that the blacksmith's shop constituted a public space, and according to the Kansas flag statute, any language that "cast contempt" on the flag in public was against the law.[71] The exercise of political power through institutions of the nation-state increasingly took precedence over liberal ideas of individual freedom. Only a few years earlier, George M. Cohan had used the word *rag* in his wildly popular song "You're a Grand

Old Rag." But by the time of Shumaker's trial the mood of the country had changed. Cohan himself briefly came under criticism when a theater critic complained about the song's title. Cohan promptly changed the wording and said that he had not intended it to be unpatriotic, but to describe how the flag had become "splendidly tattered after valiant service." But intent no longer mattered.[72]

The cult of the flag became the common sense of the nation. In a Socialist parade in Massachusetts, a red flag with the words "Finnish Socialist Branch" earned a man a prison sentence for violation of a state statue that prohibited parading with a red flag or carrying a placard with an inscription that could be construed as against the government.[73] In Montana, a court convicted E. V. Starr in 1918 for the crime of sedition after he refused to kiss an American flag. When attacked, Starr retorted, "What is this thing anyway? Nothing but a piece of cotton with a little paint on it and some other marks in the corner there. I will not kiss that thing. It might be covered with microbes." For his abusive language, the court sentenced him to the state penitentiary for up to twenty years of hard labor. When Starr appealed his case, Judge Bourquin reluctantly decided that he could not legally reverse the lower court's decision despite its "horrifying" sentence. The judge's sympathies went to the appellant, whom he believed "was more sinned against than sinning." In the judge's opinion, the mob had descended into the kind of "fanaticism" that "incited the massacre of St. Bartholomew, the tortures of the Inquisition, the fires of Smithfield, [and] the scaffolds of Salem."[74]

"AMERICA FOR AMERICANS": LEGISLATING NATIONAL COHESION

After the United States declared war, a hardening of political lines quickly led to the conflation of ethnicity and patriotism. Assimilation became a battle cry, and the cultural homogeneity of the nation-state was now infused with issues of national security. Whereas before World War I, patriots could maintain dual identities and allegiances, the war years accelerated demands for "100 percent Americanism." Far from unified about the concept of Americanization, reformers before the war advocated different positions on how to convert immigrants into Americans, aliens into citizens. Progressives like Jane Addams and Horace Kallen not only valued but promoted the cultural heritages of the new immigrants.[75] Kallen, a Jewish American professor at Columbia University, began teaching ideas he would later call "cultural pluralism" around 1906. He argued that the melting pot had failed and that immigration had strengthened rather than weakened ethnic identities.[76] To Kallen, cultural pluralism represented the United States at its best, creating "a multiplicity in a unity, an orchestration of mankind."[77] But New Nationalists like Theodore Roosevelt railed against "hyphenated Americans" and asserted the superiority of Anglo-Saxon mores. Other reformers who did not necessarily support coercive Americanization nonetheless tried to convince immigrants to abandon their ethnic cultures.

As the United States prepared to intervene in the Great War, calls for "English only," Anglo-conformity, and the subordination of all attachments to the "one dominant idea" of America prevailed in national discourse.[78] Distinctions between patriotism and Anglo-conformity became increasingly blurred. In Nebraska, an editorial gave the state its marching orders: "The issue of the day is to Americanize America."[79] Citizens with German, Polish, Italian, or Russian cultural roots were denounced as "hyphenates," while groups of "Yankee Protestants, southern Anglo-Saxons, midwestern Wasps, and western Anglos" laid claim to being the only true Americans. In a rapidly changing world, these groups bolstered their own sense of national cohesion by asserting their whiteness and identification with England against the otherness of southern and eastern Europeans.[80] This restrictive definition of Americanism was backed up in Congress by the passage in 1917 and subsequent years of immigration bills that imposed political loyalty tests on new arrivals and made it much easier to deport radicals for a wide range of actions and beliefs.[81]

In public and industrial schools, teachers turned up the heat under the melting pot. One of the most dramatic theatrical interpretations of converting ethnics into Americans came from the Ford English School. A leader in industrial Americanism, the Ford Motor Company initiated English instruction for its workers as a vehicle for shaping every aspect of a worker's life. "We not only teach a man how to earn more money," explained Samuel S. Marquis, the head of Ford's Sociological Department, "but we begin at once to teach him how to spend it. . . . The object of this English school is not only to make the men more efficient in our work in the shop, but also to prepare them for citizenship." Some criticized the school for "grotesquely exaggerated patriotism," but other employers looked to the Ford English School as a national model for how to organize workplace Americanization programs that linked patriotism and labor discipline.[82]

Each year, the graduating class of the Ford English School participated in a massive pageant. Teachers symbolically stirred an enormous melting pot, fifteen feet in diameter and almost eight feet tall, in front of a painting of a huge ship that stretched from one end of the stage to the other. Hundreds of immigrant Americans, often representing as many as fifty-two nationalities, marched onto the gangway. Dressed in the clothes from their native lands, the graduates slowly descended into the pot. The teachers, wielding ten-foot ladles, stirred the pot ever more vigorously. When the pot finally boiled over, "out came men dressed in their best American clothes and waving American flags."[83]

During the war, industrialists joined forces with conservative Progressives to replace educational programs that emphasized ethnic contributions to the national culture with a coercive and reactionary Americanism. Eventually, most liberal Progressives admitted that their efforts "to create a new culture and new nationalism for the masses" had met defeat.[84] In place of notions of cultural pluralism, slogans like "One country, one language, one flag" became the prevailing chorus.[85] Even when a group of Italian Americans carrying an Italian flag arrived at a U.S. army recruitment meeting to offer their services, the janitor blocked their entrance until they placed the Stars and Stripes at the front of their column.[86] Theodore Roosevelt, whose campaign against "hyphenated Americanism" had won the day, gave "three cheers" when he heard that a young Italian student answered the question, What does it mean to be a patriotic American? with, "It means—it means—an American-American."[87]

In such an intolerant political climate, most immigrant Americans went out of their way to prove their patriotism or kept their opinions to themselves, retreating from the public sphere for the war's duration. Immigrant communities entertained highly complex reasons for their decision to support, oppose, or remain silent on the issue of the war. Depending on the situation in the country of their origin, immigrants from opposite political tendencies suddenly found themselves making common cause for joining the war effort or withholding support.[88] In the case of ethnic groups who supported the Allies, support for countrymen in Europe bolstered their standing as American patriots. But the dual allegiances of groups who identified with the Central Powers led to charges of treason.

Determined to demonstrate their loyalty, national organizations representing "nearly every element of the foreign-born citizenship" in 1918 sent President Wilson a petition announcing plans for demonstrations in support of the United States on July Fourth.[89] Across the country, immigrant Americans held massive rallies. In Philadelphia, nearly one hundred thousand foreign-born men, women, and children staged one of the most spectacular celebrations of Independence Day the city had ever witnessed. Participants representing more than thirty nationalities assembled at Independence Hall and pledged an oath of "allegiance to the country of their adoption."[90]

Despite such patriotic displays, demands for cultural conformity grew more strident and became equated with the internal strength needed for successful combat in the war. The imposition of a hegemonic national culture was enforced through administrative and economic measures backed up by relentless public pressure. Just as a racialized imperialist ideology became a mass phenomenon in Europe, so, too, the charge of un-Americanism was used against any group whose political or cultural beliefs deviated from the mainstream of wartime politics.[91]

German Americans came under heightened suspicion and the most intense attacks for not sufficiently changing their cultural traditions. In Cleveland, a German American tried to explain the anguish of having to choose sides in a war that set "brother against brother and in many cases of son against father, a war against the sweet memories of childhood and friendship." He feared that "days of untold sorrows and bitterness are in store for us, terrible days of conflict between duty toward our county and natural sympathy for the land of our fathers."[92] Pleas for empathy, however, were not well received. "No true loyalty can be divided," wrote an America First enthusiast from Chicago. "The fact that these people have a divided loyalty simply shows that they have no right to be called Americans."[93] Demonized as "Huns," many Germans tried to pass as Dutch, Russian, or Swiss.[94] Fearful of persecution, families even petitioned the courts to legally change their German names to their English equivalents.[95] German American merchants also changed the names of their stores, as rumors ruined once thriving businesses. In New York, a small family business lost friends and customers when false stories spread that on Washington's Birthday the father had assaulted a young girl who wore an "American flag on her bosom."[96] In desperation, a Brooklyn baker offered a reward of one thousand dollars for the arrest and conviction of the person who had circulated a similar story about his having insulted the flag.[97]

The threat of internment also loomed as a real possibility. The Justice Department, with the help of the American Protection League, a vigilante volunteer organization of 350,000 members who favored deportation and summary internment of aliens, imprisoned 6,300 aliens in camps during World War I. Unquestionably, many were jailed simply for having a German accent.[98] Among those imprisoned was Dr. Karl Muck, the premier conductor of America's leading orchestra, the Boston Symphony. The Justice Department treated Muck as a dangerous enemy alien even through two investigations failed to substantiate the charges brought against him. He became a magnet for wartime hysteria as rumors circulated that he had refused to play the "Star-Spangled Banner." The Muck case became a focal point for patriotic organizations, which questioned the loyalty of all German musicians and lobbied orchestras to stop playing German music. The hatred for all things German created a profound dilemma for symphony orchestras, which were among the most visible cultural institutions in the United States. Until 1917, German composers, musicians, and conductors dominated the world of classical music. American musicians went to study at German conservatories, and German was the rehearsal language of most of the major orchestras in the United States.[99]

When the Boston Symphony prepared to go to Baltimore, Maryland's former Governor Warfield told the Police Board that Muck should not be allowed to play in the birthplace of the national anthem. At a protest meeting, Warfield provocatively asked the crowd, "What does art amount to when it is in competition with patriotism?" In New York, Theodore Roosevelt wrote a broadside telling the conductor to go home, but the Justice Department refused to "let this German get away." On 25 March 1918, Muck was arrested and sent to Fort Oglethorpe in Georgia, where he remained until 1919, when he and his wife were finally deported.[100]

Some German Americans responded to charges of un-Americanism by becoming superpatriots. For example, after a group of brewery employees of German birth purchased a flag, they viciously turned against an Austrian-born employee when he refused to salute the Stars and Stripes. The German American workers forced the owner to discharge the man by refusing to return to work unless he was fired.[101] Many German Americans were not prepared to pledge such staunch allegiance to the United States, but the overwhelming majority did not resort to either espionage or treason. Nonetheless, any act could bring severe public censure. When a woman refused to fly an American flag from her apartment, her neighbors hung one over her objections. When she tore it down and threw it on the floor, yelling, "To hell with the American flag, I want my own flag," her neighbors had her arrested. The judge sentenced her to six months in a workhouse and told the courtroom that "if he had the power to send her to jail for life he would do so."[102]

In an atmosphere of wartime xenophobia, towns banned German books from libraries, stopped the teaching of German in the public schools, changed and defaced German place names, and charged opponents of the war with being the puppets of "the masters of Germany." Theodore Roosevelt even advised shooting any German who proved to be disloyal. Separated from the real enemy by more than three thousand miles, World War I patriots turned with a fury on representations of German culture within the United States.[103] In 1900 only Berlin had a larger concentration of Germans than New York City. A prolific German-language press prospered, the public schools taught German, and a vibrant club culture thrived in the sizable German American community. By the war's end, the German American community lay in shambles: German-language presses, the "glue of the community," had suffered irreversible losses; 47 percent of German publications had disappeared, the number of dailies having dropped to twenty-six, less than half the prewar figure.[104] Americanizers had effectively eradicated German American culture, forcing the disappearance of German Americans as a publicly identifiable group.[105]

In 1919–20 the convergence of the anti-alien movement, which had successfully destroyed the ability of German Americans to exist as a vibrant and identifiable group, with the antiradical movement, which had honed its tactics in wartime suppression of the IWW, led to a campaign of state repression against the newly formed Communist Labor Party and the Communist Party. Federal agents detained thousands of members for deportation. What became known as the Red Scare drew upon deep historical roots, including the antiradical hysteria generated in the national press during the 1877 railway strike against the "dangerous classes" and the nativist traditions of anti-Catholicism and racialized nationalism. Palmer raids, so named after the attorney general, involved political persecution, unlawful searches, brutalization of defendants, excessive bail, and denial of counsel. Policies of systematic repression, manifested in "the dragnet roundups, the group prosecutions, and the mass deportations of radicals," subsided in the years after the war, but, notes William Preston Jr., the "fear and hatred of left-wing beliefs endured as an influence on official policy."[106]

CONCLUSION: "LET AMERICA BE AMERICA AGAIN"

During World War I, an alliance between government leaders, conservative political forces, industrialists, business corporations, and patriotic organizations effectively marginalized the liberal wing of Progressivism and repressed leftist opposition. "All the radical and liberal friends of your anti-imperialist war policy were either silenced or intimidated," wrote CPI Director George Creel to President Wilson after the 1918 Congressional elections. "The Department of Justice and the Post Office were allowed to silence and intimidate them."[107] Senator Hiram Johnson concluded that "the war has set back the people for a generation. They have bowed to a hundred repressive acts."[108] The retreat of middle-class liberals, the total destruction of the IWW and immobilization of the Socialist Party, and the disarming of political opposition and militant unionism shifted the politics of the United States to the right for an entire decade and established the terms of anticommunist discourse that would endure until the end of the Cold War.

During World War I, Anglo-Protestants asserted that they were the only group capable of self-government. An official patriotic culture—defined by the ascendance of national power, shaped by the language of masculinity, infused with a martial spirit, and nar-

20. A black soldier, a member of the 369th Infantry, known as the "Harlem Hell-Fighters," returns from World War I in 1919. The "Hell-Fighters" were the first black regiment sent to the European battlefields. UPI.

rowed by the imposition of racialized and anti-radical criteria defined by Anglo superiority and political intolerance—eclipsed competing interpretations. As in Europe, a nationalism developed in which loyalty was attached not just to a particular country but to an ideologically constructed and politically exclusive version of what that country should represent.[109] Black Americans returned from World War I to find that the language of patriotism no longer held out the promise of inclusion and equality under which they had fought.

In the war's aftermath, the American Legion, which replaced the Grand Army of the Republic as the nation's military conscience, spearheaded the drive to promote a conservative political

ethos and enforce "100 percent Americanism." Federal intervention in national culture continued as the government and business
elites allied to suppress the rise of radicalism and militant unionism in the strike wave of 1919; federal agencies and troops fueled
the Red Scare with raids in which radicals whose only crime was
membership in targeted organizations were rounded up, arrested,
and deported; Congress imposed immigration restrictions in 1921
and again in 1924 to guard against the influx of inferior "races";
and states throughout the 1920s enacted coercive decrees against
teaching in languages other than English. After the Red Summer
of 1919—named for the blood shed in the twenty-five race riots—
some vigilante groups receded, but a revived Ku Klux Klan gained
popularity by adding Catholics, Jews, and foreigners to its list of
un-Americans.[110]

The seeming hegemony of this militarist, racist, and exclusive
brand of patriotism, however, provoked new contradictions. Efforts to forcefully impose a sense of cultural homogeneity in a
country still profoundly divided by differences of race, class, ethnicity, gender, and region generated as much fracturing and in-
subordination as it did unity and consolidation. Janus-faced, the
culture of patriotism proceeded along an ambivalent path.[111] As
Eric Hobsbawm has noted, overly exclusive definitions of citizenship can backfire, alienating those who refuse or are denied the
terms of assimilation while encouraging superpatriots to take matters into their own hands.[112] After WWI, right-wing organizations
like the Ku Klux Klan and the American Legion promoted a "virile
Christian nationalism," each claiming to be the exclusive arbiter
of true Americanism.[113] Meanwhile, thousands of working-class
blacks felt thoroughly disillusioned with the U.S. and supported
Marcus Garvey's pan-African nationalism. Black people, Garvey
argued, had helped the United States in all of her wars—always
bringing back the "glory of the flag," having made sure that it
never "touched the dust"—and now it was time for white America
to let black people realize their own separatist mission.[114]

Ultimately, the campaign to impose political and Anglo-conformity failed despite the devastation they imposed. World War I
stands as a turning point, a time when Americanizers succeeded
in liquidating the autonomous cultural existence of German
Americans; when public and private antiradicalism succeeded in
defeating a broad range of political opposition, from the labor

militancy of the IWW to the electoral strategy of the Socialist Party; when a generation of progressives who believed in cultural pluralism had to admit defeat; when civil liberties were suspended in the name of national security; and when the civil-rights movement lost ground as African American soldiers were lynched and whites rioted against blacks who refused to submit to a separate and unequal status.

Yet, despite such unrelenting repression, the cultural and social diversity of the American people, combined with its long traditions of political debate and resistance, confounded and undermined the absolute imposition of "100 percent Americanism." WWI and its aftermath revealed one of the paradoxes of American nationalism. Even though all the institutional trappings and mechanisms of a homogeneous national culture were in place, an intolerant and racialized patriotism exacerbated divisions, forcing radicals, immigrants, and African Americans into the margins, where each continued to generate political and cultural meanings from the "in-between spaces" of the nation-state.[115]

The question whether national allegiance would serve emancipatory aims had been silenced but not settled. Between the regimes of intolerance that ruled the country during and after both world wars, the U.S. witnessed one of the most radical periods in its history, as the New Woman, the New Negro, and revived labor and leftist movements once again challenged the nation to guarantee equality as a condition of loyalty. "Let America be America again. / Let it be the dream it used to be," urged Langston Hughes in his anthem of hope, which captured the contradictory relationship between liberty and loyalty, justice and nationhood:

> O, let my land be a land where Liberty
> Is crowned with no false patriotic wreath,
> But opportunity is real, and life is free,
> Equality is in the air we breathe.
> (There's never been equality for me.
> Nor freedom in this "homeland of the free.")
> . . . .
> O, let America be America again—
> The land that never has been yet—
> And yet must be. . . .[116]

* *Notes* *

CHAPTER 1
"TO MAKE A NATION"

1. Alexis de Tocqueville to Ernest de Chabrol, 9 June 9 1831, in *Selected Letters on Politics and Society*, ed. Roger Boesche, trans. James Toupin and Roger Boesche (London: Printed for T. Davies, 1782; reprint, Berkeley: University of California Press, 1985), 38.

2. William T. Sherman, *Memoirs of Gen. W. T. Sherman, Written By Himself*, 4th ed., vol. 2 (New York: Charles L. Webster, 1891), 227.

3. The phrase was used by President Woodrow Wilson in his "July 4th Address," 1913, contained in Pennsylvania Commission, *Fiftieth Anniversary of the Battle of Gettysburg* (Harrisburg: WM. Stanley Ray, 1913), 174–76.

4. I use the term *American* to denote "of the United States of America"—even though its use appropriates the name of two continents—because this selective meaning was so important to the nationalist movement's self-identity.

5. Eric Hobsbawm, "Introduction: Inventing Traditions," in *The Invention of Tradition*, ed. Eric Hobsbawm and Terence Ranger (1983; reprint, Cambridge: Cambridge University Press, 1988), 1.

6. Eric Hobsbawm, *Nations and Nationalism since 1780: Programme, Myth, Reality* (Cambridge: Cambridge University Press, 1990), 78.

7. Benedict Anderson, *Imagined Communities: Reflections on the Origin and Spread of Nationalism*, rev. ed. (London: Verso, 1991), 7; Geoff Eley and Ronald Grigor Suny, eds., *Becoming National: A Reader* (New York: Oxford University Press, 1996), 22.

8. Traditionally, studies of nationalism have emphasized a fundamental difference between Western/civic and Eastern/ethnic forms of nationalism. The standard, Western/civic model typically refers to the existence of a historical territory, a legal-political community, and a common civic culture and ideology. The non-Western, or ethnic, concept of the nation is typically defined in terms of a "community of common descent," in which the "people" are categorized according to family lineage rather than as members of a political community subject to common laws and institutions. However, Anthony D. Smith reminds us that there are multiple, dynamic routes to the "making of 'states' and the 'building' of nations." Every nationalism contains elements in varying proportions

of both civic/territorial and ethnic/genealogical models of nation-building (*National Identity* [London: Penguin Books, 1991], 11–12, 15, 117–19). For the influence of ethnic symbols, memories, and myths on the formation of modern nation-states, see idem, *The Ethnic Origins of Nations* (Oxford: Blackwell, 1986).

9. Stuart Hall, "The Question of Cultural Identity," in *Modernity and Its Futures*, ed. Stuart Hall, David Held, and Tony McGraw (Cambridge: Polity Press in Association with the Open University, 1992), 278–79, 299.

10. Ernest Renan, "Qu'est-ce qu'une nation?" (What is a nation?) delivered at the Sorbonne, 11 March 1882, trans. Martin Thom, in *Nation and Narration*, ed. Homi K. Bhabha (London: Routledge, 1990), 19.

11. Homi K. Bhabha, "DissemiNation: Time, Narrative, and the Margins of the Modern Nation," in Bhabha, *Nation and Narration*, 310.

12. Throughout this study I refer to patriotic groups and individuals as *nationalists* even though the term was not broadly adopted until the onset of World War I, when Theodore Roosevelt popularized his creed as the "New Nationalism." Nonetheless, the term best describes the concerted efforts of activists whose lives were bound up with the destiny of the United States and who worked to create a transcendental culture in which all other loyalties and identities were subsumed into one national identity.

13. Hans Kohn's classic Cold War study stresses the uniqueness of American nationalism's essentially unchanging quest for the realization of civic ideals (*American Nationalism: An Interpretive Essay* [New York: Macmillan, 1957], x, 3–10). Recent work continuing the tradition of stressing American exceptionalism includes Arthur M. Schlesinger Jr., *The Disuniting of America: Reflections on a Multicultural Society* (1991; reprint, New York: Norton, 1992); and Liah Greenfeld, *Nationalism: Five Roads to Modernity* (Cambridge: Harvard University Press, 1992), 401–23, which argues that a preexisting national identity defined by commitment to civic principles "finally achieved a geo-political embodiment" in 1865.

14. Greenfeld, *Nationalism*, 484; Schlesinger, *Disuniting of America*, 13.

15. Schlesinger, *Disuniting of America*, 43.

16. Michael Lind, *The Next American Nation: The New Nationalism and the Fourth American Revolution* (New York: Free Press, 1995), 6.

17. Among the most important, classic books on American nationalism, nativism, and patriotism are Merle Curti, *The Roots of American Loyalty* (New York: Columbia University Press, 1946); and John Higham, *Strangers in the Land: Patterns of American Nativism, 1860–1925* (1955; reprint, New York: Atheneum, 1967). Among the groundbreaking works to analyze the role of national culture as an engine of modernization are Ernest

Gellner's *Thought and Change* (Chicago: University of Chicago Press, 1964) and his later *Nations and Nationalism* (Ithaca: Cornell University Press, 1983). Both books locate nationalism within the rise of modern capitalist societies and focus on the constructed nature of nationalism. Eric Hobsbawm and Terence Ranger's *Invention of Tradition* continued along the intellectual path set by Gellner but added a cultural analysis of how societies create national meanings through the "invention" of rituals and symbols. Benedict Anderson further moved the discussion of nations and nationalism into the territory of cultural studies with his pioneering study of how nations are "imagined" even though their members "will never know most of their fellow-members, meet them, or even hear of them, yet in the minds of each lives the image of their communion" (*Imagined Communities*, 6). Other books from the United States and England that explore relationships between culture and nationalism include Gail Bederman, *Manliness and Civilization: A Cultural History of Gender and Race in the United States, 1880–1917* (Chicago: University of Chicago Press, 1995); Bhabha, *Nation and Narration*; John Bodnar, *Remaking America: Public Memory, Commemoration, and Patriotism in the Twentieth Century* (Princeton: Princeton University Press, 1992); idem, ed., *Bonds of Affection: Americans Define Their Patriotism* (Princeton: Princeton University Press, 1996); Linda Colley, *Britons: Forging the Nation, 1701–1837* (New Haven: Yale University Press, 1992); James Donald and Stuart Hall, eds., *Politics and Ideology* (Milton Keynes, England: Open University Press, 1986); Eley and Suny, *Becoming National*; Gary Gerstle, *Working-Class Americanism: The Politics of Labor in a Textile City, 1914–1960* (Cambridge: Cambridge University Press, 1989); John R. Gillis, ed., *Commemorations: The Politics of National Identity* (Princeton: Princeton University Press, 1994); Paul Gilroy, *"There Ain't No Black in the Union Jack": The Cultural Politics of Race and Nation* (London: Unwin Hyman, 1987); Catherine Hall, *White, Male, and Middle Class: Explorations in Feminism and History* (Cambridge: Polity Press, 1992); Stuart Hall, *The Hard Road to Renewal: Thatcherism and the Crisis of the Left* (London: Verso, 1988); Hall, Held, and McGraw, *Modernity and Its Futures*; Hobsbawm and Ranger, *Invention of Tradition*; Hobsbawm, *Nations and Nationalism*; Eric Hobsbawm, *The Age of Extremes: A History of the World. 1914–1991* (New York: Pantheon Books, 1994); Michael Kammen, *Mystic Chords of Memory: The Transformation of Tradition in American Culture* (1991; reprint, New York: Vintage Books, 1993); Lind, *Next American Nation*; Andrew Parker et al., eds., *Nationalisms and Sexualities* (New York: Routledge, 1992); Raphael Samuel, ed., *Patriotism: The Making and Unmaking of British National Identity*, 3 vols. (London:

Routledge, 1989); Nina Silber, *The Romance of Reunion: Northerners and the South, 1865–1900* (Chapel Hill: University of North Carolina Press, 1993); and Wilbur Zelinsky, *Nation into State: The Shifting Symbolic Foundations of American Nationalism* (Chapel Hill: University of North Carolina Press, 1988).

18. Hobsbawm, *Nations and Nationalism,* 11.

19. Bodnar, *Bonds of Affection,* 4.

20. Joyce Appleby, "Recovering America's Historic Diversity: Beyond Exceptionalism," *Journal of American History* 79 (September 1992): 431.

21. The term *political roof* is from Ernest Gellner, quoted in Hall, "Question of Cultural Identity," 292.

22. Kammen, *Mystic Chords of Memory,* 293–94.

23. Although both Confederate and Grand Army veterans claimed to be patriots, I have generally reserved the term *patriot* for those who strove to defend the United States and consolidate its cultural and political power.

24. For an in-depth review of the history of literature on nationalism, as well as key concepts and debates, see Eley and Suny, *Becoming National,* 3–37.

25. Hall, "Question of Cultural Identity," 292.

26. Eley and Suny, *Becoming National,* 24.

27. Throughout the book I use various terms for African Americans depending on how they named themselves in different periods. For example, at the end of the nineteenth century black Americans often referred to themselves as "Afro-Americans" and "Negroes."

28. Among books that bring a historical perspective to contemporary public controversies are Robert Justin Goldstein, *Saving "Old Glory": The History of the American Flag Desecration Controversy* (Boulder: Westview, 1995); Lawrence W. Levine, *The Opening of the American Mind: Canons, Culture, and History* (Boston: Beacon, 1996); and Tom Englehardt and Edward T. Linenthal, *History Wars: The Enola Gay and Other Battles for the American Past* (New York: Metropolitan Books, 1996).

CHAPTER 2
"DYED IN THE BLOOD OF OUR FOREFATHERS": PATRIOTIC CULTURE BEFORE THE CIVIL WAR

1. Annie Laurie, "Respect the Flag," *American Monthly Magazine,* October 1893, 447–49.

2. Eric Hobsbawm, *Nations and Nationalism since 1780: Programme, Myth, Reality* (Cambridge: Cambridge University Press, 1990), 9–10.

3. Liah Greenfeld, *Nationalism: Five Roads to Modernity* (Cambridge: Harvard University Press, 1992), 409, 412, 423.

4. Whitney Smith, *The Flag Book of the United States*, rev. ed. (New York: Morrow, 1975), 45.

5. Anthony D. Smith, "State-Making and Nation-Building," in *States in History*, ed. John Hall (Oxford: Blackwell, 1986), 234–35.

6. Max Savelle, "Nationalism and Other Loyalties in the American Revolution," *American Historical Review* 67 (July 1962): 906, 914–15, 917, 919, 921–23.

7. *Crisis*, no. 13 (1783), in *Life and Works of Thomas Paine*, ed. William M. Van der Weyde III (New Rochelle, N.Y.: Thomas Paine National Historical Association, 1925), 77–79, 244–46.

8. Joyce Appleby, "Recovering America's Historic Diversity: Beyond Exceptionalism," *Journal of American History* 79 (September 1992): 421.

9. First draft of the Constitution (August 1787), Papers of the Continental and Confederation Congresses, 1774–1789, RG 360, National Archives, Washington, D.C.

10. Merle Curti, *The Roots of American Loyalty* (New York: Columbia University Press, 1946), 27–28.

11. Ralph Henry Gabriel, *The Course of American Democratic Thought: An Intellectual History since 1815* (New York: Ronald Press, 1940), 90–91.

12. Curti, *Roots of American Loyalty*, 130.

13. Joyce Appleby, "Republicanism and Ideology," *American Quarterly* 37 (fall 1985): 467.

14. The impact of classicism on the building of the capitol is demonstrated in the spring 1995 exhibit *Temple of Liberty: Building the Capitol for a New Nation*, Madison Building, Library of Congress, Washington, D.C. (hereafter cited as Temple of Liberty Exhibit, LC); early coins are exhibited at the National Museum of American History, Smithsonian Institution, Washington, D.C. (hereafter NMAH). See also Clarence P. Hornung, ed. and comp., *The American Eagle in Art and Design* (New York: Dover, 1978), v.

15. Benjamin Franklin, designer, Claude-Michel Clodion, sculptor, "Allegory of the American Revolution," 1783, Temple of Liberty Exhibit, LC.

16. William H. Gerdts, *American Neo-Classical Sculpture: The Marble Resurrection* (New York: A Studio Book, 1973), 98–99; Garry Wills, "Washington's Citizen Virtue: Greenough and Houdon," *Critical Inquiry* 10 (March 1984): 420–41. Since 1995 the statue has been located between two whimsical carousel horses at the NMAH.

17. "A View of the Capitol of the United States After the Conflagration of 1814," frontispiece in Jesse Torry, *A Portraiture of Domestic Slavery in the United States* (Philadelphia: Jesse Torry, 1817).

18. Ruth Miller Elson, *Guardians of Tradition: American Schoolbooks of the Nineteenth Century* (Lincoln: University of Nebraska Press, 1964), 282–83.

19. Thomas Jefferson to James Madison, Paris, 6 September 1789, in *The Papers of Thomas Jefferson*, ed. Julian P. Boyd, vol. 15, *27 March 1789 to 30 November 1789* (Princeton: Princeton University Press, 1958), 392.

20. John Quincy Adams to Baron Von Furstenwaerther, 4 June 1819, in "Emigration to the U. States," in *Niles Weekly Register* 18 (29 April 1820): 157–58.

21. Todd Gitlin, *The Twilight of Common Dreams: Why America Is Wracked by Culture Wars* (New York: Metropolitan Books, 1995), 46.

22. Peter J. Parish, "An Exception to Most of the Rules: What Made American Nationalism Different in the Mid-Nineteenth Century?" *Prologue*, fall 1995, 222–23.

23. Ibid., 222, 227.

24. Michael Kammen, *Mystic Chords of Memory: The Transformation of Tradition in American Culture* (1991; reprint, New York: Vintage Books, 1993), 55, 293–94.

25. Hector St. John de Crevecoeur, "Letter III: What is an American?" in *Letters from an American Farmer* (1782; reprint, New York: Penguin Books, 1983), 69.

26. As late as 1904, the DAR despaired that "no monument of any kind had been reared in the memory" of Jefferson ("Proceedings of the Thirteenth Continental Congress," *American Monthly Magazine*, 25 [July 1904], 91).

27. Nian-Sheng Huang, *Benjamin Franklin in American Thought and Culture, 1790–1990* (Philadelphia: American Philosophical Society, 1994), 31–32, 42–43, 50, 66–67. For a discussion of Stuart's portrait of Washington, see Karal Ann Marling, *George Washington Slept Here: Colonial Revivals and American Culture, 1876–1986* (Cambridge: Harvard University Press, 1988), 8–13.

28. John Bodnar, introduction to his *Bonds of Affection: Americans Define Their Patriotism* (Princeton: Princeton University Press, 1996), 4.

29. Appleby, "Recovering America's Historic Diversity," 423–24.

30. Daniel J. Boorstin, *The Americans: The National Experience* (New York: Vintage Books, 1965), 340–42.

31. John Adams to Joseph Ward, 6 June 1809, in *We the People: Voices and Images of the New Nation,* by Alfred F. Young and Terry J. Fife with Mary E. Janzen (Philadelphia: Temple University Press, 1993), 191.

32. Ibid., 192, 197.

33. George William Douglas, *The American Book of Days* (New York: H. W. Wilson, 1937), 132–33.

34. Wiley Thompson, 1832, quoted in Boorstin, *Americans,* 350.

35. Edward Tabor Linenthal shared the information about the Catholic stone being thrown into the Potomac in a letter to the author in the spring of 1996.

36. Frederick L. Harvey, *History of the Washington National Monument and of the Washington National Monument Society* (Washington, D.C.: Norman E. Elliott, 1902), 49, 108.

37. Herbert Ridgeway Collins, *Threads of History: Americana Recorded on Cloth, 1775 to the Present* (Washington, D.C.: Smithsonian Institution Press, 1979), 48.

38. States individually adopted July Fourth as an official holiday. The federal government can make proclamations, but its authority to establish national holidays is limited to the District of Columbia and to federal employees (Boorstin, *Americans,* 375; Curti, *Roots of American Loyalty,* 31–32, 35, 37–38, 41–42, 62, 65, 68, 103, 116, 120, 137, 140).

39. Michael Kammen, "The Problem of American Exceptionalism: A Reconsideration," *American Quarterly* 45 (March 1993): 7–8, 11.

40. Appleby, "Recovering America's Historic Diversity," 424.

41. Len Travers, *Celebrating the Fourth: Independence Day and the Rites of Nationalism in the Early Republic* (Amherst: University of Massachusetts Press, 1997), 152.

42. July Fourth, Nevada, Photo Files, The Huntington Library, San Marino, Calif.

43. Charles Carroll, quoted in Douglas, *American Book of Days,* 357.

44. For a fuller discussion of colonists' views on liberty and power, see Bernard Bailyn, *The Ideological Origins of the American Revolution* (Cambridge: Harvard University Press, Belknap Press, 1967), 55–58.

45. Michael Kammen, *A Season of Youth: The American Revolution and the Historical Imagination* (New York: Knopf, 1978), 96–99, 102.

46. Roger A. Fisher and Edmund B. Sullivan, *American Political Ribbons and Ribbon Badges, 1825–1981* (Lincoln, Mass.: Quarterman, 1985), 55–56, 66–68.

47. Ralph Waldo Emerson, "Native Americans," in *The Journals and Miscellaneous Notebooks of Ralph Waldo Emerson*, vol. 9, *1843–1847* (Cambridge: Harvard University Press, Belknap Press, 1971), 299–300.

48. Travers, *Celebrating the Fourth*, 222. See also Diana Karter Appelbaum, *The Glorious Fourth: An American Holiday, an American History* (New York: Facts on File, 1989).

49. Daniel Webster, "The Addition to the Capitol: Address at the Laying of the Corner Stone of the Addition to the Capitol, on the 4th of July, 1851," in *The Great Speeches and Orations of Daniel Webster* (Boston: Little, Brown, 1882), 641.

50. Kammen, *Season of Youth*, 53–55.

51. Travers, *Celebrating the Fourth*, 141–44.

52. Roman J. Zorh, "The New England Anti-Slavery Society: Pioneer Abolition Organization," *Journal of Negro History* 43 (July 1957): 158, 160; William Lloyd Garrison, quoted in Leonard Sweet, "The Fourth of July and Black Americans in the Nineteenth Century," ibid. 61 (July 1976): 261.

53. Milo M. Quaife, Melvin J. Weig, and Roy F. Appleman, *The History of the United States Flag: From the Revolution to the Present, Including a Guide to Its Use and Display* (New York: Harper & Brothers, 1961), 57, 59, 73–76.

54. Bryan Lindsay, "Anacreon on the Wagon: 'The Star-Spangled Banner' in the Service of the Cold Water Army," *Journal of Popular Culture* 4 (winter 1973): 595–600.

55. Joseph Muller, *The Star Spangled Banner: Words and Music Issued between 1814–1864* (New York: G. A. Baker, 1935), 23–24.

56. Lindsay, "Anacreon on the Wagon," 600.

57. Maj. John H. Magruder III, "A Touch of Tradition: The National Anthem," *Marine Corps Gazette*, July 1955, 47.

58. William Rea Furlong, Byron McCandless, and Harold D. Langley, *So Proudly We Hail: The History of the United States Flag* (Washington, D.C.: Smithsonian Institution Press, 1981), 186; Quaife, Weig, and Appleman, *History of the United States Flag*, 87.

59. Boleslaw D'Otrange Mastai and Marie-Louise D'Otrange Mastai, *The Stars and the Stripes: The American Flag as Art and as History from the Birth of the Republic to the Present* (New York: Knopf, 1973), 82, 96.

60. Fisher and Sullivan, *American Political Ribbons and Ribbon Badges*, 6, 29–30.

61. David Montejano, *Anglos and Mexicans in the Making of Texas, 1836–1986* (Austin: University of Texas Press, 1987), 224.

62. Ibid., 305; Edward Tabor Linenthal, *Sacred Ground: Americans and Their Battlefields*, 2nd ed. (Urbana: University of Illinois Press, 1993), 70–71.

63. Eric Hobsbawm, "Mass-Producing Traditions: Europe, 1870–1914," in *The Invention of Tradition*, ed. Eric Hobsbawm and Terence Ranger (1983; reprint, Cambridge: Cambridge University Press, 1988), 263.

64. Robert W. Johannsen, *To the Halls of Montezumas: The Mexican War in the American Imagination* (New York: Oxford University Press, 1985), 51–54, 59–61.

65. Captain W. S. Henry, *Campaign Sketches of the War with Mexico* (New York: Harper & Brothers, 1848), 215.

66. D'Otrange Mastai and D'Otrange Mastai, *The Stars and the Stripes*, 96.

67. Furlong, McCandless, and Langley, *So Proudly We Hail*, 110, 186.

68. Curti, *Roots of American Loyalty*, 154–56.

69. Howard Zinn, *A People's History of the United States, 1492–Present*, rev. ed. (1980; reprint, New York: Harper Perennial, 1995), 154.

70. Henry David Thoreau, "Resistance to Civil Government," in *Great Short Works of Henry David Thoreau*, ed. Wendell Glick (New York: Harper Perennial, 1982), 148.

71. George Lippard, *Washington and His Generals; or, Legends of the Revolution* (Philadelphia: G. B. Zieber, 1847), 524–25.

72. The Marine banner, on exhibit at the NMAH in 1995, remains on exhibit.

73. Walt Whitman, "An Emanation of Brooklyn Patriotism," 16 April 1847, in *The Gathering of the Forces: Editorials, Essays, Literary and Dramatic Reviews, and Other Material Written by Walt Whitman as Editor of the Brooklyn Daily Eagle in 1846 and 1847*, ed. Cleveland Rodgers and John Black, 2 vols. (New York: G. P. Putnam's Sons, 1920), 1:84.

74. Nancy Cunningham, "Civil War Diary," in *"Patriotism" the Story of the Civil War in America: McGuffey's Fourth Reader of the Cherryville, Indiana, District School, 1860 and 1861, with Notes by the Schoolmates on the Fly-Leaves. Anna May Thistlewaite's Story, as Told in a Diary Kept by a Classmate, Nancy Cunningham*, by Clarence E. Votaw (Philadelphia: Dorrance, 1941), 70–72.

75. Benson J. Lossing, *Pictorial History of the Civil War in the United States of America* (Philadelphia: George W. Childs, 1866), 335.

76. "The Union Forever!" *New York Times*, 21 April 1861, 1.

77. Lossing, *Pictorial History of the Civil War*, 333–43.

78. Reverend E. A. Anderson, quoted in George Henry Preble, *Our Flag: Origin and Progress of the Flag of the United States of America* (Albany: Joel Munsell, 1872), 348.

79. *Boston Transcript*, 27 April 1861, quoted in Preble, *Our Flag*, 351, 354.

80. Gail Hamilton [Mary Abigail Dodge], "A Call To My Country-Women," *Atlantic Monthly*, March 1863, 346.

81. Julia Ward Howe, "Battle Hymn of the Republic," in *Twenty-Five Army Ballads: Boys Who Wore the Blue*, comp. S. B. Jones (Omaha: Republican Publishing & Printing, 1882), 2.

82. Johannsen, *To the Halls of Montezumas*, 63, 67.

83. Peter Welsh, *Irish Green and Union Blue: The Civil War Letters of Peter Welsh, Color Sergeant, 28th Regiment, Massachusetts Volunteers*, ed. Lawrence Frederick Kohl and Margaret Cossé Richard (New York: Fordham University Press, 1986), xv, 8–11.

84. Abraham Lincoln, "First Inaugural Address—Final Text," 4 March 1861, in *The Collected Works of Abraham Lincoln*, ed. Roy P. Basler, 8 vols. (New Brunswick, N.J.: Rutgers University Press, 1953), 4:263.

85. Frederick Douglass, "Why Should a Colored Man Enlist?" *Douglass' Monthly* (Rochester, N.Y.), April 1863, 819.

86. Frederick Douglass, "The Present and Future of the Colored Race in America," speech delivered in New York, May 1893, in *The Life and Writings of Frederick Douglass*, ed. Philip S. Foner (New York: International Publishers, 1952), 347–49, 352.

87. George M. Fredrickson, *The Inner Civil War: Northern Intellectuals and the Crisis of the Union* (New York: Harper & Row, 1965), 118.

88. John Bodnar, introduction to *Bonds of Affection*, 2.

89. Abraham Lincoln, "Address Delivered at the Dedication of the Cemetery at Gettysburg," 19 November 1863, in Lincoln, *Collected Works*, 7:19–21.

90. George Henry Preble, *Origin and History of the American Flag*, new ed., 2 vols. (Philadelphia: Nicholas L. Brown, 1917), 2:563.

91. Stephen Crane, *The Red Badge of Courage and Other Stories* (1895; New York: Penguin Books, 1991), 175, 179–80.

92. I owe many insights into the developing significance of the flag to discussions in the summer of 1992 with Dr. Harold D. Langley, curator, Division of Armed Forces, NMAH.

93. Edward Everett Hale, "The Man Without a Country," *Atlantic Monthly*, December 1863, 665–79.

94. William Sloane Kennedy, "Edward Everett Hale," *Century Illustrated Monthly Magazine* 12 (January 1885): 338–43.

95. Hale, "Man Without a Country," 675.

96. Kennedy, "Edward Everett Hale," 338–43.

97. "The Man Without a Country" remained popular at least through the 1940s, when public-school children in New York routinely received a free copy (Lawrence Levine, personal communication about his own experience as a child of immigrant parents).

98. Eric Hobsbawm, *The Age of Extremes: A History of the World, 1914–1991* (New York: Pantheon Books, 1994), 44.

99. Eric L. McKitrick, *Andrew Johnson and Reconstruction* (Chicago: University of Chicago Press, 1960), 27.

100. Kate Brownlee Sherwood, "The Nation's Memorial," in *Camp-fire, Memorial-Day, and Other Poems* (Chicago: Jansen, McClurg, 1885), 65.

101. Abraham Lincoln, "Address Delivered at the Dedication of the Cemetery at Gettysburg," first draft, 19 November 1863, in Lincoln, *Collected Works*, 7:18.

CHAPTER 3
"WHEN JOHNNY COMES MARCHING HOME": THE EMERGENCE
OF THE GRAND ARMY OF THE REPUBLIC

1. Michael Kammen, *A Season of Youth: The American Revolution and the Historical Imagination* (New York: Knopf, 1978), 103; Architect of the Capitol, *Art in the United States Capitol* (Washington, D.C.: Government Printing Office, 1976), 354.

2. "Home From The Wars!" *Philadelphia Inquirer,* 24 May 1865, 1; "Grant and His Chiefs Review the Mighty Host!" ibid., 25 May 1865, 1; "Military Pageants in History," ibid., 26 May 1865, 2.

3. "The National Military Review," *Boston Post,* 26 May 1865, 1.

4. For a fuller gender analysis of Teddy Roosevelt, see Gail Bederman, *Manliness and Civilization: A Cultural History of Gender and Race in the United States, 1880–1917* (Chicago: University of Chicago Press, 1995), 13, 44.

5. Stuart McConnell, *Glorious Contentment: The Grand Army of the Republic, 1865–1900* (Chapel Hill: University of North Carolina Press, 1992), 1–3.

6. "Military Pageants in History."

7. "Grant and His Chiefs Review the Mighty Host!"

8. "The Grand Review," *Washington Evening Star,* 24 May 1865, 2.

9. "The Review of Sherman's Army," *Boston Post*, 25 May 1865, 2; and "Home From The Wars!"

10. "Scenes and Incidents: The Capitol," *Philadelphia Inquirer*, 24 May 1865, 1.

11. Graphic of "The Grand Review at Washington," Prints and Photographs Division, Library of Congress, Washington, D.C (hereafter cited as Prints and Photographs, LC).

12. "The Grand Review."

13. "Military Pageants in History."

14. Walt Whitman, *Complete Poetry and Collected Prose* (New York: Viking, 1982), 778.

15. Mary P. Ryan, *Women in Public: Between Banners and Ballots, 1825–1880* (Baltimore: John Hopkins University Press, 1990), 42.

16. "Grant and His Chiefs Review the Mighty Host!"; "Review of the Armies," *New York Times*, 25 May 1865, 8.

17. "Home From The Wars!"

18. McConnell, *Glorious Contentment*, 8.

19. "The Review of Sherman's Army"; "The Grand Review."

20. "Scenes and Incidents."

21. "Review of the Armies." Photographs of the Grand Review suggest that some black soldiers were present among the spectators (Prints and Photographs, LC).

22. "Grant and His Chiefs Review the Mighty Host!"

23. Russell F. Weigley, *History of the United States Army* (New York: Macmillan, 1967), xii, 158.

24. Mercy Otis Warren, *History of the Rise, Progress, and Termination of the American Revolution*, vol. 3 (1805; reprint, New York: AMS Press, 1970), 284.

25. Samuel Adams to Elbridge Gerry, Boston, 23 April 1784, in *The Writings of Samuel Adams, 1778–1802*, ed. Harry Alonso Cushing, vol. 4 (New York: G. P. Putnam's Sons, 1908), 301.

26. Wallace Evan Davies, *Patriotism on Parade: The Story of Veterans' and Hereditary Organizations in America, 1783–1900* (Cambridge: Harvard University Press, 1955), 2–13.

27. *Proceedings of the Convention of the Soldiers of the War of 1812, 1854* (Syracuse: Edward Hoogland, Printer, Daily Republican and National Star Office, 1854), 1, 7, 10–11.

28. Davies, *Patriotism on Parade*, 30–31, 36.

29. Ibid., 29–33; McConnell, *Glorious Contentment*, 24–25; Mary Rulkatter Dearing, *Veterans in Politics: The Story of the GAR* (Baton Rouge: Louisiana State University Press, 1952), 81, 84.

30. "Fall in Comrades," *National Tribune* (Washington, D.C.), 21 June 1892, 6.

31. The *National Tribune* had the largest circulation of the various veteran newspapers and the longest publishing record (1877–1900). Its founder and editor, George Lemon, was a GAR veteran who built his newspaper and his career by becoming a leading crusader for federal veteran pensions (McConnell, *Glorious Contentment*, 114–15, 208–9).

32. "Promises versus Performance," *National Tribune*, 17 October 1889, 1.

33. GAR, *Journal of the Seventeenth Annual Session, National Encampment, 1883* (Omaha: Republican Publishing & Printing, 1883), 54–55.

34. GAR, *Proceedings of the Fourteenth Annual Meeting of the National Encampment, 1880* (Dayton: Journal Book and Job Printing Establishment, 1880), 662–63.

35. Davies, *Patriotism on Parade*, 31, 33–35.

36. McConnell, *Glorious Contentment*, 3, 29–32, 50–51.

37. James Russell Lowell, *The Writings of James Russell Lowell*, vol. 5 (Cambridge: Riverside Press, 1890), 243–44.

38. Benedict Anderson, *Imagined Communities: Reflections on the Origins and Spread of Nationalism*, rev. ed. (London: Verso, 1991), 63–65.

39. Alfred D. Chandler Jr., *The Visible Hand: The Managerial Revolution in American Business* (Cambridge: Harvard University Press, Belknap Press, 1977), 285–86.

40. 1876 Centennial, Picture Files, Division of Domestic Life, NMAH (hereafter cited as Division of Domestic Life, NMAH).

41. Davies, *Patriotism on Parade*, 250; McConnell, *Glorious Contentment*, 84–85.

42. *Indianapolis Sentinel*, 4 and 5 July 1876, in Walter T. K. Nugent, "Seed Time of Modern Conflict: American Society at the Centennial," in *Indiana Historical Society Lectures, 1972–1973: 1876 The Centennial Year*, by Lillian B. Miller, Walter T. K. Nugent, and Wayne Moisan (Indianapolis: Indiana Historical Society, 1973), 31.

43. Lyn Spillman, *Nation and Commemoration: Creating National Identities in the United States and Australia* (Cambridge: Cambridge University Press, 1997), 39–40, 47; Robert W. Rydell, *World of Fairs: The Century-of-Progress Expositions* (Chicago: University of Chicago Press, 1993), 5.

44. Rydell, *World of Fairs*, 41; Robert W. Rydell, *All the World's a Fair: Visions of Empire at America's International Expositions, 1876–1916* (Chicago: University of Chicago Press, 1984), 18.

45. John E. Findling, ed., *Historical Dictionary of World's Fairs and Expositions, 1851–1988* (New York: Greenwood, 1990), xvii–xviii.

46. 1876 Centennial, Division of Domestic Life, NMAH.

47. 1876 Centennial souvenirs, Larry Zim and Edward J. Orth World's Fair Collection, 1733–1992, Archives Center, NMAH.

48. 1876 World's Fair Trade Cards, ibid.

49. S. B. Jones, comp., *Twenty-Five Army Ballads: Favorites of the Boys Who Wore the Blue* (Omaha: Republican Publishing & Printing, 1882), 10.

50. GAR, *Journal of the Fifteenth Annual Session of the National Encampment, 1881* (Philadelphia: Merrihew & Lippert, 1881), 761.

51. W. S. Harwood, "Secret Societies in America," *North American Review* 164 (May 1897): 617, 620, 623; Mark C. Carnes and Clyde Griffen, eds., *Meanings for Manhood: Constructions of Masculinity in Victorian America* (Chicago: University of Chicago Press, 1990), 38, 221.

52. Albert C. Stevens, *Cyclopaedia of Fraternities* (New York: Hamilton, 1899), xvi.

53. For a fuller discussion of fraternal orders, see Lynn Dumenil, *Freemasonry and American Culture, 1880–1930* (Princeton: Princeton University Press, 1984) 31–111; Mark C. Carnes, *Secret Ritual and Manhood in Victorian America* (New Haven: Yale University Press, 1989), 107–27; and Mary Ann Clawson, *Constructing Brotherhood: Class, Gender, and Fraternalism* (Princeton: Princeton University Press, 1989).

54. Bederman, *Manliness and Civilization*, 16.

55. GAR, *Journal of the Twenty-Sixth National Encampment, 1892* (Albany, N.Y.: S. H. Wentworth, 1892), 51.

56. GAR, *Journal of the Twenty-Third Annual Session of the National Encampment, 1889* (St. Louis: A. Whipple, 1889), 34.

57. GAR, *Journal of the Twenty-Fourth Annual Session of the National Encampment, 1890* (Detroit: Richmond & Backus, 1890), 9.

58. Jones, *Twenty-Five Army Ballads*, 7.

59. U.S. Bureau of the Census, *Historical Statistics of the United States, Colonial Times to 1970*, Bicentennial Edition (Washington, D.C.: Government Printing Office, 1975), pt. 2, ser. Y, no. 856, p. 1140.

60. Stuart Hall, "Notes on Deconstructing 'The Popular,' " in ed. Raphael Samuel, *People's History and Socialist Theory* (London: Routledge & Kegan Paul, 1981), 227.

61. Jones, *Twenty-Five Army Ballads*, 32–33.

62. "Scenes and Incidents of the Sixteenth Annual Encampment of the GAR, At Baltimore, June 21st–24th," *Frank Leslie's Illustrated Newspaper* (New York), 1 July 1882, 296.

63. "Meeting of the National Encampment, GAR at Minneapolis, July 21st–26th," ibid., 9 August 1884, 397–98.

64. "Illuminating the Streets on the Night of the Grand Parade," ibid., 1 October 1887, 103–4.

65. "Benefit for Grand Army Fund Promises to be Successful," *San Francisco Examiner*, 9 August 1903, 10.

66. United States Brewers' Association, "Registered Trade-Marks Applied to Malt Liquors" (New York, 1896), Warshaw Collection of Business Americana, Archives Center, NMAH (hereafter cited as Warshaw Collection, NMAH); "The History of Our Flag" (n.p., n.d.), ibid.

67. "The Man with the Medal," *National Tribune*, 28 May 1896, 5.

68. "From Bull Run to Appomattox," *San Francisco Examiner*, 16 August 1903, 2.

69. Unexcelled Fireworks Co., *Illustrated Campaign Hand Book, Annual of Arms and Tactics, and Catalogue of Equipments for Political Organizations* (n.p., 1888), 75; and American Flag Company, *Flags, Banners, and Decoration Goods of Every Description* (n.p., 1900), 20–21, Political Division, NMAH (hereafter cited as Political Division, NMAH).

70. "G.A.R. Jewelry," *National Tribune*, 22 July 1897, 8.

71. Davies, *Patriotism on Parade*, 30–36.

72. GAR, *Proceedings of the Twelfth Annual Meeting of the National Encampment, 1878* (New York: Office of the Grand Army Gazette, 1878), 553.

73. Theda Skocpol, *Protecting Soldiers and Mothers: The Political Origins of Social Policy in the United States* (Cambridge: Harvard University Press, Belknap Press, 1992), 110–12.

74. The Pension Building, with its frieze of Civil War soldiers and sailors, still stands; in 1980 it became the home of the National Building Museum (Linda Brody Lyons, *A Handbook to the Pension Building* [Washington, D.C.: National Building Museum, 1989], 10, 23, 25–26, 28–29, 32–34).

75. GAR, *Journal of the Seventeenth Annual Session, National Encampment, 1883*, 55.

76. McConnell, *Glorious Contentment*, 137–39, 156, 162.

77. For a fuller elaboration of these arguments, see Skocpol, *Protecting Soldiers and Mothers*, 102–55.

78. "Another Veto: President Cleveland Refuses to Sign the Pension Bill," *National Tribune*, 17 February 1887, 2; and George S. Merrill, "Veterans! Make Reply," ibid., 24 February 1887, 4.

79. "To 'The Confederate States,' " ibid., 23 June 1887, 4.

80. Robert B. Beath, *History of the Grand Army of the Republic* (New York: Bryan, Taylor, 1889), 14, 299–300.

81. William Penack, *For God and Country: The American Legion, 1919–1941* (Boston: Northeastern University Press, 1989), 27, 124–25, 127.

82. Photos Files, Campaign Objects, 1888–1892, Political Division, NMAH.

83. Skocpol, *Protecting Soldiers and Mothers*, 110–11.

84. Ibid., 130–32, 134–38.

85. GAR, "Chart of Membership since 1878," *Journal of the Forty-Second National Encampment, 1908* (Kansas City: John C. Bovard, 1908), 121; Skocpol, *Protecting Soldiers and Mothers*, 112.

86. Davies, *Patriotism on Parade*, 36.

87. GAR, *Journal of the Thirtieth National Encampment, 1896* (Indianapolis: Wm. B. Burford, 1896), 67.

88. GAR, *Journal of the Twenty-Sixth National Encampment, 1892*, 48.

89. Woman's Relief Corps, *Journal of the Fifteenth National Convention, 1897* (Boston: E. B. Stillings, 1897), 371–72.

90. GAR, *Journal of the Twenty-Sixth National Encampment, 1892*, 208.

Chapter 4
"Living History": Crafting Patriotic Culture
within a Divided Nation

1. Andrew S. Draper, quoted in Thomas Jefferson Morgan, *Patriotic Citizenship* (New York: American Book Company, 1895), 330.

2. Michael Kammen, *Mystic Cords of Memory: The Transformation of Tradition in American Culture* (1991; reprint, New York: Vintage Books, 1993), 293–94.

3. Stuart Hall, "The Question of Cultural Identity," in *Modernity and Its Futures*, ed. Stuart Hall, David Held, and Tony McGraw (Cambridge: Polity Press in Association with the Open University, 1992), 293–95.

4. Anthony Bimba, *The History of the American Working Class* (New York: International Publishers, 1927), 137–40; "The Late Riots," *Nation*, 2 August 1877, 68–69; "Statistical: Cheap Labor and Immigration," *Public Opinion, April–October 1886*, vol. 1 (Washington, D.C.: Public Opinion,

1886), 134–35; Robert H. Wiebe, *The Search for Order, 1877–1920* (New York: Hill & Wang, 1968).

5. Lawrence Glickman, "Inventing the 'American Standard of Living': Gender, Race, and Working Class Identity, 1880–1925," *Labor History* 34 (spring 1993): 221, 223–24, 226–27.

6. David Montgomery, *The Fall of the House of Labor: The Workplace, the State, and American Labor Activism, 1865–1925* (Cambridge: Cambridge University Press, 1987), 81.

7. Lawrence B. Glickman, *A Living Wage: American Workers and the Making of Consumer Society* (Ithaca: Cornell University Press, 1997), 6–7, 79–80.

8. Walker Connor, "Nation-Building or Nation-Destroying?" *World Politics* 24, no. 3 (1972): 320.

9. GAR, *Journal of the Twenty-Sixth National Encampment, 1892* (Albany, N.Y.: S. H. Wentworth, 1892), 81; idem, *Journal of the Fortieth National Encampment, 1906* (Philadelphia: Town Printing, 1906), 307.

10. For a fuller discussion of the origins of the theory of organic nationalism, see Merle Curti, *The Roots of American Loyalty* (New York: Columbia University Press, 1946), 171–83.

11. William H. Goetzmann, ed., *The American Hegelians: An Intellectual Episode in the History of Western America* (New York: Knopf, 1973), 5, 13–17, 156, 159–60.

12. Chaplain-in-Chief Lovering, quoted in Robert B. Beath, *History of the Grand Army of the Republic* (New York: Braun, Taylor, 1889), 176.

13. President Raymond, "Education and Citizenship," in National Education Association, *Journal of Proceedings and Addresses, Session of the Year 1892* (New York, 1893), 396–97.

14. GAR, *Journal of the Twentieth Annual Session of the National Encampment, 1886* (Washington, D.C.: Gibson Bros., 1886), 51–52.

15. Geoff Eley and Ronald Grigor Suny, eds., *Becoming National: A Reader* (New York: Oxford University Press, 1996), 21–23.

16. GAR, *Journal of the Twenty-Eighth National Encampment, 1894* (Boston: E. B. Stillings, 1894), 54; idem, *Journal of the Twenty-Third Annual Session of the National Encampment, 1889* (St. Louis: A. Whipple, 1889), 43.

17. "Hymn for Decoration Day, 1880," in *Twenty-Five Army Ballads: Boys Who Wore the Blue*, comp. S. B. Jones (Omaha: Republican Publishing and Printing House, 1882), 24–25.

18. "Memorial Day," *National Tribune* (Washington, D.C.), 28 May 1891, 4.

19. Ibid.

20. GAR, *Journal of the Twenty-Fourth Annual Session of the National Encampment, 1890* (Detroit: Richmond & Backus, 1890), 13.

21. GAR, *Proceedings of the Twelfth Annual Meeting of the National Encampment, 1878* (New York: Office of the Grand Army Gazette, 1878), 553.

22. Patriotism also became a route of civic participation in England (see Linda Colley, *Britons: Forging the Nation, 1701–1837* [New Haven: Yale University Press, 1992], 5).

23. For a discussion of how French revolutionaries used "language, images, and daily political activities. . . . to establish the basis for a new national community," see Lynn Hunt, *Politics, Culture, and Class in the French Revolution* (Berkeley: University of California Press, 1984), 12.

24. GAR, *Journal of the Thirty-Fourth National Encampment, 1900* (Philadelphia: Town Printing, 1901), 788–89.

25. Thomas C. Leonard, *Above the Battle: War Making in America from Appomattox to Versailles* (New York: Oxford University Press, 1978), 11–12.

26. The Century, *Battles and Leaders of the Civil War: The Century War Book, People's Pictorial Edition*, pts. 1–10 (New York, 1894).

27. Leonard, *Above the Battle*, 12, 15, 17, 22.

28. Stephen Crane, *The Red Badge of Courage and Other Stories* (1895; New York: Penguin Books, 1991), 187.

29. For a discussion of how World War I "tied nationalism and masculinity" even more tightly, see George L. Mosse, *The Image of Man: The Creation of Modern Masculinity* (New York: Oxford University Press, 1996), 109–10.

30. GAR, *Journal of the Thirty-Fourth National Encampment, 1900*, 788.

31. "Boys of Sixty-One Are Boys Again," *San Francisco Chronicle*, 18 August 1903, 1.

32. Front-page graphic, *San Francisco Examiner*, 17 August 1903; front page of souvenir supplement, *San Francisco Chronicle*, 17 August 1903.

33. Mary P. Ryan, *Women in Public: Between Banners and Ballots, 1825–1880* (Baltimore: Johns Hopkins University Press, 1990), 53.

34. Stuart McConnell, *Glorious Contentment: The Grand Army of the Republic, 1865–1900* (Chapel Hill: University of North Carolina Press, 1992), 177–78; "Tramp of Veterans," *Washington Evening Star*, 25 August 1897, 1.

35. "McKinley in Buffalo," *New York Times*, 25 August 1897, 5.

36. Roberts Post No. 14, Department of Vermont, GAR, "Camp Fire" (1 June 1894), Warshaw Collection, NMAH.

37. Joseph W. Morton Jr., ed., *Sparks from the Campfire; or Tales of the Old Veterans* (Philadelphia: Keystone, 1895).

38. GAR, *Journal of the Thirty-First National Encampment, 1897* (Lincoln, Nebr.: State Journal Company, 1897), 228.

39. "On Parade," *San Francisco Examiner,* 4 August 1886, 1.

40. "Twenty Seven Years After," *Washington Evening Star,* 20 September 1892, 1.

41. David Glassberg, *American Historical Pageantry: The Uses of Tradition in the Early Twentieth Century* (Chapel Hill: University of North Carolina Press, 1990), 3–4; Mary P. Ryan, "The American Parade: Representations of the Nineteenth-Century Social Order," in *The New Cultural History,* ed. Lynn Hunt (Berkeley: University of California Press, 1989), 132, 134, 136; Susan G. Davis, *Parades and Power: Street Theater in Nineteenth-Century Philadelphia* (Philadelphia: Temple University Press, 1986), 14, 19, 44, 48, 62, 67, 113, 152, 156–57, 159.

42. "Parade of the Grand Army," *Washington Post,* 21 September 1892, 1.

43. Ryan, "American Parade," 132–53.

44. "Story of the Day," *Minneapolis Tribune,* 3 September 1896, 1.

45. "Tramp of Veterans."

46. "Twenty-Seven Years After."

47. "Keep Step to Memories of Days of Sixty-One," *San Francisco Chronicle,* 20 August 1903, 1.

48. "On Parade."

49. Abraham Lincoln, "First Inaugural Address—Final Text," 4 March 1861, in *The Collected Works of Abraham Lincoln,* ed. Roy P. Basler, 8 vols. (New Brunswick, N.J.: Rutgers University Press, 1953), 4:271.

50. McConnell, *Glorious Contentment,* 82–83, 211; Wallace Evan Davies, *Patriotism on Parade: The Story of Veterans' and Hereditary Organizations in America, 1783–1900* (Cambridge: Harvard University Press, 1955), 87.

51. GAR, *Proceedings of the Twelfth Annual Meeting of the National Encampment, 1878,* 522.

52. Robert Justin Goldstein, *Political Repression in Modern America, 1870 to the Present* (Cambridge: Schenkman, 1978), xvii.

53. See, e.g., "The Late Riots."

54. "The Rioters and the Regular Army," *Nation,* 9 August 1877, 85–86.

55. *New York Times,* 24 July 1877.

56. David Montgomery, *Citizen Worker: The Experience of Workers in the United States with Democracy and the Free Market during the Nineteenth Century* (Cambridge: Cambridge University Press, 1993), 103–4.

57. Davies, *Patriotism on Parade,* 309.

58. GAR, *Journal of the Twenty-Third Annual Session of the National Encampment, 1889*, 34

59. "An Open Letter: To the President of the United States," *National Tribune*, 19 July 1894, 4.

60. "The New Insurrection," ibid., 12 July 1894, 4.

61. GAR, *Proceedings of the Twelfth Annual Meeting of the National Encampment, 1878*, 522; idem, *Journal of the Twenty-Ninth National Encampment, 1895* (Rockford, Ill.: Frank S. Horner, 1895), 133.

62. Montgomery, *Citizen Worker*, 97.

63. *In Re Debs*, in Henry Steele Commager, *Documents of American History*, 10th ed., vol. 1 (Englewood Cliffs, N.J.: Prentice Hall, 1988), 614.

64. "The Right Ring," *National Tribune*, 6 December 1894, 4.

65. GAR, *Journal of the Thirtieth National Encampment, 1896* (Indianapolis: Wm. B. Burford, 1896), 67.

66. The term *un-American* first appeared in print in 1818, in reference to the use of Italian marble in an architectural plan (*Oxford English Dictionary*, 2nd ed.).

67. John Higham, *Strangers in the Land: Patterns of American Nativism, 1860–1925* (1955; reprint, New York: Atheneum, 1967), 30, 54.

68. Robert A. Carlson, *The Americanization Syndrome: A Quest for Conformity*, rev. ed. (London: Croom Helm, 1987), 86.

69. Higham, *Strangers in the Land*, 7.

70. GAR, *Journal of the Twenty-Sixth National Encampment, 1892*, 82–83.

71. McConnell, *Glorious Contentment*, 114–15, 208–9.

72. "Undesirable Immigrants," *National Tribune*, 2 August 1888, 3–4; "A Determined Fight Against the A.P.A.," *American Tribune*, 20 June 1895, 4.

73. Montgomery, *Fall of the House of Labor*, 81–82.

74. GAR, *Journal of the Twenty-Sixth National Encampment, 1892*, 82.

75. GAR, *Journal of the Twenty-Eighth National Encampment, 1894*, 63.

76. Eric Hobsbawm, "Mass-Producing Traditions: Europe, 1870–1914," in *The Invention of Tradition*, ed. Eric Hobsbawm and Terence Ranger (1983; reprint, Cambridge: Cambridge University Press, 1988), 280.

77. Nick Salvatore, *We All Got History: The Memory Books of Amos Webber* (New York: Times Books, 1996), 159–60, 165–68.

78. Ibid., 168–69.

79. Ibid., 161–63.

80. For a contemporary analysis of racial meanings and dynamics, see Paul Gilroy, *"There Ain't No Black in the Union Jack": The Cultural Politics of Race and Nation* (London: Unwin Hyman, 1987), 17, 27–28.

81. Wallace Evan Davies, "The Problem of Race Segregation in the Grand Army of the Republic," *Journal of Southern History* 13 (August 1947): 354–56.

82. "Colored Grand Army Meeting," *Washington Bee,* 11 January 1890, 2.

83. GAR, *Journal of the Twenty-Fifth National Encampment, 1891* (Rutland, Vt.: Tuttle, 1891), 250.

84. Ibid., 254–55.

85. Ibid., 259, 262.

86. Ibid., 156–57.

87. *Christian Recorder,* 27 August 1891, 4.

88. Davies, "The Problem of Race Segregation in the Grand Army of the Republic," 365–66.

89. "The Encampment in 1892," *Washington Bee,* 10 October 1891, 2.

90. "Grand Army Encampment: The Right Sentiment," ibid., 14 May 1892, 1.

91. GAR, *Journal of the Twenty-Sixth National Encampment, 1892,* 53.

92. "In a Blaze of Glory," *Washington Evening Star,* 21 September 1892, 1.

CHAPTER 5
"OH, MY SISTERS!": SHIFTING RELATIONS OF GENDER AND RACE

1. Woman's Relief Corps (WRC), *Report of the National Organization, 1883 and Proceedings of the Second National Convention, 1884* (1884; reprint, Boston: Griffith-Stillings, 1903), 9, 11.

2. Woman's Relief Corps, Massachusetts Department Convention, *History of the Department of Massachusetts Woman's Relief Corps, Auxiliary to the Grand Army of the Republic, from Date of Organization, February 12, 1879, to January 1, 1895* (Boston: E. B. Stillings, 1895), 284–85, 312.

3. Geoff Eley and Ronald Grigor Suny, eds., *Becoming National: A Reader* (New York: Oxford University Press, 1996), 26–27.

4. My interpretation of gender and the WRC draws upon the insights of poststructuralist theory, cultural history, and social history. For a fuller discussion of debates between historians about these approaches, see

Barbara Melosh, ed., *Gender and American History since 1890* (London: Routledge, 1993), 3–8.

5. WRC, *Report of the National Organization, 1883 and Proceedings of the Second National Convention, 1884,* 9, 14–15.

6. "The Girl I Left Behind Me," Folklore Division, Library of Congress, Washington, D.C.

7. Linda K. Kerber, *Women of the Republic: Intellect and Ideology in Revolutionary America* (New York: Norton, 1980), 7–9.

8. Ruth H. Bloch, "The Gendered Meanings of Virtue in Revolutionary America," *Signs* 13 (fall 1987): 37–58.

9. Janet Montgomery Hooks, *Women's Occupations through Seven Decades,* Women's Bureau Bulletin 218 (Washington, D.C.: Government Printing Office, 1947), 10.

10. Anne Firor Scott, *Natural Allies: Women's Associations in American History* (Urbana: University of Illinois Press, 1991), 59–66.

11. Jeanie Attie, "Warwork and the Crisis of Domesticity in the North," in *Divided Houses: Gender and the Civil War,* ed. Catherine Clinton and Nina Silber (New York: Oxford University Press, 1992), 251.

12. Margaret Davis, *Mother Bickerdyke: Her Life and Labors for the Relief of Our Soldiers: Sketches of Battle Scenes and Incidents of the Sanitary Service* (San Francisco: A. T. Dewey, 1886), 32–33.

13. Hannah Ropes, *Civil War Nurse: The Diary and Letters of Hannah Ropes,* ed. and comp. John R. Brumgardt (Knoxville: University of Tennessee Press, 1980), 3, 112–13, 117.

14. Gerald F. Linderman, *Embattled Courage: The Experience of Combat in the American Civil War* (New York: Free Press, 1987), 311.

15. Woman's Relief Corps, Massachusetts Department Convention, *History of the Department of Massachusetts Woman's Relief Corps,* 283–84.

16. John Hope Franklin, *From Slavery to Freedom* (New York: Knopf, 1988), 171, 197.

17. Kathe Schick, "Lawrence Black Community," cited in Marilyn Dell Brady, "The Kansas Federation of Colored Women's Clubs, 1900–30," *Kansas History* 9 (spring 1986): 21.

18. Scott, *Natural Allies,* 67–68.

19. L. P. Brockett, M.D., and Mrs. Mary C. Vaughan, *Woman's Work in the Civil War: A Record of Heroism, Patriotism and Patience* (Philadelphia: Zeigler, McCurdy, 1867), 82, 86–87.

20. Ibid., 193–97.

21. WRC, *Journal of the Thirteenth Annual Convention, 1895* (Boston: E.B. Stillings, 1895), 42.

22. GAR, *Proceedings of the Thirteenth Annual Meeting of the National Encampment, 1879* (New York: Office of the Grand Army Gazette, 1879), 695.

23. WRC, *Journal of the Thirteenth Annual Convention, 1895*, 42.

24. WRC, *Report of the National Organization, 1883 and Proceedings of the Second National Convention, 1884*, 8, 12.

25. Mary Ann Clawson, *Constructing Brotherhood: Class, Gender, and Fraternalism* (Princeton: Princeton University Press, 1989), 187, 193–94, 200.

26. Davis, *Mother Bickerdyke*, 22–23.

27. WRC, *Report of the National Organization, 1883 and Proceedings of the Second National Convention, 1884*, 12–15.

28. Ibid.

29. WRC, *Journal of the Thirteenth Annual Convention, 1895*, 34; idem, *Journal of the Eighteenth National Convention, 1900* (Boston: E. B. Stillings, 1900), 333; idem, *Journal of the Twentieth National Convention, 1902* (Boston: Griffith-Stillings, 1902), 429.

30. See Denise Riley, *"Am I That Name?" Feminism and the Category of "Women" in History* (Minneapolis: University of Minnesota Press, 1988), 1–2; Joan Wallach Scott, *Gender and the Politics of History* (New York: Columbia University Press, 1988), 2, 4–5, 7, 10.

31. WRC, *Journal of the Ninth Annual Convention, 1891* (1891; facsim. reprint, Boston: Griffith-Stillings, 1911), 147, 328.

32. WRC, *Report of the National Organization, 1883, and Proceedings of the Second National Convention, 1884*, 10.

33. WRC, *Journal of the Fifth National Convention, 1887* (San Francisco: George Spaulding, 1887), 42–43.

34. WRC, *Journal of the Eighth Annual Convention, 1890* (Boston: E. B. Stillings, 1890), 36.

35. *The Spirit of '76* 2 (November 1895): 67.

36. Ellen Hardin Walworth, "The Origin of the National Society of the Daughters of the American Revolution," *American Monthly Magazine*, July–December 1893, 114–18.

37. Daughters of the American Revolution, *Third Report of the National Society of the Daughters of the American Revolution, October 11, 1889–1900*, 50th Cong., 2nd sess., 1901, S. Doc. 219, 45–46.

38. A chronicle of the DAR's work during the period under study can be found in their publication, *American Monthly Magazine*, 1893–1920.

39. Mollie Somerville, comp., *Washington Landmark* (Washington, D.C.: National Society, Daughters of the American Revolution, 1976), 98.

40. Janet E. Hosmer Richards, "The Great Objects of the Daughters of the American Revolution," *American Monthly Magazine*, December 1893, 492.

41. Gertrude Van Rensselaer Wickham, "The Mission of the Daughters of the American Revolution is that of Restoration, Preservation and Education," ibid., July 1893, 2.

42. DAR, *Third Report of the National Society of the Daughters of the American Revolution*, frontispiece and pp. 49, 46.

43. Martha Strayer, *The D.A.R.: An Informal History* (Washington, D.C.: Public Affairs Press, 1958), 32, 37.

44. President General Cornelia Fairbanks, quoted in "Proceedings of the Thirteenth Continental Congress," *American Monthly Magazine*, 1904, 86.

45. Harry A. Miller, "Patriotism," *American Monthly Magazine*, November 1903, 404–5.

46. "Work of the Daughters," ibid., May 1907, 630–31.

47. Hilary A. Herbert, *History of the Arlington Confederate Monument at Arlington, Virginia* (n.p.: United Daughters of the Confederacy, 1914), 22–23.

48. Ibid., 17–12.

49. Catherine Hall, *White, Male, and Middle Class: Explorations in Feminism and History* (Cambridge: Polity Press, 1992), 207.

50. Clawson, *Constructing Brotherhood*, 131–32.

51. WRC, *Journal of the Ninth Annual Convention, 1891*, 53.

52. WRC, *Journal of the Eighth Annual Convention, 1890*, 26.

53. WRC, *Journal of the Fifteenth National Convention, 1897* (Boston: E.B. Stillings, 1897), 322; idem, *Journal of the Eighteenth National Convention, 1900*, 293.

54. WRC, *Journal of the Eighth Annual Convention, 1890*, 262–63.

55. Wallace Evan Davies, "The Problem of Race Segregation in the Grand Army of the Republic," *Journal of Southern History* 13 (August 1947): 354–72.

56. For a discussion of Northern teachers who went south to instruct freedmen during Reconstruction, see Jacqueline Jones, *Soldiers of Light and Love: Northern Teachers and Georgia Blacks, 1865–1873* (Athens, Ga.: Brown Thrasher Books, 1980), 49–50, 68–69, 110.

57. WRC, *Journal of the Tenth Annual Convention, 1892* (Boston: E. B. Stillings, 1892), 59.

58. WRC, *Journal of the Fifteenth National Convention, 1897*, 320–23.

59. "Women," *Washington Bee,* 14 June 1913; "Women's Good Work," ibid., 15 March 1902; "Negroes Persecuted," ibid., 29 November 1913.

60. WRC, *Journal of the Fifteenth National Convention, 1897,* 323–25.

61. Ibid.

62. Ibid., 326–27.

63. Ibid., 329–30.

64. WRC, *Journal of the Eighteenth National Convention, 1900,* 51, 58.

65. Ibid., 294–95.

66. Ibid., 51, 297.

67. WRC, *Journal of the Twenty-Second National Convention, 1904* (Boston: Griffith-Stillings, 1904), 136.

68. For a fuller discussion of the exclusion of black women from the suffrage movement, see Robert Allen in collaboration with Pamela P. Allen, *Reluctant Reformers: Racism and Social Reform Movements in the United States* (Washington, D.C.: Howard University Press, 1983), 153–56. For an analysis of the role of the Republican Party in driving a wedge between women abolitionists and suffrage proponents, see Ellen Carol DuBois, *Feminism and Suffrage: The Emergence of an Independent Women's Movement in America, 1848–1869* (Ithaca: Cornell University Press, 1978).

69. WRC, *Journal of the Twenty-Fourth National Convention, 1906* (Boston: Griffith-Stillings, 1906), 80, 297, 299, 300.

70. WRC, *Journal of the Eleventh Annual Convention, 1893* (Boston: E. B. Stillings, 1893), 252–54, 284.

71. WRC, *Journal of the Twenty-Fifth National Convention, 1907* (Boston: Griffith-Stillings, 1907), 117.

72. WRC, *Roll of Members, Address of National President and Report of Officers of the Twenty-Ninth National Convention, 1911* (Boston: Griffith-Stillings, 1911), 141, 173.

73. Nell Irvin Painter, *Standing at Armageddon: The United States, 1877–1919* (New York: Norton, 1987), 8, 164.

74. WRC, *Roll of Members, Address of National President and Report of Officers of the Twenty-Ninth National Convention, 1911,* 425–27, 170.

CHAPTER 6
"MOTHERS TRAIN THE MASSES—STATESMEN LEAD THE FEW": WOMEN'S PLACE IN SHAPING THE NATION

1. During the nineteenth century, women typically chose to use the singular term *woman* in describing their movement. In this book, however, I use the contemporary designation *women's movement.*

2. For a discussion of women's multiple relations to the nation-state, see Floya Anthias and Nira Yuval-Davis, eds., *Woman-Nation-State* (New York: St. Martin's, 1989), 6–7.

3. Linda K. Kerber, *Women of the Republic: Intellect and Ideology in Revolutionary America* (New York: Norton, 1980), 35, 106, 110–11.

4. WRC, *Journal of the Twenty-Seventh National Convention, 1909* (Boston: Griffith-Stillings, 1909), 171.

5. Throughout this chapter I draw on issues and questions raised by Shelia Rowbotham in "Nationalist Movements and Women's Place," in *Women in Movement: Feminism and Social Action* (New York: Routledge, 1992), 102–13.

6. WRC, *Proceedings of the Fourth National Convention, 1886* (Boston: E.B. Stillings, 1886), 20–21; idem, *Journal of the Eighth Annual Convention, 1890* (Boston: E. B. Stillings, 1890), 23; idem, *Report of the National Organization, 1883 and Proceedings of the Second National Convention, 1884* (1884; reprint, Boston: Griffith-Stillings, 1903), 29.

7. WRC, *Proceedings of the Third National Convention, 1885* (1885; reprint, Boston: Griffith-Stillings, 1908), 4.

8. WRC, *Journal of the Eighth Annual Convention, 1890,* 24.

9. Louise A. Tilly and Patricia Gurin, eds., *Women, Politics, and Change* (New York: Russell Sage Foundation, 1990), 19–20, 24.

10. WRC, *Journal of the Sixteenth National Convention, 1898* (1898; reprint, Boston: Griffith-Stillings, 1911), 156.

11. WRC, *Journal of the Tenth Annual Convention, 1892* (Boston: E. B. Stillings, 1892), 33.

12. WRC, *Journal of the Eleventh Annual Convention, 1893* (Boston: E. B. Stillings, 1893), 35.

13. WRC, *Journal of the Twenty-Seventh National Convention, 1909,* 237–38.

14. WRC, *Journal of the Eleventh Annual Convention, 1893,* 203–7, 210–11.

15. WRC, *Journal of the Twelfth Annual Convention, 1894* (Boston: E. B. Stillings, 1894), 39.

16. The DAR joined preparedness forces during World War I and in the 1920s allied with the American Legion in attacking pacifists for "paving the way for Red revolution." For a fuller description of the role of right-wing women in forcing the NCW to disavow groups such as the Women's International League for Peace and Freedom, see Nancy F. Cott, *The Grounding of Modern Feminism* (New Haven: Yale University Press, 1987), 254–57.

17. "The First Hague Conference, 1899," in *The Eagle and the Dove: The American Peace Movement and Unites States Foreign Policy, 1900–1922,* ed. John Whiteclay Chambers II (New York: Garland, 1976), 87–93.

18. Julia Ward Howe, "The Message of Peace," in WRC, *Roll of Members, Address of National President and Report of the Officers of the Twenty-Ninth National Convention, 1911* (Boston: Griffith-Stillings, 1911), 195.

19. Ibid., 193–95.

20. WRC, *Journal of the Thirteenth Annual Convention, 1895* (Boston: E.B. Stillings, 1895), 160.

21. WRC, *Journal of the Eighth Annual Convention, 1890,* 24.

22. WRC, *Journal of the Thirteenth Annual Convention, 1895,* 35, 156–57.

23. Ibid., 158.

24. WRC, *Journal of the Sixteenth National Convention, 1898,* 59.

25. WRC, *Journal of the Thirty-Fourth National Convention, 1916* (Washington, D.C.: National Tribune, 1916), 103.

26. WRC, *Journal of the Twenty-Fifth National Convention, 1907* (Boston: Griffith-Stillings, 1907), 93.

27. WRC, *Proceedings of the Fourth National Convention, 1886,* 131, 153–54.

28. On the new feminism, see Cott, *Grounding of Modern Feminism,* 13–50.

29. WRC, *Journal of the Tenth Annual Convention, 1892,* 55.

30. Eric Hobsbawm, "Mass-Producing Traditions: Europe, 1870–1914," in *The Invention of Tradition,* ed. Eric Hobsbawm and Terence Ranger (1983; reprint, Cambridge: Cambridge University Press, 1988), 279.

31. The first national observation of Memorial Day took place on 30 May 1868. General Ulysses S. Grant attended the ceremony at the National Cemetery at Arlington, Virginia. New York became the first state to make Memorial Day into a legal holiday, in 1873. By 1890 it was a legal holiday in most of the Northern states. In 1968, President Lyndon B. Johnson signed legislation that shifted the observance of Memorial Day and other holidays to enable Americans to have an increased number of three-day weekends. By 1971 most states had implemented the schedule of making Memorial Day the last Monday of May (Jane M. Hatch, comp. and ed., *The American Book of Days,* 3rd ed. [New York: H. W. Wilson, 1978], 502–3).

32. G. Kurt Piehler, *Remembering War the American Way* (Washington, D.C.: Smithsonian Institution Press, 1995), 49–51.

33. WRC, *Proceedings of the Third National Convention, 1885,* 206.

34. E.g., a sentimental image of a widow and children in St. Louis in the 1870s, photo US262-63576, Prints and Photographs, LC.

35. WRC, *Journal of the Fifteenth National Convention, 1897* (Boston: E. B. Stillings, 1897), 227.

36. Gerald F. Linderman, *Embattled Courage: The Experience of Combat in the American Civil War* (New York: Free Press, 1987), 30.

37. Mary A. Livermore, *My Story of the War: A Woman's Narrative of Four Years Personal Experience.* . . . (Hartford, Conn.: A. D. Worthington, 1889), 192.

38. WRC, *Journal of the Eighteenth National Convention, 1900* (Boston: E. B. Stillings, 1900), 7.

39. WRC, *Journal of the Thirteenth Annual Convention, 1895*, 37.

40. WRC, *Journal of the Twelfth Annual Convention, 1894*, 320.

41. LeeAnn Whites, "The Civil War as a Crisis in Gender," in *Divided Houses: Gender and the Civil War*, ed. Catherine Clinton and Nine Silber (New York: Oxford University Press, 1992), 9–10, 16–17.

42. Mrs. Geo. T. Fry, "Memorial Day—Its Origin," *Confederate Veteran* 1 (May 1893): 149.

43. Eric Foner and Olivia Mahoney, exhibit curators, *America's Reconstruction: People and Politics After the Civil War*, exhibit at the Virginia Historical Society, Richmond, Virginia, spring 1996.

44. LeeAnn Whites, *The Civil War as a Crisis in Gender: Augusta, Georgia, 1860–1890* (Athens: University of Georgia Press, 1995), 13, 183–84.

45. Wallace Evan Davies, while crediting the South with creating the rituals associated with Memorial Day, proposes a different version of how Logan learned of the custom. According to Davies, the then GAR Commander-in-Chief Logan and his wife were first introduced to the practice on a trip to Richmond in the spring of 1868 (*Patriotism on Parade: The Story of Veterans' and Hereditary Organizations in America, 1783–1900* [Cambridge: Harvard University Press, 1955], 217).

46. George William Douglas, *The American Book of Days* (New York: H. W. Wilson, 1937), 230.

47. GAR, *Journal of the Fifteenth Annual Session of the National Encampment, 1881* (Philadelphia: Merrihew & Lippert, 1881), 753.

48. WRC, *Report of the National Organization, 1883 and Proceedings of the Second National Convention, 1884*, 17.

49. WRC, *Journal of the Nineteenth National Convention, 1901* (Boston: E. B. Stillings, 1901), 117–18.

50. Joseph Edwin Roy, "Letter LXIX, The National Cemeteries at the South, Atlanta, GA., May 30, 1880," in *Pilgrim's Letters: Bits of Current History* (Boston: Congregational Sunday School and Publishing Society, 1888), 187–88.

51. WRC, *Journal of the Twenty-Seventh National Convention, 1909*, 240.

52. WRC, *Journal of the Fifth National Convention, 1887* (San Francisco: George Spaulding, 1887), 33.

53. WRC, *Journal of the Ninth Annual Convention, 1891* (1891; facsim. reprint, Boston: Griffith-Stillings, 1911), 98.

54. WRC, *Proceedings of the Third National Convention, 1885*, 103, 111.

55. WRC, *Journal of the Twentieth National Convention, 1902* (Boston: Griffith-Stillings, 1902), 55.

56. WRC, *Proceedings of the Third National Convention, 1885*, 57.

57. WRC, *Journal of the Thirty-Second National Convention, 1914* (Boston: Griffith-Stillings, 1914), 69; idem, *Journal of the Twenty-Seventh National Convention, 1909*, 239.

58. Michael Zuckerman, "The Rising Generation in the Young Republic," in *Red, White, and Blue: Childhood and Citizenship*, ed. Morris J. Vogel (Philadelphia: Please Touch Museum, 1987), 7. The quotation is from a personal communication from Edward T. Linenthal in 1997.

59. WRC, *Proceedings of the Third National Convention, 1885*, 106–7, 113.

60. WRC, *Journal of the Ninth Annual Convention, 1891*, 92.

61. WRC, *Proceedings of the Fourth National Convention, 1886*, 64.

62. WRC, *Journal of the Eighth Annual Convention, 1890*, 229.

63. David W. Blight, " 'For Something beyond the Battlefield': Frederick Douglass and the Struggle for the Memory of the Civil War," *Journal of American History* 75 (September 1988): 1156–78.

64. WRC, *Journal of the Sixteenth National Convention, 1898*, 111.

65. Benedict Anderson, *Imagined Communities: Reflections on the Origin and Spread of Nationalism*, rev. ed. (London: Verso, 1991), 7.

66. The potentially powerful antiwar symbolism that could be associated with Memorial Day is dramatically captured in a scene from the 1976 book *Friendly Fire*. The father, a heartland farmer who is coming to believe that the government has allowed his son to die in an unjustified war in Viet Nam, goes to the cemetery on Memorial Day as the "Boy Scouts and Girl Scouts . . . and Women's Relief Corps . . . began assembling outside the American Legion Hall." In a quiet but profound act of protest, he removes the small U.S. flag that had been placed on his son's grave (C. D. B. Bryan, *Friendly Fire* [New York: Bantam Books, 1976], 163).

CHAPTER 7
"ONE COUNTRY, ONE FLAG, ONE PEOPLE, ONE DESTINY":
REGIONS, RACE, AND NATIONHOOD

1. Thomas Wentworth Higginson, *Army Life in a Black Regiment* (Boston: Fields, Osgood, 1870), 40.

2. Henry McNeal Turner, "On the Anniversary of Emancipation, 1866," in *Respect Black: The Writings and Speeches of Henry McNeal Turner,* comp. Edwin S. Redkey (New York: Arno Press and The New York Times, 1971), 7, 11. The article originally appeared in the *Augusta Colored American,* 13 January 1866.

3. Leon F. Litwack, "How Free Is Free?" in *Been in the Storm So Long: The Aftermath of Slavery* (New York: Knopf, 1979), 240–317; idem, "The Historian, the Filmmaker, and the Civil War," in *Ken Burn's The Civil War: Historians Respond,* ed. Robert Brent Toplin (New York: Oxford University Press, 1996), 131.

4. Leonard I. Sweet, *Black Images of America, 1784–1870* (New York: Norton, 1976), 1–5.

5. Nathaniel Paul to William Lloyd Garrison, *Liberator,* 12 April 1834, in *The Mind of the Negro as Reflected in Letters during the Crisis, 1800–1860,* ed. Carter G. Woodson (Washington, D.C.: Association of the Study of Negro Life and History, 1926), 170.

6. *Equal Suffrage: Address from the Colored Citizens of Norfolk, VA., to the People of the United States* (New Bedford, Mass.: E. Anthony & Sons, Printers, 1865); reprinted in Afro-American Series, ed. Maxwell Whiteman, Rhistoric Publication No. 216 (Philadelphia: Rhistoric Publications, 1969), 2, 8.

7. Quoted in Eric Foner, *Reconstruction: America's Unfinished Revolution, 1863–1877* (New York: Harper & Row, 1988), 115.

8. John Bodnar, "Introduction: The Attractions of Patriotism," in *Bonds of Affection: Americans Define Their Patriotism* (Princeton: Princeton University Press, 1996), 14.

9. Frederick Douglass, "January First, 1863," *Douglass' Monthly* (Rochester, N.Y.), January 1863, 769–70.

10. Frederick Douglass, "What to the Slave is the Fourth of July?" extract from an oration at Rochester, 5 July 1852, in *Frederick Douglass: Autobiographies* (New York: Library of America, 1994), 431.

11. William H. Wiggins Jr., *O Freedom! Afro-American Emancipation Celebrations* (Knoxville: University of Tennessee Press, 1987), xi, xix–xx, 34–35, 46–47, 81–82, 93–95. For a comparative discussion of "bodily prac-

tices" in revolutionary France, see Paul Connerton, *How Societies Remember* (New York: Cambridge University Press, 1989), 10–11.

12. Jacob Schirmer, Diary, 4 July 1867, 4 July 1872, in Foner, *Reconstruction*, 289.

13. Foner, *Reconstruction*, 289, 290.

14. *Sumter True Southron*, July 1876, quoted in Carter G. Woodson, *The Negro in Our History* (Washington, D.C.: Associated Publishers, 1922), 415–16.

15. *Weekly Clarion: Official Journal of the State of Mississippi*, 6, 26 July 1876.

16. *Daily Critic* (Washington, D.C.), 19, 20 July 1876.

17. Michael Kammen, *Mystic Chords of Memory: The Transformation of Tradition in American Culture* (1991; reprint, New York: Vintage Books, 1993), 121.

18. Reports of black communities celebrating July Fourth are virtually absent from black newspapers (see the Black Press Archives, Moorland-Spingarn Research Center, Howard University, Washington, D.C.).

19. Ellie Fisher, quoted in William H. Wiggins, "Juneteenth: 'They Closed the Town Up, Man!' " *American Visions: The Magazine of Afro-American Culture* 1 (May/June 1986): 41.

20. Henry W. Grady, "In Black and White: A Reply to Mr. Cable," *Century Magazine* 29 (April 1885): 911.

21. "Bishop Turner on the Civil Rights," *Christian Recorder*, 8 November 1883, 1.

22. Benjamin T. Tanner, "The Recent Supreme Court Decision," ibid., 15 November 1883, 2.

23. August Meier, *Negro Thought in America, 1880–1915: Racial Ideologies in the Age of Booker T. Washington*, rev. ed. (Ann Arbor: University of Michigan Press, 1973), 162.

24. Wm. H. Rowan to Thomas L. Jones (congressman from Kentucky), 9 July 1876, *Daily Critic*, 18 July 1876.

25. Russell F. Weigley, *The American Way of War: A History of the United States Military Strategy and Policy* (New York: Macmillan, 1973), 158–62.

26. Although it is impossible to document because official records are lacking, most military historians agree that former Confederate officers and privates served among the enlisted men during the Indian wars.

27. Clell T. Peterson, "Charles King: Soldier and Novelist," *American Book Collector* 15 (December 1965): 9–10.

28. Professor Larry Toll, Brewton-Parker College, Mount Vernon, Ga., phone interview with author, April 1993.

29. John Ford, *Rio Grande* (Hollywood: Argosy-Republic, 1950).

30. John Ford, *She Wore a Yellow Ribbon* (Hollywood: Argosy-RKO, 1949).

31. Russell F. Weigley, *Towards an American Army: Military Thought from Washington to Marshall* (New York: Columbia University Press, 1962), 127–28.

32. John Logan, "The Dangerous West Point Monopoly," in *The American Military: Readings in the History of the Military in American Society*, ed. Russell F. Weigley (Menlo Park: Addison-Wesley, 1969), 77.

33. Bvt. Maj. Gen. Emory Upton, Unites States Army, *The Military Policy of the United States*, 64th Cong., 1st sess., 1916, S. Doc. 379, 4th imp. (Washington, D.C.: Government Printing Office, 1916), ix, xi.

34. Horace Porter, "Grant's Last Campaign," *Century Magazine* 35 (November 1887): 145–47.

35. Ibid., 148–52.

36. General Grant, quoted in ibid., 150.

37. Stephen Davis, "A Matter of Sensational Interest: The Century Battles and Leaders Series," *Civil War History: A Journal of the Middle Period* 28 (December 1981): 338–43.

38. Richard Wentworth Browne, "Union War Songs and Confederate Officers," *Century Magazine* 35 (January 1888): 478.

39. Graphics from the magazine series can be seen in The Century, *Battles and Leaders of the Civil War: The Century War Book, People's Pictorial Edition*, pts. 1–10 (New York, 1894).

40. See the front-page graphic from *Frank Leslie's Illustrated Newspaper* (New York), 3 June 1865.

41. For popular lithographs of Jefferson Davis's capture, see *American Caricatures Pertaining to the Civil War: Reproduced from the Original Lithographs Published from 1856 to 1872* (New York: Brentanos, 1918).

42. Nina Silber, *The Romance of Reunion: Northerners and the South, 1865–1900* (Chapel Hill: University of North Carolina Press, 1993), 28–38.

43. *Jeff in Petticoats* (Chatham, N.Y.: H. De Marsan, n.d.), song sheet, Virginia Historical Society, Richmond, Va.

44. "Soldier and Citizen," *Century Magazine* 30 (October 1887): 950; "Let Us Have Peace!" ibid. 29 (February 1885): 638.

45. "Old Questions and New," *Century Illustrated Monthly Magazine* 29 (January 1885): 471–72.

46. "North and South," *Century Magazine* 30 (October 1885): 965.

47. Col. John A. Cutchins, *Famous Command: The Richmond Light Infantry Blues* (Richmond, Va.: Garret & Massie, 1934), 199.

48. Stuart McConnell, *Glorious Contentment: The Grand Army of the Republic, 1865–1900* (Chapel Hill: University of North Carolina Press, 1992), 192.

49. GAR, *Proceedings of the Thirteenth Annual Meeting of the National Encampment, 1879* (New York: Office of the Grand Army Gazette, 1879), 598.

50. Gaines M. Foster, *Ghosts of the Confederacy: Defeat, the Lost Cause, and the Emergence of the New South* (New York: Oxford University Press, 1987), 36–37, 55, 5, 61.

51. Ibid., 57, 47–62.

52. Ibid., 112, 108, 80.

53. Richmond, Va., real-estate map and *The Official Souvenir of the Dedication of the Monument to General Robert E. Lee* (Richmond: R. Newton Moon., n.d.), both in Richmond Archives, The Valentine: The Museum of the Life and History of Richmond, Virginia.

54. Foster, *Ghosts of the Confederacy*, 86–87.

55. "The Confederate Flag," *Confederate Veteran* 3 (December 1895): 353.

56. Quoted in ibid., 139.

57. "A Question of 'Offense,' " *National Tribune* (Washington, D.C.), 23 June 1887.

58. "The Lost Cause," ibid., 18 June 1883.

59. "The Confederate Flag Was Everywhere Conspicuously Displayed," *Harper's Weekly*, June 1890.

60. Robert Beverley Munford Jr., *Richmond Homes and Memories* (Richmond, Va.: Garrett & Massie, 1936), 45.

61. Quoted in Foster, *Ghosts of the Confederacy*, 100.

62. "Thro' Richmond's Streets They Marched Again," *New York Herald*, 30 May 1890.

63. Foster, *Ghosts of the Confederacy*, 98–103.

64. Today, tens of thousands of Southerners keep Confederate traditions alive through yearly reenactments of Civil War campaigns.

65. Tucker Hill, *Victory in Defeat: Jefferson Davis and the Lost Cause* (Richmond, Va.: Museum of the Confederacy, 1865), 6–7; *Monuments to the Dead* (n.p.: United Daughters of the Confederacy, 1914), in "Historical Records of the United Daughters of the Confederacy, Scrapbooks," comp. Mildred Lewis Rutherford, scrapbook 8, Historical Records and Scrapbooks, Museum of the Confederacy, Richmond, Va.

66. James M. Goode, *The Outdoor Sculpture of Washington: A Comprehensive Historical Guide* (Washington, D.C.: Smithsonian Institution Press, 1974), 214.

67. "The Heart of America," *Confederate Veteran* 3 (December 1895): 354–55.

68. "Our Worst Enemies," *National Tribune*, 13 January 1887.

69. "The Yank and the Reb," *Confederate Veteran* 7 (June 1899): 353.

70. Political cartoon from *Puck*, n.d., Photographic Files, Political Division, NMAH.

71. GAR, *Journal of the Twenty-Sixth National Encampment, 1892* (Albany, N.Y.: S. H. Wentworth, 1892), 213–14.

72. GAR, *Journal of the Thirty-First National Encampment, 1897* (Lincoln, Nebr.: State Journal Company, 1897), 55.

CHAPTER 8
"BLOOD BROTHERHOOD": THE RACIALIZATION OF PATRIOTISM

1. Frederick Douglass, "Address at the Grave of the Unknown Dead," Arlington, Virginia, 30 May 1871, Frederick Douglass Papers, reel 14, Manuscript Division, Library of Congress, Washington, D.C. (hereafter cited as Douglass Papers, LC).

2. Frederick Douglass, "Speech in Madison Square," New York, Decoration Day, 1878, reel 15, Douglass Papers, LC.

3. Christian A. Fleetwood, "Speech given on August 2, 1894," Papers of Christian Fleetwood, reel 1, Manuscript Division, Library of Congress, Washington, D.C.

4. GAR, *Journal of the Twenty-Sixth Annual Session, 1892* (Albany, N.Y.: S. H. Wentworth, 1892), 207.

5. Bessie Louise Pierce, *Public Opinion and the Teaching of History in the United States* (New York: Knopf, 1926), 149.

6. GAR, *Journal of the Thirty-Sixth National Encampment, 1902* (Minneapolis: Kimball Stofer, 1902), 252–53.

7. Woodrow Wilson to Richard Heath Dabney, 7 November 1886, quoted in *That Noble Dream: "The Objectivity Question" and the American Historical Profession*, by Peter Novick (Cambridge: Cambridge University Press, 1988), 78.

8. Pierce, *Public Opinion and the Teaching of History*, 13, 14–16.

9. "Patriotic School Histories," *Confederate Veteran* 5 (September 1897): 450, 146.

10. Pierce, *Public Opinion and the Teaching of History*, 136–37.

11. Fred Arthur Bailey, "Textbooks of the 'Lost Cause': Censorship and the Creation of Southern State Histories," *Georgia Historical Quarterly* 75 (fall 1991): 508–11.

12. Pierce, *Public Opinion and the Teaching of History,* 163.

13. UDC, Constitution of the United Daughters of the Confederacy, 1903, Virginia State Library and Archives, Richmond, Va.

14. Novick, *That Noble Dream,* 74–78; Ernst Breisach, *Historiography: Ancient, Medieval, and Modern* (Chicago: University of Chicago Press, 1983), 261.

15. Woodrow Wilson, *A History of the American People* (New York: Harper & Brothers, 1902), 4:271, 312, and 5:46, 60, 115–16.

16. John Burgess, *Reconstruction and the Constitution* (New York: Charles Scribner's Sons, 1902), 297–98.

17. W. E. B. Du Bois, *Black Reconstruction in America: An Essay Toward a History of the Part Which Black Folk Played in the Attempt to Reconstruct Democracy in America, 1860–1880* (1935; reprint, New York: Atheneum, 1970), 714.

18. GAR, *Journal of the Thirty-Eighth National Encampment, 1904* (Chicago: M. Umbdenstock, 1904), 67.

19. United Confederate Veterans, *Minutes of the Twentieth Annual Meeting and Reunion of the United Confederate Veterans, 1910* (New Orleans: Schumert & Warfield, 1910), 101.

20. Pierce, *Public Opinion and the Teaching of History,* 155–64.

21. WRC, *Journal of the Fifteenth National Convention, 1897* (Boston: E.B. Stillings, 1897), 373.

22. David W. Blight, "The Strange Meaning of Being Black: Du Bois' American Tragedy," in *The Souls of Black Folk by W. E. B. Du Bois,* ed. David W. Blight and Robert Gooding-Williams (Boston: Bedford Books, 1997), vii, 4.

23. W. E. B. Du Bois, *The Souls of Black Folk* (1903; reprint, New York: Knopf, Everyman's Library, 1993), 16, 28–29.

24. Blight, "Strange Meaning of Being Black," 14–15.

25. Richard White, "Civil Rights Agitation: Emancipation Days in Central New York in the 1880s," *Journal of Negro History* 78 (winter 1993): 16.

26. Very little information exists from the contemporary national press on the activities of black GAR and WRC members. In my review of the black press, however, I found repeated mention of black posts having meetings, calling for the observance of Emancipation Day, and marching on Memorial Day. See, e.g., "Our Emancipation Day: Its Celebration Proposed," *New York Freeman,* 13 December 1884; "Emancipation Day: Calli-

ous Post—Major Palmer," ibid., 20 December 1884; "Emancipation Day: Celebrating in a Rain Storm," ibid., 10 January 1885; "Emancipation Celebration," ibid., 9 January 1886; "The Battle of Antietam," ibid., 25 September 1886; and "Tramp of Veterans," *Washington Evening Star,* 25 August 1897, 1.

27. John R. Gillis, ed., *Commemorations: The Politics of National Identity* (Princeton: Princeton University Press, 1994), 10.

28. George Henry Preble, *Our Flag: Origin and Progress of the Flag of the United States of America* (Albany: Joel Munsell, 1872), 37.

29. GAR, *Journal of the Thirty-Second National Encampment, 1898* (Philadelphia: Town Printing, 1898), 49–50; "The Rebel Flags," *National Tribune* (Washington, D.C.), 23 June 1887.

30. Captain Carlton McCarthy, quoted in *The Embattled Emblem,* exhibit, summer 1993, Museum of the Confederacy, Richmond, Virginia.

31. "The Confederate Flag," *Confederate Veteran* 3 (December 1895): 353–54.

32. Father Abram J. Ryan, "The Conquered Banner," ibid., supplement to souvenir issue 42 (April 1894).

33. GAR, *Journal of the Thirty-Second National Encampment, 1898,* 49.

34. *Confederate Veteran* 7 (June 1899): 246, 255–56.

35. Gaines M. Foster, *Ghosts of the Confederacy: Defeat, the Lost Cause, and the Emergence of the New South* (New York: Oxford University Press, 1987), 154.

36. Gerald F. Linderman, *The Mirror of War: American Society and the Spanish-American War* (Ann Arbor: University of Michigan Press, 1974), 93.

37. Carl Sandburg, *Always the Young Strangers* (New York: Harcourt, Brace, 1952), 409.

38. Frederick Jackson Turner, "The Significance of the Frontier in American History," in *The Frontier in American History* (1893; reprint, New York: Henry Holt, 1958), 1–4.

39. Richard Slotkin, *Gunfighter Nation: The Myth of the Frontier in Twentieth-Century America* (New York: Atheneum, 1992), 334–35, 58, 61, 77, 83.

40. Theodore Roosevelt to Henry White, 30 April 1897, in *The Letters of Theodore Roosevelt,* ed. Elting E. Morison, 8 vols. (Cambridge: Harvard University Press, 1951–54), 1:606.

41. Linderman, *Mirror of War,* 34, 154–55.

42. *New York Journal,* 1 May 1898.

43. Graham A. Cosmas, *An Army for Empire: The United States Army in the Spanish-American War* (Columbia: University of Missouri Press, 1971), 93–94.

44. Ibid., 93, 149.

45. Office of the Adjutant-General of the Army, *Correspondence Relating to the War with Spain and Conditions Growing out of the Same Including the China Relief Expedition, between the Adjutant-Generals of the Army and Military Commanders in the United States, Cuba, Porto Rico, China, and the Philippine Islands, from April 15, 1898, to July 30, 1902*, vol. 1 (Washington, D.C.: Government Printing Office, 1902), 583–87.

46. Theodore Roosevelt, *The Rough Riders* (New York: Scribner's Sons, 1902), 20–21, 32.

47. Richard Slotkin, "Nostalgia and Progress: Theodore Roosevelt's Myth of the Frontier," *American Quarterly* 33 (winter 1981): 635.

48. Office of the Adjutant-General of the Army, *Correspondence Relating to the War with Spain*, 509–49.

49. D. D. Christian and W. Asbury, *Richmond and Her Past* (1912; reprint, Spartanburg, S.C.: The Reprint Company, 1973), 458–60; "The Richmond Blues—The American-Spanish War—1898, Jacksonville, Fla.," in Photographic Files, The Valentine: The Museum of the Life and History of Richmond, Virginia.

50. Leonard Wood and Theodore Roosevelt, quoted in David F. Trask, *The War with Spain in 1898* (New York: Macmillan, 1981), 181.

51. Office of the Adjutant-General of the Army, *Correspondence Relating to the War with Spain*, 538–39.

52. Hon. James Rankin Young, comp., *Reminiscences and Thrilling Stories of the War by Returned Heroes Containing Vivid Accounts of Personal Experiences by Officers and Men* (Chicago: C. W. Stanton, 1899), 531.

53. *New York Journal*, 2 May 1898, 1.

54. James Crawford, "The Warriors of Civilization: U.S. Soldiers, American Culture, and White Supremacy, 1898–1902" (paper presented at the annual meeting of the Organization of American Historians, Washington, D.C., April 1995).

55. Stuart Creighton Miller, "The American Soldier and the Conquest of the Philippines," in *Reappraising an Empire: New Perspectives on Philippine-American History*, ed. Peter W. Stanley (Cambridge: Committee on American–East Asian Relations of the Department of History in collaboration with the Council on East Asian Studies, Harvard University, 1984), 13–14, 19–20, 34.

56. Robert L. Beisner, *Twelve against Empire: The Anti-Imperialists, 1898–1900* (New York: McGraw-Hill, 1968), 219.

57. Slotkin, *Gunfighter Nation*, 85–87.

58. Gail Bederman, *Manliness and Civilization: A Cultural History of Gender and Race in the United States, 1880–1917* (Chicago: University of Chicago Press, 1995), 171, 184–87, 198–99, 214.

59. GAR, *Journal of the Thirty-Second National Encampment, 1898*, 193.

60. WRC, *Journal of the Sixteenth National Convention, 1898* (1898; reprint, Boston: Griffith-Stillings Press, 1911), 111–13.

61. Ibid., 216–17, 288–89.

62. Albert J. Beveridge, "Senator Albert J. Beveridge's Salute to Imperialism, 1900," in *Major Problems in American Foreign Policy: Documents and Essays*, ed. Thomas G. Paterson, vol. 1 (Lexington: Heath, 1989), 389–91.

63. Amy Kaplan, "Romancing the Empire: The Embodiment of American Masculinity in the Popular Historical Novel of the 1890s," *American Literary History* 3 (December 1990): 559, 662.

64. "Confederates Commanding U.S. Regiments," *Confederate Veteran* 6 (August 1898): 365–67.

65. Rudyard Kipling, "The White Man's Burden," *McClure's Magazine* 12 (Feb. 1899), http://www.accinet.net/~fjzwick/kipling/kipling.html, in *Anti-Imperialism in the United States, 1898–1935*, ed. Jim Zwick, Syracuse University [created 15 March 1995; updated 11 Jan. 1998].

66. Hon. J. S. Durham, "Emancipation Address," *Christian Recorder*, 10 January 1901, p. 3.

67. Willard B. Gatewood Jr., comp., *"Smoked Yankees" and the Struggle for Empire: Letters from Negro Soldiers, 1898–1902* (Fayetteville: University of Arkansas Press, 1987), 44–45; George W. Prioleau, Ninth Cavalry, to the *Cleveland Gazette*, 22 October 1898, reprinted in ibid.

68. GAR, *Journal of the Forty-Second National Encampment, 1908* (Kansas City: John C. Bovard, 1908), 169.

69. "The '98 Decoration at Camp Chase," *Confederate Veteran* 6 (August 1898): 263.

70. Wallace Evan Davies, *Patriotism on Parade: The Story of Veterans' and Hereditary Organizations in America, 1783–1900* (Cambridge: Harvard University Press, 1955), 267–72; Stuart McConnell, *Glorious Contentment: The Grand Army of the Republic, 1865–1900* (Chapel Hill: University of North Carolina Press, 1992), 181, 213–18.

71. U.S. Department of Interior, National Park Service, National Register of Historic Places Inventory—Nomination Form, "Chickamauga-

Chattanooga National Military Park," structure #776, Kentucky State Monument, 1.

72. Douglass, Frederick, "The Freedmen's Monument to Abraham Lincoln," in *The Frederick Douglass Papers*, vol. 4, 1864–80, eds. John W. Blassingame and John R. McKivigan (New Haven: Yale University Press, 1991), 428.

73. Foster, *Ghosts of the Confederacy*, 153–54.

74. James Edward Peters, *Arlington National Cemetery: Shrine to America's Heroes* (n.p.: Woodbine House, 1986), 250–53.

75. GAR, *Journal of the Fortieth National Encampment, 1906* (Philadelphia: Town Printing, 1906), 97.

76. Abraham Lincoln, quoted in ibid.

77. GAR, *Journal of the Forty-Fourth National Encampment, 1910* (Atlantic City, N.J.: n.p., 1910), 66–67.

78. GAR, *Journal of the Fortieth National Encampment, 1906*, 98–99.

79. This analysis draws upon Anne McClintock, *Imperial Leather: Race, Gender and Sexuality in the Colonial Contest* (New York: Routledge, 1995).

80. Graphic on cover of Jos. J. Kaiser, "March American Heroes" (New York: Jos. J. Kaiser Music Co., 1904), Warshaw Collection, NMAH.

81. My interpretation of Beadle's Half Dime Library is based on a phone interview with Professor James Evans, of the University of Texas, in March 1993. For an example of Prentiss Ingraham's nickel novels, see *Buck Taylor: The Comanche Captive, Beadle's Half Dime Library* 39, no. 737 (September 1891).

82. Alexander Saxton, *The Rise and Fall of the White Republic: Class Politics and Mass Culture in Nineteenth-Century America* (London: Verso, 1990), 229–330.

83. Annin & Co., *Annin & Co., Makers of Fine Flags* (New York, 1912), 161, 169, 226–27, 40–41, Political Division, NMAH.

84. GAR, *Journal of the Twenty-Sixth National Encampment, 1892*, 208.

CHAPTER 9
"I PLEDGE ALLEGIANCE . . .": MOBILIZING THE NATION'S YOUTH

1. *Public Opinion*, 3 March 1888, 510.

2. GAR, *Journal of the Thirty-Ninth National Encampment, 1905* (Boston: Griffith-Stillings, 1905), 173.

3. GAR, *Journal of the Twenty-Third Annual Session of the National Encampment, 1889* (St. Louis: A. Whipple, 1889), 41.

4. Nat Brandt, "To the Flag," *American Heritage: The Magazine of History* 22 (June 1971): 72.

5. Bessie Louise Pierce, *Public Opinion and the Teaching of History in the United States* (New York: Knopf, 1926), 29–31.

6. "The Relief Corps: News and Gossip of the Great Auxiliary," *National Tribune* (Washington, D.C.), 5 August 1897.

7. George T. Balch, *Methods of Teaching Patriotism in the Public Schools* (New York: D. Van Nostrand, 1890), xi.

8. "The Relief Corps: News and Gossip"; WRC, *Journal of the Fifteenth National Convention, 1897* (Boston: E. B. Stillings, 1897), 279; Balch, *Methods of Teaching Patriotism,* xxxv–xxxvii.

9. George T. Balch, *A Patriotic Primer for the Little Citizen,* rev. and enl. Wallace Foster (Indianapolis: Levey Bros., 1898), 12.

10. Paula Baker, "The Domestication of Politics: Women and American Political Society, 1780–1920," *American Historical Review* 89 (June 1984): 631–32.

11. Jurgen Herbst, *And Sadly Teach: Teacher Education and Professionalization in American Culture* (Madison: University of Wisconsin Press, 1989), 61, 185–86.

12. "The Relief Corps: News and Gossip."

13. Henry Ward Beecher, quoted in Balch, *Methods of Teaching Patriotism,* title page of pt. 3.

14. Balch, *Methods of Teaching Patriotism,* 5, 10–13, 15–17.

15. Ibid., 32, 8, 30–31, 44–45.

16. Eric Hobsbawm, *Nations and Nationalism since 1780: Programme, Myth, Reality* (Cambridge: Cambridge University Press, 1990), 91–92.

17. Eric Hobsbawm, "Mass-Producing Traditions: Europe, 1870–1914," in *The Invention of Tradition,* ed. Eric Hobsbawm and Terence Ranger (1983; reprint, Cambridge: Cambridge University Press, 1988), 164.

18. Wallace Foster, "All Salute the Flag," *National Tribune,* 20 October 1892.

19. Kate B. Sherwood, "Gleanings from the National Headquarters," ibid., 11 November 1893.

20. Theodore Peterson, *Magazines in the Twentieth Century* (Urbana: University of Illinois Press, 1964), 2.

21. Earl D. Babst, "F. Wayland Ayer: The Business Pioneer," in *F. Wayland Ayer: Founder,* comp. F. W. Ayer & Sons (Philadelphia: N. W. Ayer & Sons, 1923), 21–27.

22. Louise Harris, *The Flag over the Schoolhouse* (Providence, R.I.: C. A. Stephens Collection, 1971), 9–10, 13–15.

23. See *Youth's Companion*, 18 October 1892 and 10 November 1892.

24. Harris, *Flag over the Schoolhouse*, 19, 16.

25. "Our Schools' Greatest Task," *Youth's Companion*, 13 October 1892, 509; "Our Mixed Population," ibid., 10 November 1892, 596.

26. Harris, *Flag over the Schoolhouse*, 16.

27. "Who Originated Columbus School Day?" *School Journal* (n.p.), 12 November 1892, 436, Francis Bellamy Papers, Rare Books and Special Collections, Rush Rhees Library, University of Rochester, Rochester, N.Y. (hereafter cited as Bellamy Papers); *Youth's Companion*, 19 March 1891, reprinted in Harris, *Flag over the Schoolhouse*, 41.

28. *Youth's Companion*, 25 October 1888, 9 January, 3 July, 9, 30 October 1890, reprinted in Harris, *Flag over the Schoolhouse*, 21, 18, 24–25, 29, 31.

29. "Who Originated Columbus School Day?"

30. *Youth's Companion*, 4 May 1893, reprinted in Harris, *Flag over the Schoolhouse*, 86.

31. "The Newest Movement. What Mr. Francis Bellamy is Doing. A Systematic Effort to Intensify and Elevate the Teaching of Americanism in the Public Schools," newspaper clipping, 1892, and Francis Bellamy, "The Story of the Pledge of Allegiance," 33, both in Bellamy Papers.

32. "Mr. Bellamy on Socialism," *Standard* (n.p.), July 1908, ibid.

33. John W. Baer, *The Pledge of Allegiance: A Centennial History, 1892–1992* (n.p., 1992), 51, copy in Bellamy Papers. In 1891 the *Companion* revived the Lyceum, originally founded in 1826 by Daniel Webster. The *Companion* renamed it the Lyceum League of America and encouraged young men to form reading clubs to "understand their country, its politics and its problems." For the full listing of activities, see *Youth's Companion*, 29 October 1891, reprinted in Harris, *Flag over the Schoolhouse*, 96–100.

34. "Mr. Bellamy's Lecture," *Portland Daily Press*, n.d., Bellamy Papers.

35. Ibid.

36. "Mr. Bellamy on Socialism."

37. For a fuller discussion of the term *social citizenry*, see Nancy Fraser and Linda Gordon, "Contract versus Charity: Why Is There No Social Citizenship in the United States?" *Socialist Review* 22 (July–September 1992): 45–67.

38. *St. Louis Globe-Democrat*, April 1887, cited in *Public Opinion*, 30 April 1887, 49; *New York Commercial Advertiser*, July 1887, cited in ibid., 2 July 1887, 249.

39. Edward Bellamy, *Looking Backward* (Boston: Picknar, 1888; reprint, New York: New American Library, Signet Classic, 1960).

40. Ibid., 110–11.

41. Erich Fromm, foreword to Bellamy, *Looking Backward*, v; Frank Luther Mott, *Golden Multitudes: The Story of Best Sellers in the United States* (New York: R. R. Bower, 1947), 100–101.

42. Merle Curti, *The Roots of American Loyalty* (New York: Columbia University Press, 1946), 211.

43. Edward Bellamy, *Edward Bellamy Speaks Again* (Kansas City, 1937), 28, quoted in ibid.

44. Laurence Grondlund, "Nationalism," *Arena* 1 (January 1890): 158.

45. Nick Salvatore, *Eugene V. Debs: Citizen and Socialist* (Urbana: University of Illinois Press, 1982), 101.

46. Baer, *Pledge of Allegiance*, 31, 36, Bellamy Papers.

47. Francis Bellamy, "A New Plan for Counter-Attack on the Nation's Internal Foes," May 1923, ibid.

48. "Paragraph No. 15, Sworn Affidavit of Francis Bellamy, 13 August 1923," in Bellamy to Mrs. Lue Stuart Wadsworth, WRC, n.d., ibid.

49. Bellamy, "Story of the Pledge of Allegiance," 33.

50. Bellamy to Mrs. Lue Stuart Wadsworth, 12 July 1923, ibid.; and Bellamy, "Story of the Pledge of Allegiance," 37.

51. Bellamy, "Story of the Pledge of Allegiance," 37.

52. Bellamy, "New Plan for Counter-Attack."

53. *Youth's Companion*, 26 May, 14 January, 2 June 1892, reprinted in Harris, *Flag over the Schoolhouse*, 51, 48, 53.

54. Francis Bellamy to President Harrison, 12 May 1892, Bellamy Papers.

55. Francis Bellamy, untitled status report, 1892; and Department of Superintendence, "National Public School Celebration of Columbus Day: Suggestions for the Campaign," n.d., ibid.

56. Department of Superintendence, "National Public School Celebration of Columbus Day: Suggestions for the Campaign," n.d.; and Francis Bellamy, form letter to superintendents of education, 10 September 1892, ibid.

57. *National Public School Celebration Bulletin* (Boston, 1892), ibid.

58. Francis Bellamy to Mr. Ford, first letter dated 18 April 1892, 3–4, ibid.

59. Ibid.

60. Executive Committee of the National Columbian Public School Celebration, "Columbus Day Page, No. 1," ibid.

61. Francis Bellamy to Mr. Ford (first letter), 18 April 1892, 1–4, ibid.

62. Francis Bellamy to Mr. Ford, second letter dated 18 April 1892, 4–6, ibid.

63. Executive Committee of the National Columbian Public School Celebration to President Benjamin Harrison, 12 May 1892, ibid.

64. Bellamy, "Story of the Pledge of Allegiance," 34–35, 53.

65. Ibid., 35.

66. A representative sampling of congressional responses can be found in transcripts of Bellamy interviews with senators and congressmen, 1892, Bellamy Papers.

67. For a typical discussion of Columbus as an enlightenment man, see "Interview of Hon. Allen C. Duborrow, Jr. by Francis Bellamy, 1892," ibid.

68. "A Young Columbus of 1892," *Youth's Companion*, 13 October 1892.

69. "Interview with Theodore Roosevelt by Francis Bellamy," June, 1892, Bellamy Papers.

70. Francis Bellamy, John W. Dickinson, Thomas B. Stockwell, W. R. Garrett, and Ferris S. Fitch, eds., *Official Program: The National Public School Celebration of Columbus Day, October 21, 1892* (n.p.), ibid.

71. Bellamy, untitled status report, 3–4.

72. "The Celebration Begun," *New York Times*, 20 October 1892.

73. "Prominent Guests Start," ibid., 19 October 1892.

74. John E. Findling, ed., *Historical Dictionary of World's Fairs and Expositions, 1851–1988* (New York: Greenwood, 1990), 122.

75. Robert W. Rydell, *All the World's a Fair: Visions of Empire at America's International Expositions, 1876–1916* (Chicago: University of Chicago Press, 1984).

76. For a political analysis of the convergence of business, politics, industry, and culture in the construction of the Columbian Exposition, see Alan Trachtenberg, *The Incorporation of America: Culture and Society in the Gilded Age* (New York: Hill & Wang, 1982), chap. 7, "White City."

77. Gail Bederman, *Manliness and Civilization: A Cultural History of Gender and Race in the United States, 1880–1917* (Chicago: University of Chicago Press, 1995), 35–36.

78. *Huntsville (Ala.) Gazette*, May 1983, quoted in Elliott M. Rudwick and August Meier, "Black Man in the 'White City': Negroes and the Columbian Exposition, 1893," *Phylon* 26 (winter 1965): 354. For an analysis of black women's efforts to gain representation at the exposition, see Ann Masa, "Black Women in the 'White City,' " *Journal of American Studies* 8 (December 1974): 319–37.

79. Bederman, *Manliness and Civilization*, 35.

80. "In the Public Schools," *New York Times*, 20 October 1892.

81. James Upham, quoted in Bellamy, "Story of the Pledge of Allegiance," 33.

82. "Columbus Day," *Youth's Companion*, 17 November 1892, 608.

83. " 'Columbus' Song," *Chicago Tribune*, 20 October 1892.

84. "All Carried Flags: A Private Lesson in Patriotism," *New York Times*, 25 May 1892.

85. "Had a Drum and Fife Corps," *Chicago Tribune*, 20 October 1892.

86. "Official Badge of the National Public School Celebration of Columbus Day, October 21, 1492–1892," Bellamy Papers.

87. "Had a Drum and Fife Corps."

88. "Discovery Day: October 21 Proclaimed a National Holiday by the President," *New York Times*, 22 July 1892; "Young America Does Honor to the Memory of Columbus," *Chicago Daily Tribune*, 20 October 1892.

89. Bellamy et al., *Official Program*.

90. "Pledge of Allegiance," *Chicago Tribune*, 20 October 1892.

91. Bellamy et al., *Official Program*.

92. National Columbian Public School Celebration, Executive Committee, *Supplement to Official Program: The Address for Columbus Day*, 1892, Bellamy Papers.

93. "Cincinnati's School Children Parade," *Chicago Tribune*, 20 October 1892.

94. "Young America Leads Off: First of the Great Parades of Columbus Week" and "What the Boys in Line Saw," *New York Times*, 11 October 1892. Most of the country celebrated Columbus Day on 21 October. The date of Columbus Day was changed from 12 October to 21 October to make it more accurately reflect when Columbus landed in America. However, New York decided against changing the arrangements it had already made to celebrate the day on 12 October.

95. "Columbus Day," 608.

CHAPTER 10
"THE GREAT FUSING FURNACE":
AMERICANIZATION IN THE PUBLIC SCHOOLS

1. David B. Tyack and Thomas James, "Moral Majorities and the School Curriculum: Historical Perspectives on the Legalization of Virtue," *Teachers College Record* 86 (summer 1985): 513.

2. "Report of the Committee on State School Systems: Compulsory Education," in National Education Association (NEA), *Journal of Proceedings and Addresses, Session of the Year 1891* (New York, 1891), 295, 298.

3. Noah Webster, quoted in Carl F. Kaestle, *Pillars of the Republic: Common Schools and American Society* (New York: Hill & Wang, 1983), 7.

4. Benjamin Rush, *Essays Literary, Moral and Philosophical* (1786; reprint, Schenectady: Union College Press, 1988), 5, 9.

5. Kaestle, *Pillars of the Republic*, 5, 79.

6. Ibid., 62.

7. John W. Meyer et al., "Public Education as Nation-Building in America: Enrollments and Bureaucratization in the American States, 1870–1930," *American Journal of Sociology* 85 (November 1979): 592, 599, 601.

8. Kaestle, *Pillars of the Republic*, 80.

9. Lawrence A. Cremin, *American Education: The Metropolitan Experience, 1876–1980* (New York: Harper & Row, 1988), 154.

10. Kaestle, *Pillars of the Republic*, 73, 95.

11. Horace Mann, quoted in Samuel Bowles and Herbert Gintis, *Schooling in Capitalist America: Educational Reform and the Contradictions of Economic Life* (New York: Basic Books, 1976), 167.

12. Bowles and Gintis, *Schooling in Capitalist America*, 169–71.

13. Geoff Eley and Ronald Grigor Suny, eds., *Becoming National: A Reader* (New York: Oxford University Press, 1996), 9.

14. Michael B. Katz, *Reconstructing Education* (Cambridge: Harvard University Press, 1987), 6–7.

15. J. R. Preston, State Superintendent of Public Instruction, Jackson, Miss., "Teaching Patriotism," in NEA, *Journal of Proceedings and Addresses, Session of the Year 1891*, 110.

16. Eric Hobsbawm, *Nations and Nationalism since 1780: Programme, Myth, Reality* (Cambridge: Cambridge University Press, 1990), 91–93.

17. Preston, "Teaching Patriotism," 110.

18. George T. Balch, *Methods of Teaching Patriotism in the Public Schools* (New York: D. Van Nostrand, 1890), xxxv.

19. Mary M. North, quoted in WRC, *Journal of the Twenty-Eighth National Convention, 1910* (Boston: Griffith-Stillings, 1910), 166–67.

20. Thomas Jefferson Morgan, *Patriotic Citizenship* (New York: American Book Company, 1895), 10.

21. Ruth H. Bloch, "Gendered Meanings of Virtue in Revolutionary America," in *Signs* 13 (fall 1987): 47.

22. Balch, *Methods of Teaching Patriotism*, vii–viii.

23. Thomas Jefferson, *Notes on the State of Virginia* (1787; reprint, Chapel Hill: University of North Carolina Press, 1955), 34.

24. Morgan, *Patriotic Citizenship*, 10–11.

25. "To Make Lads Patriots," *National Tribune* (Washington, D.C.), 2 July 1896.

26. The NEA was formed in 1856 by men interested in organizing a national association of professional teachers (see Zalmon Richards, "Historical Sketch of the National Education Association," and William T. Harris, "The National Educational Association: Its Organization and Functions," in *Report of the Commissioner of Education for the Year 1892–93*, vol. 2 [Washington, D.C.: Government Printing Office, 1895], 1495–1502 and 1502–6).

27. Edgar B. Wesley, *NEA, The First Hundred Years: The Building of the Teaching Profession* (New York: Harper & Brothers, 1957), 117.

28. "Who Originated Columbus School Day?" *School Journal* (n.p.), 12 November 1892, 436, Bellamy Papers.

29. "The Newest Movement. What Mr. Francis Bellamy is Doing. A Systematic Effort to Intensify and Elevate the Teaching of Americanism in the Public Schools," newspaper clipping, 1892, Bellamy Papers.

30. "The Schoolhouse Flag," *Youth's Companion*, 2 July 1891, 376.

31. Wesley, *NEA*, 113–14.

32. The number of women grammar-school teachers rose as men found more lucrative employment. In Massachusetts the number of women teachers in 1837 was 3,591, or 60.2 percent of the total; by 1870 the number had risen to 10,793, or 88.2 percent (Jurgen Herbst, *And Sadly Teach: Teacher Education and Professionalization in American Culture* [Madison: University of Wisconsin Press, 1989], 185–86).

33. "The Schoolhouse Flag," 376.

34. Francis Bellamy, "A New Plan for Counter-Attack on the Nation's Internal Foes," May 1923, 9–10, Bellamy Papers.

35. Preston, "Teaching Patriotism," 102–3.

36. Anthony D. Smith, *National Identity* (London: Penguin Books, 1991), 118–19.

37. GAR, *Journal of the Twenty-Sixth National Encampment, 1892* (Albany, N.Y.: S. H. Wentworth, 1892), 50.

38. GAR, *Journal of the Twenty-Third Annual Session of the National Encampment, 1889* (St. Louis: A. Whipple, 1889), 41.

39. "Compulsory Patriotism," *National Tribune*, 26 September 1895.

40. GAR, *Journal of the Twenty-Sixth National Encampment, 1892*, 80–82.

41. WRC, *Journal of the Eighth Annual Convention, 1890* (Boston: E. B. Stillings, 1890), 87–89.

42. Charles R. Skinner, ed., *Manual of Patriotism: For Use in the Public Schools in the State of New York, Authorized by Act of the Legislature* (Albany: Brandow Printing Company, 1900), ii.

43. NEA, *Journal of Proceedings and Addresses, Session of the Year 1892* (New York, 1893), 60.

44. William A. Mowry, Superintendent of Schools, Salem, Mass., "What Special Work Should be Undertaken in the Elementary School to Prepare the Pupils for the Duties of Citizenship," in NEA, *Proceedings of the International Congress of Education of the World's Columbian Exposition, Chicago, July 25–28, 1893* (New York, 1894), 274–75.

45. Tyack and James, "Moral Majorities and the School Curriculum," 526.

46. WRC, *Journal of the Thirty-Seventh National Convention, 1919* (Washington, D.C.: National Tribune, 1919), 200–201.

47. WRC, *Journal of the Twentieth National Convention, 1902* (Boston: Griffith-Stillings, 1902), 286.

48. WRC, *Journal of the Eleventh Annual Convention, 1893* (Boston: E. B. Stillings, 1893), 285; Kate B. Sherwood, "Gleanings from the National Headquarters," *National Tribune*, 11 November 1893.

49. GAR, *Journal of the Thirty-Second National Encampment, 1898* (Philadelphia: Town Printing, 1898), 192; John George Lankevich, "The Grand Army of the Republic in New York State, 1865–1898" (Ph.D. diss., Columbia University, 1967), 23.

50. GAR, *Journal of the Twenty-Ninth National Encampment, 1895* (Rockford, Ill.: Frank S. Horner, 1895), 58, 304; Charles Frank Speierl Jr., "The Influence of the Grand Army of the Republic on Education in New Jersey, between 1866–1935" (Ph.D. diss., Fairleigh Dickinson University, 1987), 248–57.

51. GAR, *Journal of the Thirty-Third National Encampment, 1899* (Philadelphia: Town Printing, 1899), 244.

52. GAR, *Journal of the Thirty-Seventh National Encampment, 1903* (Philadelphia: Town Printing, 1903) 248.

53. GAR, *Journal of the Twenty-Sixth National Encampment, 1892*, 209.

54. GAR, *Journal of the Thirty-First National Encampment, 1897* (Lincoln, Nebr.: State Journal Company, 1897), 214–17.

55. "To Make Lads Patriots."

56. GAR, *Journal of the Thirtieth National Encampment, 1896* (Indianapolis: Wm. B. Burford, 1896), 160–61.

57. GAR, *Journal of the Thirty-Fourth National Encampment, 1900* (Philadelphia: Town Printing, 1901), 63.

58. Russell F. Weigley, *History of the United States Army* (New York: Macmillan, 1967), xi–xii, 157–58.

59. Stuart McConnell, *Glorious Contentment: The Grand Army of the Republic, 1865–1900* (Chapel Hill: University of North Carolina Press, 1992), 25–26, 197–98.

60. John A. Logan, *The Volunteer Soldier of America* (Chicago: R. S. Peale & Co., 1887), reprinted in *The American Military: Readings in the History of the Military in American Society,* ed. Russell F. Weigley (Menlo Park: Addison-Wesley, 1969), 78–79.

61. Weigley, *History of the United States Army,* 282–83.

62. GAR, *Journal of the Twenty-Ninth National Encampment, 1895,* 234–35.

63. GAR, *Journal of the Thirty-First National Encampment, 1897,* 62.

64. GAR, *Journal of the Thirty-Fifth National Encampment, 1901* (St. Louis: A. Whipple, 1901), 249.

65. All quoted in GAR, *Journal of the Twenty-Ninth National Encampment, 1895,* 232–33.

66. WRC, *Journal of the Twenty-First National Convention, 1903* (Boston: Griffith-Stillings, 1903), 425.

67. GAR, *Journal of the Twenty-Ninth National Encampment, 1895,* 233; idem, *Journal of the Thirty-First National Encampment, 1897,* 213.

68. David Montgomery, *Citizen Worker: The Experience of Workers in the United States with Democracy and the Free Market during the Nineteenth Century* (Cambridge: Cambridge University Press, 1993), 101–3.

69. Samuel Gompers to James Lynch, 26 October 1894, in *The Samuel Gompers Papers,* ed. Stuart B. Kaufman and Peter J. Albert, vol. 3, *Unrest and Depression, 1891–94* (Urbana: University of Illinois Press, 1989).

70. GAR, *Journal of the Thirty-Fifth National Encampment, 1901,* 234–35.

71. John W. Davis, *Young America's Manual: The Child's Guide to Patriotism* (New York: Educational Publishing, 1906), 18, 24, 63, 114.

72. GAR, *Journal of the Twenty-Ninth National Encampment, 1895,* 235.

73. GAR, *Journal of the Thirtieth National Encampment, 1896,* 160.

74. GAR, *Journal of the Forty-Second National Encampment, 1908* (Kansas City: John C. Bovard, 1908), 171.

75. NEA, *Journal of Proceedings and Addresses, Session of the Year 1895* (St. Paul, 1895), 32.

294

76. WRC, *Journal of the Twelfth Annual Convention, 1894* (Boston: E. B. Stillings, 1894), 239; idem, *Journal of the Twenty-First National Convention, 1903,* 174, 427.

77. WRC, *Journal of the Fourteenth National Convention, 1896* (Boston: E. B. Stillings, 1896), 185–86, 188.

78. Ibid., 189.

79. Jesse Knowlton Flanders, *Legislative Control of the Elementary Curriculum,* Contributions to Education, no. 195 (New York City: Teachers College, Columbia University, 1925), 12.

80. William Jennings Bryan, "Imperialism," 13 December 1898, in *Patriotic Eloquence Relating to the Spanish-American War and Its Issues,* comp. Robert I. Fulton and Thomas C. Trueblood (New York: Charles Scribner's Sons, 1900), 43, 350; Joseph Danna Miller, "Militarism or Manhood?" *Arena* 24 (July 1900): 379–92.

81. Skinner, *Manual of Patriotism,* i, v.

82. GAR, *Journal of the Thirty-Fourth National Encampment, 1900,* 61–62,

83. J. M. Carlisle, State Superintendent of Public Instruction, Texas, "The South and Its Problems—Teaching Patriotism in Southern Schools," in NEA, *Journal of Proceedings and Addresses, Session of the Year 1894* (St. Paul, 1895), 578.

84. Mowry, "What Special Work Should be Undertaken?" 275; Skinner, *Manual of Patriotism,* xi.

85. Skinner, *Manual of Patriotism,* xi.

86. Richard Hofstadter, *Anti-Intellectualism in American Life* (New York: Knopf, 1969), 362.

87. Mowry, "What Special Work Should be Undertaken?" 279.

88. Frank A. Hill, "Aims in Teaching Civil Government," in NEA, *Journal of Proceedings and Addresses, Session of the Year 1891,* 661.

89. Merle Curti, *The Roots of American Loyalty* (New York: Columbia University Press, 1946), 216.

90. E. Benjamin Andrews, "Patriotism and the Public Schools," *Arena* 3 (December 1890): 71–72, 76–77.

91. Hofstadter, *Anti-Intellectualism in American Life,* 305.

92. WRC, *Journal of the Twenty-Seventh National Convention, 1909* (Boston: Griffith-Stillings, 1909), 157.

93. GAR, *Journal of the Forty-Third National Encampment* (n.p., n.d.), 155.

94. Elbert Hubbard, "A Message to Garcia," in *The Patriotic Reader for Seventh and Eighth Grades and Junior High Schools,* ed. Katharine Isabel

Bemis, Mathilde Edith Holtz, and Henry Lester Smith (Boston: Houghton Mifflin, 1917), 115–19.

95. Clara Walker, Principal, School No. 16, Albany, N.Y., "Flag Day Exercises for the Grades," in *The American Flag: New York State Education Department, Sixth Annual Report,* ed. Harlan Hoyt Horner (New York, 1910), 69–73.

96. Ella Dare, "St. Paul's 'Living Flag,' " reprinted in WRC, *Journal of the Fourteenth National Convention, 1896,* 351–52.

97. A. H. McKay, "Discussion on Teaching Patriotism," in NEA, *Journal of Proceedings and Addresses, Session of the Year 1891,* 111–13.

98. *The Army and Navy Primer* (Chicago: Madison Book Co., 1903).

99. Maj. Gen. Leonard Wood, "The Civil Obligation of the Army," 15 June 1915, in Weigley, *American Military,* 47.

CHAPTER 11

"CLASPING HANDS OVER THE BLOODY DIVIDE": NATIONAL MEMORY, RACISM, AND AMNESIA

1. Rev. Newell Dwight Hillis, "Oration," in Pennsylvania Commission, *Fiftieth Anniversary of the Battle of Gettysburg* (Harrisburg: WM. Stanley Ray, 1913), 162; "Description of Charge by Pickett's Division," *Confederate Veteran* 21 (August 1913): 383–84.

2. Charles R. Nitchkey, *Gettysburg 1863 and Today* (Hicksville, N.Y.: Exposition Press, 1980), 18, 28; Robert D. Hoffsommer, "The Aftermath of Gettysburg: The Story of the Casualties," *Civil War Times Illustrated* 2 (July 1963): 35, 38.

3. For a sampling of newspaper reports, see "Gray Men Totter to Bloody Angle," *Washington Post,* 4 July 1913, 1; "New Englanders at Bloody Angle," *Boston Post,* 4 July 1913, 1; "Blue and Gray Joyfully Cheer Reunited Nation," *San Antonio Express,* 2 July 1913, 1; "Over This Wall Pickett's Men Charged," *Atlanta Constitution,* 6 July 1913, 1; "Echoes from Gettysburg," *Confederate Veteran* 21 (September 1913): 429–30; and "Battle Scene Re-enacted by the Survivors," *San Francisco Examiner,* 4 July 1913, 4.

4. Hon. J. Hampton Moore, "Speech at Bloody Angle," in Pennsylvania Commission, *Fiftieth Anniversary of the Battle of Gettysburg,* 162, 168–71; photograph, "Philadelphia Brigade Association, and Pickett's Division Association Meeting at the 'Stone Wall' and 'Bloody Angle,' on July 3rd, 1913," in ibid., between 168 and 169.

5. Homi K. Bhabha, "DissemiNation: Time, Narrative, and the Margins of the Modern Nation," in *Nation and Narration*, ed. Homi K. Bhabha (London: Routledge, 1990), 309–11.

6. The Confederate Monument is located in Jackson Circle, Arlington National Cemetery, Washington, D.C.

7. George Brown Tindall, *The Emergence of the New South, 1913–1945* (Baton Rouge: Louisiana State University Press, 1967).

8. *New York Times*, 5 March 1913; *Washington Bee*, 8 March 1913.

9. "Gettysburg Honor to Girls of '63," *New York Times*, 1 July 1913.

10. "The Great Jubilee," *National Tribune* (Washington, D.C.), 23 June 1913, 3.

11. For other examples of transformative performances, see Richard Schechner, "From Ritual to Theater and Back," in *Ritual, Play, and Performance: Readings in the Social Sciences / Theater*, ed. Richard Schechner and Mady Schuman (New York: Seabury Press, Continuum Book, 1976), 196–97, 205–7.

12. Nitchkey, *Gettysburg 1863 and Today*, 113.

13. David Glassberg, letter to author, 4 August 1996.

14. "Peace on Earth; Good Will Toward Men," *National Tribune*, 10 July 1913, 1.

15. "Special Trains Bear the Old Soldiers to Scene of Great Celebration Arranged in their Honor," ibid., 1 July 1913; photograph, "Our Veteran Guests," Pennsylvania Commission, *Fiftieth Anniversary of the Battle of Gettysburg*, between 52 and 53.

16. "G.A.R. Men See Battle Films, Gettysburg Pictured for Vets," *San Francisco Examiner*, 2 July 1913, 1.

17. Advertisement for *Gettysburg*, in *Moving Picture World* 16 (26 April 1913): 346–47.

18. "Spectacle Enthused Audience," *Motography* 10 (13 July 1913): 18.

19. Maurice Halbwachs, *The Collective Memory* (New York: Harper Colophon Books, 1980), 50–51, 70–71.

20. Jack Spears, *The Civil War on the Screen and Other Essays* (New York: A. S. Barnes, 1977), 12.

21. Eileen Bowser, *The Transformation of Cinema, 1907–1915*, vol. 2, *History of the American Cinema* (New York: Charles Scribner's Sons, 1990), 177–78.

22. Paul C. Spehr, comp., *The Civil War in Motion Pictures: A Bibliography of Films Produced in the United States since 1897* (Washington, D.C.: Library of Congress, 1961), 8, 13, 16–18, 28, 51, 67, 69.

23. Floyd France, *Two Kentucky Boys* (Thomas A. Edison, 1917), George Kleine Collection of Early Motion Pictures, and Copyright #2528, synopsis, Motion Picture Division, Library of Congress, Washington, D.C. (hereafter cited as Motion Picture, LC).

24. "Grand Emancipation Celebration," *Christian Recorder*, 10 January 1901, 6.

25. Booker T. Washington, letter to the editor, 21 December 1909, in *Washington Bee*, 1 January 1910, 1.

26. U.S. Congress, House, *Commission for Exposition Commemorating Semicentennial of Negro Freedom*, 61st Cong., 2nd sess., 29 March 1910, H. Rept. 896; idem, "Semicentennial of Negro Freedom," H. J. Res. 88, 62nd Cong., 2nd sess., *Congressional Record* (20 June 1910), 45, pt. 8.

27. U.S. Congress, Senate, Committee on Industrial Expositions, *Semicentennial Anniversary of Act of Emancipation*, 62nd Cong., 2nd sess., 2 February 1912, S. Rept. 311, 1–2.

28. U.S. Congress, Senate, *A Bill Providing for the Celebration of the Semicentennial Anniversary of the Act of Emancipation*, 62nd Cong., 2nd sess., S. 180, 6 April 1912 (first introduced as S. 180 on 6 April 1911).

29. Senate Committee on Industrial Expositions, *Semicentennial Anniversary of Act of Emancipation*, 1–2.

30. Ibid., 3; U.S. Congress, House, Subcommittee of Committee on Appropriations, *Celebration of the Semicentennial Anniversary of the Act of Emancipation, Addenda to Hearings*, 62nd Cong., 2nd sess., 1912, 3–18.

31. U.S. Congress, "Emancipation Act Celebration," S. 180, 62nd Cong., 3rd sess., *Congressional Record* (17 January 1913), 49, pt. 1.

32. For a sampling of press coverage on Emancipation Day, see Emancipation Day Celebrations, 1913, Tuskegee News Clipping File, Reel 240, Black Press Archives, Moorland-Springarn Research Center, Howard University, Washington, D.C. (hereafter cited as Tuskegee Clipping File).

33. U.S. Congress, "Anniversary Celebration of Act of Emancipation," S. 180, 62nd Cong., 2nd sess., *Congressional Record* (2 April 1912), 49, pt. 4:4179–80.

34. "Exposition to Show Advance," *Indianapolis Recorder*, 12 July 1913, 1.

35. Editorial, *Crisis* 6 (August 1913): 163; "Three Expositions," ibid. 6 (October 1913); "Exhibit Covers Many Subjects," *Afro-American Ledger*, 26 July 1913, 7.

36. "Negro Exposition Opens," *New York Sun*, 28 October 1913, 5.

37. "Keen Interest in Exposition," *Afro-American Ledger*, 4 October 1913.

38. David Glassberg, *American Historical Pageantry: The Uses of Tradition in the Early Twentieth Century* (Chapel Hill: University of North Carolina Press, 1990), 132; "Negro Exposition Opens," *New York Times*, 23 October 1913, 5.

39. W. E. B. Du Bois, *The Conservation of the Races*, American Negro Academy Occasional Papers, no. 2 (1897; reprint, New York: Arno Press, 1969), 9–12.

40. "The National Emancipation Exposition," *Crisis* 7 (November 1913): 339–41.

41. "Fifty Years of Freedom," *New York Times*, 15 December 1913, 8.

42. "Anniversary of the Battle of Gettysburg," *Washington Bee*, 24 May 1913.

43. It is difficult to substantiate the presence or number of black veterans at Gettysburg in 1913. I found only one mention of black veterans from the Union or the Confederacy, in "Echoes from Gettysburg," 431. I am grateful to David Blight for referring me to the only reference he found, in Walter H. Blake, *Hand Grips: The Story of Great Gettysburg Reunion, 1913* (Vineland, N.J.: G. E. Smith, 1913), 66–67.

44. "At Gettysburg," *Outlook* 104 (12 July 1913): 541.

45. "Address of Commander Beers," *Confederate Veteran* 21 (September 1913): 425.

46. Col. J. M. Schoonmaker, "Introductory Remarks," in Pennsylvania Commission, *Fiftieth Anniversary of the Battle of Gettysburg*, 95–96.

47. *Philadelphia Evening Bulletin*, 30 June 1913, quoted in ibid., 195.

48. " 'Rebel Yell' Awarded Governor Tener at Veterans Exercises," *Philadelphia Inquirer*, 2 July 1913.

49. Photograph in Pennsylvania Commission, *Fiftieth Anniversary of the Battle of Gettysburg*, 176; Woodrow Wilson, "July 4th Address," in ibid., 174–76.

50. W. E. B. Du Bois, *Black Reconstruction in America: An Essay toward a History of the Part Which Black Folk Played in the Attempt to Reconstruct Democracy in America, 1860–1880* (1935; reprint, New York: Atheneum, 1970), 714.

51. Booker T. Washington, "Fifty Years of Freedom," *Tuskegee Students*, 4 October 1913, Tuskegee Clipping File.

52. Leon F. Litwack, *Trouble in Mind: Black Southerners in the Age of Jim Crow* (New York: Knopf, 1998), 267–68, 281, 283–88.

53. Edward L. Ayers, *Southern Crossing: A History of the American South, 1877–1906* (New York: Oxford University Press, 1995), 108–10.

54. Richard Wright, *Black Boy* (1937; reprint, New York: Harper & Row, 1966), 83–84.

55. Richard Slotkin, *Gunfighter Nation: The Myth of the Frontier in Twentieth-Century America* (New York: Atheneum, 1992), 238–41.

56. Lary May, *Screening Out the Past: The Birth of Mass Culture and the Motion Picture Industry* (Chicago: University of Chicago Press, 1980), 80–83.

57. D. W. Griffith, *Birth of a Nation* (Hollywood: Epoch, 1915), Copyright Collection, Motion Picture, LC.

58. "The Birth of a Nation," *New York Times*, 4 March 1915, 9.

59. Hazel V. Carby, *Reconstructing Womanhood* (New York: Oxford University Press, 1987), 27, 34.

60. Griffith, *The Birth of a Nation*, Motion Picture, LC.

61. John Hope Franklin, " 'Birth of a Nation'—Propaganda as History," *Massachusetts Review* 20 (fall 1979): 424–25.

62. Woodrow Wilson, quoted in Michael P. Rogin, *"Ronald Reagan," the Movie and Other Episodes in Political Demonology* (Berkeley: University of California Press, 1987), 190.

63. Mildred Lewis Rutherford, "Reconstruction and the Ku Klux Klan," newspaper clipping, 1914, in *Historical Records of the United Daughters of the Confederacy, Scrapbooks*, comp. Mildred Lewis Rutherford, 15, Historical Records and Scrapbooks, Museum of the Confederacy, Richmond, Va.

64. Raymond Zirkel, "Dixie Doodle: 'You're the Land for Me' " (Columbus, Ohio: Buckeye Music, 1918), Patriotic Music; and J. Keirn Brennan, words, and Ernest R. Ball, music, "For Dixie and Uncle Sam" (New York: M. Witmark & Sons, 1916), Uncle Sam, both in Sam DeVincent Collection of Sheet Music, Archives Center, NMAH (hereafter cited as DeVincent Collection, NMAH).

65. Chicago Commission on Race Relations, *The Negro in Chicago: A Study of Race Relations and a Race Riot* (Chicago: University of Chicago Press, 1922), 357–58.

66. Emmett J. Scott, *Negro Migration during the War* (New York: Oxford University Press, 1920), 26–30.

67. St. Clair Drake and Horace R. Cayton, *Black Metropolis: A Study of Negro Life in a Northern City* (New York: Harcourt, Brace, 1945), 59–60.

68. Emmet J. Scott, comp., "Letters of Negro Migrants of 1916–1918," *Journal of Negro History* 4 (1919): 296, 304.

69. Carter G. Woodson, *A Century of Negro Migration* (Washington, D.C.: Association for the Study of Negro Life and History, 1918), 192.

70. Chicago Commission on Race Relations, *Negro In Chicago*, 79–80.

71. "Tells Negroes To Wage a Bloodless War for Their Constitutional Rights," *New York Age*, 29 March 1917, 1.

72. James Weldon Johnson, *Along This Way: The Autobiography of James Weldon Johnson* (New York: Viking, 1933), 310–11.

73. Grace B. House, *Soldiers of Freedom* (n.p., n.d.), 8, pamphlet, Moorland-Springarn Research Center, Howard University, Washington, D.C.; Arthur E. Barbeau and Florette Henri, *The Unknown Soldiers: Black American Troops in World War I* (Philadelphia: Temple University Press, 1974), 7.

74. Peter M. Bergman, *The Chronological History of the Negro in America* (New York: Harper & Row, 1969), 376.

75. Robert Russa Moton, *Finding a Way Out: An Autobiography* (Garden City, N.Y.: Negro University Press, 1920), 236–376.

76. Bernard C. Nalty, *Strength for the Fight: A History of Black Americans in the Military* (New York: Free Press, 1986), 108; Jane Lang Scheiber and Harry N. Scheiber, "The Wilson Administration and the Wartime Mobilization of Black Americans, 1917–1918," *Labor History* 10 (summer 1969): 441.

77. W. E. B. Du Bois, *The Autobiography of W. E. B. Du Bois: A Soliloquy on Viewing My Life from the Last Decade of Its First Century* (New York: International Publishers, 1968), 265; "The Perpetual Dilemma," *Crisis* 13 (April 1917): 271.

78. James Weldon Johnson, "The Right to Fight," *New York Age*, 12 April 1917.

79. James Weldon Johnson, "Why Should a Negro Fight?" ibid., 29 June 1918.

80. "Loyalty," *Crisis* 14 (May 1917): 23.

81. Scheiber and Scheiber, "The Wilson Administration and the Wartime Mobilization of Black Americans," 441.

82. "Now or Never," *Crisis* 17 (November 1918): 11.

83. Walter F. White, *Man Called White* (New York: Viking, 1948), 35–36.

84. "Resolutions of Washington Conference," *Crisis* 14 (June 1917): 59–60.

85. "Making the World Safe for Democracy," *Messenger* 1, no. 11 (1917): 9; Jervis Anderson, *A. Philip Randolph: A Biographical Portrait* (New York: Harcourt Brace Jovanovich, 1972), 104–8.

86. Anthony M. Platt, *E. Franklin Frazier Reconsidered* (New Brunswick, N.J.: Rutgers University Press, 1991), 35–39.

87. Benjamin E. Mays, *Born to Rebel: An Autobiography* (New York: Scribner, 1971), x, 53.

88. Charles H. Williams, *Sidelights on Negro Soldiers* (Boston: B. J. Brimmer, 1923), 18–19, 23.

89. Harry Haywood, *Black Bolshevik: Autobiography of an Afro-American Communist* (Chicago: Liberator Press, 1978), 45–46, 49–50.

90. *Baltimore Afro-American*, 1 November 1917.

91. Leon F. Litwack, "Trouble in Mind: The Bicentennial and the Afro-American Experience," *Journal of American History* 74 (September 1987): 317–25.

92. Walter J. Stevens, *Chip on My Shoulder: Autobiography of Walter J. Stevens* (Boston: Meador, 1946), 136.

93. Johnson, *Along This Way*, 319.

94. "The World Last Month," *Crisis* 14 (September 1917): 215.

95. Ida B. Wells-Barnett and Alfreda M. Duster, eds., *Crusade for Justice: The Autobiography of Ida B. Wells* (Chicago: University of Chicago Press, 1970), 383–84.

96. "Awake America" and "The Negro Silent Parade," *Crisis* 14 (September 1917): 216 and 241–44; Johnson, *Along This Way*, 320–21; "5,000 March in Silent Parade," *Baltimore Afro-American*, 4 August 1917, 1.

97. Paula Giddings, *When and Where I Enter: The Impact of Black Women on Race and Sex in America* (New York: Morrow, 1984), 7; Cynthia Neverdon-Morton, *Afro-American Women of the South and the Advancement of the Race, 1895–1925* (Knoxville: University of Tennessee Press, 1989), 74–77.

98. "Women at Prayer in Washington," *Baltimore Afro-American*, 14 July 1917, 1.

99. "Women Will Pray 'Till Wrongs Are Righted," ibid., 28 July 1917, 1.

100. Giddings, *When and Where I Enter*, 31; Carby, *Reconstructing Womanhood*, 25–39.

101. "Lynch Horrors Poison the Nation: They Develop Race Hatred and Contempt of Law," *Cleveland Gazette*, 25 August 1917, 1.

102. Nalty, *Strength for the Fight*, 112.

103. Edward M. Coffman, *The War to End All Wars: The American Military Experience in World War I* (New York: Oxford University Press, 1968), 231, 71.

104. "Lordy, Turn Your Face," in *Singing Soldiers*, comp. John J. Niles (New York: Scribner's Sons, 1927), 49–50.

105. "Trench Blues," in *Our Singing Country: A Second Volume of American Ballads and Folk Songs*, comp. John A. Lomax and Alan Lomax (New York: Macmillan, 1949), 202–4.

106. Addie W. Hunton and Kathryn M. Johnson, *Two Colored Women with the American Expeditionary Forces* (Brooklyn: Brooklyn Eagle, 1920), 235–36.

107. "Our Returned Negro Soldiers," *Charleston Messenger,* 13 September 1919, in *Voice of the Negro, 1919,* ed. Robert T. Kerlin (New York: E. P. Dutton, 1920), 37.

108. *Savannah Journal,* 4 October 1919, reprinted in ibid., 38–39.

109. Quoted in John Jacob Niles, "White Pioneers and Black," *Musical Quarterly* 18 (January 1932): 70.

110. "Returning Soldiers," *Crisis* 18 (May 1919): 14.

111. Arthur I. Waskow, *From Race Riot to Sit-in: 1919 and the 1960s* (Garden City, N.Y.: Doubleday, 1966), 12; Drake and Cayton, *Black Metropolis,* 65; William Preston Jr., *Aliens and Dissenters: Federal Suppression of Radicals, 1903–1933,* 2nd ed. (Urbana: University of Illinois Press, 1994), 217–20.

112. Carter G. Woodson, *The Negro in Our History,* 6th ed. (Washington, D.C.: Associated Publishers, 1922), 527.

113. *Houston Informer,* 11 October 1919, reprinted in Kerlin, *Voice of the Negro,* 34.

114. Nalty, *Strength for the Fight,* 126.

115. Carrie Williams Clifford, "The Black Draftee from Dixie," in *Black Sister: Poetry by Black American Women, 1746–1980,* ed. Erlene Stetson (Bloomington: Indiana University Press, 1981), 82–83.

116. Chicago Commission on Race Relations, *Negro in Chicago,* 481–83, 488.

117. Emmett J. Scott, *Scott's Official History of the American Negro in the World War* (Chicago: Homewood, 1919), 467–68.

118. Quoted in Wendell Berry, *The Hidden Wound* (San Francisco: North Point, 1989), 34.

119. Ned Cobb, quoted in Theodore Rosengarten, *All God's Dangers: The Life of Nate Shaw* (New York: Knopf, 1975), 161.

120. Langston Hughes, "The Colored Soldier," in *The Collected Poems of Langston Hughes,* ed. Arnold Rampersad (New York: Knopf, 1995), 147–48.

CHAPTER 12
"MY COUNTRY RIGHT OR WRONG": WORLD WAR I AND THE PARADOX OF AMERICAN PATRIOTISM

1. Gary Gerstle, *Working-Class Americanism: The Politics of Labor in a Textile City, 1914–1960* (Cambridge: Cambridge University Press, 1989), 1–2.

2. See, generally, Frank J. Donner, *The Age of Surveillance: The Aims and Methods of America's Intelligence System* (New York: Alfred A. Knopf, 1980); Robert Justin Goldstein, *Political Repression in Modern America, 1870 to the Present* (Cambridge: Schenkman, 1978); Max Lowenthal, *The Federal Bureau of Investigation* (New York: Harcourt Brace Jovanovich, 1950); H. C. Peterson and Gilbert C. Fite, *Opponents of War, 1917–1918* (Madison: University of Wisconsin Press, 1957); and William Preston Jr., *Aliens and Dissenters: Federal Suppression of Radicals, 1903–1933*, 2nd ed. (Urbana: University of Illinois Press, 1994).

3. Wolfgang J. Mommsen, "The Varieties of the Nation State in Modern History: Liberal, Imperialist, Fascist, and Contemporary Notions of Nation and Nationality," in *The Rise and Decline of the Nation State*, ed. Michael Mann (Oxford: Blackwell, 1990), 223.

4. Gerstle, *Working-Class Americanism*, 12.

5. John Whiteclay Chambers II, ed., *The Eagle and the Dove: The American Peace Movement and Unites States Foreign Policy, 1900–1922* (New York: Garland, 1976), 35–41.

6. "Addresses at the Woman's Peace Party Conference," 1915, reprinted in ibid., 36–37, 260–62, 266–68.

7. Socialist Party of America, "To the People of the United States," in *The American Socialists and the War*, ed. Alexander Tractenberg (New York: Rand School of Social Science, 1917), 14.

8. Eugene V. Debs, "Canton, Ohio speech, June 16, 1918," in *Great Lives Observed: Debs*, ed. Ronald Radosh (Englewood Cliffs: Prentice Hall, 1971), 66–78.

9. Nick Salvatore, *Eugene V. Debs: Citizen and Socialist* (Urbana: University of Illinois Press, 1982), 291–96; Debs, "Canton, Ohio speech."

10. "Patriotism," *The Masses* 8, no. 6 (1916): 10.

11. Charles W. Wood, "Am I A Patriot?" ibid. 8, no. 8 (1916): 8.

12. "My Country 'tis of thee," *Mother Earth* 7, no. 6 (1912): 173; front-page graphic, ibid. 9, no. 3 (1914); B. Russell Herts, "On Patriotism," ibid. 4, no. 6 (1909): 169, 171, 174.

13. Extract from the *Industrial Worker* reprinted in Philip S. Foner, *The Industrial Workers of the World, 1905–1917* (New York: International Publishers, 1965), 131.

14. *Seattle Post Intelligencer*, 19–21 July 1913, in ibid., 132.

15. *Proceedings of the Tenth Convention of the Industrial Workers of the World, 1916* (Chicago, 1917), 138, cited in ibid., 555–56.

16. Foner, *Industrial Workers of the World*, 554–55.

17. "World War and the Color Line," *Crisis* 9 (November 1914): 84.

18. "George V. Hobart's Impressive Allegory," *Washington Post*, 4 July 1915, 2.

19. Julius Mattfeld, *Variety Music Cavalcade, 1620–1969: A Chronology of Vocal and Instrumental Music Popular in the United States* (Englewood Cliffs: Prentice Hall, 1971).

20. Alfred Bryan, words, and Al Piantadosi, music, "I Didn't Raise My Boy to Be a Soldier" (New York: Leo. Feist, 1915), Music Division, Library of Congress, Washington, D.C.

21. Eddie Cavanaugh, words, and Bob Allan, music, "In Times of Peace Prepare for War" (Chicago: Will Rossiter, 1915), Patriotic Songs; Harry T. Bunce, words, and Will Donaldson, music, "Prepare the Eagle to Protect the Dove, That's the Battle Cry of Peace" (New York: F. B. Haviland, 1916), Patriotic Songs; and Carl B. Winge (words and music), "Johnny Getcha Gun: It Looks Like War" (Seattle: Echo Music, 1915), Uncle Sam, all in DeVincent Collection, NMAH.

22. *Wake Up America Parade* (New York: Thomas A. Edison, between 1914 and 1917), Motion Picture, LC.

23. Kalton C. Lahue, *Continued Next Week: A History of the Moving Picture Serial* (Norman: University of Oklahoma Press, 1964), 38, 40–41.

24. George B. Seitz, *Pearl White in the Pearl of the Army*, "The Traitor," episode 1, pt. 1; "Unmasking America's Secret Foes," episode 4, pt. 1; "The Flag Despoiler," episode 14, pt. 1 (New York: Astra Film Corporation, 1916), Motion Picture, LC.

25. Woodrow Wilson, quoted in Harry N. Scheiber, *The Wilson Administration and Civil Liberties, 1917–1921* (Ithaca: Cornell University Press, 1960), 18, 22–23.

26. Preston, *Aliens and Dissenters*, 144–45.

27. Peterson and Fite, *Opponents of War*, 17–18.

28. Goldstein, *Political Repression in Modern America*, 68–69.

29. Peterson and Fite, *Opponents of War*, 17–18.

30. George M. Cohan, "Over There" (New York: William Jerome, 1917), Music Division, Library of Congress.

31. E. Dempsey, words, and Joseph A. Burke, music, "If I Had a Son for Each Star in Old Glory, Uncle Sam I'd Give Them All to You" (New York: Leo. Feist, 1917), Uncle Sam, DeVincent Collection, NMAH.

32. E. E. Cole, words, and P. H. Sloan, music, "My Country Right or Wrong" (n.p.: Coonley School Press, 1917), Patriotic Music, ibid.

33. Don Moser, "At 75, the Boy Scouts Still Answer the Call of Adventure," *Smithsonian Magazine*, July 1985, 35–36.

34. William D. Murray, *The History of the Boy Scouts of America* (New York: Boy Scouts of America, 1937), 102–4; Allan Richard Whitmore, "Beard, Boys, and Buckskins: Daniel Carter Beard and the Preservation of the American Pioneer Tradition" (Ph.D. diss., Northwestern University, 1970), 307–21.

35. Nancy E. Allyn, "Uncle Sam Speaks: Broadsides and Posters from the National Archives," *Prologue*, winter 1985, 260.

36. Edward H. Griffith, *The Boy Who Cried Wolf: The Story of a Boy Scout*, feature (New York: Thomas A. Edison, 1917), Motion Picture, LC.

37. Frederick H. Marten, text, and Wil C. MacFarlane, music, *America First: A Boy Scout Operetta* (New York: J. Fisher & Brother, 1917), De-Vincent Collection, NMAH.

38. Theodore Roosevelt, "Address to the National Congress of Mothers," in National Congress of Parents and Teachers, *Report on the National Congress of Mothers, Held in the City of Washington, D.C., March 10–17, 1905* (n.p.: National Congress of Mothers, 1905), 79, 83–85. See also *Children Sewing Stars on Flag, Placing Flag on TR's Grave* (New York: International Film Service, 1919), Theodore Roosevelt Association Film Collection, Motion Picture, LC.

39. Theodore Roosevelt, "Race Decadence," *Outlook* 97 (8 April 1911): 766–69.

40. *Theodore Roosevelt, Great Scout*, 2d version (Oyster Bay, N.Y.: Roosevelt Memorial Association, 1925), Theodore Roosevelt Association Film Collection, Motion Picture, LC.

41. George T. Blakely, *Historians on the Homefront: American Propagandists for the Great War* (Lexington: University Press of Kentucky, 1970), 2.

42. George Creel, *How We Advertised America* (New York: Harper & Brothers, 1920), 86–87, 90, 95–96. See also Stephen Vaughan, *Holding Fast the Inner Lines: Democracy, Nationalism, and the Committee on Public Information* (Chapel Hill: University of North Carolina Press, 1980).

43. Committee on Public Information, *The President's Flag Day Address with Evidence of Germany's Plans*, special ed. (n.p.: printed for distribution by Boy Scouts of America, 1917), Flags, Warshaw Collection, NMAH.

44. Creel, *How We Advertised America*, 5–9.

45. Franklin, K. Lane, "Why We Are Fighting Germany," in Committee on Public Information, *The War Message and Facts behind It*, War Information Series No. 1 (Washington, D.C., 1917), 6.

46. Donner, *Age of Surveillance*, 32–33.

47. T. W. Gregory to Gilbert A. Currie, 12 April 1918, quoted in Peterson and Fite, *Opponents of War*, 20.

48. Jessie Knowlton Flanders, *Legislative Control of the Elementary Curriculum*, Contributions to Education, no. 195 (New York: Teachers College, Columbia University, 1925), 2, 7–10, 61–62, 177, 179.

49. "Hubert Eaves Refuses to Salute the U.S. Flag," *Chicago Defender*, 25 March 1916, reel 5, Tuskegee Clipping File.

50. Kenneth O'Reilly, *"Racial Matters": The FBI's Secret File on Black America, 1960–1972* (New York: Free Press, 1989), 9, 12.

51. The Bureau of Investigation was created in 1908. The name was changed to Federal Bureau of Investigation in 1935 (see O'Reilly, *"Racial Matters"*; and Durand Whipple to Mr. A. M. Briggs, 3 July 1917, in *Federal Surveillance of Afro-Americans, 1917–1925: The First World War, the Red Scare, and the Garvey Movement*, ed. Theodore Kornweibel, Black Studies Research Sources [Frederick, Md.: University Publications of America, 1985, microfilm]).

52. Photograph of 1896 William McKinley banner, in the Political Division, NMAH. See also Herbert Ridgeway Collins, *Threads of History: Americana Recorded on Cloth, 1775 to the Present* (Washington, D.C.: Smithsonian Institution Press, 1979), 262–320.

53. U.S. Congress, Senate, Committee on Military Affairs, "American Flag: Statement of Col. Ralph Earl Prime," 4, *American Flag: Hearings before the Committee on Military Affairs, Bills (S. 226, S. 229, S. 596, S. 1220, and S. 2504) to Prevent the Desecration of the American Flag*, 57th Cong., 1st sess., 20 February 1902, S. Doc. 22.

54. For an excellent compilation of scholarly articles and significant court cases and briefs, see Michael Kent Curtis, ed., *The Constitution and the Flag*, vols. 1, *The Flag Salute Cases*, and 2, *The Flag Burning Cases* (New York: Garland, 1993).

55. E. Benjamin Andrews, "Patriotism in the Public Schools," *Arena* 3 (December 1890): 71.

56. The patriotism generated by World War I, followed by the postwar Red Scare, quickly brought the remaining states into the extensive legal web of state-controlled flag statutes. However, Congress did not enact a national law against flag desecration until 1968, when the anti–Viet Nam War movement incorporated flags into acts of political protest (Robert Justin Goldstein, *Saving "Old Glory": The History of the American Flag Desecration Controversy* [Boulder: Westview, 1995], 18–19, 30, 40–41, 54–57).

57. Albert M. Rosenblatt, "Flag Desecration Statutes: History and Analysis," *Washington University Law Quarterly*, 1972, no. 2:193–237.

58. *Ruhstrat v. People*, Supreme Court of Illinois, 17 April 1900, in 57, *Northeastern Reporter, May 18–October 19, 1900* (St. Paul: West Publishing, 1900), 41–46.

59. Rosenblatt, "Flag Desecration Statutes," 199.

60. *Halter et al. v. State*, Supreme Court of Nebraska, 19 October 1905, in 105, *Northwestern Reporter, January 9–March 27, 1906* (St. Paul: West Publishing, 1906), 298–301.

61. *Halter v. Nebraska*, no. 174, submitted 23 January 1907, decided 4 March 1907, in 205, *United States Reports: Cases Adjusted in the Supreme Court at October Term, 1906* (New York: Banks Law Publishing, 1907), 34–46.

62. Elizabeth Gurley Flynn, *The Rebel Girl, an Autobiography: My First Life, 1906–1926*, new rev. ed. (New York: International Publishers, 1973), 229–30.

63. "Marine Punishes Man," *Milwaukee Sentinel*, 24 April 1917, 1.

64. "Insulter of Flag Is Made to Kiss It," *San Francisco Examiner*, 17 April 1917, 8.

65. "Diners Resent Slight to the Anthem," *New York Times*, 7 April 1917, 3.

66. The Texas "disloyalty act" remained in effect until 1973. During an anti–Viet Nam War protest, this law was used to sentence a man to a four-year prison term for burning a flag (Goldstein, *Saving "Old Glory,"* 80).

67. "Aliens Warned Against Desecrating American Flag," *New York Times*, 10 April 1917, 4.

68. "Twenty Days for Insult to Flag," ibid., 8.

69. Peterson and Fite, *Opponents of War*, 200–203.

70. "The State v. Shumaker, 9 November 1918, no. 21,894," in *Reports of Cases Argued and Determined in the Supreme Court of the State of Kansas, April 7, 1918–December 31, 1918*, 103 (1919; Topeka: Kansas State Printing Office, 1919), 741–43.

71. Rosenblatt, "Flag Desecration Statutes," 212–13; "The State v. Shumaker, 9 November 1918, no. 21,894," 741.

72. John McCabe, *George M. Cohan: The Man Who Owned Broadway* (Garden City, N.Y.: Doubleday, 1973), 74–75.

73. Curtis, *The Constitution and the Flag*, vol. 1, *The Flag Salute Cases*, xxiv–xxv.

74. Ex parte Starr, District Court, D. Montana, 31 January 1920, no. 794, in *The Federal Reporter: Cases Argued and Determined in the Circuit Courts*

of Appeals and District Courts of the United States and the Court of Appeals of the District of Columbia, May–June, 1920, 263 (St. Paul: West Publishing, 1920), 145–47.

75. Gary Gerstle, "The Protean Character of American Liberalism," *American Historical Review* 99 (October 1994): 1050–51.

76. Lawrence W. Levine, *The Opening of the American Mind: Canons, Culture, and History* (Boston: Beacon, 1996), 113–14.

77. Horace Kallen, "Democracy *versus* the Melting Pot," *Nation*, 18, 25 February 1915.

78. E. E. Bittenhouse, "The American Melting Pot Overwhelmed," *New York Times*, 6 May 1916, 10.

79. Richard L. Metcalf, "The Americanization of America," *Omaha World Herald*, 3 April 1917, 6.

80. Alan Dawley, *Struggles for Justice: Social Responsibility and the Liberal State* (Cambridge: Harvard University Press, Belknap Press, 1991), 181–82.

81. Preston, *Aliens and Dissenters*, chap. 3, "Naturalization and a New Law, 1912–1917," 63–87.

82. Samuel S. Marquis, "The Ford Idea in Education," in *Addresses and Proceedings of the National Education Association of the United States*, vol. 64 (n.p., 1916), 910–17; Stephen Meyer III, *The Five Dollar Day: Labor Management and Social Control in the Ford Motor Company, 1908–1921* (Albany: State University of New York Press, 1981), 157–58, 160–61; Olivier Zunz, *The Changing Face of Inequality: Urbanization, Industrial Development, and Immigrants in Detroit, 1880–1920* (Chicago: University of Chicago Press, 1982), 309–11.

83. Clinton C. DeWitt, "Industrial Teachers," in U.S. Department of the Interior, Americanization Division of the U.S. Bureau of Education, *Proceedings of the Americanization Conference* (Washington, D.C.: Government Printing Office, 1919), 119; Steve Babson, *Working Detroit: The Making of a Union Town* (Detroit: Wayne State University Press, 1986), 35.

84. Gerstle, "Protean Character of American Liberalism," 1054–55.

85. WRC, *Journal of the Thirty-Seventh National Convention, 1919* (Washington, D.C.: National Tribune, 1919), 82–83.

86. "Had no American Flag," *New York Times*, 16 April 1917, 6.

87. "Teaching Patriotism," ibid., 7 October 1917, 2.

88. David Montgomery, "Nationalism, American Patriotism, and Class Consciousness in the United States in the Epoch of World War I," in *"Struggle a Hard Battle": Essays on Working-Class Immigrants*, ed. Dirk Hoerder (Dekalb: Northern Illinois University Press, 1986), 327–51.

89. "President Calls for July 4 Celebration," *New York Times*, 25 May 1918, 7.

90. "Pledge by Foreign Born," ibid., 5 July 1918, 2.

91. For a comparative analysis, see Mommsen, "Varieties of the Nation State in Modern History," 214–17.

92. "Our German-Americans," *Des Moines Register,* 7 April 1917, 6.

93. "Loyalty Knows No Division," *Chicago Tribune*, 4 April 1917, 4.

94. Helen Z. Papanikolas, "Immigrants, Minorities, and the Great War," *Utah Historical Quarterly* 58 (fall 1990): 351–70.

95. "Dislikes His German Name," *Washington Post*, 14 April 1917, 12.

96. "Flag Insult Fake Harms Loyal Folk," *New York World,* 8 April 1917, 5.

97. "$1,000 to Run Down Flag Insult Rumor," ibid., 9 April 1917, 2.

98. Joan M. Jensen, *The Price of Vigilance* (Chicago: Rand McNally, 1968), 162–63; Goldstein, *Political Repression in Modern America*, 111–13.

99. Alan Howard Levy, "The American Symphony at War: German-American Musicians and Federal Authorities during World War I," *Mid-America: An Historical Review* 71 (January 1989): 5–7; Bliss Perry, *Life and Letters of Henry Lee Higginson* (Freeport, N.Y.: Books for Libraries, 1922), 486–87.

100. M. A. DeWolfe Howe, *The Boston Symphony Orchestra, 1881–1931* (New York: Da Capo, 1978), 133–36; J. E. Vacha, "When Wagner Was Verboten: The Campaign against German Music in World War I," *New York History* 24 (April 1983): 173, 178; "Ex-Gov. Warfield Would Mob Muck," *New York Times*, 5 November 1917, 13; Levy, "American Symphony at War," 10, 12.

101. "Austrian Wouldn't Salute," *New York Times*, 3 April 1917, 24.

102. "In Jail for Insulting Flag," ibid., 28 March 1918, 5.

103. Goldstein, *Political Repression in Modern America,* 107; John Higham, *Strangers in the Land: Patterns of American Nativism, 1860–1925* (1955; reprint, New York: Atheneum, 1967), 208–9; Vacha, "When Wagner Was Verboten," 172.

104. Frederick C. Luebke, *Bonds of Loyalty: German Americans and World War I* (Dekalb: Northern Illinois University Press, 1974), 270–71.

105. Erik Kirschbaum, *The Eradication of German Culture in the United States, 1917–1918* (Stuttgart: Akademischer Verlag / Academic Publishing House, 1986), 13–15.

106. Preston, *Aliens and Dissenters*, 1–7, 220–21, 236–37.

107. George Creel, quoted in Donald Johnson, *The Challenge to American Freedoms: World War I and the Rise of the American Civil Liberties Union* (Lexington: University Press of Kentucky, 1963), 69.

108. Hiram Johnson, quoted in Goldstein, *Political Repression in Modern America*, 167.

109. Eric Hobsbawm, *Nations and Nationalism since 1780: Programme, Myth, Reality* (Cambridge: Cambridge University Press, 1990), 92–93.

110. Dawley, *Struggles for Justice*, 257, 259, 261; William Pencak, *For God and Country: The American Legion, 1919–1941* (Boston: Northeastern University Press, 1989), 5, 37, 39, 46–47.

111. Tom Nairn uses the phrase "Janus-face of nationalism," in *The Break Up of Britain* (London: Verso, 1977). See also Homi Bhabha, ed., *Nation and Narration* (London: Routledge, 1990), 4.

112. Hobsbawm, *Nations and Nationalism*, 95.

113. Pencak, *For God and Country*, 45–47.

114. Marcus Garvey, "No Exclusive Right to the World," in *Negro Social and Political Thought, 1850–1920: Representative Texts*, ed. Howard Botz (New York: Basic Books, 1966), 575.

115. The concept of "in-between spaces" comes from Bhabha, introduction to *Nation and Narration*, 4.

116. Langston Hughes, "Let America Be America Again," in *The Collected Poems of Langston Hughes*, ed. Arnold Rampersad (New York: Knopf, 1995), 189–91.

* *Bibliography* *

PRIMARY SOURCES

Archives and Manuscript Collections

Richmond, Virginia
  Museum of the Confederacy. Historical Records and Scrapbooks.
  The Valentine: The Museum of the Life and History of Richmond, Virginia.
    Photographic Files.
  Virginia Historical Society.
Rochester, New York
  University of Rochester. Rush Rhees Library. Rare Books and Special Collections. Francis Bellamy Papers.
San Marino, California
  The Huntington Library. Photographic Files.
Stanford, California
  Stanford University. Cubberley Library. Historical Textbooks.
Washington, D.C.
  Howard University. Moorland-Spingarn Research Center. Black Press Archives. Tuskegee News Clipping File
  Library of Congress
    Manuscript Division. Papers of Christian Fleetwood. Frederick Douglass Papers. John Alexander Logan and Family Papers.
    Motion Picture Division. Early Motion Pictures: The Paper Print Collection. George Kleine Collection of Early Motion Pictures. Theodore Roosevelt Association Film Collection.
    Prints and Photographs Division. Mathew B. Brady Collection. Civil War Collection. Jacob Riis Collection. Specific Subjects Collection. Stereograph Collection. Washingtoniana Collection
  Smithsonian Institution, National Museum of American History
    Archives Center. Victor A. Blenkle Postcard Collection. Sam DeVincent Collection of Sheet Music. Warshaw Collection of Business Americana. Larry Zim and Edward J. Orth World's Fair Collection.
    Division of Political History. Photographic Files. Campaign Objects, 1894–1920.

Motion Pictures

Children Sewing Stars on Flag, Placing Flag on TR's Grave. News film. International Film Service, New York, 1919.
Ford, John. *Rio Grande.* Feature. Argosy-Republic, Hollywood, 1950.
———. *She Wore a Yellow Ribbon.* Feature. Argosy-RKO, Hollywood, 1949.

France, Floyd. *Two Kentucky Boys*. Feature. Thomas A. Edison, New York, 1917.

General Pershing Speaking to Scouts in New York. News film. International Film Service, New York, September 1919.

Griffith, D. W. *Birth of a Nation*. Feature. Epoch, 1915.

Griffith, Edward H. *The Boy Who Cried Wolf: The Story of a Boy Scout*. Feature. Thomas A. Edison, New York, 1917.

Seitz, George B. *Pearl White in the Pearl of the Army*. Serial. Astra Film Corporation, New York, 1916. Distributed by Pathe.

Theodore Roosevelt, Great Scout. 2d version. Factual compilation. by Roosevelt Memorial Association, Oyster Bay, N.Y., 1925.

Wake Up America Parade. Factual compilation. Thomas A. Edison, New York, between 1914 and 1917.

Music

Bratton, John W., words, and Harold Levery in collaboration with Geoffrey O'Hara, music. "America! Love it, or Leave it." N.p.: Belwin, 1961.

Brennan, J. Keirn, words, and Ernest R. Ball, music. "For Dixie and Uncle Sam." New York: M. Witmark & Sons, 1916.

Bryan, Alfred, words, and Al Piantadosi, music. "I Didn't Raise My Boy to Be a Soldier." New York: Leo. Feist, 1915.

Bunce, Harry T., words, and Will Donaldson, music. "Prepare the Eagle to Protect the Dove, That's the Battle Cry of Peace." New York: F. B. Haviland, 1916.

Cavanaugh, Eddie, words, and Bob Allan, music. "In Times of Peace Prepare for War." Chicago: Will Rossiter, 1915.

Cohan, George M. "Over There." New York: William Jerome, 1917.

Cole, E. E., words, and P. H. Sloan, music. "My Country Right or Wrong." N.p.: Coonley School Press, 1917.

Dempsey, E., words, and Joseph A. Burke, music. "If I Had a Son for Each Star in Old Glory, Uncle Sam I'd Give Them All to You." New York: Leo. Feist, 1917.

"The Girl I Left Behind Me." Author, exact date, and place of origin are unknown. Manuscripts containing the melody date back to 1770. Folklore Division, Library of Congress, Washington, D.C.

Grondahl, Jens K., words, and E. F. Maetzold, music. "America, My Country." Red Wing, Minn.: Red Wing, 1917.

Howe, Julia Ward. "Battle Hymn of the Republic." In *Twenty-Five Army Ballads: Boys Who Wore the Blue*, comp. S. B. Jones. Omaha: Republican Publishing & Printing, 1882.

Jeff in Petticoats. Chatman, N.Y.: H. De Marsan, n.d.

Jones, S. B., comp. *Twenty-Five Army Ballads: Boys Who Wore the Blue*. Omaha: Republican Publishing & Printing, 1882.

"Lordy, Turn Your Face." In *Singing Soldiers*, comp. John J. Niles. New York: Charles Scribner's Sons, 1927.

Marten, Frederick H., text, and Wil C. MacFarlane, music. *America First: A Boy Scout Operetta*. New York: J. Fisher & Brother, 1917.

"Trench Blues." In *Our Singing Country: A Second Volume of American Ballads and Folk Songs*, comp. John A. Lomax and Alan Lomax. New York: Macmillan, 1941.

Winge, Carl B. "Johnny Getcha Gun: It Looks Like War." Seattle: Echo Music, 1915.

Zirkle, Raymond. "Dixie Doodle: 'You're the Land for Me.' " Columbus, Ohio: Buckeye Music, 1918.

Newspapers and Serials

Afro-American Advance (Minneapolis and St. Paul). 1900.

Afro-American Ledger. 1900–1915 (Baltimore *Afro–American*).

American Monthly Magazine (Washington, D.C.). 1893–1920.

American Tribune (Indianapolis). 1895.

Atlanta Constitution. 1918.

Beadle's Half Dime Library. 1883–91.

Boston Guardian. 1904.

Broad Ax (Chicago). 1912–15.

Chicago Defender. 1909–17.

Chicago Tribune. 1892, 1916–17.

Christian Recorder (Philadelphia). 1878–1901.

Cleveland Gazette. 1892, 1898, 1902–19.

Colored American (Washington, D.C.). 1893, 1896, 1898.

Confederate Veteran (Nashville). 1893, 1895, 1897–99, 1913.

The Crisis (New York). 1910–20.

Daily Critic (Washington, D.C.). 1876, 1897.

Des Moines Register. 1917–18.

Douglass' Monthly (Rochester, N.Y.). 1863.

Frank Leslie's Illustrated Newspaper (New York). 1865, 1880–90.

Freeman (Indianapolis). 1913.

Harper's Weekly (New York). 1890.

Indianapolis Recorder. 1899–1919.

Los Angeles Times. 1917–18.

Milwaukee Sentinel. 1917.

Minneapolis Morning Tribune. 1917–18.

Mother Earth (New York). 1906–17.

Motography (Chicago). 1913–17.

Moving Picture World (New York). 1913–17.

National Tribune (Washington, D.C.). 1883–97, 1913, 1916.

New National Era (Washington, D.C.). 1870–74.

Freeman / New York Age. 1884–91, 1900–1920.

New York Journal. May 1898.

New York Times. 1861, 1865, 1877, 1892–1923, 1989, 1993–95.

New York World. 1916–17.

Omaha World Herald. 1917.

People's Advocate (Alexandria, Va.). 1876–86.

Public Opinion (New York). 1887–88.

Richmond (Va.) Planet. 1895–1919.

Saint Louis Post Dispatch. 1918.

San Francisco Examiner. 1886, 1903, 1913, 1917.

Savannah Tribune. 1899–1900.

Southern Workmen (Hampton, Va.). 1872–1919.

Standard (n.p.). 1908.

Voice of the Negro (Atlanta). 1904–7.

Washington Bee. 1880–1919.

Washington City Paper. 1995.

Washington Evening Star. 1865, 1897, 1892.

Washington Post. 1892, 1913, 1915–18, 1995.

Weekly Clarion: Official Journal of the State of Mississippi. July 1876.

Youth's Companion. 1888–93.

Other Primary Sources

Adams, John Quincy. "Emigration to the U. States." *Niles Weekly Register* 18 (29 April 1820): 157–58.

Adams, Samuel. Letter to Elbridge Gerry, Boston, 23 April 1784. In *The Writings of Samuel Adams, 1778–1802*, ed. Harry Alonso Cushing, 4:301. New York: G. P. Putnam's Sons, 1908.

American Caricatures Pertaining to the Civil War: Reproduced from the Original Lithographs Published from 1856 to 1872. New York: Brentanos, 1918.

Andrews, E. Benjamin. "Patriotism and the Public Schools." *Arena* 3 (December 1890): 71–80.

Annin & Co. *Annin & Co., Makers of Fine Flags.* New York, 1912.

The Army and Navy Primer. Chicago: Madison Book Co., 1903.

Babst, Earl D. "F. Wayland Ayer: The Business Pioneer." In *F. Wayland Ayer: Founder*, comp. F. W. Ayer & Sons. Philadelphia: N. W. Ayer & Sons, 1923.

Balch, George T. *Methods of Teaching Patriotism in the Public Schools.* New York: D. Van Nostrand. Indianapolis: Levey Bros., 1898.

Beath, Robert B. *History of the Grand Army of the Republic.* New York: Braun, Taylor, 1889.

Bellamy, Edward. *Looking Backward.* Boston: Picknar, 1888. Reprint. New York: New American Library, Signet Classic, 1960.

Beveridge, Albert J. "Senator Albert J. Beveridge's Salute to Imperialism, 1900." In *Major Problems in American Foreign Policy: Documents and Essays*, ed. Thomas G. Paterson, 1:389–91. Lexington, Mass.: Heath, 1989.

Brockett, L. P., M.D., and Mrs. Mary C. Vaughan. *Women's Work in the Civil War: A Record of Heroism, Patriotism and Patience*. Philadelphia: Zeigler, McCurdy, 1867.

Browne, Richard Wentworth. "Union War Songs and Confederate Officers." *Century Magazine* 35 (January 1888): 478.

Burgess, John. *Reconstruction and the Constitution*. New York: Charles Scribner's Sons, 1902.

Century, The. *Battles and Leaders of the Civil War: The Century War Book, People's Pictorial Edition*. New York, 1894.

Christian, D. D., and W. Asbury. *Richmond and Her Past*. 1912. Reprint. Spartanburg, S.C.: The Reprint Company, 1973.

Commager, Henry Steele. *Documents of American History*. 10th ed. Vol. 1. Englewood Cliffs, N.J.: Prentice Hall, 1988.

Committee on Public Information. *The Creel Report*. Washington, D.C.: Government Printing Office, 1920.

———. *The President's Flag Day Address with Evidence of Germany's Plans*. Special ed. N.p.: printed for distribution by Boy Scouts of America, 1917.

———. *The War Message and Facts behind It*. War Information Series No. 1. Washington, D.C., 1917.

Crane, Stephen. *The Red Badge of Courage and Other Stories*. 1895. New York: Penguin Books, 1991.

Creel, George. *How We Advertised America*. New York: Harper & Brothers, 1920.

Crevecoeur, Hector St. John de. *Letters from an American Farmer*. 1782. Reprint. New York: Penguin Books, 1983.

Daughters of the American Revolution. *Proceedings of the Continental Congress, National Society of the Daughters of the American Revolution, 1894–1920*. Place of publication varies.

———. *Third Report of the National Society of the Daughters of the American Revolution, October 11, 1889–1900*. 56th Cong., 2nd sess. 1901. S. Doc. 219.

Davis, John W. *Young America's Manual: The Child's Guide to Patriotism*. New York: Educational Publishing, 1906.

Davis, Margaret. *Mother Bickerdyke: Her Life and Labors for the Relief of Our Soldiers: Sketches of Battle Scenes and Incidents of the Sanitary Service*. San Francisco: A. T. Dewey, 1886.

Debs, Eugene V. "Canton, Ohio speech, June 16, 1918." In *Great Lives Observed: Debs*, ed. Ronald Radosh. Englewood Cliffs: Prentice Hall, 1971.

Douglass, Frederick. "The Present and Future of the Colored Race in America." Speech delivered in New York, May 1893. In *The Life and Writ-*

317

ings of Frederick Douglass, ed. Philip S. Foner. New York: International Publishers, 1952.

———. "What to the Slave is the Fourth of July?" Extract from an oration at Rochester, 5 July 1852. In *Frederick Douglass: Autobiographies*. New York: Library of America, 1994.

———. "The Freedmen's Monument to Abraham Lincoln." An address delivered in Washington, D.C., on 14 April 1876. In *The Frederick Douglass Papers*, vol. 4, 1864–80, eds. John W. Blassingame and John R. McKivigan. New Haven: Yale University, 1991.

———. "Why Should a Colored Man Enlist?" *Douglass' Monthly* (Rochester, N.Y.), April 1863, 819.

Du Bois, W. E. B. *The Autobiography of W. E. B. Du Bois: A Soliloquy on Viewing My Life from the Last Decade of Its First Century*. New York: International Publishers, 1968.

———.*Black Reconstruction in America: An Essay toward a History of the Part Which Black Folk Played in the Attempt to Reconstruct Democracy in America, 1860–1880*. 1935. Reprint. New York: Atheneum, 1970.

———. *The Conservation of the Races*. American Negro Academy Occasional Papers, no. 2. 1897. Reprint. New York: Arno Press, 1969.

———. *The Souls of Black Folk*. 1903. Reprint. New York: Knopf, Everyman's Library, 1993.

Emerson, Ralph Waldo. "Native Americans." In *The Journals and Miscellaneous Notebooks of Ralph Waldo Emerson*, vol. 9, *1843–1847*. Cambridge: Harvard University Press, Belknap Press, 1971.

Equal Suffrage: Address from the Colored Citizens of Norfolk, VA., to the People of the United States. New Bedford, Mass.: E. Anthony & Sons, Printers, 1865. Reprinted in Afro-American Series, ed. Maxwell Whiteman. Rhistoric Publication no. 216, pp. 1–26. Philadelphia: Rhistoric Publications, 1969.

Flanders, Jessie Knowlton. *Legislative Control of the Elementary Curriculum*. Contributions to Education, no. 195. New York: Teachers College, Columbia University, 1925.

Flynn, Elizabeth Gurley. *The Rebel Girl, an Autobiography: My First Life, 1906–1926*. New rev. ed. New York: International Publishers, 1973.

Foner, Eric, and Olivia Mahoney, exhibit curators. *America's Reconstruction: People and Politics After the Civil War*. Exhibit at the Virginia Historical Society, Richmond, Virginia, spring 1996.

Fulton, Robert I., and Thomas C. Trueblood, comps. *Patriotic Eloquence Relating to the Spanish-American War and Its Issues*. New York: Charles Scribner's Sons, 1900.

Garvey, Marcus. "No Exclusive Right to the World." In *Negro Social and Political Thought, 1850–1920: Representative Texts*, ed. Howard Botz. New York: Basic Books, 1966.

Gompers, Samuel. Letter to James Lynch, 26 October 1894. In *The Samuel Gompers Papers*, ed. Stuart B. Kaufman and Peter J. Albert, vol. 3, *Unrest and Depression, 1891–94*. Urbana: University of Illinois Press, 1989.

Grady, Henry W. "In Black and White: A Reply to Mr. Cable." *Century Magazine* 29 (April 1885): 909–15.

Grand Army of the Republic. *Proceedings of the . . . National Encampment, 1878–1914*. For some years the title reads, *Journal of the . . National Encampment*. Place of publication varies.

Grondlund, Laurence. "Nationalism." *Arena* 1 (January 1890): 153–65.

Hale, Edward Everett. "The Man Without a Country." *Atlantic Monthly*, December 1863, 665–79.

Hamilton, Gail [Mary Abigail Dodge]. "A Call To My Country-Women." *Atlantic Monthly*, March 1863, 346.

Harris, William T. "The National Educational Association: Its Organization and Functions." In *Report of the Commissioner of Education for the Year 1892–93*, 2:1502–6. Washington, D.C.: Government Printing Office, 1895.

Harvey, Frederick L. *History of the Washington National Monument and of the Washington Monument Society*. Washington, D.C.: Norman E. Elliot, 1902.

Harwood, W. S. "Secret Societies in America." *North American Review* 164 (May 1897): 617–24.

Haywood, Harry. *Black Bolshevik: Autobiography of an Afro-American Communist*. Chicago: Liberator, 1978.

Henry, Captain W. S. *Campaign Sketches of the War with Mexico*. New York: Harper & Brothers, 1848.

Herbert, Hilary A. *History of the Arlington Confederate Monument at Arlington, Virginia*. N.p.: United Daughters of the Confederacy, 1914.

Higginson, Thomas Wentworth. *Army Life in a Black Regiment*. Boston: Fields, Osgood, 1870.

Hill, Tucker. *Victory in Defeat: Jefferson Davis and the Lost Cause*. Richmond, Va.: Museum of the Confederacy, 1865.

Hooks, Janet Montgomery. *Women's Occupations through Seven Decades*. Women's Bureau Bulletin 218. Washington, D.C.: Government Printing Office, 1947.

Horner, Harlan Hoyt, ed. *The American Flag: New York State Education Department, Sixth Annual Report*. New York, 1910.

House, Grace B. *Soldiers of Freedom*. N.p., n.d.

Hubbard, Elbert. "A Message to Garcia." In *The Patriotic Reader for Seventh and Eighth Grades and Junior High Schools*, ed. Katharine Isabel Bemis, Mathilde Edith Holtz, and Henry Lester Smith. Boston: Houghton Mifflin, 1917.

Jefferson, Thomas. Letter to James Madison, Paris, 6 September 1789. In *The Papers of Thomas Jefferson*, ed. Julian P. Boyd, vol. 15, *27 March 1789 to 30 November 1789*. Princeton: Princeton University Press, 1958.

————. *Notes on the State of Virginia.* 1787. Reprint. Chapel Hill: University of North Carolina Press, 1955.

Johnson, James Weldon. *Along This Way: The Autobiography of James Weldon Johnson.* New York: Viking, 1933.

Kallen, Horace. "Democracy *versus* the Melting Pot." *Nation*, 18, 25 February 1915.

Kennedy, William Sloane. "Edward Everett Hale." *Century Illustrated Monthly Magazine* 12 (January 1885): 338–43.

Kerlin, Robert T., ed. *Voice of the Negro, 1919.* New York: E. P. Dutton, 1920.

Kipling, Rudyard. "The White Man's Burden." *McClure's Magazine* 12 (February 1899). http://home.ican.net/~fjzwick/ail198–35.html. In *Anti-Imperialism in the United States, 1898–1935*, ed. Jim Zwick, Syracuse University [created 15 March 1995; updated 11 January 1998].

Kornweibel, Theodore, ed. *Federal Surveillance of Afro-Americans, 1917–1925: The First World War, the Red Scare, and the Garvey Movement.* Black Studies Research Sources. Frederick, Md.: University Publications of America, 1985. Microfilm.

"The Late Riots." *Nation*, 2 August 1877, 68–69.

Laurie, Annie. "Respect the Flag." *American Monthly Magazine*, October 1893, 447–49.

"Let Us Have Peace." *Century Magazine* 29 (February 1885): 638.

Lincoln, Abraham. *The Collected Works of Abraham Lincoln.* Ed. Roy P. Basler. 8 vols. New Brunswick, N.J.: Rutgers University Press, 1953.

Lippard, George. *Washington and His Generals; or, Legends of the Revolution.* Philadelphia: G. B. Zieber, 1847.

Livermore, Mary A. *My Story of the War: A Woman's Narrative of Four Years Personal Experience.* . . . Hartford, Conn.: A. D. Worthington, 1889.

Lossing, Benson J. *Pictorial History of the Civil War in the United States of America.* Philadelphia: George W. Childs, 1866.

Lowell, James Russell. *The Writings of James Russell Lowell.* Vol. 5. Cambridge: Riverside Press, 1890.

Marquis, Samuel S. "The Ford Idea in Education." In *Addresses and Proceedings of the National Education Association of the United States*, vol. 64 (n.p., 1916), 910–17.

Mays, Benjamin E. *Born to Rebel: An Autobiography.* New York: Scribner, 1971.

McCarthy, Carlton. *Detailed Minutie of Soldier Life in the Army of Northern Virginia, 1861–1865.* Richmond, Va.: Carlton McCarthy, 1882.

Miller, Harry A. "Patriotism." *American Monthly Magazine*, November 1903, 404–5.

Miller, Joseph Danna. "Militarism or Manhood?" *Arena* 24 (July 1900): 379–92.

Morgan, Thomas Jefferson. *Patriotic Citizenship*. New York: American Book Company, 1895.

Morton, Joseph W., Jr., ed. *Sparks from the Campfire; or Tales of the Old Veterans*. Philadelphia: Keystone, 1895.

Moton, Robert Russa. *Finding a Way Out: An Autobiography*. Garden City, N.Y.: Negro University Press, 1920.

National Education Association. *Journal of Proceedings and Addresses, Session of the Year*, 1891–1918. Place of publication varies.

National Education Association. *Proceedings of the International Congress of Education of the World's Columbian Exposition, Chicago, July 25–28, 1893*. New York, 1894.

"North and South." *Century Magazine* 30 (October 1885): 965.

Office of the Adjutant-General of the Army. *Correspondence Relating to the War with Spain and Conditions Growing out of the Same Including the China Relief Expedition, between the Adjutant-Generals of the Army and Military Commanders in the United States, Cuba, Porto Rico, China, and the Philippine Islands, from April 15, 1898, to July 30, 1902*. Vol. 1. Washington, D.C.: Government Printing Office, 1902.

"Old Questions and New." *Century Illustrated Monthly Magazine* 29 (January 1885): 471–72.

Paul, Nathaniel. Letter to William Lloyd Garrison, *Liberator*, 12 April 1834. In *The Mind of the Negro as Reflected in Letters during the Crisis, 1800–1860*, ed. Carter G. Woodson. Washington, D.C.: Association of the Study of Negro Life and History, 1926.

Pennsylvania Commission. *Fiftieth Anniversary of the Battle of Gettysburg*. Harrisburg: WM. Stanley Ray, 1913.

Porter, Horace. "Grant's Last Campaign." *Century Magazine* 35 (November 1887): 145–52.

Preble, George Henry. *Origin and History of the American Flag*. New ed. 2 vols. Philadelphia: Nicholas L. Brown, 1917.

———. *Our Flag: Origin and Progress of the Flag of the United States of America*. Albany: Joel Munsell, 1872.

Prioleau, George W., Ninth Cavalry. Letter to the *Cleveland Gazette*, 22 October 1898. In *"Smoked Yankees" and the Struggle for Empire: Letters from Negro Soldiers, 1898–1902*, comp. Willard B. Gatewood Jr. Fayetteville: University of Arkansas Press, 1987.

Proceedings of the Convention of the Soldiers of the War of 1812, 1854. Syracuse: Edward Hoogland, Printer, Daily Republican and National Star Office, 1854.

Richards, Zalmon. "Historical Sketch of the National Education Association." In *Report of the Commissioner of Education for the Year 1892–93*, 2:1495–1502. Washington, D.C.: Government Printing Office, 1895.

Roosevelt, Theodore. "Address to the National Congress of Mothers." In *Report on the National Congress of Mothers, Held in the City of Washington, D.C., March 10–17, 1905*, by the National Congress of Parents and Teachers. N.p.: National Congress of Mothers, 1905.

———. *The Letters of Theodore Roosevelt*. Ed. Elting E. Morison. 8 vols. Cambridge: Harvard University Press, 1951–54.

———. *The New Nationalism*. New York: Outlook, 1910. Reprint. Englewood Cliffs: Prentice Hall, 1961.

———. "Race Decadence." *Outlook* 97 (8 April 1911): 763–69.

Roosevelt, Theodore. *The Rough Riders*. New York: Scribner's Sons, 1902.

Ropes, Hannah. *Civil War Nurse: The Diary and Letters of Hannah Ropes*. Ed. and comp. John R. Brumgardt. Knoxville: University of Tennessee Press, 1980.

Roy, Joseph Edwin. "Letter LXIX, The National Cemeteries at the South, Atlanta, GA., May 30, 1880." In *Pilgrim's Letters: Bits of Current History*. Boston: Congregational Sunday School and Publishing Society, 1888.

Rush, Benjamin. "Of the Mode of Education Proper in a Republic." In *Essays Literary, Moral and Philosophical*. 1786. Reprint. Schenectady: Union College Press, 1988.

Sandburg, Carl. *Always the Young Strangers*. New York: Harcourt, Brace, 1952.

Scott, Emmett J. *Scott's Official History of the American Negro in the World War*. Chicago: Homewood, 1919.

Sherman, William T. *Memoirs of Gen. W. T. Sherman, Written By Himself*. 4th ed. Vol. 2. New York: Charles L. Webster, 1891.

Sherwood, Kate Brownlee. *Camp-fire, Memorial-Day, and Other Poems*. Chicago: Jansen, McClurg, 1885.

Skinner, Charles R., ed. *Manual of Patriotism: For Use in the Public Schools in the State of New York, Authorized by Act of the Legislature*. Albany: Brandow, 1900.

Socialist Party of America. "To the People of the United States." In *The American Socialists and the War*, ed. Alexander Tractenberg. New York: Rand School of Social Science, 1917.

"Soldier and Citizen." *Century Magazine* 30 (October 1887): 950.

Stevens, Albert C. *Cyclopaedia of Fraternities*. New York: Hamilton, 1899.

Stevens, Walter J. *Chip on My Shoulder: Autobiography of Walter J. Stevens*. Boston: Meador, 1946.

Thoreau, Henry David. "Resistance to Civil Government." In *Great Short Works of Henry David Thoreau*, ed. Wendell Glick. New York: Harper Perennial, 1982.

Tocqueville, Alexis de. Letter to Ernest de Charbol, 9 June 1831. In *Selected Letters on Politics and Society*, ed. Roger Boesche, trans. James Toupin and Roger Boesche. London: Printed for T. Davis, 1782. Reprint. Berkeley: University of California Press, 1985.

Turner, Frederick Jackson. "The Significance of the Frontier in American History." In *The Frontier in American History.* 1893. Reprint. New York: Henry Holt, 1958.

Turner, Henry McNeal. "On the Anniversary of Emancipation, 1866." In *Respect Black: The Writings and Speeches of Henry McNeal Turner,* comp. Edwin S. Redkey, 5–12. New York: Arno Press and The New York Times, 1971.

United Confederate Veterans. *Minutes of the Twentieth Annual Meeting and Reunion of the United Confederate Veterans, 1910.* New Orleans: Schumert & Warfield, 1910.

United Daughters of the Confederacy. Constitution of the United Daughters of the Confederacy, 1903. Virginia State Library and Archives, Richmond, Va.

Upton, Bvt. Maj. Gen. Emory, United States Army. *The Military Policy of the United States.* 64th Cong., 1st sess., 1916. S. Doc. 379.

U.S. Bureau of the Census. *Historical Statistics of the United States, Colonial Times to 1970.* Bicentennial Edition. Washington, D.C.: U.S. Government Printing Office, 1975.

U.S. Congress. House of Representatives. *To Prevent Desecration of United States Flag.* 51st Cong., 1st sess., 24 May 1890. H. Rept. 2128.

U.S. Congress. Senate. Committee on Military Affairs. *American Flag: Hearings before the Committee on Military Affairs, Bills (S. 226, S. 229, S. 596, S. 1220, and S. 2504) to Prevent the Desecration of the American Flag.* 57th Cong., 1st sess., 20 February 1902. S. Doc. 22.

————. *Desecration of the American Flag.* 58th Cong., 2nd sess., 29 January 1904. S. Rept. 506.

U.S. Department of the Interior. Americanization Division of the U.S. Bureau of Education. *Proceedings of the Americanization Conference.* Washington, D.C.: Government Printing Office, 1919.

U.S. Department of Interior. National Park Services. National Register of Historic Places Inventory—Nomination Form. "Chickamauga-Chattanooga National Military Park." Structure #776, Kentucky State Monument.

U.S. Federal Bureau of Investigation. *Federal Bureau of Investigation Confidential Files.* Frederick, Md.: University Publications of America, 1989.

Van der Weyde, William M., III. *Life and Works of Thomas Paine.* New Rochelle, N.Y.: Thomas Payne National Historical Association, 1925.

Votaw, Clarence E. *"Patriotism": The Story of the Civil War in America: McGuffey's Fourth Reader of the Cherryville, Indiana, District School, 1860 and 1861, with Notes by the Schoolmates on the Fly-Leaves, Anna May Thistlewaite's Story, as Told in a Diary Kept by a Classmate, Nancy Cunningham.* Philadelphia: Dorrance, 1941.

Walworth, Ellen Hardin. "The Origin of the National Society of the Daughters of the American Revolution." *American Monthly Magazine*, July–December 1893, 114–18.

Warren, Mercy Otis. *History of the Rise, Progress, and Termination of the American Revolution*. Vol. 3. 1805. Reprint. New York: AMS Press, 1970.

Webster, Daniel. "The Addition to the Capitol: Address at the Laying of the Corner Stone of the Addition to the Capitol, on the 4th of July, 1851." In *The Great Speeches and Orations of Daniel Webster*. Boston: Little, Brown, 1882.

Wells-Barnett, Ida B., and Alfreda M. Duster, eds. *Crusade for Justice: The Autobiography of Ida B. Wells*. Chicago: University of Chicago Press, 1970.

Welsh, Peter. *Irish Green and Union Blue: The Civil War Letters of Peter Welsh, Color Sergeant, 28th Regiment, Massachusetts Volunteers*. Ed. Lawrence Frederick Kohl and Margaret Cossé Richard. New York: Fordham University Press, 1986.

Whitman, Walt. *Complete Poetry and Collected Prose*. New York: Viking, 1982.

————. *The Gathering of the Forces: Editorials, Essays, Literary and Dramatic Reviews, and Other Material Written by Walt Whitman as Editor of the Brooklyn Daily Eagle in 1846 and 1847*. Ed. Cleveland Rodgers and John Black. 2 vols. New York: G. P. Putnam's Sons, 1920.

Wickham, Gertrude Van Rensselaer. "The Mission of the Daughters of the American Revolution is that of Restoration, Preservation and Education." *American Monthly Magazine*, July 1893, 2.

Wilson, Woodrow. *A History of the American People*. Vols. 4 and 5. New York: Harper & Brothers, 1902.

————. Letter to Richard Heath Dabney, 7 November 1886. In *That Noble Dream: "The Objectivity Question" and the American Historical Professions*, by Peter Novick. Cambridge: Cambridge University Press, 1988.

Woodson, Carter G. *The Negro in Our History*. 6th ed. Washington, D.C.: Associated Publishers, 1922.

"Work of the Daughters." *American Monthly Magazine*, May 1907, 630–31.

Woman's Relief Corps, Massachusetts Department Convention. *History of the Department of Massachusetts Woman's Relief Corps, Auxiliary to the Grand Army of the Republic, from Date of Organization, February 12, 1879, to, January 1, 1895*. Boston: E. B. Stillings, 1895.

Woman's Relief Corps. *Journal of the Annual Convention of the Woman's Relief Corps, Auxiliary to the Grand Army of the Republic*, 1885–1920. Title and place of publication vary.

Wright, Richard. *Black Boy*. 1937. Reprint. New York: Harper & Row, 1966.

Young, Hon. James Rankin, comp. *Reminiscences and Thrilling Stories of the War by Returned Heroes Containing Vivid Accounts of Personal Experiences by Officers and Men*. Chicago: C. W. Stanton, 1899.

SECONDARY SOURCES

Abercrombie, Nicholas, Stephen Hill, and Bryan S. Turner. *The Penguin Dictionary of Sociology*. London: Allen Lane, 1984.

Allen, Robert, in collaboration with Pamela P. Allen. *Reluctant Reformers: Racism and Social Reform Movements in the United States*. Washington, D.C.: Howard University Press, 1983.

Allyn, Nancy E. "Uncle Sam Speaks: Broadsides and Posters from the National Archives." *Prologue*, winter 1985, 259–63.

Anderson, Benedict. *Imagined Communities: Reflections on the Origin and Spread of Nationalism*. Rev. ed. London: Verso, 1991.

———. "The New World Disorder." *New Left Review* 193 (May/June 1992): 3–13.

Anderson, Jervis. *A. Philip Randolph: A Biographical Portrait*. New York: Harcourt Brace Jovanovich, 1972.

Anthias, Floya, and Nira Yuval-Davis, eds. *Woman-Nation-State*. New York: St. Martin's, 1989.

Appelbaum, Diana Karter. *The Glorious Fourth: An American Holiday, an American History*. New York: Facts on File, 1989.

Appleby, Joyce. "Recovering America's Historic Diversity: Beyond Exceptionalism." *Journal of American History* 79 (September 1992): 419–31.

———. "Republicanism and Ideology." *American Quarterly* 37 (fall 1985): 461–73.

Architect of the Capitol. *Art in the United States Capitol*. Washington, D.C.: Government Printing Office, 1976.

Attie, Jeanie. "Warwork and the Crisis of Domesticity in the North." In *Divided Houses: Gender and the Civil War*, ed. Catherine Clinton and Nina Silber, 251–59. New York: Oxford University Press, 1992.

Ayers, Edward L. *Southern Crossing: A History of the American South, 1877–1906*. New York: Oxford University Press, 1995.

Babson, Steve. *Working Detroit: The Making of a Union Town*. Detroit: Wayne State University Press, 1986.

Baer, John W. *The Pledge of Allegiance: A Centennial History, 1892–1992*. N.p., 1992.

Bailey, Fred Arthur. "Textbooks of the 'Lost Cause': Censorship and the Creation of Southern State Histories." *Georgia Historical Quarterly* 75 (fall 1991): 507–33.

Bailyn, Bernard. *The Ideological Origins of the American Revolution*. Cambridge: Harvard University Press, Belknap Press, 1967.

Baker, Paula. "The Domestication of Politics: Women and American Political Society, 1780–1920." *American Historical Review* 89 (June 1984): 620–47.

Barbeau, Arthur E., and Florette Henri. *The Unknown Soldiers: Black American Troops in World War I*. Philadelphia: Temple University Press, 1974.

Beath, Robert B. *History of the Grand Army of the Republic*. New York: Bryan, Taylor, 1889.

Bederman, Gail. *Manliness and Civilization: A Cultural History of Gender and Race in the United States, 1880–1917*. Chicago: University of Chicago Press, 1995.

Beisner, Robert L. *Twelve against Empire: The Anti-Imperialists, 1898–1900*. New York: McGraw-Hill, 1968.

Bergman, Peter M. *The Chronological History of the Negro in America*. New York: Harper & Row, 1969.

Berry, Wendell. *The Hidden Wound*. San Francisco: North Point, 1989.

Bhabha, Homi K., ed. *Nation and Narration*. London: Routledge, 1990.

Bimba, Anthony. *The History of the American Working Class*. New York: International Publishers, 1927.

Blakely, George T. *Historians on the Homefront: American Propagandists for the Great War*. Lexington: University Press of Kentucky, 1970.

Blight, David W. " 'For Something beyond the Battlefield': Frederick Douglass and the Struggle for the Memory of the Civil War." *Journal of American History* 75 (September 1988): 1156–78.

———. "The Strange Meaning of Being Black: Du Bois' American Tragedy." In *The Souls of Black Folk by W. E. B. Du Bois*, ed. David W. Blight and Robert Gooding-Williams. Boston: Bedford Books, 1997.

Bloch, Ruth H. "Gendered Meanings of Virtue in Revolutionary America." *Signs* 13 (fall 1987): 37–58.

Bodnar, John. *Remaking America: Public Memory, Commemoration, and Patriotism in the Twentieth Century*. Princeton: Princeton University Press, 1992.

———, ed. *Bonds of Affection: Americans Define Their Patriotism*. Princeton: Princeton University Press, 1996.

Boorstin, Daniel J. *The Americans: The National Experience*. New York: Vintage Books, 1965.

Bowles, Samuel, and Herbert Gintis. *Schooling in Capitalist America: Educational Reform and the Contradictions of Economic Life*. New York: Basic Books, 1976.

Bowser, Eileen. *The Transformation of the Cinema, 1907–1915*. Vol. 2, *History of the American Cinema*. New York: Charles Scribner's Sons, 1990.

Brady, Marilyn Dell. "The Kansas Federation of Colored Women's Clubs, 1900–30." *Kansas History* 9 (spring 1986): 19–30.

Brandt, Nat. "To the Flag." *American Heritage: The Magazine of History* 22 (June 1971): 72–75.

Breisach, Ernst. *Historiography: Ancient, Medieval, and Modern*. Chicago: University of Chicago Press, 1983.

Britt, Brian. "Whistling 'Dixie': Georgia Rallies Round the Flag." *Nation*, 5 April 1993, 450–51.

Bryan, C. D. B. *Friendly Fire*. New York: Bantam Books, 1976.

Burke, Peter. "History as Social Memory." In *Memory: History, Culture, and the Mind*, ed. Thomas Butler. Oxford: Blackwell, 1989.

Butler, Thomas. *Memory: History, Culture, and the Mind*. Oxford: Blackwell, 1989.

Carby, Hazel V. *Reconstructing Womanhood*. New York: Oxford University Press, 1987.

Carlson, Robert A. *The Americanization Syndrome: A Quest for Conformity*. Rev. ed. London: Croom Helm, 1987.

Carnes, Mark C. *Secret Ritual and Manhood in Victorian America*. New Haven: Yale University Press, 1989.

Carnes, Mark C., and Clyde Griffen, eds. *Meanings for Manhood: Constructions of Masculinity in Victorian America*. Chicago: University of Chicago Press, 1990.

Chambers, John Whiteclay, II, ed. *The Eagle and the Dove: The American Peace Movement and Unites States Foreign Policy, 1900–1922*. New York: Garland, 1976.

Chandler, Alfred D., Jr. *The Visible Hand: The Managerial Revolution in American Business*. Cambridge: Harvard University Press, Belknap Press, 1977.

Chatterjee, Partha. "Colonialism, Nationalism, and Colonized Women: The Contest in India." *American Ethnologist* 16 (November 1989): 622–33.

Chicago Commission on Race Relations. *The Negro in Chicago: A Study of Race Relations and a Race Riot*. Chicago: University of Chicago Press, 1922.

Clawson, Mary Ann. *Constructing Brotherhood: Class, Gender, and Fraternalism*. Princeton: Princeton University Press, 1989.

Clifford, Carrie Williams. "The Black Draftee from Dixie." In *Black Sister: Poetry by Black American Women, 1746–1980*, ed. Erlene Stetson. Bloomington: Indiana University Press, 1981.

Clinton, Catherine, and Nina Silber, eds. *Divided Houses: Gender and the Civil War*. New York: Oxford University Press, 1992.

Coffman, Edward M. *The War to End All Wars: The American Military Experience in World War I*. New York: Oxford University Press, 1968.

Colley, Linda. *Britons: Forging the Nation, 1701–1837*. New Haven: Yale University Press, 1992.

Collins, Herbert Ridgeway. *Threads of History: Americana Recorded on Cloth, 1775 to the Present*. Washington, D.C.: Smithsonian Institution Press, 1979.

Connerton, Paul. *How Societies Remember*. New York: Cambridge University Press, 1989.

Connor, Walker. "Nation-Building or Nation-Destroying?" *World Politics* 24, no. 3 (1972): 319–35.

Cosmas, Graham A. *An Army for an Empire: The United States Army in the Spanish-American War*. Columbia: University of Missouri Press, 1971.

Cott, Nancy F. *The Grounding of Modern Feminism*. New Haven: Yale University Press, 1987.

Cremin, Lawrence A. *American Education: The Metropolitan Experience, 1876–1980*. New York: Harper & Row, 1988.

Curti, Merle. *The Roots of American Loyalty*. New York: Columbia University Press, 1946.

Curtis, Michael Kent, ed. *The Constitution and the Flag*. Vol. 1, *The Flag Salute Cases*. Vol 2, *The Flag Burning Cases*. New York: Garland, 1993.

Cutchins, Col. John A. *Famous Command: The Richmond Light Infantry Blues*. Richmond, Va.: Garret & Massie, 1934.

Davies, Wallace Evan. *Patriotism on Parade: The Story of Veterans' and Hereditary Organizations in America, 1783–1900*. Cambridge: Harvard University Press, 1955.

————. "The Problem of Race Segregation in the Grand Army of the Republic." *Journal of Southern History* 13 (August 1947): 354–72.

Davis, Susan G. *Parades and Power: Street Theater in Nineteenth-Century Philadelphia*. Philadelphia: Temple University Press, 1986.

Davis, Stephen. "A Matter of Sensational Interest: The Century Battles and Leaders Series." *Civil War History: A Journal of the Middle Period* 28 (December 1981): 338–43.

Dawley, Alan. *Struggles for Justice: Social Responsibility and the Liberal State*. Cambridge: Harvard University Press, Belknap Press, 1991.

Dearing, Mary Rulkatter. *Veterans in Politics: The Story of the GAR*. Baton Rouge: Louisiana State University Press, 1952).

DeWolfe Howe, M. A. *The Boston Symphony Orchestra, 1881–1931*. New York: Da Capo, 1978.

Donald, James, and Stuart Hall, eds. *Politics and Ideology*. Milton Keynes, England: Open University Press, 1986.

Donner, Frank J. *The Age of Surveillance: The Aims and Methods of America's Intelligence System*. New York: Knopf, 1980.

Doob, Leonard W. *Patriotism and Nationalism: Their Psychological Foundations*. New Haven: Yale University Press, 1964.

D'Otrange Mastai, Boleslaw, and Marie-Louise D'Otrange Mastai. *The Stars and the Stripes: The American Flag as Art and as History from the Birth of the Republic to the Present*. New York: Knopf, 1973.

Douglas, George William. *The American Book of Days*. New York: H. W. Wilson, 1937.

Drake, St. Clair, and Horace R. Cayton. *Black Metropolis: A Study of Negro Life in a Northern City*. New York: Harcourt, Brace, 1945.

DuBois, Ellen Carol. *Feminism and Suffrage: The Emergence of an Independent Women's Movement in America, 1848–1869*. Ithaca: Cornell University Press, 1978.

Dumenil, Lynn. *Freemasonry and American Culture, 1880–1930.* Princeton: Princeton University Press, 1984.

Eley, Geoff, and Ronald Grigor Suny, eds. *Becoming National: A Reader.* New York: Oxford University Press, 1996.

Elson, Ruth Miller. *Guardians of Tradition: American Schoolbooks of the Nineteenth Century.* Lincoln: University of Nebraska Press, 1964.

Englehardt, Tom, and Edward T. Linenthal. *History Wars: The Enola Gay and Other Battles for the American Past.* New York: Metropolitan Books, 1996.

Findling, John E., ed. *Historical Dictionary of World's Fairs and Expositions, 1851–1988.* New York: Greenwood, 1990.

Fisher, Roger A., and Edmund B. Sullivan. *American Political Ribbons and Ribbon Badges, 1825–1981.* Lincoln, Mass.: Quarterman, 1985.

Foner, Eric. *Reconstruction: America's Unfinished Revolution, 1863–1877.* New York: Harper & Row, 1988.

Foner, Philip S. *The Industrial Workers of the World, 1905–1917.* New York: International Publishers, 1965.

Foster, Gaines M. *Ghost of the Confederacy; Defeat, the Lost Cause, and the Emergence of the New South.* New York: Oxford University Press, 1987.

Franklin, John Hope. " 'Birth of a Nation'—Propaganda as History." *Massachusetts Review* 20 (fall 1979): 417–34.

———. *From Slavery to Freedom.* New York: Knopf, 1988.

Fraser, Nancy, and Linda Gordon. "Contract versus Charity: Why Is There No Social Citizenship in the United States?" *Socialist Review* 22 (July–September 1992): 45–67.

Fredrickson, George M. *The Inner Civil War: Northern Intellectuals and the Crisis of the Union.* New York: Harper & Row, 1965.

Furlong, William Rea, Byron McCandless, and Harold D. Langley. *So Proudly We Hail: The History of the United States Flag.* Washington, D.C.: Smithsonian Institution Press, 1981.

Gabriel, Ralph Henry. *The Course of American Democratic Thought: An Intellectual History since 1815.* New York: Ronald Press, 1940.

Gardels, Nathan. "Two Concepts of Nationalism: An Interview with Isaiah Berlin." *New York Review of Books,* 21 November 1991, 19.

Gatewood, Willard B., Jr., comp. *"Smoked Yankees" and the Struggle for Empire: Letters from Negro Soldiers, 1898–1902.* Fayetteville: University of Arkansas Press, 1987.

Gellner, Ernest. *Nations and Nationalism.* Ithaca: Cornell University Press, 1983.

———. *Thought and Change.* Chicago: University of Chicago Press, 1964.

Gerdts, William H. *American Neo-Classical Sculpture: The Marble Resurrection.* New York: A Studio Book, 1973.

Gerstle, Gary. "The Protean Character of American Liberalism." *American Historical Review* 99 (October 1994): 1043–73.

Gerstle, Gary. *Working-Class Americanism: The Politics of Labor in a Textile City, 1914–1960*. Cambridge: Cambridge University Press, 1989.

Giddings, Paula. *When and Where I Enter: The Impact of Black Women on Race and Sex in America*. New York: Morrow, 1984.

Gillis, John R., ed. *Commemorations: The Politics of National Identity*. Princeton: Princeton University Press, 1994.

Gilroy, Paul. *"There Ain't No Black in the Union Jack": The Cultural Politics of Race and Nation*. London: Unwin Hyman, 1987.

Gitlin, Todd. *The Twilight of Common Dreams: Why America Is Wracked by Culture Wars*. New York: Metropolitan Books, 1995.

Glassberg, David. *American Historical Pageantry: The Uses of Tradition in the Early Twentieth Century*. Chapel Hill: University of North Carolina Press, 1990.

Glickman, Lawrence B. *A Living Wage: American Workers and the Making of Consumer Society*. Ithaca: Cornell University Press, 1997.

————."Inventing the 'American Standard of Living': Gender, Race, and Working Class Identity, 1880–1925." *Labor History* 34 (spring 1993): 221–35.

Goetzmann, William H., ed. *The American Hegelians: An Intellectual Episode in the History of Western America*. New York: Knopf, 1973.

Goldstein, Robert Justin. *Political Repression in Modern America, 1870 to the Present*. Cambridge, Mass.: Schenkman, 1978.

————. *Saving "Old Glory": The History of the American Flag Desecration Controversy*. Boulder: Westview, 1995.

Goode, James M. *The Outdoor Sculpture of Washington: A Comprehensive Historical Guide*. Washington, D.C.: Smithsonian Institution Press, 1974.

Greenfeld, Liah. *Nationalism: Five Roads to Modernity*. Cambridge: Harvard University Press, 1992.

Guenter, Scot M. *The American Flag: Cultural Shifts from Creation to Codification, 1777–1924*. Rutherford: Fairleigh Dickinson University Press, 1990.

Halbwachs, Maurice. *The Collective Memory*. New York: Harper Colophon Books, 1980.

Hall, Catherine. *White, Male, and Middle Class: Explorations in Feminism and History*. Cambridge: Polity Press, 1992.

Hall, John, ed. *States in History*. Oxford: Blackwell, 1986.

Hall, Stuart. *The Hard Road to Renewal: Thatcherism and the Crisis of the Left*. London: Verso, 1988.

Hall, Stuart, David Held, and Tony McGraw, eds. *Modernity and Its Futures*. Cambridge: Polity Press in Association with the Open University, 1992.

Harrington, Mona. "Loyalties: Dual and Divided." In *Harvard Encyclopedia of American Ethnic Groups*, ed. Stephan Thernstrom. Cambridge: Harvard University Press, Belknap Press, 1980.

Harris, Louise. *The Flag over the Schoolhouse*. Providence, R.I.: C. A. Stephens Collection, 1971.

Hatch, Jane M., comp. and ed. *The American Book of Days*. 3rd ed. New York: H. W. Wilson, 1978.

Herbst, Jurgen. *And Sadly Teach: Teacher Education and Professionalization in American Culture*. Madison: University of Wisconsin Press, 1989.

Higham, John. *Strangers in the Land: Patterns of American Nativism, 1860–1925*. 1955. Reprint. New York: Atheneum, 1967.

Hobsbawm, Eric. *The Age of Extremes: A History of the World, 1914–1991*. New York: Pantheon Books, 1994.

———. "Mass-Producing Traditions: Europe, 1870–1914." In *The Invention of Tradition*, ed. Eric Hobsbawm and Terence Ranger. 1983. Reprint. Cambridge: Cambridge University Press, 1988.

———. *Nations and Nationalism since 1780: Programme, Myth, Reality*. Cambridge: Cambridge University Press, 1990.

———. "Some Reflections on 'The Break-up of Britain.' " *New Left Review* 105 (September 1977): 3–23.

Hobsbawm, Eric, and Terence Ranger, eds. *The Invention of Tradition*. 1983. Reprint. Cambridge: Cambridge University Press, 1988.

Hoffsommer, Robert D. "The Aftermath of Gettysburg: The Story of the Casualties." *Civil War Times Illustrated* 2 (July 1963): 35–38.

Hofstadter, Richard. *Anti-Intellectualism in American Life*. New York: Knopf, 1969.

Hornung, Clarence P., ed. and comp. *The American Eagle in Art and Design*. New York: Dover, 1978.

Huang, Nian-Sheng. *Benjamin Franklin in American Thought and Culture, 1790–1990*. Philadelphia: American Philosophical Society, 1994.

Hughes, Langston. *The Collected Poems of Langston Hughes*. Ed. Arnold Rampersad. New York: Knopf, 1995.

Hunt, Lynn. *Politics, Culture, and Class in the French Revolution*. Berkeley: University of California Press, 1984.

———, ed. *The New Cultural History*. Berkeley: University of California Press, 1989.

Hunton, Addie W., and Kathryn M. Johnson. *Two Colored Women with the American Expeditionary Forces*. Brooklyn: Brooklyn Eagle, 1920.

Jensen, Joan M. *The Price of Vigilance*. Chicago: Rand McNally, 1968.

Johannsen, Robert W. *To the Halls of Montezumas: The Mexican War in the American Imagination*. New York: Oxford University Press, 1985.

Johnson, Donald. *The Challenge to American Freedoms: World War I and the Rise of the American Civil Liberties Union*. Lexington: University Press of Kentucky, 1963.

Jones, Jacqueline. *Soldiers of Light and Love: Northern Teachers and Georgia Blacks, 1865–1873*. Athens, Ga.: Brown Thrasher Books, 1980.

Judt, Tony. "The New Old Nationalism." *New York Review of Books*, 26 May 1994, 44.

Kaestle, Carl F. *Pillars of the Republic: Common Schools and American Society.* New York: Hill & Wang, 1983.

Kammen, Michael. *Mystic Cords of Memory: The Transformation of Tradition in American Culture.* 1991. Reprint. New York: Vintage Books, 1993.

———. "The Problem of American Exceptionalism: A Reconsideration." *American Quarterly* 45 (March 1993): 1–43.

———. *A Season of Youth: The American Revolution and Historical Imagination.* New York: Knopf, 1978.

Kaplan, Amy. "Romancing the Empire: The Embodiment of American Masculinity in the Popular Historical Novel of the 1890s." *American Literary History* 3 (December 1990): 659–90.

Katz, Michael B. *Reconstructing Education.* Cambridge: Harvard University Press, 1987.

Kerber, Linda K. *Women of the Republic: Intellect and Ideology in Revolutionary America.* New York: Norton, 1980.

King, Anthony, ed. *Culture, Globalization, and the World System.* London: Macmillan, 1991.

Kirschbaum, Erik. *The Eradication of German Culture in the United States, 1917–1918.* Stuttgart: Akademischer Verlag / Academic Publishing House, 1986.

Kohn, Hans. *American Nationalism: An Interpretive Essay.* New York: Macmillan, 1957.

Lahue, Kalton C. *Continued Next Week: A History of the Moving Picture Serial.* Norman: University of Oklahoma Press, 1964.

Lankevich, John George. "The Grand Army of the Republic in New York State, 1865–1898." Ph.D. diss., Columbia University, 1967.

Leonard, Elizabeth D. *Yankee Women: Gender Battles in the Civil War.* New York: Norton, 1994.

Leonard, Thomas C. *Above the Battle: War Making in America from Appomattox to Versailles.* New York: Oxford University Press, 1978.

Levine, Lawrence W. "Marcus Garvey and the Politics of Revitalization." In *Black Leaders of the Twentieth Century,* ed. John Hope Franklin and August Meier. Urbana: University of Illinois Press, 1982.

———. *The Opening of the American Mind: Canons, Culture, and History.* Boston: Beacon, 1996.

Levy, Alan Howard. "The American Symphony at War: German-American Musicians and Federal Authorities during World War I." *Mid-America: An Historical Review* 71 (January 1989): 5–13.

Lind, Michael. *The Next American Nation: The New Nationalism and the Fourth American Revolution.* New York: Free Press, 1995.

Linderman, Gerald F. *Embattled Courage: The Experience of Combat in the American Civil War*. New York: Free Press, 1987.

———. *The Mirror of War: American Society and the Spanish-American War*. Ann Arbor: University of Michigan Press, 1974.

Lindsay, Bryan. "Anacreon on the Wagon: 'The Star-Spangled Banner' in the Service of the Cold Water Army." *Journal of Popular Culture* 4 (winter 1973): 595–600.

Linenthal, Edward Tabor. *Sacred Ground: Americans and Their Battlefields*. 2nd ed. Urbana: University of Illinois Press, 1993.

Linenthal, Edward Tabor, and David Chidester, eds. *American Sacred Space*. Bloomington: Indiana University Press, 1995.

Lipsitz, George. *Time Passages: Collective Memory and American Popular Culture*. Minneapolis: University of Minnesota Press, 1990.

Litwack, Leon F. *Been in the Storm So Long: The Aftermath of Slavery*. New York: Knopf, 1979.

———. "The Historian, the Filmmaker, and the Civil War." In *Ken Burn's The Civil War: Historians Respond*, ed. Robert Brent Toplin. New York: Oxford University Press, 1996.

———. *Trouble in Mind: Black Southerners in the Age of Jim Crow*. New York: Knopf, 1998.

———. "Trouble in Mind: The Bicentennial and the Afro-American Experience." *Journal of American History* 74 (September 1987): 315–37.

Litwack, Leon F., and August Meier, eds. *Black Leaders of the Nineteenth Century*. Urbana: University of Illinois Press, 1988.

Logan, John. "The Dangerous West Point Monopoly." In *The American Military: Readings in the History of the Military in American Society*, ed. Russell F. Weigley, 77–85. Menlo Park: Addison-Wesley, 1969.

Lowenthal, Max. *The Federal Bureau of Investigation*. New York: Harcourt Brace Jovanovich, 1950.

Luebke, Frederick C. *Bonds of Loyalty: German Americans and World War I*. Dekalb: Northern Illinois University Press, 1974.

Lyons, Linda Brody. *A Handbook to the Pension Building*. Washington, D.C.: National Building Museum, 1989.

Magruder, Maj. John H., III. "A Touch of Tradition." *Marine Corps Gazette*, July 1955, 47.

Mann, Michael, ed. *The Rise and Decline of the Nation State*. Oxford: Blackwell, 1990.

Marling, Karal Ann. *George Washington Slept Here: Colonial Revivals and American Culture, 1876–1986*. Cambridge: Harvard University Press, 1988.

Masa, Ann. "Black Women in the 'White City.' " *Journal of American Studies* 8 (December 1974): 319–37.

Mattfeld, Julius. *Variety Music Cavalcade, 1620–1969: A Chronology of Vocal and Instrumental Music Popular in the United States*. Englewood Cliffs: Prentice Hall, 1971.

May, Lary. *Screening Out the Past: The Birth of Mass Culture and the Motion Picture Industry*. Chicago: University of Chicago Press, 1980.

McCabe, John. *George M. Cohan: The Man Who Owned Broadway*. Garden City, N.Y.: Doubleday, 1973.

McClintock, Anne. *Imperial Leather: Race, Gender, and Sexuality in the Colonial Contest*. New York: Routledge, 1995.

McConnell, Stuart. *Glorious Contentment: The Grand Army of the Republic, 1865–1900*. Chapel Hill: University of North Carolina Press, 1992.

McKitrick, Eric L. *Andrew Johnson and Reconstruction*. Chicago: University of Chicago Press, 1960.

Meier, August. *Negro Thought in America, 1880–1915: Racial Ideologies in the Age of Booker T. Washington*. Rev. ed. Ann Arbor: University of Michigan Press, 1973.

Melosh, Barbara, ed. *Gender and American History since 1890*. London: Routledge, 1993.

Meyer, John W., David B. Tyack, Joane Nagel, and Audri Gordon. "Public Education as Nation-Building in America: Enrollments and Bureaucratization in the American States, 1870–1930." *American Journal of Sociology* 85 (November 1979): 591–613.

Meyer, Stephen, III. *The Five Dollar Day: Labor Management and Social Control in the Ford Motor Company, 1908–1921*. Albany: State University of New York Press, 1981.

Miller, Stuart Creighton. "The American Soldier and the Conquest of the Philippines." In *Reappraising an Empire: New Perspectives on Philippine-American History*, ed. Peter W. Stanley. Cambridge: Committee on American–East Asian Relations of the Department of History in collaboration with the Council on East Asian Studies, Harvard University, 1984.

Mommsen, Wolfgang J. "The Varieties of the Nation State in Modern History: Liberal, Imperialist, Fascist, and Contemporary Notions of Nation and Nationality." In *The Rise and Decline of the Nation State*, ed. Michael Mann. Oxford: Blackwell, 1990.

Montejano, David. *Anglos and Mexicans in the Making of Texas, 1836–1986*. Austin: University of Texas Press, 1987.

Montgomery, David. *Citizen Worker: The Experience of Workers in the United States with Democracy and the Free Market during the Nineteenth Century*. Cambridge: Cambridge University Press, 1993.

———. *The Fall of the House of Labor: The Workplace, the State, and American Labor Activism, 1865–1925*. Cambridge: Cambridge University Press, 1987.

Montgomery, David. "Nationalism, American Patriotism, and Class Consciousness in the United States in the Epoch of World War I." In *"Struggle a Hard Battle": Essays on Working-Class Immigrants*, ed. Dirk Hoerder. Dekalb: Northern Illinois University Press, 1986.

Morgan, Francesca. " 'Home and Country': Women, Nation, and the Daughters of the American Revolution, 1890–1930." Ph.D. diss., Columbia University, 1998.

Moser, Don. "At 75, the Boy Scouts Still Answer the Call of Adventure." *Smithsonian Magazine*, July 1985, 33–40.

Mosse, George L. *The Image of Man: The Creation of Modern Masculinity.* New York: Oxford University Press, 1996.

Mott, Frank Luther. *Golden Multitudes: The Story of Best Sellers in the United States*. New York: R. R. Bower, 1947.

Muller, Joseph. *The Star Spangled Banner: Words and Music Issued between 1814–1864*. New York: G. A. Baker, 1935.

Munford, Robert Beverley, Jr. *Richmond Homes and Memories*. Richmond, Va.: Garret & Massie, 1936.

Murray, William D. *The History of the Boy Scouts of America*. New York: Boy Scouts of America, 1937.

Nairn, Tom. *The Break Up of Britain*. London: Verso, 1977.

Nalty, Bernard C. *Strength for the Fight: A History of Black Americans in the Military*. New York: Free Press, 1986.

Neverdon-Morton, Cynthia. *Afro-American Women of the South and the Advancement of the Race, 1895–1925*. Knoxville: University of Tennessee Press, 1989.

Niles, John Jacob. "White Pioneers and Black." *Musical Quarterly* 18 (January 1932): 60–75.

Nitchkey, Charles R. *Gettysburg 1863 and Today*. Hicksville, N.Y.: Exposition Press, 1980.

Novick, Peter. *That Noble Dream: "The Objectivity Question" and the American Historical Profession*. Cambridge: Cambridge University Press, 1988.

Nugent, Walter T. K. "Seed Time of Modern Conflict: American Society at the Centennial." In *Indiana Historical Society Lectures, 1972–1973: 1876 the Centennial Year*, by Lillian B. Miller, Walter T. K. Nugent, and Wayne Moisan. Indianapolis: Indiana Historical Society, 1973.

O'Reilly, Kenneth. *"Racial Matters": The FBI's Secret File on Black America, 1960–1972*. New York: Free Press, 1989.

Painter, Nell Irvin. *Standing at Armageddon: The United States, 1877–1919*. New York: Norton, 1987.

Papanikolas, Helen Z. "Immigrants, Minorities, and the Great War." *Utah Historical Quarterly* 58 (fall 1990): 351–70.

Parish, Peter J. "An Exception to Most of the Rules: What Made American Nationalism Different in the Mid-Nineteenth Century?" *Prologue*, fall 1995, 219–29.

Parker, Andrew, Mary Russo, Doris Sommer, and Patricia Yaeger, eds. *Nationalisms and Sexualities*. New York: Routledge, 1992.

Pencak, William. *For God and Country: The American Legion, 1919–1941*. Boston: Northeastern University Press, 1989.

Periwal, Sukumar, ed. *Notions of Nationalism*. Budapest: Central European University Press, 1995.

Perry, Bliss. *Life and Letters of Henry Lee Higginson*. Freeport, N.Y.: Books for Libraries, 1922.

Peters, James Edward. *Arlington National Cemetery: Shrine to America's Heroes*. N.p.: Woodbine House, 1986.

Peterson, Clell T. "Charles King: Soldier and Novelist." *American Book Collector* 15 (December 1965): 9–10.

Peterson, H. C., and Gilbert C. Fite. *Opponents of War, 1917–1918*. Madison: University of Wisconsin Press, 1957.

Peterson, Theodore. *Magazines in the Twentieth Century*. Urbana: University of Illinois Press, 1964.

Piehler, G. Kurt. *Remembering War the American Way*. Washington, D.C.: Smithsonian Institution Press, 1995.

Pierce, Bessie Louise. *Public Opinion and the Teaching of History in the United States*. New York: Knopf, 1926.

Platt, Anthony M. *E. Franklin Frazier Reconsidered*. New Brunswick, N.J.: Rutgers University Press, 1991.

Potter, David M. *The South and Sectional Conflict*. Baton Rouge: Louisiana State University Press, 1968.

Preston, William, Jr. *Aliens and Dissenters: Federal Suppression of Radicals, 1903–1933*. 1963. 2nd ed. Urbana: University of Illinois Press, 1994.

Quaife, Milo M., Melvin J. Weig, and Roy F. Appleman. *The History of the United States Flag: From the Revolution to the Present, Including a Guide to Its Use and Display*. New York: Harper & Brothers, 1961.

Richards, Janet E. Hosmer. "The Great Objects of the Daughters of the American Revolution." *American Monthly Magazine*, December 1893, 492.

Riley, Denise. *"Am I That Name?" Feminism and the Category of "Women" in History*. Minneapolis: University of Minnesota Press, 1988.

Rogin, Michael P. *"Ronald Reagan," the Movie and Other Episodes in Political Demonology*. Berkeley: University of California Press, 1987.

Rosenblatt, Albert M. "Flag Desecration Statutes: History and Analysis." *Washington University Law Quarterly*, 1972, no. 2:193–237.

Rosengarten, Theodore. *All God's Dangers: The Life of Nate Shaw*. New York: Knopf, 1975.

Rowbotham, Shelia. *Women in Movement: Feminism and Social Action*. New York: Routledge, 1992.

Rudwick, Elliott M., and August Meier. "Black Man in the 'White City': Negroes and the Columbian Exposition, 1893." *Phylon* 26 (winter 1965): 354–61.

Rutherford, Jonathon, ed. *Identity: Community, Culture, Difference*. London: Lawrence & Wishart, 1990.

Ryan, Mary P. "The American Parade: Representations of the Nineteenth-Century Social Order." In *The New Cultural History*, ed. Lynn Hunt. Berkeley: University of California Press, 1989.

———. *Womanhood in America: From Colonial Times to the Present*. New York: Franklin Watts, 1983.

———. *Women in Public: Between Banners and Ballots, 1825–1880*. Baltimore: Johns Hopkins University Press, 1990.

Rydell, Robert W. *All the World's a Fair: Visions of Empire at America's International Expositions, 1876–1916*. Chicago: University of Chicago Press, 1984.

———. *World of Fairs: The Century-of-Progress Expositions*. Chicago: University of Chicago Press, 1993.

Said, Edward. *The World, the Text, and the Critic*. Cambridge: Harvard University Press, 1983.

Salvatore, Nick. *Eugene V. Debs: Citizen and Socialist*. Urbana: University of Illinois Press, 1982.

———. *We All Got History: The Memory Books of Amos Webber*. New York: Times Books, 1996.

Samuel, Raphael, ed. *Patriotism: The Making and Unmaking of British National Identity*. 3 vols. London: Routledge, 1989.

———. *People's History and Socialist Theory*. London: Routledge & Kegan Paul, 1981.

Savage, Kirk. "The Politics of Memory: Black Emancipation and the Civil War Monument." In *Commemorations: The Politics of National Identity*, ed., John R. Gillis. Princeton: Princeton University Press, 1994.

Savelle, Max. "Nationalism and Other Loyalties in the American Revolution." *American Historical Review* 67 (July 1962): 901–23.

Saxton, Alexander. *The Rise and Fall of the White Republic: Class Politics and Mass Culture in Nineteenth-Century America*. London: Verso, 1990.

Schechner, Richard, and Mady Schuman, eds. *Ritual, Play, and Performance: Readings in the Social Sciences / Theater*. New York: Seabury Press, Continuum Book, 1976.

Scheiber, Harry N. *The Wilson Administration and Civil Liberties, 1917–1921*. Ithaca: Cornell University Press, 1960.

Scheiber, Jane Lang, and Harry N. Scheiber. "The Wilson Administration and the Wartime Mobilization of Black Americans, 1917–1918." *Labor History* 10 (summer 1969): 433–58.

Schlesinger, Arthur M., Jr. *The Disuniting of America: Reflections on a Multicultural Society*. 1991. Reprint. New York: Norton, 1992.

Schwarz, Bill. "Conservativism, Nationalism, and Imperialism." In *Politics and Ideology*, ed. James Donald and Stuart Hall. Milton Keynes, England: Open University Press, 1986.

Scott, Anne Firor. *Natural Allies: Women's Associations in American History*. Urbana: University of Illinois Press, 1991.

Scott, Emmett J. *Negro Migration during the War*. New York: Oxford University Press, 1920.

———, comp. "Additional Letters of Negro Migrants, 1916–1918." *Journal of Negro History* 4 (1919): 412–65.

———. "Letters of Negro Migrants, 1916–1918." *Journal of Negro History* 4 (1919): 290–340.

Scott, Joan Wallach. *Gender and the Politics of History*. New York: Columbia University Press, 1988.

Silber, Nina. *The Romance of Reunion: Northerners and the South, 1865–1900*. Chapel Hill: University of North Carolina Press, 1993.

Simpson, J. A., and E. S. C. Winer, eds. *The Oxford English Dictionary*. 2nd ed. Oxford: Clarendon, 1989.

Skocpol, Theda. *Protecting Soldiers and Mothers: The Political Origins of Social Policy in the United States*. Cambridge: Harvard University Press, Belknap Press, 1992.

Slotkin, Richard. *Gunfighter Nation: The Myth of the Frontier in Twentieth-Century America*. New York: Atheneum, 1992.

———. "Nostalgia and Progress: Theodore Roosevelt's Myth of the Frontier." *American Quarterly* 33 (winter 1981): 608–37.

Smith, Anthony D. *The Ethnic Origins of Nations*. Oxford: Blackwell, 1986.

———. *National Identity*. London: Penguin Books, 1991.

Smith, Whitney. *The Flag Book of the United States*. Rev. ed. New York: Morrow, 1975.

Somerville, Mollie, comp. *Washington Landmark*. Washington, D.C.: National Society, Daughters of the American Revolution, 1976.

Spears, Jack. *The Civil War on the Screen and Other Essays*. New York: A. S. Barnes, 1977.

Spehr, Paul C., comp. *The Civil War in Motion Pictures: A Bibliography of Films Produced in the United States since 1897*. Washington, D.C.: Library of Congress, 1961.

Speierl, Charles Frank, Jr. "The Influence of the Grand Army of the Republic on Education in New Jersey, between 1866–1935." Ph.D. diss., Fairleigh Dickinson University, 1987.

Spillman, Lyn. *Nation and Commemoration: Creating National Identities in the United States and Australia.* Cambridge: Cambridge University Press, 1997.

Strayer, Martha. *The D.A.R.: An Informal History.* Washington D.C.: Public Affairs Press, 1958.

Sweet, Leonard I. *Black Images of America, 1784–1870.* New York: Norton, 1976.

———. "The Fourth of July and Black Americans in the Nineteenth Century." *Journal of Negro History* 61 (July 1976): 256–75.

Takaki, Ronald. *Iron Cages: Race and Culture in Nineteenth Century America.* New York: Oxford University Press, 1979.

Tilly, Louise A., and Patricia Gurin, eds. *Women, Politics, and Change.* New York: Russell Sage Foundation, 1990.

Tindall, George Brown. *The Emergence of the New South, 1913–1945.* Baton Rouge: Louisiana State University Press, 1967.

Torry, Jesse. *A Portraiture of Domestic Slavery in the United States.* Philadelphia: Jesse Torry, 1817.

Trachtenberg, Alan. *The Incorporation of America: Culture and Society in the Gilded Age.* New York: Hill & Wang, 1982.

Trask, David F. *The War with Spain in 1898.* New York: Macmillan, 1981.

Travers, Len. *Celebrating the Fourth: Independence Day and the Rites of Nationalism in the Early Republic.* Amherst: University of Massachusetts Press, 1997.

Tyack, David B., and Thomas James. "Moral Majorities and the School Curriculum: Historical Perspectives on the Legalization of Virtue." *Teachers College Record* 86 (summer 1985): 513–37.

Ueda, Reed. "Naturalization and Citizenship." In *Harvard Encyclopedia of American Ethnic Groups,* ed. Stephan Thernstrom. Cambridge: Harvard University Press, Belknap Press, 1980.

Vacha, J. E. "When Wagner Was Verboten: The Campaign against German Music in World War I." *New York History* 24 (April 1983): 171–88.

Vaughan, Leslie J. "Cosmopolitanism, Ethnicity, and American Identity: Randolph Bourne's 'Trans-National America.'" *Journal of American Studies* 25 (December 1991): 443–59.

Vaughan, Stephen. *Holding Fast the Inner Lines: Democracy, Nationalism, and the Committee on Public Information.* Chapel Hill: University of North Carolina Press, 1980.

Vogel, Morris J., ed. *Red, White, and Blue: Childhood and Citizenship.* Philadelphia: Please Touch Museum, 1987.

Wallerstein, Immanuel. "The Agonies of Liberalism: What Hope Progress?" *New Left Review* 204 (March/April 1994): 3–17.

———. *The Politics of World Economy: The States, the Movements, and the Civilizations.* Cambridge: Cambridge University Press, 1984.

Waskow, Arthur I. *From Race Riot to Sit-in: 1919 and the 1960s*. Garden City, N.Y.: Doubleday, 1966.

Weigley, Russell F. *The American Way of War: A History of the United States Military Strategy and Policy*. New York: Macmillan, 1973.

———. *History of the United States Army*. New York: Macmillan, 1967.

———. *Towards an American Army: Military Thought from Washington to Marshall*. New York: Columbia University Press, 1962.

———, ed. *The American Military: Readings in the History of the Military in American Society*. Menlo Park: Addison-Wesley, 1969.

Wesley, Edgar B. *NEA, The First Hundred Years: The Building of the Teaching Profession*. New York: Harper & Brothers, 1957.

White, Richard. "Civil Rights Agitation: Emancipation Days in Central New York in the 1880s." *Journal of Negro History* 78 (winter 1993): 16–24.

White, Walter F. *Man Called White*. New York: Viking, 1948.

Whites, LeeAnn. "The Civil War as a Crisis in Gender." In *Divided Houses: Gender and the Civil War*, ed. Catherine Clinton and Nina Silber. New York: Oxford University Press, 1992.

———. *The Civil War as a Crisis in Gender: Augusta, Georgia, 1860–1890*. Athens: University of Georgia Press, 1995.

Wiebe, Robert H. *The Search for Order, 1877–1920*. New York: Hill & Wang, 1968.

Wiggins, William H., Jr. "Juneteenth: 'They Closed the Town Up, Man!' " *American Visions: The Magazine of Afro-American Culture* 1 (May/June 1986): 40–45.

———. *O Freedom! Afro-American Emancipation Celebrations*. Knoxville: University of Tennessee Press, 1987.

Williams, Charles H. *Sidelights on Negro Soldiers*. Boston: B. J. Brimmer, 1923.

Williams, Raymond. *Keywords*. Rev. ed. London: Fontana, 1990.

Wills, Garry. "Washington's Citizen Virtue: Greenough and Houdon." *Critical Inquiry* 10 (March 1984): 420–41.

Whitmore, Allan Richard. "Beard, Boys, and Buckskins: Daniel Carter Beard and the Preservation of the American Pioneer Tradition." Ph.D. diss., Northwestern University, 1970.

Woodson, Carter G. *A Century of Negro Migration*. Washington, D.C.: Association for the Study of Negro Life and History, 1918.

Young, Alfred F., and Terry J. Fife, with Mary E. Janzen. *We the People: Voices and Images of the New Nation*. Philadelphia: Temple University Press, 1993.

Zelinsky, Wilbur. *Nation into State: The Shifting Symbolic Foundations of American Nationalism*. Chapel Hill: University of North Carolina Press, 1988.

Zelzier, Barbie. "Reading the Past against the Grain: The Shape of Memory Studies." *Critical Studies in Mass Communication* 12 (June 1995): 214–39.

Zinn, Howard. *A People's History of the United States, 1492—Present*. Rev. ed. 1980. Reprint. New York: Harper Perennial, 1995.

Zorh, Roman J. "The New England Anti-Slavery Society: Pioneer Abolition Organization." *Journal of Negro History* 43 (July 1957): 157–76.

Zuckerman, Michael. "The Rising Generation in the Young Republic." In *Red, White, and Blue: Childhood and Citizenship*, ed. Morris J. Vogel, 7–10. Philadelphia: Please Touch Museum, 1987.

Zunz, Olivier. *The Changing Face of Inequality: Urbanization, Industrial Development, and Immigrants in Detroit, 1880–1920*. Chicago: University of Chicago Press, 1982.

* Index *

Page numbers in italics refer to illustrations.